AF692452

TRAFFICKING IN PERSONS

PROSECUTION FROM A EUROPEAN PERSPECTIVE

To Ruud, Jochem, Huub and Fien

TRAFFICKING IN PERSONS

PROSECUTION FROM A EUROPEAN PERSPECTIVE

by

Conny Rijken

T·M·C·ASSER PRESS
The Hague

The Research for this study was financed by and carried out at Tilburg University and the T.M.C. Asser Instituut in The Hague. It was defended as a PhD thesis in the year 2003 at Tilburg University. The supervisors were: Prof.dr. E.M.H. Hirsch Ballin and Prof.dr. C.J.C.F. Fijnaut. Members of the board of examiners: Dr. W. Bruggeman, Prof.dr. M.S. Groenhuijsen, Prof.dr. G.G.J. Knoops, and Prof.dr. F.A. Nelissen.

Published by T.M.C.ASSER PRESS
P.O.Box 16163, 2500 BD The Hague, The Netherlands
<www.asserpress.nl>

ISBN 90-6704-167-X

All rights reserved.
© 2003, T.M.C.ASSER PRESS, The Hague, The Netherlands, and the author

No part of the material protected by this copyright notice may be reproduced or utilized in any form or by any means, electronic or mechanical, including photocopying, recording, or by any information storage and retrieval system, without written permission from the copyright owner.

PREFACE

Trafficking in persons is among the most appalling crimes of our time. In her wide-ranging study on the prosecution of these crimes in a European perspective, Conny Rijken correctly emphasizes pulling, pushing and enabling factors. The ease of international communication and cross-border transport serving the demands of the sex market belongs to the dark side of globalization. Governments were often slow to recognize the seriousness of these crimes and only reluctantly accepted border-crossing law enforcement. Many officials appeared to be more concerned about the infringement of national sovereignty than about the infringement of the personal dignity and integrity of the victims.

This forms the background of the theoretically as well as practically highly relevant research conducted by the author. The problems of law enforcement concerning transnational crime are one of the focal points within the Centre for Transboundary Legal Development of Tilburg University, in cooperation with the T.M.C. Asser Institute for International Law in The Hague.

The author analyses carefully the guiding concepts – including that of transnational crime and the significance of state sovereignty in law enforcement within the European Union – and confronts these insights with her own observations on the practice of law enforcement concerning trafficking in persons.

Three disparities guide the reader through the complications of prosecuting transnational crimes: between the transnational character of trafficking and the fact that strategies to combat it are based on national competences; between the availability of numerous strategies and the unwillingness or inability of states to efficiently use them; and between the requirements for the application of migration law and the requirements of criminal proceedings.

The conclusions in this book are primarily directed at those who deal with decisions on these matters. The author, nevertheless, also comes back to the fundamental question: what does it mean to have state responsibility in the field of transnational crime. Her answer is a paradox that sums up the disparities: state sovereignty deserves to be maintained, subject to the condition that those who bear responsibility are willing to share its exercise with other states, in the interest of those vulnerable people who deserve to be protected. Lawmakers and law enforcement officials as well as theorists of transboundary legal development will very much benefit from the publication of this book, which has been written with diligence and dedication.

Cyrille Fijnaut
Professor of Comparative Law

Ernst Hirsch Ballin
State Councillor and Professor
of International Law

ACKNOWLEDGEMENTS

I started this research in November 1998 after my interest in the crime of trafficking in persons as well as in the crime smuggling was aroused during my work at the immigration and naturalisation service. I finally decided to focus the study on the crime of trafficking in persons, and in the four and a half years of working on this book I did not regret this choice for one moment. The crime of trafficking in persons can rely on increased attention and developments at the European and International level on this topic, which is very inspiring.

Even more inspiring and encouraging during the years of research were my supervisors, Professor Ernst Hirsch Ballin and Professor Cyrille Fijnaut. Without the discussions with them and their comments on earlier versions of the text, this book would be of less value. Thanks are also due to Nico Keijzer and Yvonne Baaijens-van Geloven, who were prepared to provide me with the necessary comments especially during the first stage of the research.

I would like to thank the T.M.C. Asser Institute for creating the possibility to embark upon this study and for giving me the opportunity to meet interesting colleagues at the Institute.

During a three-month period I had the opportunity to conduct research in the European environment of Europol at the Trafficking in Human Beings Unit. The research which I conducted during this period, was a valuable exercise in carrying out empirical research. I would like to thank the employees at the Trafficking in Human Beings Unit for their help and congeniality.

Without the help of the Bureau National Rapporteur Mensenhandel in The Hague it would have been impossible to carry out the empirical study on the problems with regard to the prosecution of trafficking cases in the Netherlands. In this regard the prosecutors at the District Courts of Amsterdam, Rotterdam, and The Hague were very helpful in obtaining the required files, in giving me a place to study them, and in providing me with the relevant information.

Ineke Sijtsma and Peter Morris should be thanked for patiently correcting the English spelling and grammar and turning the text into digestible English.

I am very grateful that I could carry out the research at the University of Tilburg's Department of European and International Law. I appreciate the support of my colleagues and some of them were particularly helpful in the final stage of completing this book. I am happy that I can continue working at this inspiring place.

A last special word of thanks goes to the three men and the little girl in my life: Ruud, Jochem, Huub and Fien. They have taught me the essential things in life which I have never seen described in books, simply because they are beyond description.

Etten-Leur, July 2003 *Conny Rijken*

(The research was completed on 1 July 2003, documents adopted after this date are only included incidentally)

SUMMARY OF CONTENTS

Preface V
Acknowledgements VII
Table of Contents XI
Abbreviations XXI

Chapter 1
INTRODUCTION: RESEARCH QUESTION AND AIM OF THE STUDY

1.1 Introduction 1
1.2 Relevant developments in the process of globalisation 1
1.3 The effects of globalisation on the crime of trafficking in persons 5
1.4 Research question 7
1.5 Aim of the study 14
1.6 Structure of the study 16

Chapter 2
TRANSNATIONAL CRIME AND INTERNATIONAL CRIMINAL LAW

2.1 Introduction 19
2.2 The nature of international criminal law 19
2.3 The traditional categorisation of international criminal law 26
2.4 Other subdivisions relating to the traditional one 43
2.5 Transnational crime as a third group of crimes? 45
2.6 Conclusion 51

Chapter 3
DEFINING TRAFFICKING IN PERSONS

3.1 Introduction 53
3.2 History of the term 'trafficking in persons' 54
3.3 Elements of the definition of trafficking in persons 57
3.4 Use of definitions of trafficking in persons by the UN, the EU, and the IOM 66
3.5 Trafficking in persons versus smuggling persons 71
3.6 Relation of trafficking in persons to slavery and slavery-like practices 74
3.7 Trends and scope of the phenomenon 79
3.8 The relation of trafficking in persons to organised crime 81
3.9 The use of the term 'trafficking in persons' in this study 86
3.10 Is trafficking in persons a transnational crime? 87
3.11 Conclusion 89

Chapter 4
EUROPEAN POLICY DOCUMENTS TO COMBAT AND LEGAL INSTRUMENTS TO PROSECUTE TRAFFICKING IN PERSONS

4.1 Introduction 91
4.2 Overview of policy documents 92
4.3 Overview of the legal instruments 107
4.4 Conclusion 151

Chapter 5
THE EFFECTIVENESS OF POLICY DOCUMENTS TO COMBAT TRAFFICKING IN PERSONS AND LEGAL INSTRUMENTS TO PROSECUTE THIS PRACTICE

5.1 Introduction 153
5.2 General remarks on the effectiveness of the policy documents and legal instruments to combat and prosecute trafficking in persons 154
5.3 Obstacles to the application of legal instruments indicated in legal literature 164
5.4 Obstacles to the application of legal instruments on mutual legal assistance in the EU 170
5.5 Conclusion 198

Chapter 6
OBSTACLES TO THE APPLICATION OF LEGAL INSTRUMENTS TO PROSECUTE TRAFFICKING IN PERSONS IN THE NETHERLANDS

6.1 Introduction 201
6.2 Method of research 202
6.3 Problems indicated in the preliminary interviews 204
6.4 Results of the analysis of the files 213
6.5 Conclusions 238

Chapter 7
CONCLUSIONS

7.1 Summary 243
7.2 Suggestions to improve the prosecution of trafficking in persons 257
7.3 Final conclusion on this study 269

Summary 273
Samenvatting 281
Appendices 289
Bibliography 295
List of treaties, documents, and cases 303
Index 319

TABLE OF CONTENTS

Preface V
Acknowledgements VII
Summary of Contents IX
Abbreviations XXI

Chapter 1
INTRODUCTION: RESEARCH QUESTION AND AIM OF THE STUDY

1.1 Introduction 1

1.2 Relevant developments in the process of globalisation 1

1.3 The effects of globalisation on the crime of trafficking in persons 5

1.4 Research question 7
1.4.1 The changing concept of state sovereignty within the EU 8
1.4.2 Effectiveness of strategies to combat and prosecute trafficking in persons 12

1.5 Aim of the study 14
1.5.1 New initiatives to prosecute those suspected of trafficking in persons 14
1.5.2 Transformation of the use of current principles 15
1.5.3 Limitations of criminal law with regard to trafficking in persons 15

1.6 Structure of the study 16

Chapter 2
TRANSNATIONAL CRIME AND INTERNATIONAL CRIMINAL LAW

2.1 Introduction 19

2.2 The nature of international criminal law 19
2.2.1 The relation between international criminal law, national criminal law, and international law 19
2.2.2 Functions and definitions of international criminal law 22
2.2.3 The protection of human rights as one of the functions of international criminal law 25

2.3	The traditional categorisation of international criminal law	26
2.3.1	Criminal law aspects of international law	26
2.3.1.1	The characteristics of the category of criminal law aspects of international law	26
2.3.1.2	The crimes within the category of criminal law aspects of international law	28
2.3.1.3	The problem of enforcement in international crime	31
2.3.2	International aspects of national criminal law	34
2.3.2.1	The characteristics of the category of international aspects of national criminal law	34
2.3.2.2	Current jurisdiction principles	36
2.3.2.3	The crimes within the category of international aspects of national criminal law	42
2.3.3	The connection between criminal law aspects of international law and international aspects of national criminal law	42
2.4	Other subdivisions relating to the traditional one	43
2.5	Transnational crime as a third group of crimes?	45
2.5.1	Characteristics of transnational crime	45
2.5.2	The connection between transnational crime and organised crime	46
2.5.3	The meaning of the term 'transnational'	47
2.5.4	Enforcement problems in the face of transnational crime	48
2.5.5	Criteria to define transnational crime	49
2.5.6	Accommodating the group of transnational crime within the traditional categorisation	50
2.6	Conclusion	51

Chapter 3
DEFINING TRAFFICKING IN PERSONS

3.1	Introduction	53
3.2	History of the term 'trafficking in persons'	54
3.3	Elements of the definition of trafficking in persons	57
3.3.1	Recruitment and transport versus exploitation	57
3.3.2	The coercive element in the term 'trafficking in persons'	60
3.3.2.1	The meaning of coercion	61
3.3.2.2	The purpose of the trafficker	63
3.3.3	The goal of the trafficking	64
3.3.4	'Trafficking in women' or 'trafficking in persons'?	65

3.4 Use of definitions of trafficking in persons by the UN, the EU, and the IOM 66
3.4.1 Definition in the Trafficking Protocol to the UNCTOC 66
3.4.2 Other definitions within the UN body 67
3.4.3 Definitions within the European Union 68
3.4.4 Definition of the IOM 71

3.5 Trafficking in persons versus smuggling persons 71
3.5.1 Application of migration law 73

3.6 Relation of trafficking in persons to slavery and slavery-like practices 74

3.7 Trends and scope of the phenomenon 79

3.8 The relation of trafficking in persons to organised crime 81
3.8.1 Organised crime in general 82
3.8.2 The definition of organised crime in the UNCTOC 83
3.8.3 The definition of organised crime within the EU 84
3.8.4 Trafficking in persons as a form of organised crime 85

3.9 The use of the term 'trafficking in persons' in this study 86

3.10 Is trafficking in persons a transnational crime? 87

3.11 Conclusion 89

Chapter 4
EUROPEAN POLICY DOCUMENTS TO COMBAT AND LEGAL INSTRUMENTS TO PROSECUTE TRAFFICKING IN PERSONS

4.1 Introduction 91

4.2 Overview of policy documents 92
4.2.1 The concept of policy documents 92
4.2.2 Policy documents on trafficking in persons within the EU 92
4.2.2.1 Policy documents adopted by the European Parliament 92
4.2.2.2 Policy documents adopted by the European Commission 94
4.2.2.3 Policy documents adopted by the Council of the EU 96
4.2.2.4 Policy documents adopted by the European Council 97
4.2.2.5 Other policy documents within the EU 98
4.2.2.6 Policy documents on (organised) crime 99
4.2.3 Policy documents on trafficking in persons within the Council of Europe 100

4.2.4 Policy documents on trafficking in persons within the OSCE 102
4.2.5 Conclusion 106

4.3 Overview of the legal instruments 107
4.3.1 The concept of legal instruments 107
4.3.2 The institutional framework for police and judicial cooperation in criminal matters in the EU 108
4.3.2.1 The establishment of police and judicial cooperation in criminal matters 108
4.3.2.2 The decision-making process on police and judicial cooperation in criminal matters 108
4.3.2.3 The Schengen acquis 110
4.3.2.4 Europol 113
4.3.2.5 Eurojust 115
4.3.2.6 The jurisdiction of the European Court of Justice 116
4.3.2.7 The idea of a European Public Prosecutor 118
4.3.2.7.1 The idea of an EPP in the Corpus Juris 118
4.3.2.7.2 The idea of an EPP in the Green Paper 120
4.3.2.7.3 The idea of an EPP in the Draft Constitution 121
4.3.3 Legal instruments within the EU 122
4.3.3.1 The Council Framework Decision on Combating Trafficking in Human Beings 123
4.3.3.2 The EU conventions on Extradition 124
4.3.3.2.1 The Convention on Simplified Extradition Procedure between Member States of the EU 124
4.3.3.2.2 The Convention Relating to Extradition between the Member States of the EU 126
4.3.3.3 The European Arrest Warrant 128
4.3.3.4 The European Convention on Mutual Assistance in Criminal Matters between the Member States of the European Union and its protocol 130
4.3.3.5 Police and judicial cooperation under the Schengen Convention 133
4.3.3.6 Proposal for a Council Directive on the Short-Term Residence Permit 135
4.3.3.7 Some new developments adopted in the legal instruments 136
4.3.4 Legal instruments of the Council of Europe 138
4.3.4.1 The European Convention on Extradition 138
4.3.4.2 The European Convention on Mutual Assistance in Criminal Matters 140
4.3.4.3 The Convention on the Transfer of Sentenced Persons 142
4.3.4.4 The Convention on Laundering, Search, Seizure and Confiscation of the Proceeds from Crime 144
4.3.4.5 The European Convention on the Transfer of Proceedings in Criminal Matters 146
4.3.4.6 The European Agreement on Travel by Young Persons on Collective Passports between the Member Countries of the Council of Europe 148

4.3.4.7 The European Convention on the International Validity of Criminal Judgements 149
4.3.4.8 Final remarks 151

4.4 Conclusion 151

Chapter 5
THE EFFECTIVENESS OF POLICY DOCUMENTS TO COMBAT TRAFFICKING IN PERSONS AND LEGAL INSTRUMENTS TO PROSECUTE THIS PRACTICE

5.1 Introduction 153

5.2 General remarks on the effectiveness of the policy documents and legal instruments to combat and prosecute trafficking in persons 154
5.2.1 The legal basis of the policy documents and legal instruments 154
5.2.1.1 The legal basis of policy documents and legal instruments within the EU 154
5.2.1.2 The legal basis of policy documents and legal instruments within the Council of Europe 157
5.2.1.3 The legal basis of policy documents within the OSCE 158
5.2.2 Lack of legal enforcement of policies and legal instruments 159
5.2.2.1 Legal enforcement within the EU 159
5.2.2.2 Legal enforcement within the Council of Europe 160
5.2.2.3 Legal enforcement within the OSCE 161
5.2.3 The complexity caused by the multiplicity of applicable legal instruments 162
5.2.4 The limited number of ratifications of treaties and reservations to treaties 163

5.3 Obstacles to the application of legal instruments indicated in legal literature 164
5.3.1 Substantive problems 164
5.3.1.1 Locus regit actum or forum regit actum? 164
5.3.1.2 The principle of double criminality 166
5.3.1.3 The relation between cooperation in criminal matters and the principle of confidentiality 167
5.3.2 Procedural problems 168
5.3.2.1 Means of communication 168
5.3.2.2 Lack of knowledge concerning the legal systems of other states and problems in identifying the competent authorities 169
5.3.2.3 Waste of time, money, and human resources 170
5.3.3 Organisational problems; language problems 170

5.4 Obstacles to the application of legal instruments on mutual legal assistance in the EU 170
5.4.1 Substantive problems 172
5.4.1.1 Execution of requests by applying the national law of the requested state 172
5.4.1.2 Double criminality 174
5.4.1.3 The different use of terms by different states and different authorities 175
5.4.2 Procedural problems 176
5.4.2.1 The use of direct communication channels 177
5.4.2.1.1 The use of the European Judicial Network 179
5.4.2.2 Waste of time, money, and human resources 181
5.4.2.3 Communication between judicial and police authorities and within the judiciary 183
5.4.2.4 Instructions and guidelines 184
5.4.2.5 Confusion as to what formalities must be fulfilled and which channels must be used 185
5.4.2.6 Appeals as a delaying strategy 186
5.4.3 Organisational problems 186
5.4.3.1 Identification of competent judicial authorities 186
5.4.3.2 Practical problems in contacting the authorities involved 189
5.4.3.3 Language problems 189
5.4.4 Other problems 191
5.4.4.1 Problems with regard to search and seizure 191
5.4.4.2 Lack of adequate records 191
5.4.4.3 Presence of requesting authorities in the requested state 191
5.4.4.4 Frustrating the mutual legal assistance system by sending requests in minor cases 192
5.4.4.5 Lack of resources 192
5.4.5 A matrix 193
5.4.6 Recommendations 193
5.4.6.1 Informal procedures for the service of documents 193
5.4.6.2 Development of a standard form for mutual legal assistance 195
5.4.6.3 Cooperation between the Nordic countries 195
5.4.7 Cooperation with states outside the European Union 196
5.4.8 Concluding observations 197

5.5 Conclusion 198

Chapter 6
OBSTACLES TO THE APPLICATION OF LEGAL INSTRUMENTS TO PROSECUTE TRAFFICKING IN PERSONS IN THE NETHERLANDS

6.1 Introduction 201

6.2 Method of research 202

6.3 Problems indicated in the preliminary interviews 204
6.3.1 Primary problems of cooperation in criminal matters in trafficking cases in the Netherlands 204
6.3.2 Secondary problems of cooperation in criminal matters in trafficking cases in The Netherlands 209
6.3.3 Problems not specifically related to cooperation in criminal matters 210
6.3.4 Additional questions in the questionnaire 212

6.4 Results of the analysis of the files 213
6.4.1 Introduction and figures 213
6.4.2 Results of the file study 214
6.4.2.1 Substantive problems 215
6.4.2.1.1 Execution of requests by applying the national law of the requested state 215
6.4.2.1.2 Double criminality 215
6.4.2.1.3 The different use of the terms by different states and different authorities 216
6.4.2.1.4 The use of Article 197a Dutch Penal Code in trafficking cases 217
6.4.2.2 Procedural problems 218
6.4.2.2.1 The use of direct communication channels and the European Judicial Network 218
6.4.2.2.2 Wasting of time, money, and human resources (duplication of efforts) 219
6.4.2.2.3 Communication between judicial and police authorities and within the judiciary 220
6.4.2.2.4 Confusion as to what formalities must be fulfilled and which channels must be used 221
6.4.2.2.5 Appeals as a delaying strategy 222
6.4.2.2.6 Penalties 222
6.4.2.3 Organisational problems 224
6.4.2.3.1 Identification of the competent judicial authorities 224
6.4.2.3.2 Practical problems in contacting the authorities involved 225
6.4.2.3.3 Language problems 225
6.4.2.4 Additional problems following the questions based on the preliminary interviews 227
6.4.2.4.1 Residence of the victim and/or witness outside the territory of the Netherlands 227
6.4.2.4.2 The reliability of local authorities in the requested state 228
6.4.2.4.3 The establishment of a relationship based on trust with the victim by the police and the role of the trafficker 230
6.4.2.4.4 The possibility to chart the recruitment practices in the country of origin and its added value 232
6.4.2.4.5 Absence of cooperation with African countries in general and Nigeria in particular 233
6.4.2.4.6 Cooperation in criminal matters with Spain 233

6.4.2.4.7 Investigation of the suspect's financial situation and assets in other countries 234

6.4.2.5 Other problems 235
6.4.2.6 Specific problems in appeal cases 235
6.4.3 Other issues raised in the concluding interviews 236
6.4.3.1 Trafficking in persons and participation in a criminal organisation 237
6.4.3.2 The consequences of policy choices with regard to the prosecution of trafficking in persons 238

6.5 Conclusions 238
6.5.1 Conclusions from the empirical study 239
6.5.2 Is trafficking in persons a transnational crime? 240

Chapter 7
CONCLUSIONS

7.1 Summary 243
7.1.1 Introduction 243
7.1.2 Transnational crime versus national competence 244
7.1.2.1 The changing concept of state sovereignty 244
7.1.2.2 Jurisdiction: The territoriality principle, the principle of universal jurisdiction, and regional jurisdiction 246
7.1.2.3 Confidence among states in each other's systems 248
7.1.2.4 Conclusion 249
7.1.3 Juridical recognition of the phenomenon of trafficking in persons versus the unwillingness or inability of states 249
7.1.3.1 Difficulties in defining trafficking in persons 250
7.1.3.2 Many formalities and opaque procedures for mutual legal assistance 251
7.1.3.3 Lack of direct contacts within the judiciary and problems in identifying the competent person 251
7.1.3.4 Absence of global sociality and adequate (financial) resources 252
7.1.3.5 Absence of cooperation in criminal matters with some countries 253
7.1.3.6 Conclusion 254
7.1.4 Application of migration law versus the importance for prosecution and the protection of victims 254
7.1.4.1 Consequences of the application of migration law for criminal proceedings and for victims 255
7.1.4.2 Victim protection in the EU 256
7.1.4.3 Conclusion 257

7.2 Suggestions to improve the prosecution of trafficking in persons 257
7.2.1 Introduction 257

7.2.2 The approach to improve the prosecution of trafficking in persons on a national level 258
7.2.2.1 The desirability of an approach on the national level 258
7.2.2.1.1 The value of the European Arrest Warrant and the EU Convention on Simplified Extradition Procedure for the prosecution of trafficking in persons 258
7.2.2.1.2 The value of the EU Convention on Mutual Assistance for the prosecution of trafficking in persons 260
7.2.2.1.3 Streamlining the national law on mutual legal assistance 261
7.2.2.1.4 Conclusion 261
7.2.2.2 The feasibility of an approach on the national level 262
7.2.3 The approach to improve the prosecution of trafficking in persons on an EU level 262
7.2.3.1 The desirability of an approach on the EU level 262
7.2.3.1.1 The value of an EPP to prosecute trafficking in persons 263
7.2.3.1.2 Conclusion 265
7.2.3.2 The feasibility of an approach on the EU level 266
7.2.4 Conclusion 269

7.3 Final conclusion on this study 269
7.3.1 The dichotomy regarding cooperation in criminal matters 269
7.3.2 A realistic approach to improve the prosecution of trafficking in persons 270

Summary 273

Samenvatting 281

Appendices
1. Organisation chart 289
2. File screening list 291
3. Research questions of the file study 293

Bibliography 295

List of treaties, documents, and cases 303

Index 319

ABBREVIATIONS

AMA	alleenstaande minderjarige asielzoeker [unaccompanied asylum seeking child]
CEDAW	Convention on the Elimination of all forms of Discrimination Against Women
Doc.	Document
EAW	European Arrest Warrant
EC Treaty	Treaty establishing the European Community
ECJ	European Court of Justice
ECOSOC	Economic and Social Council
ECPAT	End Child Prostitution, Child Pornography and the Trafficking of Children for Sexual Purposes (previously: End Child Prostitution in Asian Tourism)
EDelPP	European Delegated Public Prosecutors
EDPP	European Director of Public Prosecution
EDU	European Drugs Unit
EJN	European Judicial Network
EP	European Parliament
EPP	European Public Prosecutor
ETS	European Treaty Series
EU	European Union
EU Treaty	Treaty on European Union
GAATW	Global Alliance Against Trafficking in Women
GA	General Assembly
GAOR	General Assembly Official Records
HR	Hoge Raad [Dutch Supreme Court]
ICCPR	International Convention on Civil and Political Rights
ICJ	International Court of Justice
ILO	International Labor Organisation
IOM	International Organisation for Migration
LNTS	League of Nations Treaty Series
NCIS	National Criminal Intelligence Service
NGO	Non-Governmental Organisation
NJB	Nederlands Juristenblad
NJCM	Nederlands Juristencomité voor de Mensenrechten
no.	Number
ODIHR	Office of Democratic Institutions and Human Rights
OJ	Official Journal
OSCE	Organization for Security and Cooperation in Europe
p. (pp.)	page (pages)
para(s)	paragraph(s)
PCIJ	Permanent Court of International Justice
Res.	Resolution

SEW	Sociaal Economische Wetgeving
SIM	Studie en Informatiecentrum Mensenrechten
UK	United Kingdom
UN	United Nations
UNCTOC	United Nations Convention on Transnational Organised Crime
UNESCO	United Nations Educational, Scientific and Cultural Organization
UNICEF	United Nations Children's Fund (previously: United Nations International Children's Emergency Fund)
UNTS	United Nations Treaty Series
WODC	Wetenschappenlijk Onderzoek- en Documentatiecentrum [Scientific Research and Documentation Centre]
WRR	Wetenschappelijke Raad voor het Regeringsbeleid [Scientific Council for the Government Policy]

CHAPTER 1
INTRODUCTION: RESEARCH QUESTION AND THE AIM OF THE STUDY

1.1 INTRODUCTION

In this Introductory Chapter, a first exploration of the subject of this study will be made. In Section 1.2, the most important developments relevant for this study in the process of globalisation from the Second World War until now will be discussed in order to explore the effects of these developments on trafficking in persons in Section 1.3. In Section 1.4, the research question will be discussed on the basis of the two main disparities in this study, namely, the disparity between the fact that trafficking in persons is a crime with a transnational element and the fact that strategies to combat it are based on national competences, and the disparity between the availability of a great number of strategies to fight and prosecute trafficking in persons and the unwillingness or inability to use them efficiently.[1] The aim of this study will be discussed in Section 1.5. Finally, the structure of this study will be set out in Section 1.6.

1.2 RELEVANT DEVELOPMENTS IN THE PROCESS OF GLOBALISATION

A new period in the process of globalisation is reflected in various developments that have taken place over the last 60 years.[2] The globalisation of socio-economic relations throughout the world characterises this period. In the context of this study, the developments contributing to the globalisation of socio-economic relations will be emphasised first, before the effects of these developments on the relations between criminals and criminal organisations are described.[3] On the basis of these effects, two developments in the way criminals and criminal organisations carry out their activities will be identified.

---

[1] The efficiency of the strategies to fight and prosecute trafficking in persons will be subject of research in Chapters 5 and 6.

[2] For a description of the term globalisation, see R. Lubbers *Globalisering: naar een nieuwe kijk op political economy,* Center for Economic Research, Tilburg University, Tilburg, 1995. M. Rupert, *Ideologies of Globalization. Contending Visions of a New World Order,* Routledge, London, 2000, pp. 43-54, R. Lubbers and J. Koorevaar, *Primary Globalization, Secondary Globalization and the Sustainable Development Paradigm – Opposing Forces in the 21st Century,* Paper for Conference on 21st Century Social Dynamics: Towards the Creative Society, Berlin, 2000. J.H. Mittelman and R. Johnston, The Globalization of Organized Crime, the Courtesan State, and the Corruption of Civil Society, in: *Global Governance,* Volume 5, issue 1, 1999, pp. 103, 108-112.

[3] Ph. Williams, Transnational Criminal Organisations and International Security, in: N. Passas, *Transnational Crime,* Dartmouth, Aldershot, 1999, pp. 31-35, in which he describes the changes of the internationalisation in relation to transnational organised crime.

Globally, technological improvements and inventions can be seen as a major development contributing to the globalisation of socio-economic relations. New communication techniques make it possible to access the whole world, and computer developments offer an abundance of electronic information for everyone using these techniques. Means of transportation have improved significantly, making it a possibility to travel around the world in a relatively short period of time, which has boosted world trade. Furthermore, commercial and (financial) transactions can be made throughout the world from any place, and many (financial) companies are now operating worldwide with offices in a large number of countries.

Another development facilitating the globalisation of socio-economic relations worldwide is the enormous increase in the number of international organisations, and consequently international laws, rules, and regulations, since the Second World War. On a global level, the establishment of the United Nations (UN) as the successor of the League of Nations is the most important organisation.[4] As the UN was specifically set up to maintain international peace and security, to develop friendly relations among nations, and to achieve international cooperation in solving international problems, the UN is primarily a political organisation. However, its effect on the establishment of socio-economic relations cannot be denied.

In this study, the main focus will be on the European level. The developments that took place in Europe and which have influenced the globalisation of socio-economic relations will be focused on first of all.

Within Europe, the major relevant developments are the end of the Cold War and the fall of the Iron Curtain when a market economy was introduced in the former communist countries. This provided countries from both the East and the West with new opportunities to intensify their trade relations. The number of joint ventures and transnational enterprises grew rapidly, together with the modes of cross-border transactions.

With regard to the establishment of (political) organisations that have facilitated the globalisation of socio-economic relations on the European level, the establishment of the European Union (before 1993, the European Communities), the Council of Europe, and the Organization for Security and Cooperation in Europe (OSCE) must be mentioned. These organisations have produced a stream of policies and instruments. These often include provisions for a united policy on specific issues and support closer relations and cooperation between the states of the European region. However, when focusing on these organisations, we have to keep in mind that they were set up with different intentions. The Council of Europe is an intergovernmental organisation aiming at the protection of human rights, pluralist democracy, and the rule of law. It creates facilities to achieve these aims, for instance, by the enactment

[4] For an overview of international institutions, see: M.N. Shaw, *International Law*, third edition, Cambridge University Press, Cambridge, 1995, pp. 742-782.

of conventions. The OSCE is active in the field of early warning, conflict prevention, crisis management, and post-conflict rehabilitation. The major part of its activities takes place in missions and field activities. The main aim of the European Union (EU) relevant for this study is to achieve an area of freedom, security, and justice.

Beside great advantages of the globalisation of socio-economic and political relations, there is also a downside to this phenomenon; the developments described above have also facilitated the establishment of relations between criminals and criminal groups from various parts of the world, and have facilitated the commission of crimes across borders.[5] Three major effects of globalisation facilitating the increase of criminal contacts and activities across borders, particularly at a European level, can be identified.

Firstly, it is widely perceived that the criminal justice systems of countries with economies in transition are particularly vulnerable to criminal activities.[6] After the fall of the Iron Curtain, many new nation states were established that used the opportunity to free themselves from communist domination. Within these new states, a system for a democratic nation and state structure had to be developed and, in the period after the collapse of the old system and before the effective functioning of the new, there was often a lack of authority. It was necessary to redefine the principles and values on which a society operates and a reorientation of relationships with the outside world.[7] In many countries with economies in transition, proper criminal legislation did not exist and law enforcement systems had to be developed. Furthermore, this transforming process often ran parallel to an increase in unemployment, lack of social security, loss of old values, uncertainty about the future, and inflation. All these aspects contribute to illegal activities by actors both from within and outside the country, as criminals and criminal groups have a preference to operate in states where they are less likely to be caught.[8] The presence in a state of one of these

[5] J.S. Solomon, Forming a More Secure Union: The Growing Problem of Organised Crime in Europe as a Challenge to National Sovereignty, in: *Dickens Journal of International Law,* Volume 13, issue 3, 1995, pp. 623-648. M. Delmas-Marty and M.A. Summers, *What Kind of Criminal Policy for Europe?* Kluwer Law International, The Hague, 1996. Ph. Williams, Transnational Criminal Organisations and International Security, in: N. Passas, *Transnational Crime,* Dartmouth, Aldershot, 1999, pp. 31- 48. T.L.H. McCormack and G.J. Simpson, The International Law Commission's Draft Code of Crimes against the Peace and Security of Mankind: An Appraisal of the Substantive Provisions, in: J. Dugard and Ch. van den Wyngaert, *International Criminal Law and Procedure,* Dartmouth, Aldershot, 1996, pp. 350-351. C. Fijnaut, Transnational Crime and the Role of the United Nations in its Containment through International Cooperation: A Challenge for the 21st Century, in: *European Journal of Crime, Criminal Law and Criminal Justice,* Volume 8, issue 2, 2000, pp. 122-123.

[6] See, for instance, M. Castells, *The Information Age, Volume III: End of Millennium,* Blackwell, Cambridge, 1998, pp. 166-205. Ph. Williams, Transnational Criminal Organisations and International Security, in: N. Passas, *Transnational Crime,* Dartmouth, Aldershot, 1999, pp. 41-45.

[7] M.C. Bassiouni and E. Vetere, Organized Crime and its Transnational Manifestations, in: M.C. Bassiouni, *International Criminal Law. Crimes,* second edition, Transnational Publishers, Inc. Ardsley, New York, 1999, pp. 898-900.

[8] M. Castells, *The Information Age, Volume III: End of Millenium*, Blackwell, Cambridge, 1998, pp.

aspects is an indication that this state might be more vulnerable to criminal activities taking place on its territory. For newly established nations, at least one of these aspects is often present.

A second major effect of globalisation facilitating the increase of criminal contacts and activities across borders is the relaxation of restrictions on border crossing, particularly within the EU. This effect of globalisation is making it easier for criminals and criminal organisations to operate across borders, and organised crime groups use immigrant networks to infiltrate other societies.[9]

A third major effect of globalisation on contacts between criminals and criminal groups is that they use the technological improvements and inventions such as modern communication and transportation facilities to commit criminal activities. Besides, the number of organised crime groups operating around the world has increased as well.[10]

The effects of globalisation on criminal activities described above have become visible in two developments in the way the criminal activities are carried out. Firstly, new forms of crime are developed as a result of the use of technology and new technological inventions. Criminals use computer technology to commit new forms of crime such as distributing illegal materials, for instance, child pornography on the Internet, the hacking of computers, credit card fraud, and money laundering. Neither the extent of these crimes nor the most effective way to deal with them have been identified and few states have enacted criminal law with the aim of combating these crimes, leaving aside the question of whether national strategies are the most adequate instruments to combat these new forms of crime.

The second development making visible a change in the way the criminal activities are carried out is the increase of international elements of the crimes committed. These international elements have many guises. It is possible that the offender resides in a country other than the one in which he is being tried, or that the *locus delicti* is in another country or in more than one country, or even that different parts of the crime took place in different countries by offenders from different states. The increase in international aspects of crimes causes problems in the investigation and prosecution of these crimes, which can be called complex crimes.

Following these two developments, practitioners may be confronted with the following questions during legal proceedings. Which country has jurisdiction to prosecute

168-170. L.I. Shelley, Post-Soviet Organised Crime, Implication for Economic, Social and Political Development, in: N. Passas, *Transnational Crime,* Dartmouth, Aldershot, 1999, pp. 163-180.

[9] M. Castells, *The Information Age, Volume III: End of Millenium,* Blackwell, Cambridge, 1998, p. 203.

[10] S. Adamoli, *Organised Crime around the World,* European Institute for Crime Prevention and Control, affiliated with the United Nations, HEUNI publications series, Helsinki, 1998, especially pp. 10-18.

the offender? Who has the right to exercise jurisdiction in case of concurrent jurisdiction, and on what grounds? Under what conditions can evidence collected by a third country be used in a trial? What obligations does a third country have as regards extradition or mutual legal assistance? How can police officers work together in collecting evidence? As a result of this increased complexity of crimes, there is an urgent need for intensified cooperation between states. Whether such intensified cooperation must originate at a national or an EU level remains to be seen.

Thus, summarising the above, as a result of globalisation of criminal activities, a group of new and complex crimes can be identified.[11] This group of crimes is distinguishable from the more traditional groups of crime in the way they are organised and the way they use licit structures. They make the need for intensified cooperation between states in order to contain them more pressing. Within the group of complex crimes, a sub-group of crimes can be identified which I will call transnational crime. This sub-group of crimes will be further elaborated in this study, leaving aside the other complex crimes and the new forms of crime. Which crimes belong to the group of transnational crime? What characterises this crime? How does transnational crime relate to other groups of crime? How can this group be defined? I will endeavour to answer these questions in Chapter 2.

To avoid the pitfall of merely offering general observations, this study will concentrate on the prosecution of the crime of trafficking in persons as one of the crimes increasingly committed in an international context. As we will see in the next section, the process of globalisation has not left trafficking in persons untouched. However, it remains to be seen whether and under what conditions trafficking in persons can be categorised as a transnational crime.[12]

1.3 THE EFFECTS OF GLOBALISATION ON THE CRIME OF TRAFFICKING IN PERSONS

Trafficking in persons is one of the crimes that is nowadays committed more often in an international context than it was before. The developments in globalisation, mentioned above, have influenced the internationalisation of trafficking in persons in two ways.[13]

Firstly, it can be said that victims of trafficking in persons are more often and more

[11] The terminology of new and complex crimes is also used but not explained in Ch. van den Wyngaert, The Transformations of International Criminal Law in Response to the Challenge of Organized Crime, in: *International Review of Penal Law,* Volume 70, issue 1-2, 1999, pp. 152-164, 173-174. The complex crimes in relation to the more traditional groups of crime will be discussed in Chapter 2.

[12] This question will be answered in Chapter 3.

[13] B. de Ruyver, et al., *Strategies of the EU and the US in Combating Transnational Organised Crime,* Maklu, Antwerp, 2002, pp. 387-388. L. Hauber, The Trafficking of Women for Prostitution: A Growing Problem within the European Union, in: *Boston College International & Comparative Law Review,* Volume 21, issue 1, 1998, pp. 183-199.

easily moved from one place to another place and from one country to another.[14] The organisation of the trafficking has become easier through the use of modern communication techniques and the various forms of transportation that can be used to transport victims from one place to another. With the use of these techniques, the traffickers are for instance more able to serve the specific demands of the sex market. This demand in Western countries is an important pull factor maintaining the existence of trafficking in persons from poor countries. However, globally there is an increase in trafficking not only from countries from South to North and from East to West but between countries in the South as well.[15] Trafficking within Europe mainly takes place from Central and Eastern European countries to Western European countries. Within the EU, transportation is further facilitated by the abolition of border controls following the Schengen Convention.[16]

Secondly, it is widely observed that poverty and unemployment affect women more often than men. Consequently, the effects of globalisation for states in transition described in Section 1.2 affect women disproportionately, making them vulnerable to trafficking practices. It is widely recognised that poverty and underdevelopment is one of the main reasons for the existence of trafficking in persons.[17] Therefore, trafficking mainly takes place from poor, underdeveloped countries to rich, Western countries. According to a study of the International Organisation for Migration (IOM), the main reasons for the increase in the number of persons trafficked from Central and Eastern European countries to Western Europe is the fact that these countries are in the transition to a market economy, which leads to high rates of unemployment and poverty. Furthermore, the travel restrictions that have been lifted in the Eastern European countries have facilitated trafficking. For people living in Eastern Europe, especially women, employment in Western European countries with a lower unemployment rate and a higher standard of living is an attractive alternative.[18] For similar reasons, the number of women and young girls from Western African countries that are trafficked to Western Europe has increased as well.[19]

---

[14] See, for instance, Europol 1999 General Situation Report on Trafficking in Human Beings, Open Version, Europol, December 2000, File no: 2565-35rev1, pp. 35-36.

[15] L. Lap-Chew and M. Wijers, *Trafficking in Women, Forced Labour, and Slavery-Like Practices in Marriage, Domestic Labour, and Prostitution,* Foundation against Trafficking in Women, Utrecht, 1997, pp. 86-87. Report of the Special Rapporteur on violence against women, its causes and consequences, Ms. Radhika Coomaraswamy, Commission on Human Rights, fifty-third session, E/CN.4/1997/47, 12 February 1997, paras 72, 79, 82, 83, 85, 87, 88.

[16] Convention applying the Schengen Agreement of 14 June 1985 between the governments of the states of the Benelux Economic Union, the Federal Republic of Germany and the French Republic, on the gradual abolition of checks at their common borders, signed on 19 June 1990, in force since March 1995 (the Schengen Convention).

[17] See also Chapter 3, Section 3.3.2.1.

[18] C. Fijnaut, Transnational Crime and the Role of the United Nations in its Containment through International Cooperation: A Challenge for the 21st Century, in: *European Journal of Crime, Criminal Law and Criminal Justice,* Volume 8, issue 2, 2000, p. 123.

[19] R. van Dijk, et al., *Een schijn van Voodoo,* African Studies Centre, Leyden, December 1999, pp. 1-5. Nigerian Democratic Movement in the Netherlands and Terre des Hommes, *Handel in Nigeriaanse*

When considering trafficking in persons, we first have to keep in mind the problem of defining the crime. One of the main complaints in several policy documents agreed on at a European level is the lack of an overall definition of trafficking in persons, and the lack of criminalisation of trafficking in persons in some states. Until recently, there has not been a single comprehensive definition of trafficking in persons neither at the European nor at the international level; on the contrary, the term trafficking in persons was used in many different ways.[20] The question of whether the 'cross-border' aspect is an element of the crime has not been consistently addressed either. Trafficking in persons is one of the crimes that is often committed in an international context, but not necessarily. For trafficking in persons within the EU, the international dimension is often present, increasing the need for more cooperation among the member states to prosecute this crime. However, trafficking in persons can also take place in one and the same country. As long as there was no agreement on how the term 'trafficking in persons' must be used, the characteristics of this crime could not be defined. Questions to be answered with regard to the definition are: does trafficking in persons always take place for the purpose of sexual exploitation? What is the relation with slavery and slavery-like practices and can the Slavery Conventions be applied in this regard? What is the connection with smuggling of persons? Why do we use the term 'trafficking in persons' instead of 'trafficking in women'?[21] These questions will be answered when the term 'trafficking in persons' is analysed in more depth in this study.

As we have seen, cross-border crime needs intensified cooperation in criminal matters between states for effective prosecution. If trafficking in persons must be considered a transnational crime, methods to improve the prosecution of the crime trafficking in persons developed in this study may also be useful to prosecute transnational crime in general. Therefore, it is relevant to find out whether trafficking in persons must be considered a transnational crime.

1.4 RESEARCH QUESTION

After an exploration of the phenomena of transnational crime and trafficking in persons, this study will specifically focus on the prosecution of trafficking in persons. The research question of this study will be discussed on the basis of the two main disparities described in Section 1.1 and which follow from the developments de-

---

meisjes naar Nederland, Amsterdam, September 1999, pp. 3-7. F. Vellinga, *West-Afrikaanse AMA's,* Police North-East Gelderland, Apeldoorn, May 1999, pp. 7-9. Bureau Nationaal Rapporteur Mensenhandel, *Mensenhandel, Aanvullende kwantitatieve gegevens,* second report, Bureau NRM, The Hague, 2003, pp. 23-24.

[20] For different views on the definition problems, see J. Chuang, Redirecting the Debate over Trafficking in Women: Definitions, Paradigms, and Contexts, in: *Harvard Human Rights Journal,* Volume 11, issue spring, 1998, pp. 65-107. Y. Klerk, Definition of 'Traffic in Person', *SIM-special,* issue 17, Utrecht, 1995, pp. 13-21.

[21] Advisory Committee on Human Rights and Foreign Policy of the Dutch Ministry of Foreign Affairs, *The Traffic in Persons,* Advice no. 14, The Hague, 1992.

scribed above. The first disparity is related to the changing role of the nation state as a consequence of globalisation. In this regard, the changing concept of state sovereignty will be focused upon and the question will be discussed whether state sovereignty facilitates or impedes the effective prosecution of trafficking in persons. The disparity underlying this question is between the fact that trafficking in persons is a crime with transnational elements and the fact that strategies to combat it are based on national competences. The second disparity that will be discussed is between the availability of numerous policy documents and legal instruments[22] adopted to fight trafficking in persons directly, or indirectly by facilitating its prosecution, and the unwillingness or inability of states to use them efficiently or to transform them into concrete action in national law to suppress and prosecute trafficking in persons.

As stated in Section 1.2, the main focus in this study will be on efforts taken to combat trafficking in persons in Europe. The efforts taken within the EU will be of primary concern. The EU is an interesting area for this study as basic constitutional principles are already institutionalised[23] and the integration process in criminal matters is a rather new area in the entire integration process, with many new features. It must be borne in mind that the EU will be enlarged with 10 new member states from the Central and Eastern European region on 1 May 2004.[24] Since many of these states are countries of origin or transit in trafficking cases, the enlargement may create a major opportunity to fight trafficking in persons more effectively. Other important actors in the European context are the Council of Europe and the OSCE. The efforts of these organisations will be the subject of research as far as they influence the fight against trafficking in persons within the EU.

1.4.1 The changing concept of state sovereignty within the EU[25]

The first disparity, namely between the fact that trafficking in persons is a crime often with transnational features and the fact that strategies to combat it are largely

[22] In this study, the phrase 'policy documents and legal instruments' is used to indicate the whole collection of agreements that might be used to combat trafficking in persons. In general, policy documents are non-binding documents that are specifically adopted to combat trafficking in persons while legal instruments are binding and address trafficking in persons directly or indirectly by facilitating its prosecution. All these strategies will be discussed in Chapter 4 and their effectiveness will be evaluated in Chapters 5 and 6. In general, it can be said that the legal instruments contribute to achieving the goals that are formulated in the policy documents.

[23] N. MacCormick, Democracy, Subsidiarity, and Citizenship in the 'European Commonwealth', in: N. MacCormick, *Constructing Legal Systems: 'European Union' in Legal Theory,* Kluwer Academic Publishers, Dordrecht, 1997, pp. 333-339.

[24] These 10 new member states are: Cyprus, the Czech Republic, Estonia, Hungary, Latvia, Lithuania, Malta, Poland, Slovakia, and Slovenia.

[25] See, for instance, the various contributions in: A. van Staden, *De nationale staat, onhoudbaar maar onmisbaar? Het perspectief van Europese integratie en mondialisering,* Van Gorcum, Assen, 1996. Most of the authors agree on the idea that the sovereignty of states has declined in favour of the European Union. However, they do not agree on whether this decline has also led to the erosion of the importance of the nation state. Some argue that, because of the decline of sovereignty of states, the im-

based on national competences, can best be discussed on the basis of the changing concept of state sovereignty.[26] The developments in the process of globalisation have not left the concept of state sovereignty untouched. The legitimisation of the sovereignty of states must be sought in the need of citizens for protection and legal security.[27] Following this legitimisation, states are obliged to set up a legal system that protects their citizens. If states are unable to guarantee safety within their territory and, for instance, to prevent the illegal transportation of goods and persons to and from their territory, they lose much of their credibility. Then the sovereignty of a state no longer reflects factual control over its territory.[28] Consequently, in these cases, states are obliged to undertake extra efforts to protect their citizens and to retain the legitimisation of their sovereign powers. In order to protect citizens against cross-border crime, these efforts must consist of an intensified cooperation in criminal matters with other states. In the nation state as it exists today, based on the concept of the sovereignty and equality of states,[29] states organise their own criminal laws and procedures, but this strategy seems to be insufficient to protect citizens effectively. In this regard, it can be argued that sovereignty, when adopted as a principle to resist interference from other states in criminal law issues, is an obstacle for the effective protection of citizens.[30] When states use their sovereignty to maintain their authority in criminal matters and are not prepared to share those powers with other states, the nation state with its rigidly national criminal strategies are left without an effective system to combat flexible and internationally operating criminals and criminal groups.[31]

Criminal law is closely related to the safety and public order of states and is therefore important to states. Many states use criminal law as a way to underline their identity and the settled values of their society, and are therefore not inclined to give

portance of the nation state has automatically decreased as well while others argue that, because some of the sovereign powers are transmitted to the European Union, the importance of the nation state has increased because they remain the final institutions that can veto the subjects.

[26] The concept of state sovereignty as an exclusive and comprehensive power for law and the maintenance of law on a specific territory can no longer be upheld. It seems that the concept of state sovereignty is nowadays not strictly defined and is dependent on the context in which it is used. See, for instance: E.M.H. Hirsch Ballin, Soevereiniteit in de Europese Unie, in: *NJB*, Volume 72, issue 44, 1997, pp. 2006-2007, 2010. A. Cassese, *International Law,* Oxford University Press, Oxford, 2001, pp. 88-90.

[27] E.M.H. Hirsch Ballin, *Wereldburgers: personen in het internationale recht,* W.E.J. Tjeenk Willink, Zwolle, 1995, pp. 19-21.

[28] Ph. Williams, Transnational Criminal Organisations and International Security, in: N. Passas, *Transnational Crime,* Dartmouth, Aldershot, 1999, p. 45.

[29] Article 2 of the Charter of the United Nations.

[30] B. van Roermund, Jurisprudential Dilemmas of European Law. More moderate and with an overview of the federal and the nation-state approach, R. Bellamy and D. Castiglione, Building the Union: The Nature of Sovereignty in the Political Architecture of Europe. Both in: N. MacCormick, *Constructing Legal Systems: 'European Union' in Legal Theory,* Kluwer Academic Publishers, Dordrecht, 1997, pp. 362-365 and pp. 421-445, respectively.

[31] M. Castells, *The Information Age, Volume III: End of Millenium,* Blackwell, Cambridge, 1998, p. 203.

up their authority when criminal matters are at issue.[32] They want to stick to their sovereign powers in this area and therefore cooperation in this field is not easy to establish. Differences on criminal law issues between states remain because of the lack of harmonisation of substantive and procedural criminal law, causing lacunas between the various systems.[33] Criminals use this lack of coherence to determine which country provides the best opportunities to commit crimes with the lowest risk of being caught.[34] Criminal organisations operating across borders challenge aspects of state sovereignty, namely the security and protection of citizens. They uncover the permeability of national borders and penetrate societies without being hindered by border controls and other restrictive measures. Furthermore, they undermine the system of law and order in a society. As the ability to impose law and order is one of the essential components of state sovereignty, these organisations weaken state sovereignty, which, in the long term may lead to the loss of the legitimisation of state sovereignty.

Dealing with the transnational ramification of criminals and criminal groups requires concerted action on the part of states in order to fill the gaps in national responses and the deficiencies in international cooperation.[35] As stated before, the fight against criminal groups operating across borders can only be effective when intensified cooperation in criminal matters with other states takes place and when states are prepared to share competences in the criminal law field with other states.[36] These competences can be shared on the national or the non-national level. Although no authority on the international or European level exists that has the power to initiate and enforce strategies against cross-border crime as states do not allow a

[32] N. Passas, *Transnational Crime,* Dartmouth, Aldershot, 1999, introduction, pp. xiii-xviii and xxiv. L.S. Sunga, *The Emerging System of International Criminal Law. Developments in Codification and Implementation,* Kluwer Law International, The Hague, 1997, pp. 335-340. A.H.J. Swart, Human Rights and the Abolition of Traditional Principles, in: A. Eser and O. Lagodny (eds.), *Principles and Procedures for a New Transnational Criminal Law,* Max Planck Institute, Freiburg im Breisgau, 1992, pp. 512-513. W. Frijhoff, Eigenzinnig Nederland, Europa en de toekomst van een cultuurnatie, in: A. van Staden, *De nationale staat, onhoudbaar maar onmisbaar? Het perspectief van Europese integratie en mondialisering,* Van Gorcum, Assen, 1996, pp. 125-130.

[33] Ph. Williams, Transnational Criminal Organisations and International Security, in: N. Passas, *Transnational Crime,* Dartmouth, Aldershot, 1999, pp. 46-47. L.F.M. Besselink, *Europese Unie en nationale soevereiniteit. Tussen supranationaliteit en soevereiniteit: over het niet-communautaire recht van de Europese Unie*, W.E.J. Tjeenk Willink, Deventer, 1997, pp. 153-158.

[34] See, for instance, P. Arlacchi, The Dynamics of Illegal Markets, and N. Passas, Globalization and Transnational Crime: Effects of Criminogenic Asymmetries, both in: Ph. Williams and D. Vlassis (eds), *Combating Transnational Crime. Concepts, Activities and Responses,* International Scientific and Professional Advisory Council of the United Nations, Frank Cass, London, 2001, pp. 7-12 and 22-56, respectively.

[35] Report of the Secretary-General on the implementation of General Assembly Resolution 49/150 on the Naples Political Declaration and Global Action against Organised Transnational Crime, A/50/433, 18 September 1995.

[36] Also, WRR, *De toekomst van de Nationale Rechtsstaat,* Sdu Publishers, The Hague, 2002, pp. 72-85. The authors of the report even go further stating that the international legal order must make a demand on all states to guarantee legal order.

higher authority to structure and regulate their legal order,[37] initiatives to set up institutions on a supranational level to enforce international criminal law[38] and steps to facilitate international cooperation in criminal matters at a non-national level seem to indicate a change to state sovereignty.[39] However, as long as there does not exist an authority with the comprehensive power to enforce international criminal law, cooperation in criminal matters, badly needed for the enforcement of international criminal law, remains in the hands of states.

In recent years, the lack of an adequate answer to trafficking in persons has been the subject of debate on many occasions.[40] The prosecution of trafficking in persons is a matter of international cooperation, which necessarily goes beyond the single competence of individual states. The question of how to use current jurisdiction principles to facilitate cooperation in criminal matters will have to be addressed. Furthermore, confidence in each other's systems must be seen as a prerequisite for international cooperation. The question that arises is whether this confidence is present between EU (acceding) states or to what extent this issue causes problems with regard to cooperation in criminal matters. It is assumed that policies and instruments currently used to prosecute trafficking in persons are not effective and that a different approach to this type of crime is needed because of its specific implications. Whether such an approach must originate on a national or an EU level, or both, can only be answered when the reasons are clear as to why the efforts to prosecute the traffickers have so far not been effective. Furthermore, the concept of state sovereignty may help us to answer the question of whether an approach from the EU level is desirable and feasible.

---

[37] Different, see H. Kelsen and R.W. Tucker, *Principles of International Law,* second edition, Holt, Rinehart and Winston, New York, 1966, pp. 581-585, who state that only one entity can be sovereign, thus excluding the sovereignty of all other states by granting sovereignty to one state.

[38] These institutions are: The International Tribunal for the Prosecution of Persons Responsible for Serious Violations of International Humanitarian Law Committed in the Territory of the Former Yugoslavia since 1991, Security Council Resolution 827, 1993 (the Yugoslavia Tribunal). The International Tribunal for the Prosecution of Persons Responsible for Genocide and Other Serious Violations of International Humanitarian Law Committed in the Territory of Rwanda and Rwandan Citizens responsible for genocide committed in the territory of neighbouring States between 1 January 1994 and 31 December 1994, Security Council Resolution 955, 1994 (the Rwanda Tribunal). Rome Statute of the International Criminal Court, A/Conf.183/10, adopted 17 July 1998.

[39] A. Klip, Soevereiniteit in het strafrecht, in: G.J.M. Corstens and M.S. Groenhuijsen (eds.), *Recht en Rede, Liber Amicorum Nico Keijzer*, Gouda Quint, Deventer, 2000, pp. 139-152. J.H. Mittelman and R. Johnston, The Globalization of Organized Crime, the Courtesan State, and the Corruption of Civil Society, in: *Global Governance,* Volume 5, issue 1, 1999, pp. 114-116.

[40] For instance, within the UN during the preparatory meetings for the UN Convention on Transnational Organised Crime, within the EU with the development of an area of freedom, security, and justice, and especially within the area of police and judicial cooperation in criminal matters, resulting in a scoreboard each half year with all the current developments and the state of affairs in this field.

1.4.2 Effectiveness of strategies to combat and prosecute trafficking in persons

The second disparity referred to in Section 1.1 consists of the contradiction between the availability of a great number of strategies to fight and prosecute trafficking in persons and the unwillingness or inability of states to efficiently use these strategies. Until the early 1990s, trafficking in persons was not a big issue on the political agenda, neither in the member states of the EU nor on the European level. There seems to have been a change in this situation as the intention to combat and prosecute trafficking in persons can be found in many policy documents and legal instruments adopted by various institutions at the European level since that time. One of the most important instruments in which these intentions can be found is Article 29 of the EU Treaty.[41] The creation of an area of freedom, security, and justice became the main objective of the third pillar,[42] which is to be realised by 'preventing and combating crime, organised or otherwise, in particular ... trafficking in persons...'. A start to elaborate this aim was made during the meeting of the European Council in Tampere on 15 and 16 October 1999.[43] Besides the fight against illegal immigration and the suppression of trafficking in human beings was made one of the spearheads of the Council of the EU, which is the main decision-making organ in the third pillar.[44] All the objectives expressed in the policy documents and legal instruments contributing to this aim show great dedication on various levels to combating and prosecuting the trafficking in persons. In spite of the great dedication expressed in these agreements, it must be admitted that the effect so far has been rather limited as the willingness or ability of states to use them or to transform them into concrete actions to suppress and prosecute trafficking in persons is often lacking. The number of persons, especially women, trafficked from Western African countries and Central and Eastern European countries to Western Europe has increased, and the prosecution of trafficking cases is still problematic, as we will see in this study.[45]

Besides the policy documents and legal instruments directly addressing trafficking in persons, a number of legal instruments have been enacted that address trafficking in persons indirectly, namely by facilitating its prosecution. Especially in the last decade, increased efforts to harmonise criminal law and to improve cooperation in criminal matters have formed part of EU policy.[46] This has resulted in the develop-

[41] The EU Treaty was first amended by the Treaty of Amsterdam and later by the Treaty of Nice. When the EU Treaty is referred to in this study, the last amended version of the treaty with the provisions of the Treaty of Nice is meant, unless indicated otherwise. In that case, reference is made to the Treaty of Maastricht or the Treaty of Amsterdam. The Treaty of Nice has been in force since 1 February 2003, OJ C 80, 10.3.2001.

[42] The Pillar structure of the EU will be further elaborated in Chapter 4, Section 4.3.2.

[43] Tampere European Council, 15 and 16 October 1999, Presidency Conclusions.

[44] An elaborate overview of the policy documents adopted on the European level with regard to trafficking in persons is the subject of Chapter 4, Section 4.3.3.1.

[45] See Chapter 3, Section 3.7 and Chapter 6.

[46] See, for instance, Article 31(1)(e) EU Treaty.

ment of various instruments to combat (organised) crime in general, such as the EU Convention on Mutual Assistance in Criminal Matters,[47] the European Arrest Warrant,[48] and the two EU conventions on extradition.[49] Most of these instruments are based on conventions enacted within the framework of the Council of Europe. Since the end of the Second World War, the Council of Europe has made great efforts to improve cooperation in criminal matters, which have resulted in a list of international legal instruments, for example, on jurisdiction, extradition, mutual legal assistance, transfer of criminal proceedings, and transfer of enforcement of foreign judgements. Together with existing instruments, such as the Schengen Agreement, the Convention Applying the Schengen Agreement, and other instruments in the third pillar, they form an impressive collection of legal instruments to facilitate the prosecution of (organised) crime in general and thus to facilitate the prosecution of the suspects involved in trafficking in persons.

In this study, the policy documents specifically addressing trafficking in persons as well as the legal instruments that might facilitate the prosecution of those accused of trafficking in persons will be identified and discussed. Afterwards, the effectiveness of these policy documents and legal instruments will be explored. It would be beyond the scope of this study, and it would not contribute to a clear picture of the relevant problems either, to generally examine the effectiveness of all the instruments aimed at combating (organised) crime. Therefore, an examination will be made as far as it is relevant for the prosecution of those accused of trafficking in persons. It is presupposed that the internationalisation of trafficking in persons and, consequently, the increased complexity of this crime described in Section 1.3, raises particular problems as regards its prosecution. Thus, the main question in this study will be: to what extent do legal instruments contribute to the effective prosecution of those suspected of trafficking in persons? In order to find an answer to this main question, the following questions will play a leading role in this study: Are the legal instruments to prosecute trafficking in persons used? And, if any, what are the obstacles for an effective use of the legal instruments?

Following these questions, the main focus in this study will be on the legal instruments. Since these cannot be discussed and examined without referring to the policies on which they are based, the policy documents directly referring to trafficking in persons will be discussed in this study as well.

[47] Council Act of 29 May 2000, Establishing, in Accordance with Article 34 of the Treaty on European Union, the Convention on Mutual Assistance in Criminal Matters between the Member States of the European Union, OJ C 197, 12.7.2000.

[48] Council Framework Decision of 13 June 2002 on the European Arrest Warrant and the Surrender Procedures between the Member States, OJ L 190, 18.7.2002, pp. 1-20.

[49] The Convention on Simplified Extradition Procedure between the Member States of the European Union, OJ C 78, 30.3.1995, and the Convention Relating to Extradition between the Member States of the European Union, OJ C 313, 23.10.1996.

1.5 AIM OF THE STUDY

The aim of this study follows from the premise that the internationalisation of trafficking in persons generates particular problems for the prosecution of this crime. The aim of this study is to identify the obstacles to the use of policy documents and legal instruments adopted to suppress and prosecute trafficking in persons in order to improve the prosecution of alleged traffickers. The question will be answered whether it is desirable and feasible that the approach for improvement originates on the national or the EU level or on both. It is not my aim in this study to develop a complete new approach to fighting trafficking in persons but the recommendations given at the end of this study may serve as starting points to develop such an approach.

Before solutions can be developed, the obstacles must be further identified. These obstacles can consist of, for instance, the fact that the instruments include vague terms, or that procedures laid down in the instruments are too time-consuming and therefore are not taken into account because states have other priorities. Maybe states do not have enough confidence in each other's systems for effective cooperation. This study seeks to clarify the obstacles. Only after the identification and analysis of the obstacles will it be possible to suggest solutions to improve the cooperation between the EU member states in order to improve the prosecution of trafficking in persons. The improvement can be sought in two directions, namely, in new initiatives and in the modification of the use of current principles.

1.5.1 **New initiatives to prosecute those suspected of trafficking in persons**

A first new initiative for a collective strategy under the EU Treaty is the setting up of Eurojust. The contribution of Eurojust to the prosecution of those suspected of trafficking in persons will be examined. Although Eurojust is an intergovernmental organisation comparable to Europol, it must be considered a new instrument as it concerns judicial authorities. A second new initiative that will be examined is the proposal for a European Public Prosecutor, originally a proposal to combat Eurofraud.[50] It will be judged on its value to prosecute those suspected of trafficking in persons. Thirdly, the replacement of aspects of the national legal order with a European legal order to prosecute trafficking in persons might be another solution contributing to the aim of this study. The question will be answered whether setting up a strategy originating at EU level to prosecute trafficking in persons is desirable and feasible.

---

[50] M. Delmas-Marty and Ch. van den Wyngaert, *Corpus Juris,* Intersentia Rechtswetenschappen, Antwerp, 1998.

1.5.2 Transformation of the use of current principles

Questions on mutual legal assistance, extradition, transfer of criminal proceedings, and mutual recognition of decisions, arising in the context of trafficking in persons, will be addressed in relation to current developments in the field of cooperation in criminal matters within the EU. The purpose is to find indications of how to transform the use of the principles on these issues so that they can facilitate the use of legal instruments to prosecute traffickers. The principles that limit the prosecution of trafficking in persons will subsequently be identified. General principles originating from extradition law, such as *double criminality* and the *speciality rule*, and jurisdiction principles, such as the *universality principle,* will be the subject of research in order to answer the question of whether a transformation of the use of these principles will be helpful to apply and change the legal instruments in order to improve the prosecution of trafficking in persons. A transformation of the use of some of these principles has already been adopted in the European Arrest Warrant, the EU Convention on Mutual Assistance, and the EU Conventions on Extradition. Therefore, the potential of these instruments to prosecute those suspected of trafficking in persons more effectively will be tested on in order to answer the question of whether such a transformation can really contribute to the improvement of the prosecution of trafficking in persons.

1.5.3 Limitations of criminal law with regard to trafficking in persons

It has to be emphasised that not all the problems related to trafficking in persons can be solved by criminal law. For example, poverty in the home countries of the trafficked persons and the differences in living standards between the various parts of the world are important reasons why people leave their countries. Criminal law is not the adequate instrument to end or reduce this poverty, but development aid may be more appropriate. Another field in which progress can be made to prevent trafficking in persons is migration law. Most of the EU countries limit legal migration for employment purposes, so migrants have to find an alternative in the illegal scene. Traffickers use the vulnerable position of these persons to arrange employment for them.[51] For persons outside the EU, it is almost impossible to obtain a work permit because of the free movement of persons within the EU, and consequently the preference of member states for employees from other member states. If the rules for employment for immigrants are less strict, the necessity to use the illegal way will be less urgent because of the existence of lawful possibilities for employment for immigrants. In this regard, it is regrettable that most of the current EU member states will suspend the application of the provisions on the free movement of workers for citizens of the applicant countries for three years.

[51] International Organisation for Migration, *Trafficking and Prostitution: The Growing Exploitation of Migrant Women from Central and Eastern Europe,* Migration Information Programme, Budapest, 1995, pp. 12-14.

Migration law is also in another way related to trafficking in persons. Most of the persons who are trafficked are staying in the EU without a valid residence permit. Consequently, the legal position of trafficked persons is often very weak. When decisions are taken on the granting of residence permits or on expulsion, the vulnerable position of the trafficked persons has to be taken into account; these persons must be treated as victims rather than as offenders. Thus, migration law and the regulation of prostitution are other ways to address the suppression of trafficking in persons.[52]

Preferably, aid for the countries of origin, action in the area of immigration law, and criminal law solutions should be fine-tuned. In this study, the main focus will be on the criminal law aspects of prosecuting traffickers; aspects of immigration law will be dealt with only as far as is relevant for this study.

1.6 STRUCTURE OF THE STUDY

Before the analysis of policy documents and legal instruments to combat and prosecute trafficking in persons can be made, some clarification about the relevant terms is needed. In Chapter 2, the area of international criminal law and crimes in international criminal law will be explored. The characteristics of a new, third group of international crime, namely, transnational crime, will be identified and its relation with other (international) crimes will be analysed. Chapter 3 deals with the definition of trafficking in persons, the extent of the phenomenon, and the modus operandi of the traffickers. When different persons, organisations, and states use different terminology and definitions for the same conduct or phenomenon, it will be impossible to develop an effective strategy to suppress and prosecute the crime of trafficking in persons. In this chapter, the term 'trafficking in persons' will be explored and the question of under what conditions trafficking in persons must be considered a transnational crime will be answered on the basis of criteria developed in Chapter 2. Furthermore, the definition of trafficking in persons to be used in this study will be given. Its relation to other phenomena such as slavery, slavery-like practices, forced labour, and smuggling people will be outlined. In Chapter 4, the current policy documents and legal instruments available on the European level, namely within the EU, the Council of Europe, and the OSCE, to combat and prosecute the crime of trafficking in persons will be discussed. In Chapter 5, the effectiveness of the policy documents and legal instruments focusing on trafficking in persons and cooperation in criminal matters, as discussed in Chapter 4, will be examined. Firstly, some gen-

[52] J. Wiarda, Trends in de wetgeving inzake mensensmokkel en mensenhandel, *Tijdschrift voor Criminologie,* Volume 43, issue 4, 2001, pp. 370-371. M. Smit, Mensenhandel: een moderne vorm van slavernij, *Tijdschrift voor Criminologie,* Volume 43, issue 4, 2001, p. 384. In 2002, a first evaluation was made of the effects of the legalisation of prostitution in the Netherlands that was realised in October 2000. The results of this study show that the expected effect that criminal activities were eliminated from regulated legal prostitution has been rather limited so far. Further research is necessary to make more definite statements on this issue. A. Daalder, Het bordeelverbod opgeheven, Prostitutie 2000-2001, WODC report 200, 2002.

eral remarks will be made on the reasons for the ineffectiveness of the policy documents and legal instruments. Secondly, an analysis will be made of the obstacles to the use of legal instruments as indicated in the legal literature. Thirdly, a study will be made of the evaluations of the mutual legal assistance systems of the member states of the EU, executed by the Multidisciplinary Group on Organised Crime of the Council of the EU. In Chapter 6, the effectiveness of the system of cooperation in criminal matters in trafficking cases in the Netherlands will be examined on the basis of a file study of the trafficking cases that were registered in the years 1999 and 2000 at the courts of Amsterdam, The Hague, and Rotterdam. Prior to this file study, I conducted interviews with public prosecutors specialised in trafficking issues in order to obtain a first impression of the problems concerning the prosecution of the traffickers in the Netherlands. The file study itself is based on the problems indicated on the basis of the analysis of the evaluation reports in Chapter 5 and the problems mentioned in the orientating interviews.

After the problems involved in and the obstacles to an effective use of instruments to prosecute trafficking in persons are identified, a summary of the obstacles to the prosecution of alleged traffickers will be given in Chapter 7. Suggestions to improve the prosecution of trafficking in persons shall be elaborated on the basis of the pros and cons of both national and EU approaches. By focusing on the European Arrest Warrant, the EU Convention on Mutual Assistance, and the EU Convention on Simplified Extradition Procedure between the member states of the EU, I will discuss whether the transformation of the use of the current principles adopted in these instruments will contribute to a more effective prosecution of trafficking in persons on the national level, once they are in force. Eurojust and the proposal for the installation of a European Public Prosecutor will be judged in Chapter 7 as new initiatives that may contribute to an effective prosecution of the crime on the EU level. On the basis of this analysis, the final conclusion will be drawn with the recommendation for a realistic approach to prosecuting trafficking in persons. An answer will be given to the question of how the changing concept of state sovereignty can contribute to the application of this realistic approach to prosecute trafficking in persons.

CHAPTER 2
TRANSNATIONAL CRIME AND INTERNATIONAL CRIMINAL LAW

2.1 INTRODUCTION

Since the crime of trafficking in persons is surrounded by implications of an international criminal nature, an approach from an international criminal law perspective to the phenomenon seems obvious. It is often indicated that trafficking in persons can be seen as a transnational crime, however, without this term being further analysed. This chapter aims to identify the characteristics of transnational crime and to clarify the connection between transnational crime and international criminal law. Before this connection can be clarified and the characteristics identified, we have to take a closer look at the system of international criminal law. To this end, an overview of the dominant views concerning the functions of international criminal law and the leading principles of jurisdiction in international criminal law will be given. I will discuss the traditional division of international criminal law between the criminal law aspects of international law, on the one hand, and the international aspects of national criminal law, on the other. Both these categories correspond to a certain group of crimes, which will be discussed as well. Using the internationalisation of criminal activities that was discussed in Chapter 1 as a starting point, I will distinguish a third group of crimes, namely, transnational crime. Following the characterisation of this third group, the question must be answered whether this group of crimes can be accommodated within the traditional two categories of international criminal law. Furthermore, the question must be answered whether the crime of trafficking in persons fits the description of this third group of crimes. This last question shall be answered in Chapter 3.

2.2 THE NATURE OF INTERNATIONAL CRIMINAL LAW

2.2.1 The relation between international criminal law, national criminal law, and international law

Before analysing the relation between trafficking in persons and international criminal law in the next chapter, some exploration on the content of the latter has to be made. Whether something like international criminal law exists, depends on the point of reference. If international criminal law must be seen as a further development of a system similar to municipal criminal law, binding for a defined community and enforced by authoritative institutions functioning in their own capacity, the conclusion must be drawn that such a system of international criminal law does not exist. When starting from an international law point of view, in which international criminal law is a subdivision of international law and based on principles such as consent between states and dependent on the will of the states, it can be said that such a form of international criminal law does exist. Notwithstanding the fact that the question of whether international criminal law exists is not undisputed, most of the legal authors agree on the existence of international criminal law as a separate discipline as we will see in the next section.

It can be said that international criminal law is situated on the boundary between criminal law and international law or in the words of Wise: 'In its widest, most commodious sense, international criminal law covers all problems lying on the borderline between international and criminal law.'[1] It is that discipline of law where the penal aspects of international law and the international aspects of national criminal law converge.[2] This is often called the dichotomy of international criminal law. This dichotomy causes a division in international criminal law that will be discussed in Section 2.3.

Criminal law on the national level, on the one hand, is limited by the principle of sovereignty, which means that national criminal law is designed for a particular territory and a specific legal order, namely, that of a particular state. The power of national criminal law outside that state is limited. On the basis of state sovereignty, interference with the criminal procedures in another state is not allowed and states do not have to accept interference from other states in criminal matters. Territoriality still remains the primary basis for criminal jurisdiction.[3] In this sense sovereignty must be seen as a limitation for intensified cooperation in criminal matters. On the other hand, international law, as it is agreed by states on the basis of their sovereign powers, provide some mechanisms to extend a state's power in criminal matters, and facilitate states in the performance of their duties in the field of criminal law. In this way sovereignty must be seen as a basis for the creation of mechanisms for intensified cooperation. These two approaches of state sovereignty play an important role when discussing the improvement of cooperation in criminal matters for the prosecution of trafficking in persons in Chapter 7. In that chapter the changing concept of state sovereignty will be further elaborated by taking into account these two approaches.

International law is based on consent between states and normally formulated to impose obligations on states while municipal criminal law is directed at individuals.[4] Therefore, individual criminal responsibility in international criminal law cannot be applied without further modification. Individual criminal responsibility has to be established in treaties of international criminal law,[5] although it cannot be excluded

---

[1] E.M. Wise, Terrorism and the Problems of an International Criminal Law, in: J. Dugard and Ch. van den Wyngaert, *International Criminal Law and Procedure*, Dartmouth, Aldershot, 1996, p. 39.

[2] J.J. Paust, et al., *International Criminal Law: Cases and Materials,* Carolina Academic Press, Durham, North Carolina, 1996, pp. 3-19.

[3] K. Kittichaisaree, *International Criminal Law,* Oxford University Press, Oxford, 2001, pp. 4-6. Section 2.3.2.2 below.

[4] K. Kittichaisaree, *International Criminal Law,* Oxford University Press, Oxford, 2001, p. 10.

[5] M.C. Bassiouni, *International Criminal Law, Crimes,* second edition, Transnational Publishers, Inc. Ardsley, New York, 1999, pp. 21-23.

that individual criminal responsibility for international crimes also exists without a conventional basis. International criminal law finds its basis, at least partly, in international law. With regard to the relation between international law and national law, Kelsen stated that no subject exclusively belongs to domestic jurisdiction. 'There are no matters which, by their very nature, are reserved to regulation by national law and are not susceptible of regulation by international law.'[6] International law includes the ability to regulate all matters. It depends on the circumstances of a case whether provisions of international law are the most appropriate to deal with the case. Regulation by international law depends on whether international aspects are present in a particular case and whether national law exists on the subject. According to Kelsen, the primary function of international law is to determine the territorial, personal, temporal, and material spheres of validity of the national legal orders and to coordinate them. This characterisation of international law can also be applied to international criminal law since it rules the material, territorial and personal aspects of international crimes. For the enforcement of international criminal law, the application of national criminal law is essential. The enforcement of international criminal law is almost completely dependent on national courts, except in the case of international tribunals, where international criminal law can be enforced directly.[7] Consequently, international criminal law and national criminal law are inextricably bound: the effect of international criminal law is very limited when national criminal law cannot be used to enforce it.[8] There is a trend in international law to regulate matters that originally were regulated only by national law.[9] When international criminal law is considered to be a part of international law, which is a common approach, this trend applies for international criminal law as well.[10] With the enormous increase of initiatives and agreements at the international level in the field of criminal law and cooperation in criminal matters, this trend cannot be denied.[11]

---

[6] H. Kelsen and R.W. Tucker, *Principles of International Law,* second edition, Holt, Rinehart and Winston, Inc. New York, 1966, p. 291.

[7] For instance, The International Tribunal for the Prosecution of Persons Responsible for Serious Violations of International Humanitarian Law Committed in the Territory of the Former Yugoslavia since 1991, Security Council Resolution 827, 1993. The International Tribunal for the Prosecution of Persons Responsible for Genocide and Other Serious Violations of International Humanitarian Law Committed in the Territory of Rwanda and Rwandan Citizens responsible for genocide committed in the territory of neighbouring States between 1 January 1994 and 31 December 1994, Security Council Resolution 955, 1994. Rome Statute of the International Criminal Court, A/Conf.183/10, adopted 17 July 1998.

[8] J.J. Paust, et al., *International Criminal Law: Cases and Materials,* Carolina Academic Press, Durham, North Carolina, 1996, pp. 7-8, 15-16.

[9] H. Kelsen and R.W. Tucker, *Principles of International Law,* second edition, Holt, Rinehart and Winston, Inc. New York, 1966, pp. 290-293, 301, 304-306. Examples of such matters are, for instance, the rights of disabled persons and the minimum age for marriage.

[10] For a discussion of whether International Criminal Law is part of International Law, see L.S. Sunga, *The Emerging System of International Criminal Law. Developments in Codification and Implementation,* Kluwer Law International, The Hague, 1997, pp. 323-340.

[11] Such initiatives include, for instance, the establishment of Europol and Eurojust. Agreements on the international level in the field of criminal law are, for instance, the UN Convention of Transnational

2.2.2 Functions and definitions of international criminal law

Legal authors use different definitions of international criminal law. By summarising the most important views the following picture can be drawn.[12] Some writers argue that there is not something like international criminal law at all, some see international criminal law as a small part of international law, and some believe that there may be a system of international criminal law but that it is not enforceable in the relations between states. In this last view, the establishment of an international body capable of enforcing judicial decisions is needed. Another opinion states that one of the major difficulties in the notion of international criminal law is that it has a strong tendency to combine public international legal norms with the international aspects of domestic criminal law. According to these authors, the main reason for the problem of enforceability is a lack of norms at the international level as international criminal law must be seen as the law of sovereign states. Therefore, the existence of a proper penal system on the supranational level is impossible because of the equality of states.

One of the writers who explicitly deny the existence of international criminal law is Schwarzenberger. According to Schwarzenberger, all forms of international criminal law have their roots in national procedures. He argues that international criminal law is used in at least six different meanings,[13] in none of which he finds evidence for the existence of international criminal law. For him, the two prerequisites for the existence of international criminal law are that it consists of rules of a prohibitive character and that these are endowed with specific penal sanctions.[14] Neither the former nor the latter can be found in international criminal law, according to Schwarzenberger. He is of the opinion that, as long as the national states are the violators as well as the dispensers of justice, international criminal law in its true sense cannot exist and remains the monopoly of the strong states.[15] Together with Malekian, he is of the opinion that the veto of the five permanent members of the Security Council is one of the reasons for the non-existence of international criminal law and must

---

Organised Crime A/55/383, signed 12-15 December 2000, (not yet in force), the Convention on Cyber Crime (ETS no. 185, signed 23 November 2001, not yet in force) and the Criminal Law Convention on Corruption (ETS no. 173, in force since 1 July 2002), both from the Council of Europe.

[12] F. Malekian, *International Criminal Law: The Legal and Critical Analysis of International Crimes,* Malekian, Uppsala, 1991, pp. 3-10.

[13] International criminal law in the meaning of the territorial scope of municipal criminal law; in the meaning of internationally prescribed municipal criminal law; in the meaning of internationally authorised municipal criminal law; in the meaning of municipal criminal law common to civilised nations; in the meaning of international cooperation in the administration of municipal criminal justice; and international criminal law in the material sense of the term.

[14] G. Schwarzenberger, The Problem of an International Criminal Law, in: *International Criminal Law and Procedure,* J. Dugard and Ch. van den Wyngaert, Dartmouth, Aldershot, 1996, pp. 14ff.

[15] F. Malekian, *The Monopolization of International Criminal Law in the United Nations. A Jurisprudential Approach,* second edition, Almqvist & Wiksell International, Stockholm, 1995, pp. 55-59.

be seen as an obstacle in the development of international criminal law. He states:[16]

> in such a situation an international criminal law that is meant to be applied to the world powers is a contradiction in terms. It presupposes an international authority which is superior to these states. In reality, however, any attempt to enforce an international criminal code against either the Soviet Union or the United States would be war under another name. ... If, and when, the swords of war are taken from their present guardians, then, and only then, will the international community be strong enough to wield the sword of universal criminal justice.

According to Malekian, the purpose of international criminal law is 'to deter international crimes from being committed which may jeopardize the international legal order and its peace'.[17] He considers the United Nations of decisive importance for determining the contents of international criminal law. He states that the aim of securing international peace and security, as is outlined in Chapter VII of the Charter of the UN, can only be achieved within the system of international criminal law, especially when defining the international crimes at the basis of Chapter VII of the UN Charter. These crimes are: war crimes, aggression, genocide, and apartheid. According to Malekian, international criminal law, in its current situation, can only be a result of a compromise between the permanent members of the Security Council. In this regard, he allocates too much influence in international criminal law to the Security Council and applies a very limited concept of international criminal law, namely that international criminal law only consists of the criminal law aspects of international law resulting in the formulation of some core international crimes. Consequently, international criminal law, in the opinion of Malekian and Schwarzenberger must be observed and enforced on a supranational level. When the view is adopted that the international aspects of domestic criminal law are a substantive part of international criminal law as well, the need for a supranational enforcement mechanism is less tangible and the role of the five permanent members of the Security Council is much more limited, since the equality of states is better guaranteed in this part of international criminal law. However, Malekian also argues that the development of international criminal law depends on the political will of each individual state to support this development, which is a more moderate and realistic point of view.

It is generally accepted that the main function of international criminal law is to prevent criminal violations against national or international orders.[18] This includes the protection of human rights as one of the functions of international criminal law.[19] In

---

[16] G. Schwarzenberger, The Problem of an International Criminal Law, in: *International Criminal Law and Procedure,* J. Dugard, and Ch. van den Wyngaert, Dartmouth, Aldershot, 1996, pp. 33-34.

[17] F. Malekian, *The Monopolization of International Criminal Law in the United Nations. A Jurisprudential Approach,* second edition, Almqvist & Wiksell International, Stockholm, 1995 p. 26.

[18] F. Malekian, *International Criminal Law: The Legal and Critical Analysis of International Crimes,* Malekian, Uppsala, 1991, p. 1.

[19] See Section 2.2.3 below.

Malekian's opinion a positivist view with regard to international criminal law is not satisfactory because moral, economic, and legal values as well as political factors play an important role in establishing international criminal law.

Based upon the different definitions, Malekian comes to the conclusion that international criminal law has two clear aims.[20] The first is 'to secure the international legal order and therefore to maintain international perpetual peace.' For this purpose, the conduct that forms a violation of world peace and security has to be codified in international criminal law. The second aim of international criminal law is 'to secure domestic legal systems where they are unable to implement their own legal systems as a result of international aspects in a certain case.' Therefore, agreements on cooperation in criminal matters between states are needed to guarantee the prosecution and conviction of offenders who have committed such crimes.

From these two aims of international criminal law, it follows that it has two characteristics. The first characteristic is that it contains a body of international agreements in which the international community criminalises certain conduct. The second characteristic is that it contains a set of instruments that regulates the application of national criminal law in case international aspects complicate the applicability and enforcement of law. The difference between the former and the latter is that the former ideally is enforceable internationally, while the latter is only enforceable among a certain number of states. The former may, in certain situations, be considered as a principle of *jus cogens.* Provisions recognised as such have to be obeyed by all states at all times, regardless of their participation in an international criminal convention according to the International Court of Justice (ICJ).[21] Although this provides a dichotomy in international criminal law, it has to be admitted that the enforceability of international criminal law of both types depends upon political considerations, since the enforceability of international criminal law has always depended mainly on the willingness of the states to apply these provisions in their national courts. Furthermore, the inability to enforce sanctions on an international level is one of the aspects that frustrate the development of international criminal law.[22] Instead, states undertake, via international criminal conventions, to transform provisions of international criminal law into national law in order to establish the jurisdiction of national courts. The International Criminal Court that was officially established on 1 July 2002, is the first structural institution to weaken this practice of giving primacy to

[20] F. Malekian, *International Criminal Law: The Legal and Critical Analysis of International Crimes,* Malekian, Uppsala, 1991, pp. 9-10.

[21] Barcelona Traction, Light and Power Limited, *Belgium* v. *Spain*, ICJ (1962-1970). A norm *jus cogens* is a norm accepted and recognised by the international community of States as a whole as a norm from which no derogation is permitted and which can be modified only by a subsequent norm of general international law having the same character, according to Article 53 of the Vienna Convention on the Law of Treaties, 1155 UNTS 331, entered into force, 27 January 1980.

[22] F. Malekian, *The Monopolization of International Criminal Law in the United Nations. A Jurisprudential Approach,* second edition, Almqvist & Wiksell International, Stockholm, 1995, pp. 40-41.

apply international criminal law before national courts, by providing a complementary provision at the international level.

2.2.3 The protection of human rights as one of the functions of international criminal law

One development that can be traced in international criminal law in general is an increased focus on human rights. The impact of violations of human rights treaties and values on neighbouring countries and the world community provides arguments to justify actions against these violations. This development can be transposed to the field of international criminal law. In many treaties, the penalised conduct that is referred to as international crimes are violations of human rights and basic values.[23] In this sense, international criminal law and human rights protection are intertwined. In addition to this increased attention for human rights, the problem of enforcing human rights law is another reason for the increased role of human rights in international criminal law. Negotiations, reporting procedures, investigating procedures, and the enactment of general comments by several monitoring committees are not enough to enforce human rights provisions in treaties. Power based on Chapter VII of the UN Charter might in some exceptional cases be used under strict conditions and serve as a remedy to enforce human rights. This is another way in which international criminal law and human rights are dependent on each other. However, humanitarian motives to legitimise this power are always accompanied by political, economic and legal motives and therefore the relation with international criminal law is complicated.[24] Not only with regard to the substantive part of international criminal law has human rights obtained increased attention but also with regard to the procedural part. Especially in the field of cooperation in criminal matters human rights play a still increasing role for instance as regards the possible exceptions to extradition or the application of double criminality.[25] Another indication that international criminal law and human rights protection are linked is the increased attention in recent years for the victim during criminal proceedings as well as for the protection of the procedural rights of the suspect.[26]

---

[23] M.C. Bassiouni, *International Criminal Law. Crimes*, second edition, Transnational Publishers, Inc. Ardsley, New York, 1999, pp. 46-48. For instance, the violation of a person's physical integrity as a basis for the Torture Convention, the violation of the right to life as a basis for war crimes and crimes against humanity.

[24] F. Malekian, *The monopolization of International Criminal Law in the United Nations, A Jurisprudential Approach,* second edition, Almqvist & Wiksell International, Stockholm, 1995, pp. 143-144.

[25] A.H.J. Swart, Human Rights and the Abolition of Traditional Principles, and Ch. van den Wyngaert, Rethinking the Law of International Criminal Cooperation: The Restrictive Function of International Human Rights Through Individual-Oriented Bars, both in: A. Eser and O. Lagodny (eds.), *Principles and Procedures for a New Transnational Criminal Law,* Max Planck Institute, Freiburg im Breisau, 1992, pp. 507-512 and 489-503 respectively.

[26] For instance, C. Chinkin, The Protection of Victims and Witnesses, in: G.K. McDonald and O. Swaak-Goldman, *Substantive and Procedural Aspects of International Criminal Law. The Experience of International and National Courts,* Kluwer Law International, The Hague, 2000, pp. 455-478.

2.3 THE TRADITIONAL CATEGORISATION OF INTERNATIONAL CRIMINAL LAW

The two functions in international criminal law outlined in Section 2.2.2 above[27] correspond with a division in international criminal law that is frequently mentioned in the literature and which was already referred to in the introduction. It concerns the distinction between criminal law aspects of international law and international aspects of national criminal law. In the literature many distinctions have been made in international criminal law but most of them can be traced to this principal categorisation. Both categories of international criminal law will be discussed below. Bassiouni states that international criminal law has developed along these two different paths to become complementary and co-extensive.[28]

2.3.1 **Criminal law aspects of international law**

2.3.1.1 *The characteristics of the category of criminal law aspects of international law*

International law has long been influenced by the natural law approach. In the 19th century, positivism became the leading view. After the First and Second World Wars, natural law recovered its position and again became influential for the content of international law. The recovered influence of natural law became evident in the law applied in the Tokyo and Nuremberg Tribunals. The positivists had to admit that recognising only codified law as applicable law could lead to undesirable results. By strictly obeying only codified norms, harmful national-socialist regimes could not be prevented from flourishing again.[29] Moral values (as part of the doctrine of natural law) were again allowed to play a role on the juridical scene.

With these developments, a new phase in international criminal law commenced. Before the judgements at Nuremberg and Tokyo, some types of conduct were internationally criminalised, like slavery and piracy. But it remained unclear under what circumstances conduct becomes an international crime and what the content of international criminal law is. The judgements after the Second World War provided some clarification. For these tribunals, new law had been created to prosecute the perpetrators of war crimes, which accelerated the development of international criminal law. After these temporary tribunals, the UN considered the establishment of a permanent international court in 1948 in the context of the adoption of the Conven-

[27] Namely, the function to secure the international legal order and thus to maintain international perpetual peace, and the function to secure domestic legal systems where a state is unable to implement its own legal system as a result of international aspects in a certain case.

[28] M.C. Bassiouni, *International Criminal Law. Crimes,* second edition, Transnational Publishers, Inc. Ardsley, New York, 1999, pp. 8-14.

[29] A. Verdross, Dynamisches Naturrecht, in: H. Kelsen, A. Merkl and A. Verdross. *Die Wiener Rechtstheoretische Schule,* part I, Europa Verlag, Vienna, pp. 933ff.

tion on the Prevention and Punishment of the Crime of Genocide.[30] Because of the Cold War and differences in opinion this effort was suspended between 1954 and 1989. Another reason that it took so long is that an international definition of criminal behaviour is difficult to establish. There is no set of substantive prescriptive rules sufficient to serve as a mechanism to penalise international criminal behaviour, which does not make it easy to find agreements. In 1989, the UN General Assembly requested the International Law Commission to draft a report addressing the issue of establishing an international criminal court with jurisdiction to try persons alleged to have committed international crimes.[31] Finally, with the adoption of the Statute of Rome in July 1998, the establishment of an International Criminal Court became a real option.

Other developments which are extremely important for the development of international criminal law, especially in defining certain international crimes, is the establishment of the Yugoslavia Tribunal and the Rwanda Tribunal. If we look at the judgements of these tribunals, we have to conclude that the case law established by the Nuremberg and Tokyo Tribunals is still valuable to determine the content of some international crimes.[32] Following these developments, it must be admitted that the development of international crimes often came as a result of the enforcement of provisions on international human rights law.

This is one side of the development of international criminal law, namely, that of the criminal law aspects of international law. In this category, we find the 'rules and principles of public international law that impose obligations on states with respect to the content of their domestic criminal law or procedure.'[33] Many of these rules and principles can be found in international human rights conventions and other general conventions.

The part of international criminal law concerning criminal law aspects of international law essentially deals with substantive international criminal law or international crimes. The category of criminal law aspects of international law includes the crimes that cause a violation of interests identified by the world community as common interests of humankind, in other words, crimes against the international community. This category is defined as those aspects of the international legal system that regulate conduct through international legal obligations. It deals with the conduct of individuals that violates certain internationally defined provisions.

[30] Press Release, 3 April 1998, L/2863, Preparatory Committee on International Criminal Court.

[31] C.A.Res.44/39, UN GAOR, 44th Sess., UN Doc. A/Res/44/39 (1989) and A/RES/46/54.

[32] M. Boot, *Nullum Crimen Sine Lege and the Subject Matter Jurisdiction of the International Criminal Court*, Intersentia, Antwerp, 2002, pp. 237-240, 457-474. K. Kittichaisaree, *International Criminal Law*, Oxford University Press, Oxford, 2001, pp. 17-38, 44-55. M.C. Bassiouni, *International Criminal Law. Crimes*, second edition, Transnational Publishers, Inc. Ardsley, New York, 1999, p. 12.

[33] E.M. Wise, Terrorism and the Problems of an International Criminal Law, in: J. Dugard and Ch. van den Wyngaert, *International Criminal Law and Procedure*, Dartmouth, Aldershot, 1996, p. 42.

2.3.1.2 *The crimes within the category of criminal law aspects of international law*

According to Bassiouni, from the conventions in the category of criminal law aspects of international law, ten penal characteristics can be deduced, including the criminalisation of certain types of conduct irrespective of particular enforcement modalities and mechanisms.[34] Within this category a group of international crimes can be identified. In general, these international crimes can be found either in international criminal conventions or in customary international criminal law, which has the character of *de lege lata.* However, when the conduct described in international conventions must be considered as an international crime, is a source for controversy as well.[35] The International Law Commission has described an international crime as 'an internationally wrongful act, which results from the breach by the state of an international obligation so essential for the protection of fundamental interests of the international community that its breach is recognized as a crime by that community.'[36] According to Bassiouni, a crime is an international crime if it meets the following four requirements.[37]

1. the prohibited conduct affects a significant international interest (including threats to peace and security);
2. the prohibited conduct constitutes an egregious conduct deemed offensive to the commonly shared values of the world community (including conduct shocking to the conscience of humanity);
3. the prohibited conduct involves more than one state (transnational implications) in its planning, preparation, or commission, through the diversity of the nationality of either its perpetrators or its victims. Or because the means employed transcend national boundaries;
4. the conduct bears upon an internationally protected interest, which does not rise to the level, required by (1) or (2) but which cannot be prevented or controlled without its international criminalisation.

---

[34] M.C. Bassiouni, *International Criminal Law. Crimes*, second edition, Transnational Publishers, Inc. Ardsley, New York, 1999, pp. 47-48. These ten penal characteristics are: explicit recognition of proscribed conduct as constituting an international crime, or a crime under international law, or as a crime; implicit recognition of the penal nature of the act by establishing a duty to prohibit, prevent, prosecute, punish, or the like; criminalization of the proscribed conduct; duty or right to prosecute; duty or right to punish the proscribed conduct; duty or right to extradite; duty or right to cooperate in prosecution, punishment; establishment of a criminal jurisdictional basis; reference to the establishment of an international criminal court or an international tribunal with penal characteristics; elimination of the defence of superior orders.

[35] F. Malekian, *The Monopolization of International Criminal Law in the United Nations. A Jurisprudential Approach,* second edition, Almqvist & Wiksell International, Stockholm, 1995, p. 51.

[36] Art. 19(2), Draft Articles on State Responsibility, in: Report of the International Law Commission to the General Assembly, UN Doc. A/31/10 (1976). In the more recently adopted Draft Articles on State Responsibility the term 'international crime' is not used. A description of an internationally wrongful act can be found in Articles 2 and 12, Responsibility of States for Internationally Wrongful Acts, GA Res. 56/83, 28 January 2002.

[37] M.C. Bassiouni, *International Criminal Law. Crimes*, second edition, Transnational Publishers, Inc. Ardsley, New York, 1999, p. 33.

Whether these requirements must be met cumulatively before a certain conduct can be considered to be an international crime remains unclear. Following these criteria Bassiouni has adopted a list of 25 categories of international crimes,[38] which has been and still is subject to both criticism and praise. The list of 25 offences is further divided into (a) international crimes; (b) international delicts; and (c) international infractions.[39]

A common characteristic of international crimes is that they are shocking for the world community. The reasoning behind the notion of an international crime is to express the very serious character of an internationally unlawful act that is potentially harmful to the community of nations. An international crime emerges when a serious violation of an international obligation of fundamental importance for the security of international legal order has occurred.[40] With regard to more formal aspects, to be categorised as an international crime, the conduct must at least[41]

- be recognised as an international crime in either a treaty, under customary law, or in the writing of scholars, or
- be recognised as a violation of international law in the general principles of international law and there must be a pending draft convention before the UN for this violation.

According to Bassiouni, the international element must be deemed to be present if the conduct constitutes a direct threat to world peace and security or if it shocks the conscience of the world community or constitutes an indirect threat to world peace and security due to the magnitude of the offence.[42] The transnational element is present when 'the offensive conduct affects the interests of more than one state, the offensive conduct includes the citizens of more than one state, or the offensive con-

[38] M.C. Bassiouni, *International Criminal Law. Crimes,* second edition, Transnational Publishers, Inc. Ardsley, New York, 1999, pp. 32ff. These are: aggression; genocide; crimes against humanity; war crimes; crimes against United Nations and associated personnel; unlawful possession or use or emplacement of weapons; theft of nuclear materials; mercenarism; apartheid; slavery and slave-related practices; torture and other forms of cruel, inhuman, or degrading treatment; unlawful human experimentation; piracy; aircraft hijacking and unlawful acts against international air safety; unlawful acts against the safety of maritime navigation and the safety of platforms on the high seas; threat and use of force against internationally protected persons; taking of civilian hostages; unlawful use of the mail; unlawful traffic in drugs and related drug offences; destruction and/or theft of national treasures; unlawful acts against certain internationally protected elements of the environment; international traffic in obscene materials; falsification and counterfeiting; unlawful interference with submarine cables; bribery of foreign public officials.

[39] M.C. Bassiouni, *International Criminal Law. Crimes,* second edition, Transnational Publishers, Inc. Ardsley, New York, 1999, pp. 97-100.

[40] F. Malekian, *International Criminal Law: The Legal and Critical Analysis of International Crimes,* Malekian, Uppsala, 1991, pp. 19-24.

[41] M.C. Bassiouni, *International Criminal Law. Crimes,* second edition, Transnational publishers, Inc. Ardsley, New York, 1999, pp. 4-8.

[42] M.C. Bassiouni, *International Criminal Law. Crimes,* second edition, Transnational publishers, Inc. Ardsley, New York, 1999, pp. 95-100.

duct involves means or methods which transcend national boundaries'.[43] The international crimes listed by Bassiouni that do not have this transnational or international element must be seen to have emerged from international necessity.[44]

International law as such has not determined the criteria that must be met before conduct can be qualified as an international crime. Nevertheless, contemporary multilateral treaties creating international crimes tend to follow a similar pattern in that they[45]

- declare certain conduct to be criminal under international law,
- exclude the defence of superior orders, and
- provide for the prosecution of the suspect before an international or a national court. In the latter case, they oblige states to try or to extradite an offender.

According to Bassiouni, before a certain conduct can be declared criminal under international law, the following process takes place. The existence of writings postulating certain philosophies became the premise for more specific theoretical writings, which in turn gave impetus to certain international undertakings, followed by the formulation of specific normative proscriptions and then the shaping of sanctioning devices.[46] Another pattern for the establishment of international crimes is the following; (1) the conduct in question is deemed criminal in the municipal order; (2) an expression of its international prohibition emerges in scholarly writings and international gatherings; (3) a (draft) treaty is elaborated usually at first only to qualify the conduct in violation of international law; (4) one or more additional conventions usually ensure that the conduct in question is an international crime for which there is universal jurisdiction to prosecute.[47]

Malekian is of the opinion that the only acceptable method for identifying the existence of an international crime is the adoption of certain international rules. These rules can be adopted by custom, by norm, or by conventional rule in the practice of nations. In his view, the most important thing is that the codification of international crimes has to be established through consensus.[48]

---

[43] B.M. Yarnold, The Doctrinal Basis for the International Criminalization Process, in: M.C. Bassiouni, *International Criminal Law. Crimes,* second edition, Transnational Publishers, Inc. Ardsley, New York, 1999, pp. 131-132.

[44] B.M. Yarnold, The Doctrinal Basis for the International Criminalization Process, in: M.C. Bassiouni, *International Criminal Law. Crimes*, second edition, Transnational Publishers, Inc. Ardsley, New York, 1999, pp. 151-152.

[45] J. Dugard and Ch. van den Wyngaert, *International Criminal Law and Procedure,* Dartmouth, Aldershot, 1996, Introduction.

[46] M.C. Bassiouni, An Appraisal of the Growth and Developing Trends of International Criminal Law, in: *International Review of Penal Law*, Volume 45, 1974, p. 409.

[47] M.C. Bassiouni, An Appraisal of the Growth and Developing Trends of International Criminal Law, in: *International Review of Penal Law,* Volume 45, 1974, p. 422.

[48] F. Malekian, *International Criminal Law: The Legal and Critical Analysis of International Crimes,* Malekian, Uppsala, 1991, pp. 23-24.

In conclusion, no general agreement exists among authors on the doctrinal foundations that constitute the legal basis for including a given act in the group of international crimes, but today, all international crimes that are listed by Bassiouni are codified in treaties or have some conventional endorsement. Consent seems to exist on the fact that a certain conduct must affect world order and gravely violate human rights values before it can be considered an international crime.

2.3.1.3 *The problem of enforcement in international crime*

However, the enforcement of acts against these international crimes remains the greatest problem in international criminal law. A deeper orientation of the problems that exist concerning the enforceability of international crimes must be made in order to understand the (in)efficiency of international criminal law.

Various writers have elaborated the causes of the (in)efficient enforcement of international criminal law. According to Bassiouni, the reasons for the ineffectiveness of international criminal law are the following.[49]

1 It places the sole duty to act in conformity with treaty obligations on the states;
2 It provides no authoritative control of the states to ensure compliance;
3 It does not provide a mechanism for the resolution of conflicts that emerge between states;
4 It does not provide safeguards for those individuals who are the objects of cooperative undertakings between states;
5 It does not have an overall framework;
6 It does not have standards or general rules for the drafting of its specific proscriptions;
7 It has no uniform standards or general rules applicable to the specific provisions of the system to ensure compliance by enforcing agents;
8 Its application and enforcement is uneven and subject to those domestic political considerations affecting the enforcing agent.

Summarising, it can be said that the problems arise as a consequence of the sovereignty and equality of states as they do not tolerate a higher entity or higher legal order to which the states have to conform, unless it is agreed by all the (participating) states.

Malekian blames the ineffectiveness of international criminal law on the fact that the system of international criminal law is in the hands of political authorities. In his view, the legal system is subordinated to the political system as a consequence of Chapter VII of the UN Charter.[50] He further states that 'the lack of enforceability in

---

[49] M.C. Bassiouni, *A Draft International Criminal Code and Draft Statute for an International Criminal Tribunal,* Nijhoff, Dordrecht, 1987, p. 53.

[50] F. Malekian, *International Criminal Law. The Legal and Critical Analysis of International Crime,* Malekian, Uppsala, 1991, pp. 50-51.

international criminal law is due to many controversies, and because of political, economic, and legal conflicts among the drafting states of a convention, the quality of the conventions has decreased and less attention is being paid to procedural matters. The enforcement machinery for international criminal conventions is not effective and success is dependent on national policy and the willingness of individual states.'[51] He is convinced that the solution to making international criminal law more effective lies in an international criminal law, which is entirely based upon the international criminal responsibility of states and not on rules and regulations.

Another approach to enforceability is given by Chayes & Handler. They state that, if the principal source of non-compliance is not wilful disobedience but the lack of capability or clarity or priority, the coercive enforcement of treaty provisions will not work. The alternative they give is called the 'managerial model', which relies primarily on a cooperative, problem-solving approach. They are convinced that compliance with treaties can be reached with this model by ensuring transparency, dispute settlement, capacity building, and persuasion.[52] However, lack of capability, clarity, or priority obviously follows from a lack of political will to act in compliance with the treaty provisions, which does not mean that coercive enforcement is the effective remedy.

As Bhattacharyya says, one of the main reasons that an international criminal justice system is not yet in force is that criminal prosecution is inherently linked with notions of national sovereignty and the control over persons and territory which are fundamental to that notion.[53]

These reasons for the ineffectiveness of international criminal law have to be kept in mind when analysing the obstacles to the use of legal instruments to prosecute suspects of trafficking in persons since they may also affect the effective use of the legal instruments.[54]

Other reasons for the inefficiency are the absence of an international police force to investigate international crimes and the fact that international crimes are often committed by state officials, who can invoke the principle of immunity. Examples of such crimes are genocide, torture, and war crimes. Although the Nuremberg and Tokyo Tribunals established that individuals are responsible for their own acts even in case of superior orders and that they cannot hide themselves behind their commanders, the prosecution of the perpetrators can be complicated and politically sensitive.

---

[51] F. Malekian, *International Criminal Law. The Legal and Critical Analysis of International Crimes,* Malekian, Uppsala, 1991, pp. 51-53.

[52] A. Chayes and A. Handler-Chayes, *The New Sovereignty. Compliance with International Regulatory Agreement,* Harvard University Press, Cambridge, 1995, pp. 22-28.

[53] R. Bhattacharyya, Establishing a Rule-of-Law International Criminal Justice System, in: *Texas International Law Journal,* Volume 31, issue 1, 1996, pp. 95-96.

[54] The effectiveness of the legal instruments will be particularly focused upon in Chapters 4, 5, and 6.

The political relations must also be taken into account with regard to the prosecution of other international crimes as this prosecution can be easily explained as interference with domestic affairs, which is prohibited as a consequence of the equality of states. The opinions about the desirability of this political influence are diverse. Rosalyn Higgins says that it is desirable that the policy factors are dealt with systematically and openly.[55] As a matter of fact, we cannot deny political influence on international law especially not in international criminal law. The case of General Augusto Pinochet may illustrate the fact that a complex set of political factors is of influence on the enforceability of international criminal law.

The former Chilean President Augusto Pinochet, visited the Netherlands in 1994, when he was suspected of violating the Torture Convention.[56] This convention contains an obligation for state parties either to prosecute or to extradite a suspected person who is within the territory of their country. Although the Netherlands was a party to the convention, the Dutch public prosecutor did not take any action to prosecute Pinochet. He justified his non-action explaining that, although there was an obligation to prosecute or extradite, the Netherlands did not have jurisdiction because there was no request from another state to extradite. The suggestion was that an obligation to prosecute only existed, and thus jurisdiction, when there was a negative response to a request to extradite.[57] A second ground not to prosecute was that, according to the public prosecutor, the prosecution of Pinochet in the Netherlands would be disproportional and presumptuous. A third reason why the public prosecutor was of the opinion that the Netherlands did not have jurisdiction was that Pinochet enjoyed immunity as a former head of a state.[58] As we know now, Pinochet could not invoke immunity to escape prosecution.[59] The Netherlands being a party to the convention had accepted its treaty obligations through ratification. The motivation of the public prosecutor is therefore inexplicable. Making the decision that there was no jurisdiction to prosecute Pinochet in the Netherlands at that time, the Dutch authorities seemed to be actuated by fear for the maintenance of the Dutch public order and some practical and factual problems. It is likely that the resistance

---

[55] R. Higgins, *Problems & Process. International Law and How We Use it,* Clarendon Press, Oxford, 1994, pp. 2-12.

[56] Convention against Torture and Other Cruel, Inhuman or Degrading Treatment or Punishments, GA Res. 39/46 annex, 39 UN GAOR Supp. (no. 51) at 197, entered into force 26 June 1987.

[57] Although, during the preparations of this convention, the Netherlands did not agree to adopt the principle of universal jurisdiction in the Torture Convention, it later agreed on this matter. Unlike Brazil, the Netherlands did not set the condition that prosecution in the Netherlands can only take place after a negative answer to a request for extradition has been received. *Kamerstukken II*, 1985-1986, 19 617 (R1312), no. 3, pp. 6-8, 15-16.

[58] M. Kamminga and M. Tijssen, Pinochet, Nederland en het VN-Verdrag tegen Foltering, in: *NJCM-Bulletin*, Volume 20, issue 8, 1995, pp. 986-995. Ch. Ingelse and H. van der Wilt, De Zaak Pinochet. Over Universele Rechtsmacht en Hollandse Benepenheid, in: *NJB,* Volume 72, issue 8, 1996, pp. 280-285.

[59] UK House of Lords: *Regina* v. *Bartle and the Commissioner of Police for the Metropolis and Others, Ex Parte Pinochet*, 24 March 1999. E.M.H. Hirsch Ballin, De zaak-Pinochet, in: *Ars Aequi,* Volume 49, issue 6, 2000, pp. 481-488.

of some officials to the principle '*aut dedere aut judicare*' also played a role in this decision. In October 1998, Pinochet was arrested in Great Britain at the request of a Spanish judge who accused Pinochet of violating the Torture Convention. In two sessions, the Law Lords of England decided that Pinochet could not invoke immunity as a former head of state for his conduct. Finally, Great Britain did not extradite Pinochet to Spain because of his poor health.

The Dutch response to the situation in 1994 is a clear example of political considerations forming an obstacle to the enforceability of international criminal law. The Netherlands sought a provision in the Torture Convention to avoid jurisdiction, with the result that the Torture Convention could not be enforced. The British, on the contrary, sought a basis for jurisdiction in the convention.

Another example of the interference of political motives in international criminal law is the establishment of the future International Criminal Court. It took from 1948 until 1998 before agreement could be reached on its establishment. Many provisions of the Statute of Rome are included as the result of political compromises, which is unavoidable when an agreement must be reached.[60] Furthermore, most of the international crimes identified today are politically motivated. International (criminal) law specialists played a minor role in this process of codification.[61] This may be seen as a reconfirmation of the primacy of state sovereignty and the equality of states, which is at the same time an obstacle to enforcing international criminal law on a more international level. For an optimal enforcement of this law there should be a criminal court at the international level dealing with the prosecution of international crimes. As long as the International Criminal Court is not fully operational, an effective enforceability of international criminal law is lacking and remains in the hands of individual states beside temporary courts. This brings us to the second category of international criminal law.

2.3.2 International aspects of national criminal law

2.3.2.1 *The characteristics of the category of international aspects of national criminal law*

Following the analysis by several authors this category can be described as those aspects of the international legal system and of municipal legal systems that regulate international cooperation in those criminal matters involving individuals who have violated the criminal laws of a given state. It finds its existence in the necessity for states to cooperate in criminal cases because of the internationalisation of these

[60] T.L.H. McCormack and G.J. Simpson, A New International Criminal Law Regime? in: *Netherlands International Law Review,* Volume 42, issue 2, 1995, p. 206.

[61] B.M. Yarnold, The Doctrinal Basis for the International Criminalization Process, in: M.C. Bassiouni, *International Criminal Law. Crimes,* second edition, Transnational Publishers, Inc. Ardsley, New York, 1999, p. 152.

cases. In this category the focus is on national criminal procedure and on the conduct that is normally criminalised in national substantive criminal law in most states. Especially with regard to the investigation and prosecution of these crimes, the international aspect of this category has to be taken into account. To make a flexible and efficient criminal procedure possible, many national criminal laws contain rules concerning police and judicial cooperation. Inter-state cooperation may take the following forms.[62]

- Extradition, the traditional example of international cooperation by which a person is transferred from one state to another in order to stand trial or for the enforcement of sanctions in the latter.
- Mutual legal assistance, i.e., the communication of relevant information and evidence from one state to another.
- Enforcement in one state of a judgement rendered in another state.
- Transfer of proceedings and delimitation of competences to organise proceedings actually begun or planned in a more efficient way so that the state that is best placed prosecutes and enforces the sanction to be imposed.

The development of international instruments to facilitate national criminal procedure as part of international criminal law took place along a different track than the development of criminal law aspects of international law.[63] It concerns the evolution and enforcement of domestic criminal law when international aspects are involved. Extradition of criminals has always played an important role as a catalyst for the development of this part of international criminal law. The cooperation between states during the last decades became increasingly formalised and detailed, and numerous bilateral and multilateral treaties on cooperation in criminal matters have been concluded.[64] These forms of cooperation are only necessary because there does not exist one global criminal law system that is applied in the same way in all states. As states are largely free to organise their national criminal law as they see fit, differences between these systems will remain. However, it is understandable that states do not give up their sovereignty on these matters because their power in this area relates to the safety and the security of the society and of the citizens of a state. Therefore, it is a very delicate matter and cautiousness has to be exercised when discussing or manipulating this pattern. Furthermore, keeping the sovereign power in this field is a way for states to express their values and identity, although, as we will see in Chapter 7, sovereignty can also be used to facilitate cooperation in criminal matters.

This category contains more procedural law regulation, for instance, extradition, recognition of foreign penal judgements, transfer of criminal proceedings, mutual le-

---

[62] F. Malekian, *International Criminal Law: The Legal and Critical Analysis of International Crimes*, Malekian, Uppsala, 1991, pp. 29-30.

[63] M.C. Bassiouni, The Penal Characteristics of Conventional International Criminal Law, in: J. Dugard and Ch. van den Wyngaert, *International Criminal Law and Procedure*, Dartmouth, Aldershot, 1996, pp. 329-332.

[64] Those instruments relevant for the prosecution of trafficking in persons will be discussed in Chapter 4.

gal assistance in criminal cases, but also agreements to combat specific crimes, e.g., the UN Convention against Illicit Traffic in Narcotic Drugs and Psychotropic Substances. Indirect enforcement of international criminal law is the way to prosecute those suspected of having committed of these crimes, namely, via national courts. However, before the prosecution of a suspect can commence the question of which state may claim jurisdiction has to be answered.

2.3.2.2 *Current jurisdiction principles*

One point of international criminal law that meets wide agreement is that, as far as the granting of jurisdiction is concerned, the territoriality principle is the leading principle in international criminal law, although its application is not without difficulties. The adoption of this principle is inherent in the territoriality of states. The issue of jurisdiction is important to answer the question of which state, in a particular case, is the most appropriate state to prosecute a suspect in order to avoid conflict of jurisdiction and to prevent that perpetrators remain unpunished. Beside the territoriality principle, extraterritorial jurisdiction can be established by applying the active nationality (or personality) principle, the passive nationality (or personality) principle, the protective principle, and the universality principle.[65]

The territoriality principle
In the strict sense, this principle means that the state on whose territory a crime takes place has jurisdiction, regardless of whether the offender is a national. All crimes committed on the territory of a state may come before the municipal courts of that state. The prominence of this principle is in accordance with the role of sovereignty and equality of states in international criminal law.[66] Exceptions to this principle are allowed in only a limited number of cases, e.g., criminal immunity of heads of states.

The place where the crime was committed, the *locus delicti,* has to be determined before a state can claim jurisdiction on the basis of the territoriality principle. Because of the transnational element of many criminal activities nowadays, it cannot be denied that it has become more difficult to determine the *locus delicti*. In many cases, parts of the crime were committed in different states, so there is not one individual state that has jurisdiction. As we will see in Section 2.5, for some crimes, the

[65] P. Malanczuk, *Akehurst's Modern Introduction to International Law,* Routledge, London, 1997, pp. 110-117. I. Brownlie, *Principles of Public International Law,* Clarendon Press, Oxford, 1990, pp. 300-306. D.J. Harris, *Cases and Materials on International Law,* Sweet & Maxwell, London, 1998, pp. 264-294. J.J. Paust, et al., *International Criminal Law: Cases and Materials,* Carolina Academic Press, Durham, North Carolina, 1996, pp. 17-34. C.L. Blakesly and O. Lagodny, Competing National Laws: Network or Jungle? in: A. Eser and O. Lagodny (eds.), *Principles and Procedures for a New Transnational Criminal Law,* Max Planck Institute, Freiburg im Breisgau, 1992, pp. 47-65. J.M. Sjöcrona and A.M.M. Orie, *Internationaal Strafrecht,* Kluwer, Deventer, 2002, pp. 44-71.

[66] J.J. Paust, et al., *International Criminal Law: Cases and Materials,* Carolina Academic Press, Durham, North Carolina, 1996, pp. 17-19.

fact that parts of the crime are committed in different states is even inextricably bound up with the nature of the crime. A strict interpretation of the territoriality principle will exclude all the elements of an offence that took place outside the territory of the state that is claiming jurisdiction. The consequence of the strict application of the territoriality principle is that the investigation and prosecution of the transnational or international crime as a whole is impossible. However, there are different ways to determine the *locus delicti* so that the territory principle can be applied in such a way that jurisdiction may also be claimed when only a part of the crime took place in the state that claims jurisdiction. There are four traditional ways to determine the *locus delicti.*[67] First, under the doctrine of the actual conduct, the place where the act was commenced is decisive for determining the *locus delicti.* This doctrine is often referred to as the subjective territoriality principle. The second is the doctrine of the instrument, which means that the *locus delicti* is the place where the instrument used by the offender had its effect. The third doctrine, the 'effects doctrine', is based on the fact that the *locus delicti* is determined in the state where the injurious effect, although not the act or omission itself, took place. This doctrine is also called the objective territoriality principle.[68] The fourth doctrine is the application of the concept of 'ubiquity'. In the common understanding of this doctrine, it means a parallel application of the subjective and objective territoriality principles. A more far-reaching interpretation of the concept of 'ubiquity' is that the *locus delicti* is each place in which any part of the offence took place or where the result occurred. The jurisdiction following from this interpretation concerns the whole offence and not only the part that took place in a particular state. The only requirement of this concept is that every part of the offence must be punishable in itself.[69]

There is an increasing trend by states towards a more extensive interpretation of the territoriality principle by using the four theories mentioned above.[70] Besides, states are inclined to a flexible interpretation of these theories and they address the question of jurisdiction from a pragmatic point of view.[71] A consequence of this broad

[67] H.D. Wolswijk, *Locus delicti en rechtsmacht,* Gouda Quint, Deventer, 1998, pp. 90-91, 95-109. T. vander Beken, *Forumkeuze in het internationale strafrecht. Verdeling van misdrijven met aanknopingspunten in meerdere staten,* Maklu, Antwerp, 1999, pp. 49-53.

[68] P. Malanczuk, *Akehurst's Modern Introduction to International Law*, Routeledge, London, 1997, pp. 110-111.

[69] J.J. Paust, et al., *International Criminal Law: Cases and Materials,* Carolina Academic Press, Durham, North Carolina, 1996, pp. 20-25.

[70] T. vander Beken, *Forumkeuze in het internationale strafrecht. Verdeling van misdrijven met aanknopingspunten in meerdere staten,* Maklu, Antwerp, 1999, pp. 407-410. *Separate opinions* of judges Higgins, Kooijmans, and Buergenthal of the ICJ in the *Democratic Republic of the Congo* v. *Belgium* case, 14 February 2002, who state that Article 5 paragraph 3 of the Torture Convention 'has come to be referred to as "universal jurisdiction", though it is really an obligatory territorial jurisdiction over persons, albeit in relation to acts committed elsewhere.'

[71] T. vander Beken, *Forumkeuze in het internationale strafrecht. Verdeling van misdrijven met aanknopingspunten in meerdere staten,* Maklu, Antwerp, 1999, pp. 72-75. K. Frimpong, Punishing Offences Committed Abroad: Practical (National) Relevance or Theoretical Claim, in: A. Eser and O. Lagodny

interpretation of the territoriality principle is the evanescence of the distinction with the extraterritoriality principles that will be discussed below. The fact that the territoriality principle is being broadly interpreted nowadays makes it clear that states prefer to exercise jurisdiction themselves and do not want to be dependent on other states in this regard.

The active nationality principle

For this principle, the nationality of the offender is decisive in the granting of jurisdiction. The state of whom the offender is a national claims jurisdiction when the active nationality principle is applied. In general, this principle can only be used if the accommodating state does not claim jurisdiction and the offence is of a certain gravity. The application of this principle means that the effect of a national law is not limited to the territory of a state but that it operates outside the state as well.

An example of such extraterritorial legislation by adopting the active nationality principle is the prosecution of those who have committed child abuse abroad by some states. Rich Western tourists frequently sexually abuse children in poor countries and try to evade prosecution in these countries. By applying the active nationality principle, these offenders can be tried in their home countries. Such legislation enables perpetrators to be prosecuted in their own countries for crimes committed abroad. Impressive research on the effects of the application of the active nationality principle as a tool to combat sexual exploitation of children was made by the ECPAT Europe Law Enforcement Group.[72] It studied 15 cases in which the active nationality principle was applied to prosecute perpetrators who had sexually abused minors abroad. The selected cases were conducted in Europe and Asia (including Japan).[73] The conclusion of this study was that extraterritorial legislation for the crime of child abuse abroad serves as a welcome ground to grant jurisdiction. In many of these cases, the offender had returned to his home country, which made it difficult for the state where the offence was committed to prosecute this person. This problem is compounded by the fact that there may not be an extradition treaty with the home country of the offender and, even if there is, the home country may have adopted an exception to the extradition of nationals. Thus, the active nationality principle serves to prevent that offenders escape with impunity. This does not mean that there are no problems when combating these crimes by applying extraterritorial legislation, as the problems with regard to mutual legal assistance that will be analysed in Chapter 5 also occur in these cases. Furthermore, the majority of the countries where the offences are committed are not a party to the Council of Europe and there-

(eds.), *Principles and Procedures for a New Transnational Criminal Law,* Max Planck Institute, Freiburg im Breisgau, 1992, pp. 37-38.

[72] ECPAT Europe Law Enforcement Group, Defence for Children International, *Extraterritorial Legislation as a Tool to Combat Sexual Exploitation of Children,* Amsterdam, April 1999.

[73] The countries where the crimes were committed in the described cases are, Cambodia (1 case), Czech Republic (1 case), The Philippines (5 cases), Romania (1 case), Sri Lanka (5 cases), Thailand (3 cases).

fore not a party to the conventions enacted by the Council of Europe, and bilateral conventions on mutual legal assistance with these countries are often absent.

The passive nationality principle

Under the passive nationality principle, a state may claim jurisdiction because the victim of a crime is a national of that state. In general, it is presumed that nationals are protected abroad by the accommodating state. Only in exceptional cases if this protection is not granted, and if the liberty, safety, or life of the national is in danger, the state of the victim may invoke the passive nationality principle. This principle is applied only when the offence did not take place on the territory of the claiming state, because, in all cases, the territoriality principle takes priority. An example of the application of this principle is the American Servicemembers' Protection Act of 2002 in the United States.[74] Section 3008 of this Act authorises the President of the United States 'to use all means necessary and appropriate to bring about the release of any person described in subsection (b) who is being detained or imprisoned by, on behalf of, or at the request of the International Criminal Court'. The persons described in subsection (b) are covered United States persons, covered allied persons, and individuals detained or imprisoned for official actions taken while the individual was a covered United States person or a covered allied person and in the case of a covered allied person, upon the request of such government. The purpose of this section is to prevent those persons from being prosecuted by the International Criminal Court.

The protective principle

When the offence did not take place on the territory of a state and the territoriality principle cannot be applied, the protective principle can bring a solution in only a limited number of cases, namely, in cases in which the violation of a state's interest justifies the claim for jurisdiction. This violation can consist of a threat to the security or the prestige of a state or an offence against the territorial integrity or independence of a state. Such crimes are, for instance, acts of hijacking and other terrorist activities. The nationality of the offender is irrelevant. The reasoning behind this principle is that a state must be able to protect itself against persons conducting acts that undermine the foundations of that state. The requirement of double criminality does not need to be fulfilled and it seems that the principle of *ne bis in idem* is applied less strictly. Since the terrorist attacks on the Twin Towers in New York and the Pentagon in Washington DC on 11 September 2001, the protective principle has been applied more often and more extensively.

The universality principle

This principle applies to crimes that threaten the international community as a whole in such a grave way that it is justified that each state of the international community may claim jurisdiction although the crime took place outside its territory. The uni-

[74] American Servicemembers' Protection Act of 2002, H.R. 4775, confirmed by President Bush on 2 August 2002.

versality principle generally concerns crimes that are codified in international conventions and are criminalised in all national penal codes or are acts considered punishable by every state. In its strictest sense, a special connection with the offender or the victims is not required and it otherwise needs no special connection with the crime, although it is generally accepted that a state can only claim jurisdiction when the offender resides on the territory of that state.[75] Furthermore, it is preferred that the state in which the crime took place is granted jurisdiction in the first place. This principle has recently met with increased attention, namely, in the *Pinochet* case,[76] the *Bouterse* case,[77] the *Belgium* v. *Congo* case before the ICJ,[78] and again in the *Sharon* case in Belgium.[79] Universal jurisdiction is not easily granted and, in general, it can be said that a certain link with the crime, the offender, or the victims is necessary before a state may claim jurisdiction.[80] The president of the ICJ stated in the *Belgium* v. *Congo* case:[81]

> Additionally, they [states] may exercise jurisdiction in cases of piracy and in the situations of subsidiary universal jurisdiction provided for by various conventions if the offender is present on their territory. But apart from these cases, international law does not accept universal jurisdiction; still less does it accept universal jurisdiction *in absentia.*[82]

---

[75] See, for instance, the explanatory memorandum to the Dutch International Crimes Act, especially the section on universal jurisdiction, *Kamerstukken II,* 2001-2002, 28 337, no. 3, pp. 16-19. See also the *separate opinion* of judge G. Guillaume of the ICJ in the Arrest Warrant case of 11 April 2000, *Democratic Republic of the Congo* v. *Belgium,* 14 February 2002. For a different view, see the *separate opinions* of judges Higgins, Kooijmans, and Buergenthal of the ICJ in the same case.

[76] UK House of Lords: *Regina* v. *Bartle and the Commissioner of Police for the Metropolis and Others, Ex Parte Pinochet,* 24 March 1999. E.M.H. Hirsch Ballin, De zaak-Pinochet, in: *Ars Aequi,* Volume 49, issue 6, 2000, pp. 481-488.

[77] HR, no. 749/01, 18 September 2001.

[78] *Democratic Republic of the Congo* v. *Belgium,* (also referred to as the Yerodia case), ICJ 14 February, 2002.

[79] Decision taken by the Court of Appeal in Brussels on 26 June 2002 following a complaint filed against Sharon concerning the massacres in the refugee camps Sabra and Shatila in 1982. The cases against Sharon and against Yerodia were based on the Belgian law on the punishment of grave violations of international humanitarian law of 16 June 1993, which does not require the presence of the suspect on Belgian territory as a prerequisite to exercising jurisdiction. Following national and international criticism, this law was amended in April 2003, which limited its application. However, under certain conditions it is still possible to establish procedures against a suspect who is not present on Belgian territory. Wetsontwerp tot wijziging van de wet van 16 juni 1993 betreffende de bestraffing van ernstige schendingen van het internationaal humanitair recht en van artikel 144*ter* van het Gerechtelijk Wetboek, DOC 50 2265/010.

[80] Explanatory text to the proposed Dutch International Crimes Act, *Kamerstukken II,* 2001-2002, 28 337, no. 3, p. 18. M. Matthijssen-Boot and R. van Elst, Wetsvoorstel internationale misdrijven, in: *NJB,* Volume 77, issue 35, 2002, pp. 1748-1750.

[81] *Democratic Republic of the Congo* v. *Belgium,* ICJ, 14 February 2002, point 16. E.M.H. Hirsch Ballin, Yerodia. Rechtsmacht, immuniteit en vervolgingsbeleid, in: *Ars Aequi,* Volume 51, issue 11, pp. 743-747.

[82] For a different opinion in this case, see the *dissenting opinion* of judge *ad hoc* Van den Wyngaert and the *separate opinions* of judges Higgins, Kooijmans, and Buergenthal.

Following this brief overview of the leading principles on the granting of jurisdiction in international criminal law, the conclusion is that the territoriality principle, until today, remains the main starting point for asserting jurisdiction. As stated above, the territoriality principle is mainly based on the sovereignty of states, namely, that states do not have to tolerate interference from other states or other entities on their territory. However, as was argued in Section 1.2 of Chapter 1, the role of state sovereignty is changing. Consequently, the importance of the territoriality principle for granting jurisdiction may change as well, creating other and new mechanisms to grant jurisdiction. As we have seen, a sharp line between the territoriality principle and the extraterritoriality principles is not easy to draw and states try to use these principles to extend their possibilities to claim jurisdiction. As a result, states increasingly face problems of cooperation in criminal matters when prosecuting a suspect who has committed the crime (partly) abroad. Therefore, the extensive use of claiming jurisdiction is not always a satisfactory solution and sometimes the amelioration of cooperation in criminal matters between states must be preferred.[83]

The principles discussed above are based on the fact that only one state can claim jurisdiction and that the prosecuting state must be identified before prosecution or even the investigation can commence. The fact that only one individual state can assert jurisdiction in a certain case may lead to restrictions to the possibilities for the investigation and prosecution of offences. When those parts of a crime that took place outside a state's territory have to be investigated or prosecuted, the regime of mutual legal assistance has to be applied. In exceptional cases, jurisdiction to prosecute may be taken over by another state in the course of the process when the exercise of jurisdiction by that other state seems more appropriate. But why should it be desirable that only one individual state has jurisdiction for cross-border crime? Why should it be necessary to determine which state has jurisdiction before procedures can commence? There are many problems regarding translations and the gathering of evidence during the procedure. The assignment of jurisdiction to only one state will not contribute to a smooth procedure. Furthermore, in some cases, granting jurisdiction to a state after more information on a case is known seems to be more efficient. To view the prosecution of a suspect as the responsibility of an individual state seems unfair and untenable. Perhaps it is time to introduce a shared responsibility for investigation and prosecution among states to combat cross-border crimes. Recommendations to adopt such a shared responsibility will be elaborated in Chapter 7.

[83] C.L. Blakesly and O. Lagodny, Competing National Laws: Network or Jungle? In: A. Eser and O. Lagodny (eds.), *Principles and Procedures for a New Transnational Criminal Law*, Max Planck Institute, Freiburg im Breisgau, 1992, pp. 98-100.

2.3.2.3 *The crimes within the category of international aspects of national criminal law*

Parallel to the group of crimes within the category of criminal law aspects of international law a group of crimes can be identified as originating in the category of international aspects of national criminal law. This group normally concerns crimes against the municipal legal order with an international aspect, in other words, criminal cases involving a foreign element. The crimes committed in this category are not necessarily directly shocking to the conscience of the international community but are committed against the municipal legal order, sometimes the municipal legal order of another state or more than one state. In the category of international aspects of national criminal law, we find national crimes with an international aspect other than the international crimes in the category of criminal law aspects of international law discussed so far. This international aspect is not a constitutive element of the crime but the international aspect is generated in the way in which the crime is committed. Examples of crimes in this category are crimes that are (in part) committed outside the territory of one state or crimes the perpetrator of which is not a citizen of the state, claiming jurisdiction. Normally it concerns common crimes that are penalised in most nations, e.g., murder, theft, traffic offences, violations of the public order.

2.3.3 The connection between criminal law aspects of international law and international aspects of national criminal law

This traditional division raises doubts about the coherence and the content of international criminal law. The category of criminal law aspects of international law deals more with an enforcement problem of substantive criminal law whereas the category of international aspects of national criminal law deals more with an enforcement problem of procedural criminal law. However, the connecting link between these two categories is that international criminal law in general relies on the national legal system to enforce criminal sanctions and that international criminal law calls for the development of instruments that facilitate the application of domestic criminal law. In this sense, the two categories are interrelated and are both essential for the existence of international criminal law. Because the structural enforcement of international criminal law from a supranational level has not yet been regulated, many of the conventions containing international crimes include the principle *aut dedere aut judicare*, referring to national criminal laws for enforcement.[84]

Current developments show that these two traditional groups of international criminal law have an increasing number of similarities. On the one hand, the category of criminal law aspects of international law now also includes many provisions on pro-

[84] M.C. Bassiouni, The Penal Characteristics of Conventional International Criminal Law, in: *International Criminal Law and Procedure,* J. Dugard and Ch. van den Wyngaert, Dartmouth, Aldershot, 1996, pp. 336-338.

cedural law, specifically drafted for the ad hoc Yugoslavia and Rwanda tribunals and the permanent International Criminal Court.[85] On the other hand, it can no longer be upheld that the category of international aspects of national criminal law only concerns the procedural aspects between states in order to overcome the international aspects. For instance, at the European level, a number of decisions were taken by the Council of the EU with the aim being to adopt common definitions of criminal conduct for the whole EU. This harmonising opportunity is explicitly provided for in Article 31 paragraph 1(e) EU Treaty.

2.4 OTHER SUBDIVISIONS RELATING TO THE TRADITIONAL ONE

Kelsen distinguished between general and particular international law. General international law is customary law valid for all states belonging to the international community. Particular international law is only directly valid for some states, and comprises, for the most part, norms created by treaties valid only for the contracting parties, but it may also be created by a particular custom in the establishment of which only some states participate.[86] He further detected a tendency that 'international law more and more shows the trend to regulate matters which originally were positively regulated only by national law, the tendency to restrict more and more the so-called domestic jurisdiction of the states.'[87] The distinction between general and particular international law can also be applied in order to make a distinction in international criminal law. The general part of international criminal law contains these provisions of international criminal law that are valid for all states. As there is no treaty in international criminal law that is signed and ratified by the whole community of states this category is limited to the crimes under *jus cogens* and customary law, or to refer to Bassiouni, the international crimes. The particular part of international criminal law contains the treaties related to criminal procedure which are established between states. One of the characteristics of these instruments is that it leaves the domestic jurisdiction untouched.

Mueller and Besharov distinguish between adjective and substantive international criminal law. Adjective international criminal law is a conduct norm that fully recognises the existence of two sovereign states. It provides for mutual assistance or accommodation in a conflict situation that arises precisely because of the existence of independent sovereign entities. They name this type the accommodation type and it includes all conflicts of national criminal law, international judicial assistance, and extradition. Substantive international criminal law is that part of municipal criminal law that nations have ceded for the sake of the common good of a greater commu-

[85] G.K. McDonald, Trial Procedures and Practices, in: G.K. McDonald and O. Swaak-Goldman, *Substantive and Procedural Aspects of International Criminal Law,* Kluwer Law International, The Hague, pp. 551-558.

[86] H. Kelsen and R.W. Tucker, *Principles of International Law,* second edition, Holt, Rinehart and Winston, Inc. New York, 1966, pp. 288-290.

[87] H. Kelsen and R.W. Tucker, *Principles of International Law,* second edition, Holt, Rinehart and Winston, Inc. New York, 1966, p. 301.

nity or interest and that they have entrusted for the purpose of administration to a larger jurisdictional unit, without giving up their own sovereignty.[88] Again the division can be traced back to the traditional division. In this categorisation we see the pattern of the distinction between international aspects of national criminal law and criminal law aspects of international law described before. Adjective international criminal law then has the characteristics of the international aspects of national criminal law and substantive international criminal law those of criminal law aspects of international law. The outcome remains the same in this approach, namely, that 'international criminal law will rely on the municipal legal system to enforce its sanctions and on the international legal system to provide means by which a given municipal system will be required to carry out that task,'[89] as long as states are not inclined to give up (parts of) their sovereign powers.

Another distinction that can be mentioned here is that between interstate criminal law and supranational criminal law. The first is the criminal law between states, comparable with the adjective type mentioned above, or the international aspects of national criminal law. The latter is criminal law on a level above the states, comparable with the substantive type mentioned above, and the criminal law aspects of international law.

Beside commonly made distinctions, Wise adds a third category: International Criminal Law *stricto sensu*.[90] What can be classified under this heading is not clear. When the International Criminal Court comes into formal existence, the law applied in this court may fall within this category, he argues. Furthermore the 'rules of international law that obligate states to cooperate in repressing various kinds of conduct ostensibly reprehended by the world at large' belong to this category as well.[91] With this subscription the law applied in the Nuremberg and Tokyo Tribunals, and the Yugoslavia and Rwanda Tribunals seem to belong to international criminal law *stricto sensu* as well. However, the distinction between this form of international criminal law and international criminal law as criminal law aspects of international law is not clearly expounded by Wise. For him the criminal law aspects of international law concern international standards of criminal justice, that is, principles or rules of public international law that impose obligations on states with respect to the content of their domestic criminal law and criminal procedure. The category of international criminal law *stricto sensu* is the law applicable in an international criminal court. With this categorisation, Wise seems to make a division within the first category.

[88] G.O.W. Mueller and D.J. Besharov, Evolution and Enforcement of International Criminal Law, in: M.C. Bassiouni, *International Criminal Law. Crimes,* second edition, Transnational Publishers, Inc. Ardsley, New York, 1986, pp. 258-259.

[89] M.C. Bassiouni, An Appraisal of the Growth and Developing Trends of International Criminal Law, in: *International Review of Penal Law*, Volume 45, 1974, p. 430.

[90] E.M. Wise, Terrorism and the Problems of an International Criminal Law, in: J. Dugard and Ch. van den Wyngaert, *International Criminal Law and Procedure,* Dartmouth, Aldershot, 1996, pp. 37-59.

[91] E.M. Wise, Terrorism and the Problems of an International Criminal Law, in: J. Dugard and Ch. van den Wyngaert, *International Criminal Law and Procedure*, Dartmouth, Aldershot, 1996, p. 44.

2.5 TRANSNATIONAL CRIME AS A THIRD GROUP OF CRIMES?

Within international criminal law, a specific group of crimes can be distinguished that cannot directly be allocated to either of the two groups of crime indicated above that correspond to the traditional categorisation in international criminal law. It concerns crimes that have their roots in more than one country, and therefore have very strong international connections. In this study, this group of crimes is called 'transnational crime'.

2.5.1 **Characteristics of transnational crime**

The term transnational crime is not a new term, but although it is regularly used in literature, it is never compared with the traditional dichotomy made in international criminal law. Furthermore, there is no elaborate study on the content of this type of crime. Before addressing the procedural implications of this category, I will concentrate on the concept of this group of crimes. As outlined by Bhattacharyya, crimes of international concern consist in crimes that have an international component and crimes with a transnational component: [92]

> An international element exists where the conduct in question rises to the level where it constitutes an offense against the world community. Thus, international crimes are crimes which constitute a direct threat to world peace and security, that is, those which are committed directly against the territory of one state by another state. Also considered international crimes are those acts that are so egregious that they shock the conscience of the world community, or those which constitute an indirect threat by rising to the level of threatening world peace and security due to the magnitude of the offense.

Transnational crimes are those where

> the offensive conduct affects the interests of more than one state ... includes the citizens of more than one state, or involves means or methods which transcend national boundaries. In this sense the transnational element is more limited in its impact on world order than is the international element. International jurisdiction in these cases arises largely due to conflicting assertions of jurisdiction by two or more states.

Thus, transnational crime can be shocking to the conscience of the international community but not in the same way as the group of international crimes described in the first category. The shocking effect of international crime, such as genocide and torture, originates from its nature, the way the crime is carried out, the scale of the crime, and often the involvement of officials. Although some transnational crimes are equally grave in their nature as international crime, the shocking effect of transnational crime is generated by the way a crime is performed and the size of the crime, and less by the nature of the crime itself, as is the case with international

[92] R. Bhattacharyya, Establishing a Rule-of-Law International Criminal Justice System, in: *Texas International Law Journal,* Volume 31, issue1, 1996, pp. 66-67.

crimes. Because more countries are involved, transnational crime can affect many people.[93] The main characteristic of transnational crime is that a certain level of organisation is required to commit these crimes, but this does not mean that they are necessarily committed by organised criminal groups. However, the crimes committed by these organised groups generally belong to this group when the crimes have connections with more than one country. The international aspect and, consequently, the complexity of the crimes in this group aggravate the problems of prosecuting the offenders who have committed these crimes. Therefore, solutions must be sought beyond the national level. Until now, the response to suppress and prosecute transnational crime has mainly been based on national competence, but it seems that a response from a non-national level would be more logical.

In the literature, the term 'transnational crime' is often confused with international crime. A distinction often made between international crimes and transnational crimes is that the former are 'those prohibited by international law including treaties and custom' while the latter 'are often regarded as those acts which are criminalised by the laws of more than one country'.[94] In the views of these authors, transnational crime is not considered to be a distinct group of crimes but as ordinary crime with special 'transnational' features, for instance, the offenders or victims are located in, or operate in, more than one country. This view is not shared in this study.

2.5.2 The connection between transnational crime and organised crime

Another point of discussion is the connection between transnational crime and organised crime. Criminal organisations are increasingly engaged in activities that tend to cross national borders. The globalisation of trade and consumer demand for luxury products have made it natural for criminal organisations to move from national activity to operations across borders. Furthermore, it is likely that organised crime will increasingly operate across borders in the future in order to exploit market opportunities in other states.

Transnational crime is committed by individuals, often organised in a group, against other individuals or against a state. Whether organised crime belongs to this group depends on the way the activities of the group are executed and on the definition of organised crime. If the illegal activities of the group take place in one and the same country and the members of the group originate from one country (which is uncommon), they must be considered as not belonging to the group of transnational crime.[95] In general, the transnational element is not seen as a constitutive element of

[93] M.C. Bassiouni, et al., *International Criminal Law. Cases and Materials,* Carolina Academic Press, Durham, North Carolina, 1996, pp. 18-19.

[94] N. Passas, *Transnational Crime,* Dartmouth, Aldershot, 1999, Introduction, p. xiii.

[95] See also: C. Fijnaut, Transnational Crime and the Role of the United Nations in Its Containment through International Cooperation: A Challenge for the 21st Century, in: *European Journal of Crime, Criminal Law and Criminal Justice,* Volume 8, issue 2, 2000, pp. 119-120.

organised crime but it is seen as such for transnational crime. The commission of transnational crime assumes a certain level of organisation, not necessarily an organised crime group, consisting of either loose or close contacts in other countries with people of whom it is known that they are prepared to participate in crime. These contacts are facilitated by the internationalisation of communications.[96] The different activities that have to be carried out to commit these crimes make these contacts inevitable for the offenders. For instance, in the case of drugs trafficking, which must be considered a transnational crime as we will see below, the various activities can consist of growing coca plants, modifying the plants, transporting the coca paste, modifying the paste, and distributing the cocaine. It is unlikely that one and the same person or group of persons executes all these activities, but it is not absolutely necessary that an organised crime group execute these activities. The relation of trafficking in persons with the concept of organised crime will be elaborated in Chapter 3.

2.5.3 The meaning of the term 'transnational'

The relevance of determining whether a crime is transnational, lies in the fact that, when a crime is transnational, states are obliged to cooperate with other states to effectively combat the crime. When states are confronted with transnational crime, they cannot say that the combating of that crime is an internal matter, trying to waive interference from other states. However, when a crime is labelled transnational, there is a risk that states will be reluctant to combat it, arguing that it is not their responsibility to fight this crime because of its transnational character.

The description of the term 'transnational' in the United Nations Convention on Transnational Organised Crime (UNCTOC) might be helpful in determining transnational crime.[97] According to Article 3 (2) of the UNCTOC, an offence is transnational in nature if one of the following alternative conditions is met.

- It is committed in more than one state;
- It is committed in one state but a substantial part of its preparation, planning, direction or control takes place in another state;
- It is committed in one state but involves an organised criminal group that engages in criminal activities in more than one state; or
- It is committed in one state but has substantial effects in another state.

This broad concept of the term 'transnational' means that an offence can be labelled transnational without goods or persons actually crossing the border. Williams and

[96] C. Fijnaut, Transnational Crime and the Role of the United Nations in Its Containment through International Cooperation: A Challenge for the 21st Century, in: *European Journal of Crime, Criminal Law and Criminal Justice,* Volume 8, issue 2, 2000, pp. 122-123.

[97] C. Rijken and V. Kronenberger, The United Nations Convention on Transnational Organised Crime and the European Union, in: V. Kronenberger, *The EU and the International Legal Order,* Asser Press, The Hague, 2001, pp. 487-490.

Savona opt for a stricter interpretation, stating that 'the term "transnational" is generally used to refer to the movement of information, money, physical objects, people, or other tangible or intangible items across state boundaries ...'[98] The broad concept of the term 'transnational' does not only include the actual crossing of a border but also the involvement of more countries in other ways. Because of the transnational character of the crime, the criminal activity often manifests itself as a form of trafficking or smuggling.

2.5.4 **Enforcement problems in the face of transnational crime**

Neither national criminal law nor international criminal law in its current form seem to be adequate tools for effective criminal prosecution of transnational crime because of the complexity of this type of crime caused by the transnational element.

The enforcement problem of legal instruments caused by this complexity is one of the difficulties when combating transnational crime. The perpetrators of this type of crime often use the gaps that result from the differences between the national criminal systems to escape prosecution. The criminal procedural laws of the states involved are not adapted to each other. Efforts in international and national criminal law are being made to find a solution to the problem of enforceability, as the enforcement of provisions in instruments to combat criminal behaviour continues to be a problem. The principles included in these documents, such as the *aut dedere aut judicare* principle or the universality principle as they are interpreted nowadays, do not bring a solution to the problem of enforceability.

As we have seen, the group of crimes identified in the category of international aspects of national criminal law also have a cross-border element. Crimes within the second category include, for example, theft by an Italian in Russia, murder by an American in France. In these cases, we can speak of ordinary crimes with a cross-border aspect. Many instruments on cooperation in criminal matters have already been established to solve problems that occur with regard to these crimes. Many countries have treaties on extradition, mutual legal assistance, transfer of proceedings, transfer of suspects, and execution of foreign judgements. However, these instruments are also used to combat transnational crime. The transnational element and the complexity of the international aspects in this category make a more intensive and flexible application of these instruments necessary. Obstacles to this intensive and flexible application seem to be caused by the lack of ability or willingness of states to use these instruments efficiently or to transform them into concrete actions. Therefore, it seems that a non-national approach is more effective. The following features may have an impact on the existence of problems in the procedure to enforce instruments to combat transnational crime.

---

[98] Ph. Williams and E.U. Savona, *The United Nations and Transnational Organised Crime,* Cass., London, 1996, pp. 4-5.

- Is the act considered a crime in all the states involved?
- In case of concurrent jurisdiction, which state is the most appropriate to commence the criminal procedure? Who decides on what grounds which state is the most appropriate?
- Do the states involved have similar criminal law systems?
- Are the states involved party to the relevant conventions on cooperation in criminal matters?

As stated before, it is clear that states want to hold on to their power to decide on the policy concerning crime and security in their own territory. The effect of criminal policy is limited to the state's territory while this is not the case for the effect of crimes and the acts of criminals as they are not hindered by state borders. The result is a conflict of interests between persistence on sovereign power as a way to prevent interference from other states in criminal matters and the need to extend the possibilities in the prosecution of transnational crime. Cooperation between states in criminal matters therefore depends in the first place on the will of states to change their sovereign power in criminal matters.

2.5.5 **Criteria to define transnational crime**

Following the above, the conclusion must be drawn that transnational crime must be considered a third group of crimes, distinguishable from the group of international crimes and the group of national crimes with an international element. To be able to draw a line between transnational crimes and the other two groups of crimes, the characteristics of transnational crime must be clearly identified. As follows from the above analysis, a crime, in order to be considered a transnational crime and therefore belonging to the third group of crimes, must meet the following criteria.
a. A certain level of organisation is needed to commit these crimes but not necessarily an organised crime group.
b. It affects the interests of more than one state because citizens of more than one state are involved or (part of) the crime took place in more than one state.
c. The fact that more states are involved aggravates the problems involved in prosecuting these crimes.
d. Effective solutions to these problems are sought beyond national borders.

The first two criteria have to be met cumulatively. The third and fourth are additional criteria that inevitably follow from the first and second criteria. However, it has to be determined to what extent those criteria are fulfilled as well before adequate solutions to transnational crime can be developed.

Crimes belonging to this group include trafficking in drugs and narcotic substances and smuggling people, cars, art and protected cultural objects. On the national and international levels, these crimes have been the subject of debate on many occasions. On the national as well as on the international level, states have committed themselves to combat these forms of crime on many occasions. Many of these crimes are also prohibited in international treaties but the problem of enforceability as a result of the absence of an effective law enforcement system and the transnational element have thwarted an effective policy to combat these crimes. It is remarkable that the international agreements in which such crimes are penalised devote much text to cooperation in criminal matters and coordination, which is not so often the case with international crimes.[99] This is probably because transnational crime can be better combated by cooperation and coordination than international crimes, which need a supranational approach.

2.5.6 Accommodating the group of transnational crime within the traditional categorisation

Now the question can be answered as to whether transnational crime can be allocated to either of the two categories of international criminal law, namely, that of the criminal law aspects of international law or of the international aspects of national criminal law. As stated before, transnational crime is considered a crime that requires a certain level of organisation for its execution. Its specific transnational feature causes its complexity and is the element which distinguishes it from other crimes. This complexity makes the need for intensive coordination of and cooperation towards solutions to these crimes a necessity. The question of whether the national level and the concept of the nation state as they exist today are appropriate to combat transnational crime is increasingly answered in the negative. In the fight against transnational crime, we see a development towards more coordination and centralisation in the effort to suppress these crimes on a regional or international level. Of course, national criminal law is still the level on which prosecution takes place but many obligations nowadays originate on the international or regional level.[100] To combat these transnational crimes, cooperation between states is indispensable and has to be further developed. In the context of this study, the cooperation preferably originates on the EU level and exceeds the national level. Thus the approach to prosecuting transnational crime differs from that of the other two categories. However, the exact content of these solutions is not yet clear.

This does not provide us with an answer to the question of whether the group of transnational crime, although distinguishable from the other two groups of crime, can be allocated to one of the two traditional categories of international criminal law. The fundamental distinction between these two categories of international criminal law is that one is based on international law and the other on national law. The original basis of transnational crime must be sought in national law, although transnational crime is often and increasingly codified in international and regional conventions and agreements. Solutions to the enforcement problems of the crimes within the two traditional categories must also be sought for one category on the in-

[99] See, for instance, the three protocols to the UNCTOC on smuggling persons, trafficking in human beings and trafficking in firearms.

[100] See A. Bossard, *Transnational Crime and Criminal Law,* The Office of International Criminal Justice, University of Illinois, Chicago, 1990, pp. 117-140.

ternational and for the other mainly on the national level. For the enforcement problems of transnational crime, the solution must be sought beyond the national level, which does not automatically mean on the international level. The instruments on cooperation in this regard developed so far often operate on a regional level, for instance the EU level, and only sometimes on the global level. However, the individual states are still the drafters of these instruments and the enforcement of these instruments is completely dependent on the willingness and possibilities of the individual states. Although much has already been achieved in this regard at the EU level, it is still too early to speak of a new criminal legal order on an EU level that operates beside the national and the international levels. Therefore, the answer to the question of whether transnational crime can be allocated to the traditional categorisation in international criminal law must be answered in the affirmative. With the current state of affairs, transnational crime must be considered a separate subgroup of crimes within the category of international aspects of national criminal law. Because of the transnational feature of these crimes, their prosecution on an EU level seems to be justified. It cannot be excluded that, in the future, such an approach may lead to the development of a new third criminal legal order on the EU level that will justify a separate third category of transnational crime.[101] As we will see in Chapter 4, cautious steps in that direction have already been taken by the EU, although there are also developments demonstrating the opposite, namely a strengthening of the position of states.[102]

2.6 CONCLUSION

International criminal law is commonly divided into two categories, namely, the criminal law aspects of international law and the international aspects of national criminal law. Both categories cover a particular group of crimes. However, a third group of crimes can be distinguished that must be considered a sub-category of the crimes in the category of international aspects of national criminal law as long as a regional or EU legal order is not fully developed. The crimes within this group can be called transnational crimes. Before a crime can be considered a transnational crime, the four criteria developed in this chapter must be fulfilled. These criteria are: (1) a certain level of organisation is needed to commit the crime, (2) it affects the interests of more than one state, (3) the involvement of more states aggravates the problems involved in prosecuting transnational crime, (4) effective solutions are sought beyond national borders. The first two criteria have to be fulfilled cumulatively while the third and fourth criteria inevitably follow from the first and second and therefore must be considered additional criteria. The enforcement problems existing in international criminal procedural law are explicitly present in this group.

[101] The concept of a regional law-making process was already recognised but not described by Bassiouni. M.C. Bassiouni, Policy Considerations on Inter-State Cooperation in Criminal Matters, in: A. Eser and O. Lagodny (eds.), *Principles and Procedures for a New Transnational Criminal Law,* Max Planck Institute, Freiburg im Breisgau, 1992, pp. 815-817.

[102] See Chapter 7, Section 7.2.3.2.

These problems are a result of the absence of a competent international law enforcement authority to take decisions with regard to criminal procedure.

Sovereign power as currently used by states seems to be inefficient for the fight against transnational crime and solutions to combating this crime must be sought beyond the national borders. This means that it is justified and necessary to find a different approach to prosecute transnational crime, which, in the future, may lead to a new category of international criminal law. However, before such an approach can be developed, the obstacles to the enforcement of current instruments must be identified first. As stated in Chapter I, this study will concentrate on the crime of trafficking in persons. Therefore, in the next chapter, I will examine whether the crime of trafficking in persons fulfils the four criteria developed in this chapter and therefore can be considered a transnational crime, justifying a different approach to its prosecution.

CHAPTER 3
DEFINING TRAFFICKING IN PERSONS

3.1 INTRODUCTION

The term 'trafficking in persons' is used in many different ways and is often confused with other terms. Until recently, there has not been a generally accepted definition of the term and countries and both national and international organisations use different interpretations of the concept.[1] Some say that trafficking in persons can only occur in relation to prostitution, while others use the term to include various forms of forced labour. The use of a form of force or coercion is not always seen as an essential element of the crime.[2] In this chapter, the definition of trafficking in persons will be explored and I will examine whether trafficking in persons must be considered a transnational crime by answering the question of whether the criteria for a crime to qualify as a transnational crime, as discussed in Chapter 2, are met. The main question in this regard is under what conditions trafficking in persons can be considered a transnational crime. In order to adequately answer this question and to address the problem, it is important to clarify the elements of the definition. The definition will be relevant to determine which strategy is most adequate. In this way, a clear and well-defined concept will contribute to the effectiveness of prosecuting trafficking in persons.

There is a lack of accurate and reliable data on the scope of the problem. It is generally known that trafficking in persons is a worldwide phenomenon that mostly takes place from Southern to Northern countries, from Eastern to Western countries and increasingly between Southern countries.[3] The exact scope of the problem is difficult to determine because of its illegal character.

This chapter starts with an overview of how the term 'trafficking in persons' and, in older documents, 'trafficking in women' has been used over the years. An analysis of the elements of the definition and an overview of the definitions used by several international organisations, especially in the Trafficking Protocol to the United Nations Convention on Transnational Organised Crime (the Trafficking Protocol),[4] and

---

[1] For an overview of international definitions, see G. Vermeulen, International Trafficking in Women and Children, General Report, in: *International Review of Penal Law,* Volume 72, issue 3-4, 2001, pp. 855-866.

[2] See, for instance, preparatory meetings for the Protocol on Trafficking in Persons Especially Women and Children, A/AC/254/4/add.3/Rev.5 and A/AC/254/4/add.3/Rev.7.

[3] Report of the Special Rapporteur on Violence against Women, its Causes and Consequences, Commission on Human Rights, 53rd Sess., UN Doc. E/CN.4/1997/47 (1997) p. 19.

[4] Protocol to Prevent, Suppress and Punish Trafficking in Persons, Especially Women and Children Supplementing the United Nations Convention against Transnational Organised Crime, GA Res. 55/25, annex II 55 UN GAOR Supp. (no. 49) at 60, UN Doc. A/45/49 (Vol. 1) (2001).

the EU Council Framework Decision on Combating Trafficking in Human Beings[5] will then be given. A comparison with related phenomena such as smuggling people, slavery and slavery-like practices, and organised crime, will be included as well. A separate section will address the definition of trafficking in persons as it is used in this study.

3.2 HISTORY OF THE TERM 'TRAFFICKING IN PERSONS'

The first effort to combat trafficking in women on the international level, resulting in an international legal instrument, is the 1904 International Agreement for the Suppression of the White Slave Trade, signed by sixteen European states.[6] This agreement makes it illegal to entice and/or procure women and girls and to lead them away for purposes of prostitution in another country. The goal of this agreement is more the protection of women than the punishment of the trafficker.[7] Violence, intimidation, misuse of authority, or any other form of coercion is an element of trafficking in adult women. Force in this sense is not required for minors. According to the text of the agreement, it concerns the recruitment of prostitutes rather than the exploitation of prostitutes. On 4 May 1910, the International Convention for the Suppression of the White Slave Traffic was signed.[8] This treaty contains provisions to punish traffickers. It addresses not only trafficking into another country, but also refers to trafficking within one country.[9] It meets the same conditions for the use of coercion as the 1904 agreement, which means that coercion is required to prosecute the trafficker in the case of adult women but not in the case of minors.[10] Some people argue that this second convention also prohibits the exploitation of prostitutes. The closing statement of the convention, however, is clear in the sense that it does not apply to exploitation of prostitutes. It states:

> The case of the retention, against her will, of a woman or girl in a house of prostitution could not, in spite of its gravity, be included in the present Convention, because it is exclusively a question of internal legislation.

To complement these two international arrangements, two conventions were drafted by the League of Nations on 30 September 1921, and on 11 October 1933: The In-

[5] Council Framework Decision of 19 July 2002 on Combating Trafficking in Human Beings, OJ L 203, 1.8.2002, pp. 1-4.

[6] International Agreement for the Suppression of the White Slave Trade, 18 May 1904, 35 Stat. 426, 1 LNTS 83.

[7] S. Farrior, The International Law on Trafficking in Women and Children for Prostitution: Making it Live Up to its Potential, in: *Harvard Human Rights Journal,* Volume 10, issue spring, 1997, p. 216.

[8] International Convention for the Suppression of the White Slave Traffic, 4 May 1910, III LNTS 278.

[9] Advisory Committee on Human Rights and Foreign policy of the Dutch Ministry of Foreign Affairs, *The Traffic in Persons*, Advice no. 14, The Hague, 1992, pp. 28-29. R. Haveman, *Voorwaarden voor strafbaarstelling van vrouwenhandel*, Gouda Quint, The Hague, 1998, pp. 126ff.

[10] R. Haveman, *Voorwaarden voor strafbaarstelling van vrouwenhandel*, Gouda Quint, The Hague, 1998, pp. 126ff.

ternational Convention to Suppress the Traffic in Women and Children and The International Convention for the Suppression of the Traffic in Women of Full Age, respectively.[11] The most important achievement of the former is that it includes the trafficking in underage boys as well. By virtue of the latter convention, traffickers can be punished when they bring a woman into another country for the purpose of prostitution, irrespective of whether she has given her consent. In short, the element of 'trafficking with the purpose of bringing a woman into prostitution in another country' is the essential qualification for the existence of trafficking in women in this convention. Recruitment and transport of women, even with the consent of these women, for the purpose of prostitution are punishable by law if it concerns trafficking in women from one country to another. The difference with the earlier agreement and conventions is that coercion is no longer an essential element of the offence as long as it involves trafficking in women from one country to another. For internal trafficking, the requirement of coercion remains essential. According to the convention, the trafficking, that is, the recruitment and transport, has to be coercive. It does not say anything about the requirement of force with regard to prostitution or labour, although voluntary prostitution is hard to imagine when recruitment and transport have taken place against the will of the victim. These four instruments for suppressing trafficking in women apply only to the trafficking process and not to the exploitation of the trafficked individuals. In more recent treaties and agreements, this distinction is not always made.

The first attempt to address trafficking and exploitation simultaneously is the UN Convention signed on 2 December 1949 entitled the 'Convention for the Suppression of the Traffic in Persons and of the Exploitation of the Prostitution of Others'.[12] It replaced the four earlier instruments and deals with both trafficking and exploitation. Article 1 of this convention states:

> The Parties to the present Convention agree to punish any person who, to gratify the passions of another:
> 1. Procures, entices or leads away, for purposes of prostitution, another person, even with the consent of that person;
> 2. Exploits the prostitution of another person, even with the consent of that person.

Furthermore, individuals who keep, manage, or (partly) finance a brothel, or who provide accommodation for the purpose of the prostitution of others are punishable, according to Article 2. In this convention, forced prostitution or exploitation is not distinguished from prostitution or exploitation with the consent of the person in question. Thus, trafficking in this convention means bringing someone into prostitu-

---

[11] Convention for the Suppression of Traffic in Women and Children, 30 September 1921, 9 LNTS 415, and the International Convention for the Suppression of the Traffic in Women of Full Age, 11 October 1933, 150 LNTS 431.

[12] Convention for the Suppression of the Traffic in Persons and of the Exploitation of the Prostitution of Others, in force since 25 July 1951, 96 UNTS 271.

tion. This treaty has only been ratified by 75 states. Two reasons can be given for the limited interest in this treaty.

The first reason is that this convention also includes the voluntary recruitment and exploitation of voluntary prostitution, which was, until then, considered to belong to the national jurisdiction of the states.[13] The second reason can be found in its weak enforcement provisions. State parties have to submit reports annually to the UN Secretary-General, giving information about efforts taken to implement the convention. The Secretary-General is directed to publish these reports and to send them to other countries. There is no independent organ that has the authority to promulgate recommendations or to question the reports. The Working Group on Contemporary Forms of Slavery has reviewed these reports since 1974.[14]

Since there are different views on the tolerability of prostitution, prostitution is not always considered a punishable activity. The convention reflects an abolitionist view of prostitution.[15] Abolitionists criticise the regulation of prostitution and the interference from the authorities in regulating prostitution and want the complete abolishment of prostitution. They consider prostitution a moral evil. The former special UN rapporteur on the suppression of the trafficking in persons and the exploitation of the prostitution of others, J. Fernand-Laurent, was in favour of this abolitionist approach because he views prostitution under all circumstances a form of slavery.[16] In more recent documents of the UN, the abolitionist view is not always supported. Although an approach to view prostitution as ordinary work is not supported, it seems that the UN is more hesitant towards the total rejection of prostitution. For example, an amendment by Morocco to Article 6 of the Convention on the Elimination of All Forms of Discrimination against Women (CEDAW) to include prostitution as one of the phenomena that has to be suppressed was not adopted.[17]

In many countries, abolitionism is the dominant view with respect to brothels while prostitution as such is not prohibited. The Netherlands did not ratify the Convention of 1949, because the abolitionist view represented in the convention is incompatible with the policy in which prostitution and brothels are tolerated. Since October 2000, brothels have been legalised under certain circumstances under Dutch law[18] and therefore it is unlikely that the Netherlands will become a party to the treaty in the future.

---

[13] J. Chuang, Redirecting the Debate over Trafficking in Women: Definitions, Paradigms, and Contexts, in: *Harvard Human Rights Journal*, Volume 11, issue spring, 1998, p. 75.

[14] See Section 3.6 below.

[15] Normally, abolitionism in criminal law means the total withdrawal and abolishment of criminal law. In relation to prostitution, it can mean the discontinuation of all involvement of the authorities concerning prostitution, including its regulation. In this view, all prostitution is forced and is automatically a violation of human rights, and therefore has to be abandoned.

[16] R. Haveman, *Voorwaarden voor strafbaarstelling van vrouwenhandel*, Gouda Quint, The Hague, 1998, p. 249.

[17] L.A. Rehof, *Guide to the Travaux Préparatoires of the United Nations Convention on the Elimination of All Forms of Discrimination against Women,* Nijhoff, Dordrecht, 1993, pp. 90-91.

[18] Article 250a of the Dutch Penal Code.

There are organisations trying to update or rewrite the convention of 1949.[19] Other organisations are calling for a protocol to the 1949 convention based on the human right of self-determination, which only penalises forced prostitution and which focuses more on the element of 'force' in the definition.[20] As will be shown in this chapter, coercion, as an element of trafficking in persons, has been and still is a source of confusion in understanding the meaning of this crime.

In conclusion, in the first half of the 20th century the term trafficking in women, at that time the commonly used term, underwent two changes. The first is the change from the criminalisation of forced trafficking to the criminalisation of trafficking with the consent of a person as well. The second development is that, at the beginning of the 20th century, only the trafficking was criminalised, which meant the recruitment and transportation of the trafficked persons. The 1949 Convention also explicitly addressed the exploitation of the trafficked people as well. Consequently, the convention considered forced prostitution as a matter of international concern, whereas it had previously been seen as a case of strictly internal jurisdiction.

3.3 ELEMENTS OF THE DEFINITION OF TRAFFICKING IN PERSONS

In order to clarify the term 'trafficking in persons', the different elements of the phenomenon will be discussed below. The elements that will, successively, pass in review are: the two phases of recruitment and transport, on the one hand, and exploitation on the other, the coercive element, the goal of the trafficking, and the use of the word 'women' or 'persons' in the definition. The discussion on the international level within international organisations and NGOs will be reflected upon. Some indications will already be given of the use of the term 'trafficking in persons' in this study.

3.3.1 **Recruitment and transport versus exploitation**

Internationally, the phenomenon of 'trafficking in persons' is nowadays generally divided into recruitment and transport of persons, on the one hand, and the exploitation of persons, on the other. The title of the 1949 Convention for the Suppression of the Traffic in Persons and of the Exploitation of the Prostitution of Others reflects this distinction, which can also be found in Article 1 of this convention. By making a distinction between the two phenomena, it is easier to address each problem separately than to find comprehensive strategies to deal with both. As the two phenom-

[19] For instance, the proposal for a new 'Convention on the Elimination of All Forms of Sexual Exploitation of Women' presented by UNESCO and the 'Coalition against Trafficking in Women', which rejects the distinctions between 'free' and 'forced' prostitution (Penn State report 1992). Report of the Working Group on Contemporary Forms of Slavery, E/CN/4/Sub.2/1991/41, Annex I, paras 35-41.

[20] L. Zegveld, The Combat of Traffic in Persons within the Framework of the United Nations, in: M. Klap, Y. Klerk and J.A. Smith (eds.), *Combating traffic in Persons: Proceedings of the Conference on Traffic in Persons held from 15-19 November 1994 in Utrecht and Maastricht,* SIM-special, no. 17, Utrecht, 1995, p. 35.

ena are completely different in their appearance and origin, each phenomenon needs specific actions to combat it.

As said before, the 1949 convention was the first attempt to address trafficking and exploitation in one instrument. In the period after the Second World War, most of the treaties and agreements on this subject dealt with both trafficking and exploitation, often for the purpose of prostitution. However, this development did not help to clarify the two phenomena.

The distinction between trafficking and exploitation is also made in the CEDAW Convention.[21] Article 6 of the CEDAW Convention states that all state parties should 'take all appropriate measures, including legislation, to suppress all forms of traffic in women and exploitation of prostitution of women'. At first sight, exploitation seems to focus only on prostitution while the purpose of the trafficking is not limited. However, the exploitation of other forms of forced labour or with other intentions is also included in this article, as a result of General Recommendation 19 on violence against women, enacted by the CEDAW committee.[22] Paragraph 14 of this recommendation states that there are new forms of sexual exploitation, such as sex tourism, the recruitment of domestic labour from developing countries to work in developed countries, and arranged marriages between women from developing countries and foreign nationals.[23]

Although many current instruments address recruitment and transport as well as exploitation, they often do not make a distinction between the two. An example of the lack of clarity about the meaning of the term trafficking in persons can be found in a report by Dutch researchers concerning women who have emigrated without mediation by traffickers. In this passage, the working and living conditions of several of these women as well as their reasons for coming to the Netherlands are reasons to justify calling them victims of traffic in women.[24] A definition is to be found elsewhere in the survey: traffic in women is described as the systematic and economic exploitation of female sexuality; a process in which women lose the power and the self-determination over their own bodies, their sexuality, and their lives.[25] This description limits trafficking in persons to the exploitative phase of the crime. This is not how the term of 'trafficking in persons' should be interpreted and it is not used

[21] Convention on the Elimination of All Forms of Discrimination against Women, GA Res. 34/180 34 UN GAOR Supp. (no. 46) at 193, UN Doc. A/34/46, entered into force on 3 September 1981.

[22] The CEDAW committee monitors this convention and is empowered to formulate general recommendations about the interpretation and scope of the treaty.

[23] CEDAW committee general recommendation no. 19 (1992) on Violence against Women.

[24] N. van der Vleuten, *Survey on 'Traffic in Women'*, Vena working paper no. 91/1, Policies and Policy Research in an International Context, Research and Documentation Centre Women and Autonomy, Leyden University, 1991, p. 3.

[25] N. van der Vleuten, *Survey on 'Traffic in Women'* Vena working paper no. 91/1, Policies and Policy Research in an International Context, Research and Documentation Centre Women and Autonomy, Leyden University, 1991, p. 13.

in this way in international law, although it is a general trend that the exploitative phase is more focused upon nowadays and that the term trafficking also refers to this phase.

However, to be able to understand the essence of the problem of trafficking in persons we must determine the relation between the two phases of the phenomenon. The definitions developed by the Global Alliance Against Traffic in Women (GAATW) may be helpful in this regard.

The GAATW, a coalition of non-governmental organisations working towards the elimination of trafficking in women, has introduced a new definition that is used by many other NGOs. They distinguish between trafficking and forced labour/slavery-like practices.

The GAATW defines trafficking as:[26]

> All acts involved in the recruitment and/or transportation of a person within and across national borders for work or services by means of violence or threat of violence, abuse of authority or dominant position, debt bondage, deception or other forms of coercion.

Their definition of 'forced labour and slavery-like practices' is:

> The extraction of work or services from any person or the appropriation of the legal identity and/or physical person of any person by means of violence or threat of violence, abuse of authority or dominant position, debt bondage, deception or other forms of coercion.

However, the question remains whether the exploitative phase, in terms of the GAATW definition 'the forced labour or slavery-like practice', must have taken place before an act can be considered as a crime of trafficking in persons. The elements of the crime are literally fulfilled when the intention of the trafficker is aimed at bringing the trafficked person into the exploitative situation. Strictly speaking, it is not necessary that exploitation itself has taken place, although in order to prove that it was the intention of the trafficker to bring the person into an exploitative situation, it is often necessary that exploitation has taken place.

According to the GAATW, exploitation must be understood as forced labour/slavery-like practices, but the two are not synonymous. It seems that 'forced labour/ slavery-like practices' is a broad term that also refers to situations in which powers attaching to the right of ownership are exercised over a person. This is referred to as 'the appropriation of the legal identity and/or physical person'.[27] For the suppression

[26] Global Alliance Against Traffic in Women and the Foundation for Women in cooperation with the Foundation against Trafficking in Women: Standard Minimum Rules for the Treatment of Victims of Trafficking in Persons, Forced Labour and Slavery-Like Practices.

[27] L. Lap-Chew and M. Wijers, *Trafficking in Women, Forced Labor, and Slavery-Like Practices in*

of trafficking in persons, it is advisable to adopt a broad interpretation of the term 'exploitation' and therefore it must be understood in this broad sense.

In the definition of the GAATW the term trafficking only refers to the recruitment and transport phase. The exploitative phase is seen as separated from the trafficking phase, although the two are linked by the phrase in the trafficking definition 'for work or services'. The distinction in the GAATW definition between these two phases stresses that the two phenomena can occur independently of each other. A person can be forced into some kind of labour without being trafficked. In my view, the crime of trafficking does not occur in such cases. It is more difficult to imagine the opposite situation, in which a person is trafficked for voluntary labour. Although this situation is hard to imagine, it cannot be completely eliminated. Such a strict division of the two phases of trafficking in persons is not consistent with the use of the term by other international and regional organisations, as we will see below.

3.3.2 The coercive element in the term 'trafficking in persons'

In the instruments on trafficking in persons before 1933, coercion was an essential element in the definition. The 1933 Convention introduced the criminalisation of voluntary trafficking to another country. This was the case until the 1980s when trafficking in persons resurfaced on the agenda. In many definitions dating from that time, coercion was seen as a prerequisite for trafficking in persons. However, it is not self-evident that coercion is an essential component. The two most extreme views on the role of coercion in relation to trafficking in persons are the following.

1. Coercion is the criminal element of trafficking in persons that needs to be focused upon. Therefore, the focus in the struggle against trafficking in persons has to be on the element of force. In this view, prostitution can be seen as a normal form of labour. Therefore, it is not the kind of labour but the circumstances under which it is performed that is important. It is 'not the work or services as such, but the way those are organised (both in terms of the recruitment and the working conditions) that makes it a problem to the women involved: that is 'forced'.[28] The focus in this approach is on the coercive element.
2. Prostitution is per se coercive. Not only the pressure but the prostitution itself has to be eliminated. It is impossible to treat forced prostitution on the same basis as forced labour/slavery-like practices. In the case of prostitution, the work itself has to be abolished. For prostitution, the emphasis is on the kind of labour while, for forced labour/slavery-like practices, the coercive conditions are the reason to abolish these practices. If prostitution is eliminated, the trafficking will automatically stop, is the reasoning behind this approach.

Marriage, Domestic Labor, and Prostitution, Foundation against Trafficking in Women, Utrecht, 1997, p. 39.

[28] L. Lap-Chew and M. Wijers, *Trafficking in Women, Forced Labor, and Slavery-like Practices in Marriage, Domestic Labor, and Prostitution*, Foundation against Trafficking in Women, Utrecht, 1997, p. 35.

These two points of view are totally opposed. The requirement of coercion as a constitutive element of trafficking in persons as adopted in the first view, is a confirmation of the autonomy of women and the capacity of self-determination. In this approach, the empowerment of women can contribute to combating trafficking in persons because it allows women to make their own decisions. The second, abolitionist view, in which the consent of the person trafficked (generally a woman) is irrelevant, is a denial of the capacity of a person to make her own choice. It is another way of saying that the prostitute does not know what is best for her and that she needs some help to protect her.

It is possible for a person to consent to transport or recruitment, but as soon as some form of coercion is used, it becomes trafficking, taking into account that exploitation is the purpose of the activity. Furthermore, it is relevant to determine whether the coercion concerns recruitment and transport or exploitation, or both. Most recent definitions show us that, for the phase of recruitment and transport, there is consensus on the fact that a form of coercion is required. If this was not required, it would become completely dependent on the intention of the trafficker whether the activity concerns trafficking, smuggling, or even ordinary travel. Whether coercion also refers to exploitation as well is a subject for further discussion. As we have seen there is no agreement on the matter of whether exploitation of prostitution includes a coercive element in itself or not. As stated above, it is hard to imagine a situation in which coercive recruitment and transport is followed by voluntary exploitation. It is highly questionable whether such an activity can be considered as trafficking. However, for a clear understanding of the definition and taking into account the right to self-determination and the emancipation of women, the element of coercion in the definition of trafficking in persons must be considered to concern the exploitative phase as well. This means that a woman can also freely choose to work as a prostitute and because in these cases the coercion in the exploitative phase is absent it does not meet the requirements of the definition of trafficking in persons. However, we have to keep in mind that coercion is broadly defined in this study as we will see below.

Another question, which was briefly referred to above, is whether the exploitation phase must have taken place before the crime of trafficking in persons has taken place. In my opinion, this is not strictly necessary and the forced recruitment or transportation alone will qualify the acts as trafficking in persons. However, the purpose of the traffickers to exploit the trafficked person must be present from the beginning, which may be difficult to prove.

3.3.2.1 *The meaning of coercion*

The next question is: what is the content of the coercive element? Is it only as it is recognised in criminal law or also coercion caused by economic means? To start with the second question, if economic circumstances are included in the definition of coercion, problems with the prosecution of the trafficker may arise. The use of coercion by the trafficker will be more difficult to prove if economic circumstances can be seen as a form of coercion. The trafficker will try to hide behind the concept of economic coercion to escape punishment. Besides, it is difficult to prove whether the economic situation has forced a person into prostitution. Furthermore, the distinction between trafficked persons and other economic refugees can become problematic when economic hardship is taken into account as a form of coercion, as the protection granted to victims of trafficking is not granted to economic refugees.[29] However, as we will see below, the criteria to distinguish between trafficking and smuggling can be used to draw a line between these two phenomena. For these reasons economic hardship must generally not be included in the definition of coercion.[30] In general, the economically and socially marginalized persons, especially women, easily fall victim to illegal practices from traffickers.[31] Because of the feminisation of poverty, women and children are especially affected by and vulnerable to poverty and will be increasingly victimised in the future.[32] Under these circumstances, the right to freedom and the right to self-determination are easily violated. Therefore, some authors promote education and training of women, as well as employment opportunities as key factors for empowering women and enabling them to overcome poverty as a defence against traffickers.[33]

The question of the elements of the coercive element can be further answered by making reference to the description of the GAATW. The GAATW limits coercion to 'violence or threat of violence, abuse of authority or dominant position, debt bondage, deception, or other forms of coercion'.[34] The different forms of coercion can have the following features.[35]

- Violence or threat of violence, including deprivation of freedom of movement, and of personal choice.

---

[29] L.A. Malone, Economic Hardship as Coercion under the Protocol on International Trafficking in Persons by Organized Crime Elements, in: *Fordham International Law Journal,* Volume 25, issue 54, 2001, pp. 91-94.

[30] Different, L.A. Malone, Economic Hardship as Coercion under the Protocol on International Trafficking in Persons by Organized Crime Elements, in: *Fordham International Law Journal,* Volume 25, issue 54, 2001, pp. 89-92.

[31] Report of the Working Group on Contemporary Forms of Slavery, Draft Programme of Action on the Traffic in Persons and the Exploitation of the Prostitution of Others, E/CN/4/sub.2/1995/28/add.1, p. 18.

[32] See, for instance, World Population Report 2000, United Nations Population Fund. For the situation in the Americas see International Human Rights Law Institute, DePaul University College of Law, *In Modern Bondage: Sex Trafficking in the Americas,* IHRLI, DePaul University, Chicago, 2002, pp. 26-35.

[33] R. Haveman, *Voorwaarden voor strafbaarstelling van vrouwenhandel*, Gouda Quint, The Hague, 1998, pp. 257-263. Advisory Committee on Human Rights and Foreign Policy of the Dutch Ministry of Foreign Affairs, *The Traffic in Persons*, Advice no. 14, The Hague, 1992, p. 2.

[34] Global Alliance Against Traffic in Women and the Foundation for Women in cooperation with the Foundation against Trafficking in Women: Standard Minimum Rules for the Treatment of Victims of Trafficking in Persons, Forced Labour, and Slavery-Like Practices.

[35] L. Lap-Chew and M. Wijers, *Trafficking in Women, Forced Labor, and Slavery-Like Practices in Marriage, Domestic Labor, and Prostitution*, Foundation against Trafficking in Women, Utrecht, 1997, p. 38.

- Deception: with regard to, among other things, working conditions or the nature of the work to be done.
- Abuse of authority or dominant position: this can range from confiscating personal documents in order to place another person in a dependent position, to abusing one's dominant social position or natural parental authority or abusing the vulnerable position of persons without legal status.
- Debt bondage: i.e., pledging the personal services or labour of oneself or another person as security for a debt, if the value of these services or this labour as reasonably assessed is not applied towards the liquidation of the debt, or the length and nature of these services or this labour are not limited and defined.

These forms of coercion cover the situations in trafficking cases in which force is used. The descriptions are formulated in open terms, leaving space to include other forms of coercion as well.

In my view, coercion must be interpreted broadly, also including, for instance, bad working conditions, low payment, and no control over leisure time. Even if a person has consented to such working conditions, the existence of trafficking in persons is not excluded.

3.3.2.2 *The purpose of the trafficker*

In recent definitions of trafficking in persons, such as in the Trafficking Protocol to the UNCTOC and the Council Framework Decision on Combating Trafficking in Human Beings within the EU, trafficking takes place 'for the purpose of exploitation.' It is not always easy to determine whether coercion exists and when it occurs. The intention of the trafficker and the consent of the person trafficked are relevant issues in this context. If a person is misled, for instance, by being promised work as a waitress but is later forced to work as a prostitute, the misleading action only becomes known after the person is transported. At the moment of transport, the coercive element, in this case deception, is difficult to prove, and can only be demonstrated by the intent of the trafficker. The intent of the trafficker, as a subjective element, is difficult to prove if he has not yet carried out his actions. Does the consent of the person in these cases mean that the crime of trafficking has not taken place? Or is the intent of the trafficker the key to accepting the existence of trafficking in persons? If the original consent of the person is decisive, it can mean that, when she entered into the activity, the coercion at a later stage is not relevant in determining the existence of trafficking.[36] Many victims are not taken seriously because they agreed to work as prostitutes in advance or have worked as prostitutes in the past. The bad circumstances under which they have to work and the misleading information from the trafficker are often insufficient evidence to prove trafficking in

[36] Although the number of men falling victim to trafficking in persons is growing, the majority of the victims is female and therefore the victims are referred to in the female form in this study.

persons.[37] Fortunately, the opinions in this regard are changing which means that the evidence for coercion can be constituted by the coercive working conditions regardless of whether the trafficked person has previously consented to the work.[38] However, the existence of trafficking in persons is still hard to prove when the exploitation has not take place.

3.3.3 The goal of the trafficking

Trafficking in persons is often associated with prostitution (forced or not) or work in the sex industry. By limiting the purpose of trafficking in persons to prostitution, many situations in which persons are trafficked for other kinds of work or services, for instance domestic labour, factory labour, and commercial marriages, are excluded.

The Advisory Committee on Human Rights and Foreign Policy of the Dutch Ministry of Foreign Affairs (hereafter the advisory committee) in its comment on 'The Traffic in People' asked what consequences the use of a broader definition would have. The committee wondered whether it would be preferable to use the term 'trafficking in persons' not only when someone is trafficked for the purpose of prostitution but for other purposes as well.[39] In the newly proposed definition of the advisory committee the purpose of the crime of trafficking is not limited to prostitution; the reason for the trafficking is to bring the person into the actual and unlawful power of another, thus not per se to exploit the person. The decisive element is coercion and not the purpose of the trafficking.[40] What must be fought is the forcing of people to do something against their will.[41]

---

[37] J. Vocks and J. Nijboer, *Land van belofte. Een onderzoek naar slachtoffers van vrouwenhandel uit Centraal- en Oost-Europa,* Rijksuniversiteit Groningen, December 1999, p. 54.

[38] See, for instance, Article 1 of the Framework Decision on Combating Trafficking in Human Beings. Under (d) it states that payments or benefits that are given or received to achieve the consent of a person having control over another person must be considered as a coercive means in relation to trafficking in persons. Furthermore, paragraph 2 of this article states that the consent of the victim to the intended or actual exploitation is irrelevant if a form of coercion described under a-d of paragraph 1 is used.

[39] Advisory Committee on Human Rights and Foreign Policy of the Dutch Ministry of Foreign Affairs, *The Traffic in Persons*, Advice no. 14, The Hague, 1992, pp. 13-14.

[40] R. Haveman, Slavernij of reguliere arbeid. Prostitutie en vrouwenhandel in internationaal perspectief, in: *Nemesis*, Volume 11, issue 4, 1995, p. 102.

[41] For a critical note on this definition, see Y. Klerk, Definition of 'Traffic in Persons', in: M. Klap, Y. Klerk, and J.A. Smith (eds.), *Combating Traffic in Persons: Proceedings of the Conference on Traffic in Persons held from 15-19 November 1994 in Utrecht and Maastricht,* SIM-special no. 17, Utrecht, 1995, pp. 20-21. She sums up three disadvantages of the definition. Firstly, it excludes the trafficking of people within a country. Secondly, only the transporting person can be marked as a trafficker and not the person who holds a person in his/her actual but unlawful power. Her third remark is that, literally, the definition also covers a situation in which a person kidnaps a victim and hands him over to a guard. According to Klerk, traffic in persons should at least be limited to situations in which some form of work is exacted from the victim. When it is not limited to situations in which some form of work is exacted the distinction with the crime of smuggling in persons is difficult to make, as we will see in Section 3.5.

The statement of the Council of Europe made at the seminar on trafficking in women and forced prostitution, held in Strasbourg, 25-27 September 1991, contributed the approach to widen the definition of trafficking and to reject a definition in which the trafficking is restricted to the purpose of prostitution. It was thought advisable to 'consider extending the scope of relevant existing international instruments to all forms of trafficking in persons, irrespective of the activity persons are trafficked for.'[42]

Another supporter of a broader definition is the expert group of the Commission on the Status of Women convened in 1993, which stated that the concept of 'Trafficking in persons' should be extended to encompass trafficking for other activities, such as forced domestic labour, false marriages, clandestine employment, and false adoptions.[43]

In most definitions, the trafficking takes place for the purpose of some form of exploitation. For instance, according to the definition of the GAATW, it is necessary that the trafficking be undertaken 'for work or services'. In this content attention is focused on transport and recruitment. If the definition does not include some form of exploitation as the goal of the trafficking, it can be easily confused with other crimes that violate personal freedom, such as kidnapping.

It seems to follow from J. Chuang's article on trafficking in women that the definition in international law only concerns forced transport for forced prostitution.[44] This is consistent with the 1949 Convention some say, but not with Article 6 of the CEDAW Convention and General Recommendation 19 to this convention, as was explained before.[45]

As follows from this analysis, in recent years there has been more willingness to broaden the term and make it applicable to other forms of forced labour. In this study, the term of trafficking in persons is not limited to the purpose of prostitution but applies to all forms of exploitation.

3.3.4 'Trafficking in women' or 'trafficking in persons'?

Although trafficking in persons concerns for the greater part trafficking in women, it seems to be in accordance with recent international standards such as the Trafficking Protocol to the UNCTOC and the Council Framework Decision on Combating Traf-

[42] Council of Europe, Strasbourg, 25-27 September 1991, Seminar on action against traffic in women and forced prostitution as violations of human rights and human dignity, EC/prost (91) 13 prov. Sub II.

[43] Economic and Social Council, Commission on the Status of Women, Measures to Eradicate Violence against Women in the Family and Society, 21 January 1994.

[44] J. Chuang, Redirecting the Debate over Trafficking in Women: Definitions, Paradigms, and Contexts, in: *Harvard Human Rights Journal*, Volume 11, issue spring, 1998, pp. 78-79.

[45] See Section 3.3.1 above.

ficking in Human Beings[46] to use the term of trafficking in persons or trafficking in human beings. Trafficking in men, especially in underage boys, is increasing which justifies the use of the term trafficking in persons. Besides, the term trafficking in women is generally associated with prostitution. Although the majority of persons are trafficked for the purpose of prostitution, the term in this study is not used in this restrictive way. On the contrary, it can be said that trafficking in persons is a sex-neutral term and does not reflect the group of victims. Another reason for choosing the term 'trafficking in women' could be that the term 'trafficking in persons' is more easily confused with other terms such as smuggling people and smuggling aliens. Taking these remarks into account, it seems to be more in accordance with recent developments to use the term trafficking in persons in this study instead of trafficking in women.

3.4 USE OF DEFINITIONS OF TRAFFICKING IN PERSONS BY THE UN, THE EU, AND THE IOM

It is useful to consider different definitions of trafficking in persons. It gives an idea of the elements of the definition and an indication of the development of the term in recent years and gives a picture of the difficulties involved in defining the crime. As we will see, organisations often use a definition of trafficking in persons that best suits their activities. They concentrate on different elements of their definitions, depending on their interest. The main elements that play a role in the definitions are the purpose of the trafficking and the use of coercion.

3.4.1 **Definition in the Trafficking Protocol to the UNCTOC**

The definition used in the Trafficking Protocol to the UNCTOC, in article 3(a), reads as follows.

> Trafficking in persons shall mean the recruitment, transportation, transfer, harbouring or receipt of persons, by means of the threat or use of force or other forms of coercion, of abduction, of fraud, of deception, of the abuse of power or of a position of vulnerability or of the giving or receiving of payments or benefits to achieve the consent of a person having control over another person, for the purpose of exploitation. Exploitation shall include, at a minimum, the exploitation of the prostitution of others or other forms of sexual exploitation, forced labour or services, slavery or practices similar to slavery, servitude or the removal of organs.

For the first time, states reached agreement on a definition of trafficking in persons on a broad international level. In this definition, the two phases of trafficking in persons, namely, recruitment and transport, on the one hand, and exploitation, on the other, are merged. During the negotiations for this protocol, the elements of 'force' and 'consent' caused extensive discussion among the participating states.[47] They

[46] See Section 3.4.3 below.

[47] See, for instance, A/AC.254/4/Add.3/Rev.5, para 34.

disagreed on the point of whether prostitution could be practiced voluntarily or not and thus on the point of whether 'force' and 'consent' were constitutive elements in the definition especially for the phase of exploitation.[48] Here, the states in favour of the abolitionist view had to face those opposing this view. Finally, the discussion was decided with the inclusion of article 3(b). This paragraph states that the consent of a victim of trafficking in persons to the intended exploitation is irrelevant where a form of coercion, listed in article 3(a), has been used. In this sentence, it is covertly said that it is also possible to consent to the exploitation but it avoids the answer to the question of whether prostitution includes a form of coercion in itself.[49] Following the *travaux préparatoires* to the protocol, it is up to the participating states themselves how they address prostitution in their domestic laws.[50] From the phrase 'or any other forms of coercion' in article 3(a) it can be concluded that the coercive means listed in this article must not be considered to be exhaustive. Thus, the coercive element must be understood in a broad sense also including forced labour, slavery, and slavery-like practices.

Another item for discussion was the question of whether the physical crossing of a border was essential for the fulfilment of the elements of the definition. Until the final draft of the protocol, the inclusion of the term 'international' with regard to trafficking was discussed.[51] Although the UNCTOC only concerns crimes that are transnational in nature and involve an organised crime group, this does not mean that the factual movement from one country to another is always required.[52]

3.4.2 **Other definitions within the UN body**

The United Nations General Assembly definition of trafficking in persons does not require coercion as a necessary element of the crime. It defines trafficking as:[53]

> the illicit and clandestine movement of persons across national or international borders, largely from developing countries and some countries with economies in transition, with the end goal of forcing women and girl children into sexually or economically oppressive and exploitative situations for the profit of recruiters, traffickers and crime syndicates, as well as other illegal activities related to trafficking, such as forced domestic labour, false marriages, clandestine employment and false adoption.

---

[48] A/AC.254/4/Add.3/Rev.7, para 10.

[49] Also C. Rijken and V. Kronenberger, The United Nations Convention on Transnational Organised Crime and the European Union, in: V. Kronenberger, *The EU and the International Legal Order,* Asser Press, The Hague, 2001, pp. 503-505. The abolitionists on the other hand saw the adoption of this paragraph as a confirmation that prostitution in itself is coercive and cannot be consented to.

[50] *Travaux préparatoires*, Interpretative notes for the official records of the negotiation of the Protocol to Prevent, Suppress and Punish Trafficking in Persons, Especially Women and Children, Supplementing the United Nations Convention against Transnational Organised Crime, A/55/383/Add.1.

[51] See, for instance, A/AC.254/4/Add.3/Rev.5, A/AC.254/4/Add.3/Rev.6, A/AC.254/4/Add.3/Rev.7.

[52] For an explanation of the term 'transnational' see, Chapter 2, Section 2.5.3.

[53] Report of the Special Rapporteur on Violence against Women, its Causes and Consequences, UN ESCOR, Commission on Human Rights, 53rd Sess., UN Doc. E/CN.4/1997/47 (1997), p. 19.

In this definition, recruitment and transport and exploitative practices are inextricably linked to each other. A remarkable item is that trafficking takes place for the purpose of forced exploitative situations while, in most definitions, the force primarily focuses on the phase of recruitment and transport. Whether the oppressive and exploitative situations are part of the definition or only the goal of the trafficking is not immediately clear. By a literal interpretation of the definition, the oppressive and exploitative situations seem to be the subject of the purpose and not a prerequisite for the trafficking itself. A consequence of this definition is that, in most cases, forced exploitation must have taken place before evidence to prove the crime of trafficking can be collected. The trafficker shall not be inclined to admit his intent to exploit the trafficked persons if he has been caught during the recruitment or transport. This problem also exists regarding definitions adopted by other oganisations as we will see below. The requirement of 'clandestine movement of persons across national or international borders', thus the factual border crossing, seems to originate from means to regulate migration.

The Commission on the Status of Women prepares reports, issues recommendations to the Economic and Social Council, and plays a vital role as the preparatory body for the UN World Conferences on Women. This commission tries to draw attention to trafficking in women and girls and urges governments to take adequate measures to end these practices. Unfortunately, the Commission is not of great importance in the struggle against trafficking in persons.[54]

At its 50th session (1994), the Human Rights Commission announced the appointment of Ms. Coomaraswamy, special rapporteur on Violence against Women, and she indicated that her mandate includes trafficking in women.[55] However, her mandate is so broad that it is impossible to address all the items included in it adequately. Her mandate ended in April 2003 and her successor still has to be appointed.

3.4.3 **Definitions within the European Union**

The harmonisation of the definition of trafficking in persons was achieved in July 2002. In December 2000 the Commission made a proposal for a Framework Decision on Combating Trafficking in Human Beings. The original proposal distinguished between trafficking in human beings for the purpose of labour exploitation and trafficking in human beings for the purpose of sexual exploitation. However, following comments on this distinction, these two articles were merged, resulting in the following definition in the final Council Framework Decision.[56]

---

[54] S. Farrior, The International Law on Trafficking in Women and Children for Prostitution: Making it Live Up to its Potential, in: *Harvard Human Rights Journal,* Volume 10, issue spring, 1997, pp. 248-249.

[55] Commission on Human Rights Res. 1994/45 ESCOR, 50th Sess., Supp. no. 4, UN Doc. E/1994/24 (1994).

[56] Council Framework Decision of 19 July 2002 on Combating Trafficking in Human Beings, OJ L 203, 1.8.2002, pp. 1-4.

Each Member State shall take the necessary measures to ensure that the following acts are punishable:

the recruitment, transportation, transfer, harbouring, subsequent reception of a person, including exchange or transfer of control over that person, where:

(a) use is made of coercion, force or threat, including abduction, or
(b) use is made of deceit or fraud, or
(c) there is an abuse of authority or of a position of vulnerability, which is such that the person has no real and acceptable alternative but to submit to the abuse involved, or
(d) payments or benefits are given or received to achieve the consent of a person having control over another person

for the purpose of exploitation of that person's labour or services, including at least forced or compulsory labour or services, slavery or practices similar to slavery or servitude, or for the purpose of the exploitation of the prostitution of others or other forms of sexual exploitation, including in pornography.

As stated in the preamble and as follows from the formulation of this article, the Trafficking Protocol to the UNCTOC was the guiding text for the establishment of the framework decision. Unlike the Trafficking Protocol, it is not necessary for the framework decision that the crime is transnational in nature and is committed by an organised crime group. The border crossing as such is not a requirement in the definition. This means that also trafficking within a country or within the EU is included in this framework decision. The decision was published on 1 August 2002 but will become fully operational on 1 August 2004 as by then the member states must have taken the necessary measures to comply with the decision.[57]

In the original text of the proposal, paragraph (d) of Articles 1 and 2 adopted an open phrase with regard to the term abuse: it stated 'there is another form or abuse'. This means a broad interpretation of the term 'abuse' and consequently a broad application of the term 'coercion', including those coercive acts that are not common practice at the moment but may become so in the future. It is regrettable that such an open phrase has not been adopted in the final text of the framework decision.

Furthermore, the term 'exploitation' in the Trafficking Protocol must be understood more comprehensively than in the framework decision, where exploitation is limited, in short, to labour exploitation and sexual exploitation. For instance, exploitation through the removal of organs is not included in the framework decision.[58]

In 1996, the European Parliament (EP) adopted the following definition of trafficking in human beings.[59]

---

[57] Article 10 of the Council Framework Decision on Combating Trafficking in Human Beings.

[58] For further comments on the content of this Framework Decision, see Chapter 4, Section 4.3.3.1.

[59] Resolution on Trafficking in Human Beings, A4-0326/95.

> The illegal action of someone who, directly or indirectly, encourages a citizen from a third country to enter or stay in another country in order to exploit that person by using deceit or any other form of coercion or by abusing that person's vulnerable situation or administrative status.

The emphasis of the EP is on coercion, which is seen as an essential element of the definition.[60] It is not clear to which part of the definition coercion refers. Is it the illegal action to encourage a person to enter or stay in another country, or the exploitation of that person, or both? The purpose of the trafficking must be the exploitation of the trafficked person. Whether the trafficker himself has to exploit the trafficked person or whether the exploitation can be executed by a third person is not clear. The EP adds border crossing as an explicit element of the definition. For what kind of work or service the trafficked person is exploited after the trafficking (for labour or not) seems not to be relevant. Trafficking is in no sense limited to labour but can take place for various reasons, as long as the trafficker can profit from the victim. Again, it is not clear whether the factual exploitation is part of the definition.

In 1996, the European Commission defined trafficking in women as follows.[61]

> The transport of women from third countries into the European Union (including perhaps subsequent movement between member states) for the purpose of sexual exploitation.

The transport itself need not be coercive at first sight, but the communication further states that,

> trafficking for the purpose of sexual exploitation covers women who have suffered intimidation and/or violence at the hands of their traffickers. Initial consent may not be relevant, as some enter the trafficking chain knowing they will work as prostitutes, but who are then deprived of their basic human rights, in conditions which are akin to slavery.

It follows from this phrase that the definition includes coerced recruitment, transport, and sexual exploitation. Similar to the definition of the EP, the Commission requires activity across borders, at first instance meaning the borders of the EU. The exploitative purpose of the trafficker is limited to sexual exploitation. Furthermore, because of the insertion of the phrase 'at the hands of their traffickers', this definition seems to be limited, as the traffickers must have executed the intimidation and/or violence themselves. If they have only caused and not executed the intimidation and/or violence, for instance by placing the victims in the hands of other persons who use violence, they are not accountable if the definition is taken literally. The Commission also addresses the consent of the trafficked women, which cannot be a justification for the existence of the phenomenon if coercion is used.

---

[60] Resolution on Trafficking in Human Beings, OJ C 032, 5.2.1996, p. 88, para 31.

[61] Communication from the European Commission to the Council and the European Parliament on Trafficking in Women for Sexual Exploitation, COM(96)567 final, Brussels, 11 November 1996.

3.4.4 **Definition of the IOM**

The International Organisation for Migration (IOM) is a non-governmental organisation that places trafficking in persons on the agenda on various occasions. Its counter-trafficking activities are geared toward the prevention of trafficking in persons, particularly women and children, and the protection of migrants' rights. It defines trafficking in women as 'any illicit transporting of migrant women and/or trade in them for economic or other personal gain.'[62] This may include the following elements.[63]

- Facilitating the illegal movement of migrant women to other countries, with or without their consent or knowledge.
- Deceiving migrant women about the purpose of the migration, legal or illegal.
- Physically or sexually abusing migrant women, or financially exploiting them en route and/or in the country of destination.
- Kidnapping or coercing migrant women for the purpose of trafficking them.
- Selling women, or trading in women for the purpose of employment, marriage, prostitution or other forms of profit-making abuse.

Following a paper published by the IOM, an act must be considered as 'trafficking' when an international border is crossed, a facilitator ('trafficker') is involved, money, or another form of payment, changes hands, and entry and/or stay in the country of destination are illegal.[64] Much remains unclear in these definitions, but it is obvious that here trafficking is not clearly distinguished from smuggling. Whether the profit-making abuse has to be performed by the trafficker and whether coercion is essential in the definition cannot be deduced from this description.

3.5 TRAFFICKING IN PERSONS VERSUS SMUGGLING PERSONS

Trafficking in persons is often confused with smuggling persons.[65] The implementation of stricter migration laws in order to suppress trafficking in persons has contributed to this confusion. The difference between these two terms is clearly described by the UN Secretary-General in his report to the 50th session of the General Assembly in 1995. The report states in paragraph 17: [66]

---

[62] IOM, *Trafficking in Women to Italy for Sexual Exploitation*, Migration Information Programme, Geneva, 1996.

[63] IOM, Statement by Mr. Marco Gramegna, Preparatory meeting on Trafficking in Women, Brussels, 1-2 December 1995.

[64] IOM, Trafficking of Women to the European Union: Characteristics, Trends and Policy Issues. Conference paper submitted by the IOM at the Conference on Trafficking in Women for Sexual Exploitation, Vienna, June 1996, p. 2.

[65] Bureau Nationaal Rapporteur Mensenhandel, *Mensenhandel. Eerste rapportage van de Nationaal Rapporteur*, Bureau NRM, The Hague, 2002, pp. 3-4.

[66] Report of the Secretary-General, Traffic in Women and Girls, A/50/369, 24 August 1995, para 17.

> Trafficking across international borders is by definition illegal. The question must be asked, however, whether trafficking is the same as illegal migration. It would seem that the two are related, but different. Migration across frontiers without documentation does not have to be coerced or exploitative. At the same time, persons can be trafficked with their consent. A distinction could be made in terms of the purpose for which borders are crossed and whether movement occurs through the instrumentality of another person. Under this distinction, trafficking of women and girls would be defined in terms of 'the end goal of forcing women and girl children into sexually or economically oppressive and exploitative situations' and the fact that it is done 'for the profit of recruiters, traffickers and crime syndicates'.

In this statement, the Secretary-General refers to the definition given by the General Assembly. The purpose of the movement is the distinguishing element, together with the use of force. When smuggling people, the crossing of a border is the profitable action, while, in the case of trafficking, the profit is the exploitation.

Regulations to combat trafficking in persons often have an effect to control illegal migration, for instance, the granting of a temporary residence permit to victims of trafficking that cooperate with the authorities to prosecute the traffickers. In the EU the majority of the trafficked persons enter a country without the required residence permit and remain illegal in the country of destination,[67] which also contributes to the confusion between trafficking and smuggling.

A latent or overt wish to migrate can lead to trafficking in persons. Because of restrictive immigration policies in most of the Western countries, it has become more difficult to emigrate. Therefore, people who want to emigrate seek help in organising the formalities. The people who offer their services sometimes take advantage of the potential emigrants, and transport them to Western states to exploit them. Informing persons, especially women, while still in their home country, about the situation that may await them in the rich industrialised countries may reduce the smuggling of and trafficking in persons.[68]

Summarising the above, it cannot be denied that trafficking in persons has a connection with illegal migration.[69] In many cases, smuggling is followed by exploitation. This conduct has to be qualified as trafficking in persons when it was the intention of the trafficker to exploit the person. The interference of the smugglers often extends after arrival at the destination and the smuggled persons are under pressure to pay the smugglers or to do diverse kinds of jobs and activities. When a form of coer-

[67] L. Lap-Chew and M. Wijers, *Trafficking in Women, Forced Labour, and Slavery-like Practices in Marriage, Domestic Labour, and Prostitution,* Foundation against Trafficking in Women, Utrecht, 1997, pp. 86-90.

[68] Also, Report of the Working Group on Contemporary Forms of Slavery, Draft programme of action on the traffic in persons and the exploitation of the prostitution of others, E/CN/4/sub.2/1995/28/add.1, para 13.

[69] G. Vermeulen, International Trafficking in Women and Children, General Report, in: *International Review of Penal Law,* Volume 72, issue 3-4, 2001, pp. 841-848, 866-869.

cion is used, the act can be categorised as exploitation. When this was the intention of the smuggler, trafficking in person has taken place.

It is important to distinguish between trafficking in persons and smuggling people in the first place for the protection and help that must be given to victims of trafficking. If trafficking in persons is confused with smuggling people, it may occur that the assistance to and protection of the victim of trafficking is denied. In the second place, it is important to distinguish between the two phenomena for choosing the right remedies to fight the criminal activity as the two phenomena require a different approach. Therefore, the distinguishing elements will pass in review below.

- One of the most obvious differences between trafficking and smuggling is that persons who are smuggled in principle consent to the illegal transport, while, as we have seen, the forced recruitment and/or transport is one of the characteristics of trafficking. That does not mean, however, that the smuggler does not abuse the consent or the vulnerable situation of the smuggled person. People who are smuggled are often forced to pay exorbitant sums of money to the smuggler and the confidence of the migrants is often violated by dangerous means of transport.
- A related difference is the use of coercion. Trafficking in persons cannot take place without coercion, which is one of the essential elements of the offence. Coercion is not a prerequisite for smuggling.
- Trafficking is an offence with victims while smuggling is said to be a victimless offence.
- The victims of trafficking in persons are often women, while the smuggled people are both men and women, and the 'victim' of the crime of smuggling is the state whose borders are illegally crossed.
- For the crime of smuggling crossing the border is a prerequisite while this is not the case for trafficking, although the victims are often trafficked from one country to another.
- Smuggling people takes place within a defined period of time, namely, until the smuggled person is in the country of destination. Trafficking in persons often does not take place in a defined period of time and it is difficult to determine when the act of trafficking ends.

3.5.1 **Application of migration law**

As stated before, the majority of the trafficked persons stay in the EU in the country in which they end up without a residence permit. It is commonly known that these persons are in a vulnerable situation. It is often dangerous for them to be sent back to their homeland because of reprisals by the trafficker or the social stigma they suffer if it becomes known that they have worked as a prostitute, despite the coercive situation. International law contains no provisions that prohibit states to apply migration laws to prosecute these persons for illegal stay or that prevent them from expulsion or forced return. In Belgium, Italy, the Netherlands, and Spain victims of trafficking in persons can get a temporary residence permit on the basis of migration law.[70] However, these provisions are primarily enacted to serve the criminal proceedings as the victims can only obtain such a permit if they are willing to press charges against the traffickers. When the victims are no longer needed as witnesses and the court has handled the case, they will often have to leave the country after all. Only after strict conditions are fulfilled can the victims apply for a permanent residence permit. On the European level, a proposal for a Council Directive on the Short-Term Residence Permit for victims of trafficking was made in February 2002.[71] The aim of this proposal is not the protection of victims or witnesses but the granting of a temporary permit if victims cooperate with the authorities. In my view, it is a missed opportunity that the protection of victims and witnesses is not explicitly aimed at in this proposal as the cooperation with authorities can often only be obtained and expected when a certain form of protection is granted to the victim.[72]

In many cases, the migration laws demand that the victims be sent back to their home country. These regulations are an extra threshold for the victims to protest against their situation and provide the traffickers with an extra instrument to threaten the victims. In Chapter 6 we will see that the fact that victims are sent back to their home country shortly after their arrest is a major obstacle in criminal proceedings against traffickers. In many cases, victims do not want to return to their home country as they are often stigmatised and socially excluded when they return. Already in 1993, the European Parliament called upon member states to provide permanent residency status in cases in which the personal safety of the victim would be endangered upon return to her home country. The GAATW Standard Minimum Rules prohibit the treatment of trafficked persons as illegal immigrants, and requires that the destination state provide residency status to the trafficked person in order to ensure that she has the option of legal recourse.[73] It is time that such a (temporary) residence permit is introduced at the EU level and that victim protection is provided.

3.6 RELATION OF TRAFFICKING IN PERSONS TO SLAVERY AND SLAVERY-LIKE PRACTICES

The crime of slavery can be seen as one of the few crimes that has achieved the status of *jus cogens* in international law.[74] Slavery as such has been addressed and prohibited in many international treaties and other instruments.[75] According to Farrior,

---

[70] L. Hauber, The Trafficking of Women for Prostitution: A Growing Problem within the European Union, in: *Boston College International & Comparative Law Review,* Volume 21, issue 1, 1998, p. 195.

[71] Proposal for a Council Directive on the Short-Term Residence Permit, Issued to Victims of Action to Facilitate Illegal Immigration or Trafficking in Human Beings who Cooperate with the Competent Authorities, Brussels, 11.02.2002, COM(2002) 71 final.

[72] See Chapter 4, Section 4.3.3.6.

[73] Global Alliance Against Traffic in Women and the Foundation for Women in cooperation with the Foundation against Trafficking in Women: Standard Minimum Rules for the Treatment of Victims of Trafficking in Persons, Forced Labour, and Slavery-Like Practices.

[74] M.C. Bassiouni, Enslavement as an International Crime, in: *New York University Journal of International Law and Politics,* Volume 23, issue 2, 1991, p. 445. On the concepts of *Jus cogens*, see, I. Brownlie, *Principles of Public International Law,* Clarendon Press, Oxford, 1990, pp. 512-515.

[75] For an overview of the instruments, see M.C. Bassiouni, Enslavement as an International Crime,

victims of trafficking for prostitution fit the definition of slavery as specified in Article 1 of the 1926 Slavery Convention.[76] This article reads as follows:

> (1) Slavery is the status or condition of a person over whom any or all of the powers attaching to the right of ownership are exercised.
> (2) The slave trade includes all acts involved in the capture, acquisition or disposal of a person with intent to reduce him to slavery; all acts involved in the acquisition of a slave with a view to selling or exchanging him: all acts of disposal by sale or exchange of a slave acquired with a view to being sold or exchanged, and, in general, every act of trade or transport in slaves.

It can be said that the distinction between slavery and the slave trade resembles the distinction between 'exploitation' and 'recruitment and transport' of the crime of trafficking in persons.[77] The definition in the 1926 Convention is rather narrow in the sense that it refers to the traditional form of slavery. The content of slavery has been extended in the Supplementary Convention of 1957, which also defines slavery-like practices.[78] With this supplement, the slavery conventions were introduced in the UN machinery. In Article 1, the supplement gives a description of debt bondage, serfdom, and other practices related to slavery. It gives a definition of 'slave trade' in Article 7, which is almost the same as the definition in the Slavery Convention of 1926. The purpose of the trade, according to this definition, is slavery. It is therefore more limited than the definitions in which the purpose is not mentioned or is defined in more detail. As follows from the subscription of slavery-like practices it is not immediately clear whether the slavery conventions can be applied to trafficking in persons. Four slavery-like practices are included in the supplement.[79]

1. Debt bondage: when an individual's services are pledged as collateral for a debt, but the services are undervalued so that the debt can never be paid off.
2. Serfdom: the binding of an individual to live and work on another's land without being able to leave.
3. The condemnation of any institution or practice whereby a woman is sold by her family for the purpose of entering into a marriage and has no right to refuse; a family has the right to transfer a wife to another person; and a woman may be inherited by another person when her husband dies.

---

in: *New York University Journal of International Law and Politics,* Volume 23, issue 2, 1991, pp. 445-517.

[76] Slavery Convention of 1926, 25 September 1926, 60 LNTS 253, entered into force on 9 March 1927. S. Farrior, The International Law on Trafficking in Women and Children for Prostitution: Making it Live Up to its Potential, in: *Harvard Human Rights Journal,* Volume 10, issue spring, 1997, p. 221.

[77] C. Rijken, Van asielzoekster tot prostituee. De aanpak van handel in Nigeriaanse alleenstaande minderjarige asielzoeksters, in: *Nemesis,* Volume 16, issue 1, 2000, pp. 4-11. Bureau Nationaal Rapporteur Mensenhandel, *Mensenhandel. Eerste rapportage van de Nationaal Rapporteur,* Bureau NRM, The Hague, 2002, pp. 26-27.

[78] Supplementary Convention on the Abolition of Slavery, the Slave Trade, and Institutions and Practices Similar to Slavery, 226 UNTS 3, entered into force on 30 April 1957.

[79] K. Zoglin, United Nations Action against Slavery: A Critical Evaluation, in: *Human Rights Quarterly,* Volume 8, issue 1, 1986, p. 312.

4. Practices in which a minor is delivered by his or her parent or guardian to another person for the purpose of the exploitation of the minor or his or her labour.

At first sight, some forms of trafficking seem to fit the definition and forced marriage is covered as well by the term 'slavery-like practices'.

According to the 1926 Convention, forced labour can develop into conditions analogous to slavery.[80] This means that forced labour is not *per se* a practice for which the slavery conventions can be applied. Two conventions of the International Labour Organisation (ILO) deserve mentioning here. The first is the Forced Labour Convention, adopted in 1930, and the second is the Abolition of Forced Labour Convention of 1957.[81] In both conventions, forced labour is defined as 'all work or service, which is exacted from a person under the menace of any penalty and for which the said person has not offered himself voluntarily'. In this respect, the trafficking in children has been the greatest concern for the ILO. The exploitation of persons trafficked seems to fit in the ILO definition of forced labour, as the victims are not working voluntarily and they are often threatened when they do not follow the instructions of their traffickers. If trafficking can be seen as forced labour and if forced labour can develop into conditions analogous to slavery, as stated in Article 5 of the 1926 Slavery Convention, the slavery conventions might apply to trafficking in persons. Before this conclusion can be drawn a further study of the term 'slavery and slavery-like practices' is needed.

The International Convention on Civil and Political Rights (ICCPR) contains a provision on slavery. Article 8 of the ICCPR states that slavery and the slave trade in all their forms shall be prohibited. Slavery and the slave trade are not defined for this convention but have to be explained in the narrow traditional meaning of the Slavery Convention. However, the term 'slave trade' does not include trafficking in persons, as was made clear when France made a proposal to substitute the term slave trade with traffic in human beings.[82] This idea was rejected because Article 8 (1) has to be understood as slavery and the slave trade in their original narrow sense excluding trafficking in persons as slavery. The article also mentions two other related phenomena, namely, servitude (paragraph 2) and forced or compulsory labour (paragraph 3). Servitude in this convention is defined as slavery-like practices including serfdom, debt bondage and all forms of traffic in persons and children (including child labour or prostitution and compulsory inheritance of women).[83] Consequently trafficking in persons must be considered a slavery-like practice. Exceptions are

[80] Article 5, 1926 Slavery Convention.

[81] Forced Labor Convention, ILO Convention 29, 28 June 1930, 39 UNTS 55, and Abolition of Forced Labor Convention, ILO Convention 105, 25 June 1957, 320 UNTS 291.

[82] M.J. Bossuyt, *Guide to the 'Travaux Préparatoires' of the International Covenant on Civil and Political Rights*, Nijhoff, Dordrecht, 1987, p. 165.

[83] M. Nowak, *UN Covenant on Civil and Political Rights, CCPR Commentary*, N.P. Engel Publisher, Kehl, Strasbourg, 1993, pp. 148-149.

only possible in relation to forced or compulsory labour and are limited to forced labour [84]

- in the case of detention;
- in the case of military service;
- in the case of emergency or calamity threatening the life or well-being of the community;
- when services form part of normal civil obligations.

Thus, trafficking in persons is forbidden by the ICCPR and must not be understood as falling within the definition of slavery but as a slavery-like practice.

At the international level, another interpretation of the term slavery or enslavement can be found in the case law of the Yugoslavia Tribunal and in the statute of the International Criminal Court. In the *Foča* case, the Yugoslavia Tribunal considered the enforced sexual exploitation of some Muslim girls and women, under certain circumstances, to amount to enslavement as a crime against humanity, although no reference is made in the statute of the Yugoslavia Tribunal to sexual enslavement.[85] The statute of the International Criminal Court has defined crimes against humanity and war crimes as including sexual slavery and enforced prostitution.[86] Sexual slavery, in their interpretation, covers trafficking in persons.[87] Furthermore, the Charter of the Women's International War Crimes Tribunal 2000 for the Trial of Japanese Military Slavery states that crimes against humanity include sexual slavery, rape, and other forms of sexual violence, enslavement, torture, deportation, persecution, murder, and extermination. According to the tribunal, 'enslavement' also concerns 'forced or deceptive transfer of a human being as one's property.'[88] The tribunal found Emperor Hirohito guilty in being responsible for rape and sexual slavery as a crime against humanity.[89]

On the European level, the European Convention of Human Rights and Fundamental Freedoms contains provisions on slavery. Article 4 states:

[84] Article 8 paragraph 3(c), United Nations Convention on Civil and Political Rights.

[85] A. de Brouwer, Note to *the Kunarac, Kovac and Vukovic* case (Foča), in: *Tilburg Foreign Law Review*, Volume 9, issue 2, 2001, pp. 221-236.

[86] Article 7(1)(g) of the ICC Statute. M. Boot, *Nullum Crimen Sine Lege and the Subject Matter Jurisdiction of the International Criminal Court,* Intersentia, Antwerp, 2002, pp. 500-517.

[87] R. Lee and H. Friman (eds.), *The International Criminal Court. Elements of Crimes and Rules of Procedure and Evidence,* Transnational Publishers, Ardsley, 2001, pp. 93 and 190-193. ICC: Finalised Draft Text of the Elements of Crimes, PCNICC/2000/INF/3/Add.2.

[88] L.A. Malone, Economic Hardship as Coercion under the Protocol on International Trafficking in Persons by Organized Crime Elements, in: *Fordham International Law Journal,* Volume 25, issue 1, 2001, pp. 72-73.

[89] Judgement of the Women's International War Crimes Tribunal 2000 for the Trial of Japanese Military Sexual Slavery in the matter of *the Prosecutors and the Peoples of the Asia-Pacific Region* v. *Emperor Hirohito et al. and the Government of Japan*, 12 December 2001. The judgements of this tribunal are non-binding as they have no legal basis.

1. No one shall be held in slavery or servitude.
2. No one shall be required to perform forced or compulsory labour.

It remains to be seen whether the European Commission on Human Rights and the European Court of Human Rights will apply this provision to trafficking in persons.

The US Supreme Court has a rather narrow interpretation of the term of slavery in that it refers to the situation before and during the civil war when black people were imported, held, and sold for labour through physical or legal coercion.[90] Later, the reference to race was eliminated from the provision, but the meaning remained the same. This also counts for the definition of involuntary servitude, which only exists if coerced by law or physical force. Although there was some willingness to broaden the definition in the Shackney[91] and Mussry[92] cases, the Supreme Court finally reverted to its earlier definition in the Kozminski[93] case. This narrow definition could be considered to contradict the Supplementary Slavery Convention of 1957 to which the US is a party.

In analysing the provisions on slavery and slavery-like practices, the conclusion must be drawn that the term 'slavery' as such is often used in a narrow sense. However, there seems to be a gap between international provisions and national criminal law. In international law, the drafters are far more inclined to adopt a broad interpretation of the terms slavery and slavery-like practices, which include trafficking in persons. In national law and national case law, we see that slavery and slavery-like practices are often narrowly defined and refer to old concepts.[94] The Supplementary Convention of 1957, however, extended the concept of slavery to also include slavery-like practices, and therefore also to include trafficking in persons.

The surplus value to apply the slavery conventions in trafficking cases mainly depends on the effective enforcement of these conventions. The mechanism to verify whether states act in compliance with these treaties is the state-report procedure. State parties have to submit regular reports on the measures they have taken to implement the Slavery Convention to the UN Sub-Commission on Prevention of Discrimination and Protection of Minorities.[95] The convention has a penal nature and contains a duty to prosecute violations of the convention in Articles 2, 3, and 6. The 1957 Supplementary Convention contains a similar provision in Article 8 para-

---

[90] J. Asher, How the United States is Violating its International Agreements to Combat Slavery, in: *Emory International Law Review,* Volume 8, issue 1, 1994, pp. 218-223.

[91] *United States* v. *Shackney*, 333 F.2d 475 (2nd Cir. 1981).

[92] *United States* v. *Mussry*, 726 F.2d 1448, 1453 (9th Cir. 1984).

[93] *United States* v. *Kozminski*, 821 F.2d 1186 (6th Cir. 1987).

[94] J. Asher, How the United States is Violating its International Agreements to Combat Slavery, in: *Emory International Law Review,* Volume 8, issue 1, 1994, pp. 215-253. Also Dutch Penal Law Articles 274-277.

[95] Article 7, 1926 Slavery Convention. Also Report of the Working Group on Contemporary Forms of Slavery, E/CN.4/Sub.2/1991/41, para 159.

graphs 2 and 3. This monitoring system is rather weak and depends on the goodwill of state parties to provide the sub-commission with this information.

In 1974, the Sub-Commission on Prevention of Discrimination and Protection of Minorities, authorised by the Economic and Social Council, established the Working Group on Contemporary Forms of Slavery, which considers trafficking in women to be a form of slavery. The working group has five members and their aim is to review developments in the field of the slave trade in all its practices and manifestations, including the slavery-like practices of the traffic in persons and the prostitution of others as defined in the two slavery conventions and the trafficking convention of 1949. This working group only meets eight days a year. The main theme of their 1991 session was 'prevention of trafficking in persons and the exploitation of the prostitution of others'. The working group is responsible for drafting treaties and programmes of action. Because of the broad interpretation of its mandate, the working group faces a wide range of problems concerning the violation of the rights of women and children such as female genital circumcision and the crime of honour.[96]

In conclusion the forced recruitment, transportation, and exploitative activities as elements in the crime of trafficking in persons, must be understood to be included in the term slavery-like practices and therefore the slavery conventions are applicable with regard to trafficking in persons. The slave trade, however, has to take place for the purpose of slavery. Although no reference is made to slavery-like practices, slavery in this context must be understood as amended by the 1957 supplement, thus including slavery-like practices as well. Following this statement the provisions on slave trade can be applied with regard to trafficking in persons as well. Trafficking in persons can thus be regarded as a slavery-like practice and in that case the principle of *jus cogens* might be applicable. However, national laws, as yet, often do not reflect the interpretation of trafficking in persons as a slavery-like practice. In this study, the term trafficking in persons is not defined from the international perspective but from a national and regional; mostly an EU perspective and therefore the slavery conventions will not contribute at large to the suppression of trafficking in persons, especially since the monitoring mechanism of these conventions is rather weak.

3.7 TRENDS AND SCOPE OF THE PHENOMENON

One of the main problems when dealing with trafficking in persons is the lack of reliable statistical data and information on the number of persons being trafficked. This lack is rooted partly in the complexity of the crime itself and partly in the absence of a central point for collecting and analysing these data. This section cannot

[96] K. Zoglin, United Nations Action against Slavery: A Critical Evaluation, in: *Human Rights Quarterly*, Volume 8, issue 1, 1986, pp. 317-318.

be considered as giving an overall estimation of the number of persons trafficked but only gives an indication of the scope and the current trends.

In the majority of trafficking cases, the victims are recruited in their home country by persons they know, for instance a friend or a relative.[97] In this phase, they are often misled by promises that they can earn a large amount of money in a short period of time in Western Europe. Although it is not always explicated to them that they have to work as a prostitute, they often know that they are going to work in the sex industry. When they find themselves being exploited in prostitution, traffickers are not hesitant to use coercive measures, including physical and psychological violence.[98] Victims are often limited in their mobility and have no say in the working conditions and hours. Furthermore, victims of trafficking do not stay long in one and the same place. When they have been exploited for a while in a certain place, they are often transported to another place or country. This is to prevent the victims from settling in a certain place and becoming familiar with the local authorities or organisations.[99]

The tendency that persons from Central and Eastern European countries increasingly become victims of trafficking is reported in several documents.[100] The main source countries seem to be Ukraine, Hungary, Czech Republic, Bulgaria, Poland, Romania, Russia, and Albania.[101] Other important source countries are Thailand, China, Vietnam, Ghana, Morocco, Nigeria, Sierra Leone, Brazil, Columbia, and the Dominican Republic. Cautious estimates by Europol show that, in the EU, several thousands of persons become victims of trafficking in persons every year. According to

---

[97] J. Vocks and J. Nijboer, *Land van belofte. Een onderzoek naar slachtoffers van vrouwenhandel uit Centraal- en Oost-Europa,* Rijksuniversiteit Groningen, December 1999, pp. 34-36.

[98] P. van Baeveghem, et al., *Trafficking in Migrants through Poland,* Maklu, Antwerp, 1999, pp. 35-39, 49-51. Europol General Situation Report on Trafficking in Human Beings, Open Version, Europol, December 2000, File-no: 2565-35rev1, pp. 28-30.

[99] See, for instance, Europol General Situation Report on Trafficking in Human Beings, Open Version, Europol, December 2000, File-no: 2565-35rev1, pp. 35-36. Bureau Nationaal Rapporteur Mensenhandel, *Mensenhandel. Aanvullende kwantitatieve gegevens,* second report, Bureau NRM, The Hague, 2003, pp. 52-54. For the modus operandi in the Americas, see International Human Rights Law Institute, DePaul University College of Law, *In Modern Bondage: Sex Trafficking in the Americas,* IHRLI, DePaul University, Chicago, 2002, pp. 40-46 and 51-55.

[100] P. Sörensen, European Parliament, Report on the Communication from the Commission to the Council and the European Parliament for Further Actions in the Fight against Trafficking in Women, Brussels, 2 May 2000, A5-0127/2000, Final, p. 6. J. Vocks and J. Nijboer, *Land van belofte. Een onderzoek naar slachtoffers van vrouwenhandel uit Centraal- en Oost-Europa,* Rijksuniversiteit Groningen, December 1999, p. 5. The Europol Report, 'Trafficking in Women within the European Union', estimates that 90% of the victims in the EU originate from Central and Eastern Europe. UNICEF, UNOHCHR, OSCE, *Trafficking in Human Beings in South-Eastern Europe,* UNICEF, 2002, pp. 4-9.

[101] According to the second report of the Rapporteur on trafficking in human beings 53% of the victims registered between 1995 and 2001 originated from Central and Eastern European countries. Bureau Nationaal Rapporteur Mensenhandel, *Mensenhandel. Aanvullende kwantitatieve gegevens,* second report, Bureau NRM, The Hague, 2003, pp. 7-8.

the IOM an estimated four million people are trafficked worldwide and 500,000 victims of trafficking enter Western Europe annually.[102] With the broad definition of trafficking used by the IOM in mind, this high estimate is not surprising. Estimates by the European Commission indicate that each year, tens of thousands of human beings, especially women and children, are trafficked for exploitative purposes globally.[103]

One of the new trends of the phenomenon in recent years has been the involvement of Albanian prostitution networks in Europe.[104] Within Europe, the Albanian prostitution networks are particularly active in Italy (where figures over the last three years show that 50% of the exploited women are Albanian) as well as in France, Belgium, and the United Kingdom.[105] Their place of recruitment is not limited to Albania but they expand their territory for the recruitment of persons to other Eastern European countries as well. The transport of the victims usually takes place by train or by boat and Italy is the stepping-stone for further transport within the EU. The networks often use forged documents in order to enter a country. The Albanian traffickers often reside in another country than the country in which the persons are exploited and frequently move from one country to another in order to diminish the risk of being caught. Transport of victims from Central and Eastern European countries is generally organised over land while the victims from Africa and the Americas mainly arrive in Europe by plane.[106] Other new trends are the increased trafficking between countries in the Southern part of the world and the increase of underage boys who are trafficked.

3.8 THE RELATION OF TRAFFICKING IN PERSONS TO ORGANISED CRIME

We have seen in Chapter 2 that a crime becomes more difficult to suppress and often more serious if it is cross-border in nature. A crime can also be characterised as to how it is carried out. When the performance meets certain criteria, the crime can be labelled an organised crime. Until December 2000, when the UNCTOC was adopted, there was no agreement on the rise of the elements of organised crime in the literature and among organisations. There are many types of organised crime groups. There is no single organisational or behavioural paradigm that identifies a

[102] P. Sörensen, European Parliament, Report on the Communication from the Commission to the Council and the European Parliament for Further Actions in the Fight against Trafficking in Women, Brussels, 2 May 2000, A5-0127/2000, Final, p. 6.

[103] Communication from the Commission to the Council and the European Parliament, Combating Trafficking in Human Beings and Combating the Sexual Exploitation of Children and Child Pornography, proposals for Framework Decisions, Brussels, 21.12.2000, COM (2000) 854 final, introduction.

[104] UNICEF, UNOHCHR, OSCE, *Trafficking in Human Beings in South-Eastern Europe,* UNICEF, 2002, pp. 125, 130-131. Bureau Nationaal Rapporteur Mensenhandel, *Mensenhandel. Aanvullende kwantitatieve gegevens,* second report, Bureau NRM, The Hague, 2003, p. 41

[105] Europol Report on Albanian prostitution networks, The Hague, 18 April 2000, not published.

[106] Bureau Nationaal Rapporteur Mensenhandel, *Mensenhandel. Aanvullende kwantitatieve gegevens,* second report, Bureau NRM, The Hague, 2003, pp. 49-51.

constant and accessible feature. Criminal organisations vary in size, scale, binding mechanisms, range of activities, geographical scope, relationship with the power structures at home and in host states, internal organisation and structure, and the combination of instruments that they use to promote their criminal enterprises and to protect themselves against government and law enforcement efforts.[107] Therefore, it took a long time before one comprehensive definition that covers all forms of what is called 'organised crime' could be accepted on an international level.

Criminal organisations flourish in countries where authority has been eroded and the state is weak. In Central and Eastern European countries the opening of borders and the growing globalisation of the economy and politics, plus the fall of the Iron Curtain, have created a favourable environment for the growing unification and interdependence of the activities of criminal organisations that operate across borders.[108] One of the characteristics of organised crime groups is that the inter-jurisdictional and international barriers and differences are used to enlarge their profits. In this section, an analysis of the definition of organised crime as it is used in the UNCTOC will be discussed and an analysis will be made as to under what circumstances trafficking in human beings must be considered to be an organised crime.

3.8.1 Organised crime in general

One of the results of the lack of information on organised crime, is the lack of effective countermeasures. Therefore, determining the meaning of the term and its characteristics is crucial. The essential characteristic of the term 'organised crime' is that it denotes a process or method of committing crimes, not a distinct type of crime itself, nor even a distinct type of criminal.[109] All forms of crime can, when carried out using a certain pattern, be labelled as organised crime. However, some crimes are more frequently carried out as organised crimes such as fraud, trafficking offences, and money laundering. The essential elements of organised crime must be deduced from the process or method whereby certain criminals carry out criminal activities, increasingly within the international arena.

According to Williams and Savona, a broad consensus has now emerged on the conditions that have to be met before the term 'organised crime' may be considered applicable.[110] Participants in criminal organisations are persons associated for the purpose of engaging in criminal activity on a more or less sustained basis. The activities of organised crime groups require a significant degree of cooperation and organisation to provide the illicit goods and services. Furthermore, both violence and corruption are tactics that these groups tend to resort to for self-protection, the

[107] Economic and Social Council E/CN.15/1996/2, 4 April 1996, para 6.

[108] See Chapter 1, Section 1.2.

[109] M.E. Beare, *Criminal Conspiracies, Organised Crime in Canada*, Nelson Canada, Scarborough, 1996, p. 14.

[110] Ph. Williams and E.U. Savona (eds.), *The United Nations and Transnational Organised Crime*, Portland, London, 1996, pp. 3-7.

settlement of disputes and the facilitation of illicit business activities. Organised crime closely resembles a social exchange network in the community. Williams and Savona are convinced of the great variety in the structures of the criminal organisations. Some groups are organised hierarchically while others are more loosely structured, flexible and highly adaptable. Some are highly specialised and focus on one kind of activity while others engage in a broader range of criminal activities.

The Naples Political Declaration and Global Action Plan[111] lists six characteristics of organised crime.

a. Group organisation to commit crime.
b. Hierarchical links or personal relations which enable leaders to control the group.
c. The use of violence, intimidation, and corruption to earn profits or control territories or markets.
d. The laundering of illicit proceeds to further criminal activity and to infiltrate the legitimate economy.
e. A potential for expansion into any new activity beyond national borders.
f. Cooperation with other organised transnational criminal groups.

The transnational element plays an important role in these characteristics. Although organised crime groups often have a transnational component, it must not be considered a constitutional element for organised crime as some organised crime groups still operate within one and the same country. It would lead to an omission in the fight against organised crime which criminal organisations could take advantage of if these groups were to be excluded from the definition of organised crime. Furthermore, it is remarkable that a form of violence indicated under c is one of the characteristics. Although it is commonly known that organised crime groups often use violence to obtain their goals, it must not be seen as a prerequisite for the existence of an organised crime group, in order to avoid a definition that is too narrow.

3.8.2 The definition of organised crime in the UNCTOC

According to article 2(a) of the UNCTOC, an 'organised criminal group' means 'a structured group of three or more persons, existing for a period of time and acting in concert with the aim of committing one or more serious crimes or offences established in accordance with this Convention, in order to obtain, directly or indirectly, a financial or other material benefit'. In this definition, the following characteristic elements of organised crime can be identified.
- A structure of three or more persons.
- Continuity.
- Concerted action aimed at committing offences and serious crimes.
- The intent to obtain a financial or other material benefit.

[111] Economic and Social Council E/CN.15/1996/2, 4 April 1996.

As can be read in Article 2(c), a structured group means a group that is not randomly formed for the immediate commission of an offence and that does not need to have formally defined roles for its members, continuity of its membership or a developed structure. As indicated in the '*travaux préparatoires*' the phrase 'intent to obtain a financial or other material benefit' must be interpreted broadly.[112] It may, for example, also include sexual gratification, which is the case for members of child pornography rings.

3.8.3 The definition of organised crime within the EU

Although several definitions are circulating within the EU, the definition in the Joint Action on Making it a Criminal Offence to Participate in a Criminal Organisation in the Member States of the EU must now be considered the leading one.[113] According to this document, a criminal organisation means

> a structured association established over a period of time, of more than two persons, acting in concert with a view to committing offences which are punishable by deprivation of liberty or a detention order of a maximum of at least four years or a more serious penalty, whether such offences are an end in themselves or a means of obtaining material benefits and, where appropriate, of improperly influencing the operation of public authorities. The offences referred to in the first subparagraph include those mentioned in Article 2 of the Europol Convention and in the Annex thereto and carry a sentence at least equivalent to that provided for in the first subparagraph.

If we take a closer look at both the definitions in the UNCTOC and the definition in this Joint Action, we see that these instruments use the same system in identifying the activities of organised crime groups. Both documents have the approach in which a conceptual description of the activities of the criminal organisation is combined with a list of criminal activities of the criminal organisation.[114] The advantage of such an approach is that new forms of crimes can be accommodated under this definition rather easily without the necessity to modify the document.

Nevertheless, these two definitions differ with regard to the role of the intent to obtain material benefit. In the definition of the UNCTOC, this intent must be considered as the final purpose of the organised crime group while, in the definition of the EU, the material benefit is not necessarily the final goal of the organisation. Therefore, the definition of the European Union is broader than the definition of the

[112] Official records (*travaux préparatoires*) of the negotiation on the United Nations Convention against Transnational Organised Crime, doc. A/AC.254/33, 4 July 2000, p. 3.

[113] Joint Action of 21 December 1998 on Making it a Criminal Offence to Participate in a Criminal Organisation in the Member States of the European Union, OJ L 351, 29.12.1998, p. 1.

[114] Ch. van den Wyngaert, The Transformations of International Criminal Law in Response to the Challenge of Organised Crime, in: *International Review of Penal Law,* Volume 70, issue 1-2, 1999, pp. 153-155.

UNCTOC and it may be feared that it will become a loophole which criminal organisations could take advantage of.[115]

Furthermore, the UNCTOC can only be applied when the offence performed by the organised crime group is transnational in nature,[116] although this does not mean that the activities of the organised crime group are inherently transnational. Both criteria must be fulfilled before the UNCTOC can be applied.

3.8.4 **Trafficking in persons as a form of organised crime**

As can be seen in the cases described in the UN-report on violence against women, its causes and consequences, trafficking in persons has many different features.[117] Criminals often work together in a more or less organised structure. Often, more than one country is involved, i.e., the country of residence and the country of destination, and probably one or more transit countries. Trafficking in persons is one of the crimes that is characterised by the increased involvement of organised criminal groups.[118] The ECOSOC has recognised that organised international criminal groups are becoming increasingly dangerous and active in international trafficking in persons.[119] For example, the crime has become a major international business in Central and South America. It is said that international organised criminal networks basically control trafficking in persons.[120] All over the world, organised crime groups deal with trafficking in persons, from Denmark, Sweden, and Finland to Latin America and from China to Nigeria and South Africa.

The question of whether trafficking in persons must be considered as an organised crime depends on its occurrence and this question must again be answered every time. If we examine the criteria of the definition in the UNCTOC, the following remarks can be made. With regard to the criterion of 'a structure of more than two persons' and with the broad description of a structured group of article 2(c) in mind, it can be said that this criterion will easily be fulfilled in trafficking cases. As we have seen, the crime of trafficking normally consists of two phases, namely recruitment and trafficking, in the first place, and exploitation, in the second. In general these two activities are executed by different persons, not seldomly persons who have done business with each other before and who cooperate with each other because

[115] C. Rijken and V. Kronenberger, The United Nations Convention on Transnational Organised Crime and the European Union, in: V. Kronenberger, *The EU and the International Legal Order,* Asser Press, The Hague, 2001, pp. 489-490.

[116] For the description of the transnational element, see Chapter 2, Section 2.5.3.

[117] Report of the Special Rapporteur on Violence against Women, its Causes and Consequences, Ms. R. Coomaraswamy, E/CN.4/1997/47, 12 February 1997, Chapter 4, E.CN.4/1995/42, Chapter 3.

[118] B. de Ruyver, et al., *Strategies of the EU and the US in Combating Transnational Organised Crime,* Maklu, Antwerp, 2002, p. 388.

[119] ECOSOC Resolution 1998/20, 44th plenary meeting, 28 July 1998.

[120] S. Adamoli, et al., *Organised Crime around the World,* European Institute for Crime Prevention and Control, affiliated with the United Nations, HEUNI, Helsinki, 1998, pp. 26-30.

they know the other person is willing to engage in the trafficking of persons. However, the traffickers can also be persons who know each other vaguely or via another person and do business with each other occasionally. In these cases, the structured group is not easy to prove. Whether the criterion of 'continuity' is fulfilled depends on the circumstances. No general picture of trafficking can be drawn as it differs between regions and changes over time. It is recognised that persons originating from Nigeria who are involved in the trafficking in persons are often acting on their own account and structures are not very tight.[121] The criterion of 'concerted action aimed at committing offences and serious crimes' must be considered to be fulfilled, as trafficking in persons must be considered a serious crime. Furthermore, it is clear that obtaining financial benefit is the intention of the crime of trafficking in persons.

In conclusion, it can be stated that, in many cases, the criteria of the definition of organised crime are fulfilled although some problems may occur in the evidence for the 'existence for a period of time' of the organisation. When this criterion is not met trafficking in persons cannot be considered an organised crime. It always depends on the circumstances whether the question of the existence of an organised crime group must be answered in the affirmative. The fact that a special protocol on trafficking in persons is attached to the UNCTOC indicates that this crime must be considered as generally committed by organised crime groups. According to Mr. Pino Arlacchi (Under-Secretary-General, and Executive Director of the UN Office for Drug Control and Crime Prevention) 'trafficking in people requires a level of resources that can only be offered by elaborate criminal organisations.'[122]

3.9 THE USE OF THE TERM 'TRAFFICKING IN PERSONS' IN THIS STUDY

Having analysed the elements of the phenomenon, reviewed the most leading and most recently developed definitions, and studied some related practices of trafficking in persons, the definition of trafficking in persons, as it will be used in this study can now be given.

In this study, a distinction will be made between factual trafficking, i.e., recruitment and transport, and exploitation, i.e., forced labour/slavery-like practices although not as strictly as made by the GAATW. I will concentrate on both phenomena insofar as it takes place within Europe and in particular within the EU and from third countries to the EU. Trafficking, in this study, always involves a transnational element, which at the same time seems to be the problematic element in relation to the prosecution of the traffickers. However, to satisfy this transnational element, the factual border crossing is not strictly required as the crime can, for example, be coordinated from another country.

121 C. Rijken, Van asielzoekster tot prostituee. De aanpak van handel in Nigeriaanse alleenstaande minderjarige asielzoeksters, in: *Nemesis*, Volume 16, issue 1, 2000, pp. 4-11.

122 UN Office for Drug Control and Crime Prevention, *A Convention against Transnational Crime*, Mr. Pino Arlacchi, Under-Secretary-General, Executive Director, Buenos Aires, Argentina, 31 August 1998.

Coercion is not limited to physical force, and includes, but is not limited to, violence or threat of violence, deception, abuse of authority or dominant position, and debt bondage, as defined by the GAATW. As stated before, coercion in this study must be interpreted broadly, also including, for instance, bad working conditions, low payment, and no control over leisure time, even if a person has consented to such circumstances. A person's economic situation falls outside the definition of coercion but can be seen as a major factor that provides opportunities to use coercion against a person in a vulnerable position. Coercion, in my view, is the essential element in the crime of trafficking in persons.

As follows from the various definitions, the link between trafficking in persons and prostitution seems obvious. There is also a link between trafficking and other forms of economic, sexual, or social exploitation.[123] The recent inclination to broaden the aim of trafficking to include other forms of forced labour and exploitative situations will be adopted in the definition used in this study and includes, for example, domestic labour and clandestine marriages. It is not strictly necessary that the exploitation has actually taken place, the ill-intent of the trafficker is decisive.

Furthermore, trafficking in minors is on the increase and several instruments have been developed to address this problem.[124] As the suppression of trafficking in minors has specific implications, and needs an even more specific treatment, the issue of trafficking in children will not be discussed.

Considering the above, the following definition of trafficking in persons will be used in this study:

> Trafficking in persons means all acts involved in the coercive transnational recruitment and/or transportation of a person for forced exploitation.

3.10 IS TRAFFICKING IN PERSONS A TRANSNATIONAL CRIME?

Now that the term trafficking in persons has been analysed, the elements of the crime have been discussed, and the definition for this study has been formulated, it is possible to answer the question of whether trafficking in persons must be considered a transnational crime. This section aims to provide an answer to this question on the basis of the four criteria of transnational crime developed in Chapter 2.

- The *first* criterion is that a certain level of organisation is needed to commit these crimes, but not necessarily an organised crime group.

[123] Report of the Special Rapporteur on Violence against Women, its Causes and Consequences, Ms. R. Coomaraswamy, E/CN.4/1997/47, 12 February 1997, para 102.

[124] For instance, Optional Protocol to the Convention on the Rights of the Child on the Sale of Children, Child Prostitution and Child Pornography, GA Res. 54/263, Annex II, 54 UN GAOR Supp. (no. 49) UN Doc. A/54/49 (2000), entered into force on 18 January 2002.

The crime of trafficking in persons consists of two phases, namely, the recruitment and transport phase, on the one hand, and the exploitation phase, on the other. Although the latter need not necessarily have taken place, this phase has generally commenced; otherwise the intended exploitation would be almost impossible to prove. For the employment of the persons trafficked, contacts are needed with persons who are willing to participate in the illegal activity. Furthermore, recruitment and transportation often take place in different steps, often including falsification of documents, advertisements, transfer from one place to another, the purchase of flight tickets, arrangements for the accommodation of victims, etc. It is very unlikely that one and the same person executes all these activities, especially when it concerns trafficking across borders. The conclusion can therefore be drawn that, for the perpetration of trafficking in persons, a certain level of organisation (consisting of different contacts to execute parts of the crime) is necessary.

- The *second* criterion is that it affects the interests of more than one state because citizens of more than one state are involved or part of the crime took place in more than one state.

As was stated in Chapter 2, the factual and physical act of goods or persons crossing the border is not strictly required to meet this criterion. The involvement of more than one state is already present when, for instance, the crime takes place in one and the same country but is organised from another country. Trafficking in persons often takes place from countries with a less stable economic and legal system to countries in which these systems are well organised, thus normally between different countries. However, as was stated before, it is not strictly necessary that the trafficking takes place between countries as it can also occur within one and the same country. With the broad concept of the requirement that more than one state is involved, this criterion will be met in the majority of cases. Furthermore, the definition of trafficking in persons as used in this study includes the transnational element of the involvement of more than one state, which means that this criterion is inevitably fulfilled.

- The *third* criterion is that the fact that more states are involved aggravates the problems involved in prosecuting transnational crime.

One of the consequences that more than one state is involved in trafficking in persons is that, for the investigation and prosecution of the crime, international instruments must be applied in addition to national laws. Some of these international instruments are specifically developed to suppress trafficking in persons while others are developed more generally to facilitate cooperation and coordination in fighting crime.[125] Extra obstacles arise when international provisions must be applied. However, the nature and the scope of these obstacles with regard to the prosecution of trafficking in persons still remain unclear. Although it is likely that the prosecution

125 Both these agreements will be discussed in Chapter 4.

problems are aggravated by the fact that more than one state is involved, further research is necessary to discover the nature and scope of the obstacles to enforce these instruments.[126] Only then can the question of whether the third criterion is met be answered definitively.

- The *fourth* criterion is that effective solutions to these problems must be sought beyond national borders.

So far, criminal law based on the sovereignty of states has appeared not to be effective and too complicated to fight and prosecute trafficking in persons. If the involvement of different states aggravates problems in the prosecution of trafficking in persons, it is logical that solutions must be sought in cooperation with other countries, i.e., beyond the national borders. Because this study focuses on Europe and the EU in particular, effective solutions must be sought on the EU level. This can consist of either a more flexible and intensive application of current instruments, the modification of these instruments, or the development of new ones. This means that, if the third criterion is fulfilled, the fourth criterion is automatically met.

In conclusion, and with a reservation concerning the third criterion, it is likely that trafficking in persons must be considered a transnational crime.

3.11 CONCLUSION

In this chapter, the elements of the crime of trafficking in persons were addressed in detail and the difference with smuggling people and slavery and slavery-like practices was explicated. The conclusion was drawn that trafficking in persons must be considered a slavery-like practice and therefore the slavery conventions are applicable in the case of trafficking in persons, if trafficking in persons is considered from an international point of view. In this study, the term trafficking in persons is not defined from the international perspective and, therefore, an analysis of the contribution of the slavery conventions to the prosecution of those suspected of trafficking in persons, is beyond the scope of this study. The question of whether and under what conditions trafficking in persons must be considered an organised crime was answered and trends and figures on the phenomenon were discussed. What follows from the analysis of the definition of trafficking in persons is that the crime of trafficking can be divided into two phases, namely, recruitment and transport, on the one hand, and exploitation, on the other. It is in accordance with recent views that coercion must be seen as a constitutive element of the crime. Furthermore, the intentions of the trafficker are important in order to determine the purpose of the trafficking.

The question was answered whether the phenomenon of trafficking in persons must be considered a transnational crime. To that end, the four criteria for transnational

[126] This will be explored in Chapters 5 and 6.

crime that were developed in Chapter 2 were applied to the phenomenon of trafficking in persons. The provisional conclusion was drawn that trafficking in persons must be regarded as a transnational crime although it could not yet be decided whether the third and fourth criteria apply. Therefore, a definitive answer to the question of whether the involvement of more than one state aggravates the problems involved in prosecuting trafficking in persons cannot yet be given, as the content and the size of these problems have first to be clarified. An exploration of the relevant legal instruments to prosecute traffickers is required to find out which prosecution problems exist and whether these problems are aggravated by the involvement of more than one state. This exploration will take place in Chapter 5 and Chapter 6, after the relevant documents and instruments have been discussed in the next chapter. It is presumed that if the third criterion is met, namely, that the involvement of more than one state in trafficking aggravates the problems involved in prosecuting trafficking in persons the fourth criteria, namely, that the remedy must be sought beyond the national level, is automatically fulfilled.

CHAPTER 4
EUROPEAN POLICY DOCUMENTS TO COMBAT AND LEGAL INSTRUMENTS TO PROSECUTE TRAFFICKING IN PERSONS

4.1 INTRODUCTION

Until the beginning of the 1990s trafficking in persons was neither in most of the member states of the EU nor at the European level a big issue on the political agenda. As we will see there seems to be a turn in this practice as the intention to combat trafficking in persons can now be found in many policy documents and legal instruments adopted by various institutions in Europe since that time. Therefore, it seems likely that the lack of juridical recognition of the phenomenon is not as problematic as is often thought. The effective application of the legal instruments and the transformation of policy documents into concrete action in national law seem to be surrounded with more difficulties. As I argued in Chapter 3, it follows from the first and second criteria that problems in prosecuting trafficking in persons may be aggravated by the involvement of more than one state. The solution to these problems must then be sought beyond national borders. Before a definitive answer can be given on whether the prosecution problems are aggravated by the fact that more than one state is involved, these problems have to be studied in more depth. However, before these problems can be identified, it must be clear what policy documents and legal instruments are relevant and what their content is. This chapter aims to give an overview of and some background information on these policy documents and legal instruments. The criterion used to identify these documents and instruments is whether they may contribute to suppress trafficking in persons. Many of the legal instruments that meet this criterion focus on cooperation in criminal matters and coordination in general and were not specifically developed to prosecute those suspected of trafficking in persons. However, the prosecution of the traffickers is indirectly addressed and advocated by these documents and therefore they are highly relevant for this research. Especially those policy documents and legal instruments that were developed within the framework of the EU will be focused upon, but also those relevant documents and instruments enacted by the Council of Europe and by the OSCE.

In this chapter first the relevant policy documents in the EU will pass in review followed by the documents enacted by the Council of Europe. As the OSCE has developed its own strategy with regard to trafficking in persons and has subsequently enacted several policy documents on this subject, the efforts made by the OSCE are discussed as well. As the documents enacted by the OSCE concern exclusively policy documents they are discussed under this category only. Then the relevant legal instruments in the EU and the Council of Europe will be focused upon. Before the legal instruments will be discussed the legal framework of the EU with regard to police and judicial cooperation in criminal matters will be focused upon.

In the recently enacted instruments on mutual assistance and extradition in the EU some interesting developments become visible. It is a change in the way of cooperating that reflects the understanding that intensified cooperation between member states is required to combat some serious crimes more effectively and the increased willingness of the member states as regards intensified cooperation in the field of police and judicial cooperation in criminal matters. This change is characterised by the adoption of the transformation of the use of current principles on extradition and mutual assistance. When discussing the legal instruments more elaborately in this chapter this change will be further analysed.

4.2 OVERVIEW OF POLICY DOCUMENTS

4.2.1 **The concept of policy documents**

The policy documents that will be discussed in this study contain goals and targets to be achieved, in the field of (organised) crime in general and of trafficking in persons in particular. Furthermore, a great variety of policies adopted in these documents to combat trafficking in persons exist within Europe. Many documents address this phenomenon from numerous different points of view. The policies often make direct reference to the phenomenon, give an indication of existing problems, and formulate aims to be achieved in this regard. Sometimes, the strategy to be followed to achieve these aims is given as well. The main characteristic of these policies is that they are in general not legally binding and do not create enforceable rights for individuals. They will be discussed in this chapter, firstly, to show that the suppression of trafficking in persons is taken seriously nowadays, and, secondly, because they are important in connection with the legal instruments as the latter may contribute to achieving the goals and aims laid down in these policies.

4.2.2 **Policy documents on trafficking in persons within the EU**[1]

4.2.2.1 *Policy documents adopted by the European Parliament*

Since 1986, the European Parliament (EP) has regularly enacted resolutions on the position of women in general and on trafficking in women in particular.[2] In point 13 of the 1986 Resolution, reference is made to the improvement in the training of police officers dealing with victims of sexual crimes, which means that, according to

[1] For an overview, see J.W. de Zwaan and A.J. Bultena, *Ruimte van vrijheid, veiligheid en rechtvaardigheid. De samenwerking op het gebied van Justitie en Binnenlandse Zaken in de Europese Unie*, Sdu publishers, The Hague, 2002, pp. 344-355. Because the authors do not distinguish between policy documents and legal instruments the overview in their book contains both agreements.

[2] OJ C 176, 14.7.1986, pp. 73-83. OJ C 120, 16.5.1989, pp. 352-355. OJ C 268, 4.10.1993, pp. 141-142. OJ C 032, 5.2.1996, pp. 88-93. OJ C 304, 6.10.1997, pp. 55-59.

the EP, the response of police officers to these victims was not sufficient. It was recommended in this resolution that the victims be able to report trafficking to the competent authorities without running the risk of being deported. Other reasons given for the lack of complaints to the police by trafficked women forced into prostitution are language difficulties, isolation, and threats from those who exploit them. According to the Resolution of 14 April 1989, the general pattern of trafficking in persons is from poor countries to wealthy European countries. It states that if women in poor countries had access to employment, education, and social rehabilitation, they would cease to work as prostitutes. Furthermore, it is recommended to legalise the residence situation of the victims in case there is evidence that repatriation could endanger their personal safety or that they might become victims of exploitation again. In the Resolution on Trade in Women of 16 September 1993, Europol was introduced as the appropriate organisation to participate in the fight against trafficking in women. Some kind of witness protection is introduced in this resolution as well, namely, a legal right to residence and protection during and after legal proceedings. The Resolution of 18 January 1996 indicates trafficking in women as a preferred area of activity for international organised crime. In this resolution, the lack of a clear definition of trafficking is seen as a problem and it proposes a clarification of the term 'trafficking in human beings'. It stresses the need for police and judicial cooperation to combat trafficking in persons between the member states. More recently, a report has been produced on the communication from the Commission to the Council and the EP 'Combating Organised Crime: Further Action in the Fight against Trafficking in Women' by Patsy Sörensen, member of the Committee on Women's Rights and Equal Opportunities of the EP.[3] She points out that one of the obstacles is that policy statements have, in general, not been adequately translated into penal legislation. Furthermore, the lack of specific legal provisions on trafficking in women in some member states and applicant countries and the divergent legal systems and the lack of cooperation within and between the judicial authorities in the countries of origin, transit, and destination allow traffickers to operate with impunity. Sörensen supports a multidisciplinary approach to combating trafficking in women. Her recommendations concern, among other things, immigration law, witness protection, prevention by informing in the state of origin, cooperation on political, judicial, and police levels, and cooperation with NGOs. She also stresses that the future International Criminal Court might be an effective instrument for combating trafficking in women. One of her recommendations is to focus more on confiscating the profits of the traffickers when combating trafficking in women because the earning of large amounts of money is the main reason why women are trafficked.

Some common features mentioned in all these documents can be identified. First of all, the imbalance of international economic relations is seen as one of the important reasons for the existence of trafficking in persons. To combat the offence, both de-

[3] Report on the Communication from the Commission to the Council and the European Parliament for Further Action on the Fight against Trafficking in Women, 2 May 2000, Final A5-0127/2000.

velopment policy and policy on international cooperation with the developing countries and the countries of Central and Eastern Europe is necessary. Closely linked to this imbalance is the statement in the resolutions that aid in the countries of origin to prevent persons, and especially women, from being trafficked, for example, by supporting women's information projects and employment projects, will contribute to the prevention of trafficking in persons. Another complaint is the lack of an overall definition on the European level. The member states are therefore requested to adopt legislation in which trafficking in women is punished and to adopt a definition in which the same elements are addressed. Furthermore, it is stated that aid for returning victims is necessary to prevent them from becoming social outcasts in their home country. Balanced policy for the provision of employment, education, vocational training and equal opportunities for women is needed. Another strategy that is recommended in most of the documents is an intensified use of measures on cooperation in criminal matters. And finally, the increase in the trafficking of minors and (minor) boys is noticed.

4.2.2.2 *Policy documents adopted by the European Commission*

The European Commission has produced two communications on trafficking in women for the purpose of sexual exploitation.[4] The aim of the 1996 document is to provoke a discussion on the policy to stimulate a comprehensive European approach in the fight against trafficking in women. The document aims to include detailed proposals that are easy to realise. The recommendations of the Conference of the Commission held in Vienna in June 1996 served as a guideline for this document. Some of the recommendations are highlighted here. Again, poverty and marginalisation of women in the country of origin are seen as a main contributor to the existence of trafficking in women. Therefore, cooperation with third countries is essential in combating trafficking in women. This cooperation has to focus on reintegration into society when victims of trafficking return to their home country to prevent them from being rejected by society and on the strengthening of the position of women in all kinds of ways in the countries from which the women originate. It gives a brief overview of the *modus operandi* of traffickers. The document stresses several times that a multidisciplinary international approach is needed to adequately combat trafficking in women. A temporary residence status for victims who are willing to cooperate in criminal procedures against the traffickers is recommended. The expulsion of victims because of their illegal status is counterproductive in the prosecution of traffickers. Again, the lack of coherence between judicial systems and the lack of judicial cooperation between the member states are seen as some of the main reasons why the traffickers manage to escape prosecution. This report again states that enforcement officers are not inclined to regard women who are victims of trafficking as victims of a crime. Therefore, specific training of enforcement officers to raise awareness of the situation of and an appropriate response to the victims are

[4] Trafficking in Women for Sexual Exploitation, COM(1996) 567, Brussels, 20.11.1996, and New Strategies to Combat Trafficking in Women, COM(1998) 726, Brussels, 09.12.1998.

proposed. Finally, it is stated that the fight against trafficking in women can only be successful if the member states are willing to reserve a budget for this purpose.

The 1998 COM Document on New Strategies to Combat Trafficking in Women aims to keep this issue high on the political agenda in the EU, to strengthen cooperation on international and European levels and a multidisciplinary approach. Despite the title of the document, it does not contain many new strategies. Again, the prevention of trafficking in the countries of origin is stressed as well as the importance of educating police officers and the relation between immigration law and trafficking. The protection of victims is further elaborated in this document than in the former and includes the willingness to draft legislation on a temporary residence status for victims. New strategies on police and judicial cooperation cannot be found in the document although the importance of cooperation with applicant countries and other third countries is stressed once more. The economic position, poverty and unemployment of women in the countries of origin are still areas of concern.

On 3 June 2003, a COM Document on the development of a common policy on illegal immigration, smuggling and trafficking in human beings, external borders and the return of illegal residents, was adopted by the Commission.[5] In this document trafficking in persons is approach from the illegal immigration perspective and strategies are based on combating illegal immigration. Although the Council Framework Decision on Combating Trafficking in Human Beings is mentioned in this document, no further specific references and recommendations are made with regard to trafficking in persons.

In order to facilitate mutual confidence between the member states of the EU, the Commission produced a Green Paper on the Procedural Safeguards for Suspects in Criminal Proceedings throughout the European Union in February 2003.[6] Although this Green Paper does not specifically concern trafficking in persons, it is worth mentioning here as it is an important document for cooperation in criminal matters between the member states of the EU. In this Green Paper, the Commission is very cautious in criticising states for not acting in accordance with the European Convention on Human Rights (to which all the (acceding) member states are party). It also states that the rights guaranteed in this convention are interpreted differently in the different member states of the EU, which may lead to inequality in the position of the suspect and contains the risk that mutual confidence will be violated. As the mutual recognition of decisions in criminal matters is now an important principle in cooperation in criminal matters between the member states, this inequality is un-

[5] Communication from the Commission to the European Parliament and the Council in View of the European Council of Thessaloniki on the Development of a Common Policy on Illegal Immigration, Smuggling and Trafficking of Human Beings, External Borders and the Return of Illegal Residents, COM(2003) 323 final, Brussels, 3.6.2003.

[6] Green Paper from the Commission on the Procedural Safeguards for Suspects in Criminal Proceedings throughout the European Union, COM(2003) 75 final, Brussels, 19.2.2003.

desirable. The Green Paper was compiled to produce an overview of the possible minimum of procedural safeguards that have to be guaranteed in criminal proceedings in order to improve confidence between the member states in each other's legal systems. The Green Paper was also prepared as a consulting paper to collect more information on the necessity of a new instrument on this matter and the possible content of such an instrument. Furthermore, the Green Paper was meant to provide a consistent and uniform interpretation of the rights referred to in the Green Paper. In order to verify whether a state acts in compliance with the common minimum standards within the EU, the Commission has proposed to develop a monitoring or evaluation mechanism. The framework decision to follow up this Green Paper is now scheduled for December 2003.

4.2.2.3 *Policy documents adopted by the Council of the EU*

The Council of the EU is also responsible for the adoption of several documents on trafficking in persons. An important document is the Joint Action[7] of the Council of the EU from 29 November 1996 to Determine an Incentive and Exchange Programme for Persons Responsible for Actions against Trafficking in Human Beings and Sexual Exploitation of Children.[8] The Joint Action of 24 February 1997, to suppress trafficking in human beings and sexual exploitation of children, is another important document.[9] This document aims to adjust the different definitions of trafficking in women in the different member states by stating the characteristics of this phenomenon without the aim to establish one overall definition. In this first step towards harmonising the legislation, attention is paid to mutual legal assistance and witness protection as well. The provisions in this joint action include the intention to stimulate cooperation between the member states. It requires great commitment on the part of the member states to share information, to allow information exchange on a local level, and to cooperate with other organisations involved.

Following this joint action a new document was enacted: The Hague Ministerial Declaration on European Guidelines for Effective Measures to Prevent and Combat Trafficking in Women for the Purpose of Sexual Exploitation.[10] The member states of the EU reaffirmed their commitment to maximise cooperation in the fight against trafficking in human beings. In this declaration, it is stressed that trafficking in per-

[7] I stated in Section 4.2.1 that policy documents concern documents that are not legally binding and do not create enforceable rights for citizens. The status of joint actions is a point of discussion, see Chapter 5, Section 5.2.1.1.

[8] Joint Action of 29 November 1996 Adopted by the Council on the Basis of Article K.3 of the Treaty on European Union, Establishing an Incentive and Exchange Programme for Persons Responsible for Combating Trade in Human Beings and the Sexual Exploitation of Children, OJ L 322, 12.12.1996, p. 7.

[9] Joint Action of 24 February 1997 Adopted by the Council on the Basis of Article K.3 of the Treaty on European Union Concerning Action to Combat Trafficking in Human Beings and Sexual Exploitation of Children, OJ L 063, 4.3.1997, pp. 2-6.

[10] The Hague Ministerial Declaration on European Guidelines for Effective Measures to Prevent and Combat Trafficking in Women for the Purpose of Sexual Exploitation, The Hague, 26 April 1997.

sons requires a special approach because of the specific aspects of this crime. Furthermore, a multidisciplinary and coordinated approach on national, European, and international levels, involving all players concerned, is required to tackle this phenomenon. Guidelines are given in this declaration on cooperation between the member states, between member states and candidate countries, with countries of origin, with the UN system, and with Interpol. Furthermore, guidelines are given on prevention both in the countries of origin and of destination and include the establishment of a national rapporteur on trafficking in human beings in each member state. So far, only the Netherlands, Belgium, and Sweden have appointed a national rapporteur; and the United Kingdom and Italy are considering the appointment of a national rapporteur.[11] It is also stressed that the investigation and prosecution of trafficking cases must be targeted at perpetrators and not at those who are the victims of such practices. To that end, a special section addresses the measures to encourage and assist victims to report to the police and to act as a witness. These measures include granting the victims a temporary residence status during criminal procedures, witness protection programmes, the confiscation of the proceeds of trafficking in persons, and compensation for the victims of trafficking in persons.

4.2.2.4 *Policy documents adopted by the European Council*

Although the European Council expressed its concern as to the existence and the volume of trafficking in persons during several meetings, the subject was dealt with more in depth during the European Council in Tampere. The Presidential Conclusions of the European Council in Tampere, Finland, made a first attempt to realise an area of freedom, security, and justice.[12] It was stressed in point 5 of these conclusions that better compatibility and more convergence between the legal systems of member states must be achieved in order to prevent criminals from using gaps in the systems to avoid punishment. Every form of trafficking in persons has to be prevented and closer cooperation with the countries of origin and transit as well as information campaigns have to be established. Legislation on the European level to penalise trafficking in persons and economic exploitation of immigrants must be enacted. Closer cooperation with Europol to dismantle the criminal networks involved in these crimes is recommended. It also contains provisions on the improvement of the legal cooperation between the member states, especially mutual recognition of legal decisions and access to the courts and authorities in all the member states. As regards the prevention of trafficking in persons, it proposes joint investigative teams for the suppression of organised crime, in particular, among other things, trafficking in persons, in which representatives of Europol can participate.

[11] Bureau Nationaal Rapporteur Mensenhandel, *Mensenhandel, Eerste rapportage van de Nationaal Rapporteur,* Bureau NRM, The Hague, 2002, pp. 68-69.

[12] Presidency Conclusions Tampere European Council, 15 and 16 October 1999, General Secretary, SI (1999) 800 Brussels, 16 October 1999.

4.2.2.5 *Other policy documents within the EU*

Within the framework of the EU two programmes specially focusing on trafficking in human beings were adopted. On 29 November 1996, the Stop programme was adopted.[13] According to Article 1 paragraph 1, this programme was established for the period 1996 to 2000 to develop coordinated initiatives on the combating of trade in human beings and the sexual exploitation of children. It focused on disappearances of minors and on the use of telecommunications facilities for the purposes of trade in human beings and the sexual exploitation of children as well. The persons responsible in this area are the addressees of this programme: judges, public prosecutors, police departments, civil servants, public services concerned with immigration and border controls and with social and tax legislation. In 2001, the follow-up to this programme, the Stop II programme, was adopted. The Daphne programme for the 2000 to 2003 period was adopted on 24 January 2000.[14] The programme aims to contribute towards ensuring a high level of protection against violence including violence in the form of sexual exploitation and abuse. A proposal to extend this programme was made in February 2003.[15]

Another policy document is the Proposal for a Comprehensive Plan to Combat Illegal Immigration and Trafficking in Human Beings in the European Union.[16] Despite its name, this plan mainly concerns the combating of illegal immigration while trafficking in human beings is only referred to intermittently. Therefore, it cannot be considered a comprehensive plan to combat trafficking in persons.

In October 2002, the Brussels Declaration was the final outcome of the European Conference on Preventing and Combating Trafficking in Human Beings – Global Challenge for the 21st Century from 18 to 20 September 2002. This text was adopted by the Council of the European Union in its meeting of 8 May 2003 and will be published in the Official Journal.[17] The declaration contains further steps towards reinforcing efforts to implement best practices identified in a comprehensive and coordinated European approach. The annex to this declaration contains recommendations, standards, and best practices including the improvement of direct contacts

[13] Joint Action Establishing an Incentive and Exchange Programme for Persons Responsible for Combating Trade in Human Beings and the Sexual Exploitation of Children OJ L 322, 12.12.1996, pp. 7-10.

[14] Decision Adopting a Programme of Community Action on Preventive Measures to Fight Violence against Children, Young Persons and Women, OJ L 034, 9.2.2000, pp. 1-5.

[15] Proposal for a Decision of the European Parliament and the Council Establishing a Second Phase of a Programme of Community Action (2004-2008) to Prevent Violence against Children, Young People and Women and to Protect Victims and Groups At-Risk (the Daphne II programme), COM(2003) 54 final, Brussels, 4.2.2003. This proposal will be voted on in the EP in July 2003.

[16] Proposal for a Comprehensive Plan to Combat Illegal Immigration and Trafficking in Human Beings in the European Union, OJ C 142, 14.6.2002, pp. 23-36.

[17] Brussels Declaration on Preventing and Combating Trafficking in Human Beings, Doc. 7800/03.

between competent authorities, research, training, and awareness raising. It pays particular attention to victim protection and assistance, and police and judicial cooperation. The latter must be facilitated by the development of legislative provisions including adequate penalties, the use of direct contacts, the ratification and implementation of the EU Convention on Mutual Legal Assistance and the EU Framework Decision on Combating Trafficking in Human Beings, and the setting up of joint investigative teams. Furthermore, the use of existing police and magistrates' liaison networks should be strengthened. Since it was also recommended to set up an Expert Group on Trafficking in Human Beings, the Commission has adopted a decision to this end.[18] The Commission may consult this Expert Group on any matter relating to trafficking and the Expert Group will issue opinions or reports to the Commission at the latter's request or on its own initiative.

4.2.2.6 *Policy documents on (organised) crime*

In this section, policy documents on (organised) crime will be discussed. Although these documents were not specifically formulated to suppress trafficking in persons, this crime is often referred to more in general in these documents.

The European Judicial Network was officially established on 25 September 1998. It was prepared by the Joint Action Concerning a Framework for the Exchange of Liaison Magistrates to Improve Judicial Cooperation Between the Member States of the European Union[19] and by the contact points referred to in the Joint Action on the Creation of a European Judicial Network.[20] This second joint action came as a result of the introduction of the Justice and Home Affairs pillar in the Treaty of Maastricht[21] and some initiatives following this Treaty and was also recommended in the 1997 Action Plan to Combat Organised Crime.[22] The Network meets regularly and is active as an intermediary with the task of facilitating judicial cooperation between member states, and providing legal and practical information on mutual legal assistance to practitioners. The contact points identified by each member state elaborate this task. According to Article 1 paragraph 3, the joint action on the exchange of liaison magistrates aims to increase the speed and effectiveness of judicial cooperation and to promote the pooling of information on the legal and judicial systems of the member states and to improve their operation. The final result must be a decrease in the occurrence of transnational crime. The magistrates must therefore es-

---

[18] Commission Decision of 25 March 2003, Setting Up a Consultative Group, to be known as the 'Experts Group on Trafficking in Human Beings', OJ L 79, 26.3.2003, pp. 25-27.

[19] Joint Action of 22 April 1996 Adopted by the Council on the Basis of Article K.3 of the Treaty on European Union, Concerning a Framework for the Exchange of Liaison Magistrates to Improve Judicial Cooperation between the Member States of the European Union, OJ L 105, 27.4.1996, p. 1.

[20] Joint Action of 29 June 1998 Adopted by the Council on the Basis of Article K.3 of the Treaty on European Union, on the Creation of a European Judicial Network, OJ L 191, 7.7.1998, p. 4.

[21] Treaty of Maastricht, signed in Maastricht, 7 February 1992 and in force since 1 November 1993, OJ C 224, 31.8.1992.

[22] See the section below.

tablish direct links with the competent departments and judicial authorities of the host state and exchange statistics and other information designed to promote the mutual understanding of the legal systems and legal databases of the states concerned. The exchange of liaison officers takes place on the basis of bilateral or multilateral agreements.

The following documents complete the overview of the documents that might be relevant to combat trafficking in persons. The Joint Action of 5 December 1997 Establishing a Mechanism For Evaluating the Application and Implementation at National Level of International Undertakings in the Fight against Organised Crime provides for teams to evaluate the incorporation of the provisions on organised crime at the national level.[23] The evaluation reports following this joint action are analysed in depth in Chapter 5. Another development is the 1997 Action Plan to Combat Organised Crime,[24] the 1998 working plan on the implementation of the Action Plan,[25] the first follow-up to the 1997 Action Plan,[26] and the second follow-up.[27] For the implementation of the 1997 Action Plan and the successive documents, a Joint Action Establishing a Programme of Exchanges, Training and Cooperation For Persons Responsible For the Suppression of Organised Crime for the 1998 to 2002 period was adopted: the Falcone programme.[28] The aim of the programme is, among other things, to reduce obstacles, which may exist to increased cooperation between member states in combating organised crime, particularly in the customs, police, and judicial fields.[29]

4.2.3 Policy documents on trafficking in persons within the Council of Europe

Another organisation within Europe, with a wide range of member states, is the Council of Europe.[30] Until recently, trafficking in persons was not a priority on the

[23] Joint Action of 5 December 1997 Adopted by the Council on the Basis of Article K.3 of the Treaty on European Union, Establishing a Mechanism for Evaluating the Application and Implementation at National Level of International Undertakings in the Fight against Organised Crime, OJ L 344, 15.12.1997, pp. 7-9.

[24] Action Plan to Combat Organised Crime, Adopted by the Council on 28 April 1997, OJ C 251, 15.8.1997, p. 1.

[25] Implementation of Action Plan to Combat Organized Crime, Brussels, 29 September 1998, 11537/98, Crimorg. 139.

[26] Action Plan of the Council and the Commission on How Best to Implement the Provisions of the Treaty of Amsterdam on an Area of Freedom, Security and Justice. The text was adopted by the Justice and Home Affairs Council on 3 December 1998, OJ C 19, 23.1.1999, pp. 1-15.

[27] The Prevention and Control of Organised Crime: A European Union Strategy for the Beginning of the New Millennium, OJ C 124, 3.5.2000, pp. 1-33.

[28] Joint Action of 19 March 1998 Adopted by the Council on the Basis of Article K.3 of the Treaty on European Union, Establishing a Programme of Exchanges, Training and Cooperation for Persons Responsible for Action to Combat Organised Crime (Falcone Programme), OJ L 99, 31.3.1998, p. 8.

[29] Joint Action of 19 March 1998 Adopted by the Council on the Basis of Article K.3 of the Treaty on European Union, Establishing a Programme of Exchanges, Training and Cooperation for Persons Responsible for Action to Combat Organised Crime (Falcone Programme), OJ L 99, 31.3.1998, point 5.

[30] The current 45 member states are: Albania, Andorra, Armenia, Austria, Azerbaijan, Belgium,

agenda within the Council of Europe. The steering committee for equality between women and men raised the issue now and then and some recommendations concerning trafficking in persons were enacted. A policy in which this subject was addressed on a more structural basis was realised with the establishment of the Multi-Sectoral Group on Action against Trafficking in Human Beings for the Purpose of Sexual Exploitation under the authority of the Steering Committee for Equality between Women and Men in December 1997. The task of this group is to plan and prepare actions that the Council of Europe could undertake in this field. More specifically, the group has to identify priority fields of actions, suggest the modalities of cooperation to be established with other competent international bodies and NGOs, and to prepare a draft recommendation, which was proposed in the 1997 recommendation.[31] In this recommendation[32] the Council of Europe exposed its grave concern about the 'dramatic increase' in trafficking in persons. The Assembly felt the need for urgent action and thought the Council of Europe ideally placed to take the lead in combating trafficking in persons and forced prostitution. The Assembly recommended to elaborate a convention on trafficking in women and forced prostitution within the framework of the Council of Europe, to be open for ratification to non-member states as well. The recommendation further urged member states to increase awareness of the phenomenon, improve international cooperation on the combat of trafficking, realise training for immigration staff, adopt measures to confiscate the traffickers' profits, and to provide assistance to the victims (for example, by providing residence permits), and other legal actions. In a reaction to this recommendation, the idea of developing a European convention on trafficking in women was not warmly welcomed and it was preferred to put forward a recommendation on the idea of adopting a convention on this issue first.[33]

The multi-sectoral group adopted this recommendation on 19 May 2000.[34] It was recommended that the governments of the member states review their legislation and practice with regard to trafficking in persons. According to the appendix to this recommendation, this includes the enactment of legislation and practical measures to ensure the protection of the rights and interests of victims such as rehabilitation

Bosnia and Herzegovina, Bulgaria, Croatia, Cyprus, Czech Republic, Denmark, Estonia, Finland, France, Georgia, Germany, Greece, Hungary, Iceland, Ireland, Italy, Latvia, Liechtenstein, Lithuania, Luxembourg, Malta, Moldova, Netherlands, Norway, Poland, Portugal, Romania, Russian Federation, San Marino, Serbia and Montenegro, Slovakia, Slovenia, Spain, Sweden, Switzerland, Former Yugoslav Republic of Macedonia, Turkey, Ukraine, United Kingdom.

31 Specific Terms of Reference from the Multi-Sectoral Group on Action against Trafficking in Human Beings for the Purpose of Sexual Exploitation, 587th Meeting of the Ministers' Deputies, 1 April 1997, Appendix 2.

32 Traffic in Women and Forced Prostitution in Council of Europe Member States, Parliamentary Assembly, Recommendation 1325 (1997).

33 Reply to Parliamentary Assembly Recommendation 1325 (1997) adopted by the deputies in the 645th meeting on 20 October 1998, point 7.

34 Recommendation no. R(2000)11 of the Committee of Ministers to Member States on Action against Trafficking in Human Beings for the Purpose of Sexual Exploitation, Adopted by the Committee of Ministers on 19 May 2000, at the 710th Meeting of the Ministers' Deputies.

programmes and provisions to punish traffickers. A multidisciplinary approach is suggested to accomplish efficient and effective strategies. Bilateral and multilateral agreements must be used to achieve cooperation between countries of origin, transit, and destination. Such agreements may concern the exchange of information, mutual legal assistance, confiscation of profits, and coordination of responsibilities. The collection of data must be encouraged to achieve a better concept of the scope of the phenomenon. Raising awareness and providing information on the issue is seen as another activity to be undertaken by the member states. Strengthening the position of women, starting with avoiding gender stereotypes in schools, is another aim in the recommendation. Furthermore, the improvement of social status and economic conditions can contribute to this aim. Special training programmes for all persons who may come into contact with victims in order to recognise victims and to assist them adequately are provided as well. The appendix contains an elaborate plan for the assistance of victims. No actions were suggested to adopt a convention on trafficking in persons.

Furthermore, on 15 March 2000, a report on Violence against Women in Europe was published.[35] It gives an overview of different forms of violence against women, including trafficking, and encourages states to ratify some relevant documents. The recommendations at the end of the document address the whole phenomenon of violence against women and consequently are rather general.

A second group of specialists was established in 2000, namely, the Group of Specialists on the Impact of the Use of New Information Technologies on Trafficking in Human Beings for the Purpose of Sexual Exploitation, also under the authority of the Steering Committee for Equality between Women and Men. The task of this group is reflected by the name of the group. It is in particular instructed to collect data on the techniques used by traffickers, their modus operandi, and the legislation in the member states on this issue.[36]

4.2.4 **Policy documents on trafficking in persons within the OSCE**

The OSCE has spread its activities over a great area within Europe. Nowadays, it has a broad list of states party to the OSCE.[37] The OSCE has long identified traf-

[35] Committee on Equal Opportunities for Women and Men, *Violence against Women in Europe*, Rapporteur Mrs. Ruth-Gaby Vermot-Mangold, Council of Europe, Parliamentary Assembly, 15 March 2000, Doc. 8667.

[36] Terms of Reference of a Group of Specialists on the Impact of the Use of New Information Technologies on Trafficking in Human Beings for the Purpose of Sexual Exploitation.

[37] The 55 participating states in the OSCE are: Albania, Andorra, Armenia, Austria, Azerbaijan, Belarus, Belgium, Bosnia and Herzegovina, Bulgaria, Canada, Croatia, Cyprus, Czech Republic, Denmark, Estonia, Finland, France, Georgia, Germany, Greece, Holy See, Hungary, Iceland, Ireland, Italy, Kazakhstan, Kyrgyzstan, Latvia, Liechtenstein, Lithuania, Luxembourg, Malta, Moldova, Monaco, Netherlands, Norway, Poland, Portugal, Romania, Russian Federation, San Marino, Slovak Republic, Slovenia, Spain, Sweden, Switzerland, Tajikistan, Former Yugoslav Republic of Macedonia, Turkey, Turkmenistan, Ukraine, United Kingdom, United States of America, Uzbekistan, Yugoslavia.

ficking as a migration issue. The first OSCE commitment that specifically addresses trafficking in human beings is the Moscow Document of 1991, in which the participating states have committed themselves to taking action against trafficking in women. It states that[38]

> The participating states will ... seek to eliminate all forms of violence against women, and all forms of traffic in women and exploitation of prostitution of women, including by ensuring adequate legal prohibitions against such acts and other appropriate measures.

The topic of trafficking in persons was further addressed on an ad hoc basis in the Stockholm Declaration of 1996, where the OSCE Parliamentary Assembly expressed grave concern about the practice of trafficking within and beyond OSCE borders.[39] Furthermore, it was addressed during the OSCE Ministerial Council in 1998, where human trafficking was also identified as one of the new risks and challenges to security.[40] The OSCE addressed the topic of traffic in women for the first time on a structural basis in a background paper in 1999.[41] The OSCE Office of Democratic Institutions and Human Rights (ODIHR) has followed up this background paper with a proposed action plan and concrete suggestions for OSCE projects and initiatives.

The background paper first gives an overview of the patterns and practices. An increase in the number of women trafficked from Central and Eastern European countries is reported. The economic dimension in the country of origin with high rates of poverty, unemployment, and low payment is seen as a reason why women are placed in a vulnerable position for traffickers. The OSCE reports that the current law and policy of its participating states do not treat trafficking as a serious human rights issue and most law enforcement strategies target the people who are trafficked, not the criminal networks that traffic them. Furthermore, it states that most of the participating countries do not have adequate legislation to combat trafficking in persons and that trafficking in persons has low priority in most countries. The immediate deportation, pursuant to the state's immigration law, of trafficked persons caught residing or working in the country illegally, is seen as one of the biggest obstacles to the effective prosecution of trafficking cases and victim protection.[42] Better police coop-

---

[38] Conference on Security and Cooperation in Europe, Third Conference on the Human Dimension of the OSCE, Moscow, 10 September – 15 October 1991, para 40.7.

[39] Stockholm Declaration, adopted by the OSCE Parliamentary Assembly, 9 July 1996, Towards a Common and Comprehensive Security Model for Europe in the Twenty-First Century, Chapter III, para 84.

[40] Seventh Meeting of the Ministerial Council of the OSCE, December 1998, Oslo Ministerial Declaration.

[41] Organization for Security and Cooperation in Europe, *Trafficking in Human Beings: Implications for the OSCE,* Review Conference, September 1999, ODIHR Background Paper, p. 4.

[42] This also follows from the file study and will be discussed in Chapter 6, Sections 6.3.1 and 6.4.2.4.1.

eration between destination and origin countries may lead to more traffickers being caught and punished, since many cases are dropped for lack of evidence. Protection programmes in the country of origin for people who have been trafficked are recommended as they are now in a vulnerable position with the risk of being re-trafficked or excluded by their families. Recommendations in this background paper for the participating states include:

- increasing awareness among police, judicial, and immigration authorities.
- initiating information campaigns to generate public awareness about trafficking in its different forms.
- training police and immigration authorities to identify trafficking situations and victims of trafficking.
- treating trafficked persons as victims and potential witnesses rather than as criminals and providing temporary residence permits to enable victims to receive appropriate care and legal assistance.
- developing national strategies to combat trafficking, including legislative measures and victim protection measures.

The ODIHR has supported several projects in recent years in the fight against trafficking in women, such as training seminars and a joint project with the IOM.[43] The ODIHR has furthermore appointed an Adviser on Trafficking Issues to help the OSCE on how to best contribute to the fight against trafficking. Some OSCE field missions have dealt with the issue on an ad hoc basis. As many of the Eastern and Central European countries are members of the OSCE this organisation also has possibilities for actions in these countries, often countries of origin. Actions can, for instance, consist of protection of victims when they return to their home country, information campaigns to warn potential victims, and establishing cooperation between the several states. The OSCE has declared that it is particularly suitable for taking action to address the problem of trafficking because it has the institutions and bodies to operate on political and project levels and has a widespread network in particular regional areas such as South Eastern Europe, Central Asia, and Ukraine. Attention to trafficking in persons and other gender issues can be incorporated rather easily in this network. Relevant activities in this region concentrate mainly on support for women's NGOs, police training, anti-corruption and anti-crime initiatives, human rights monitoring, judicial reform, and legislative assistance.[44] In Central Asia, the OSCE can take steps to address trafficking and the causes of trafficking. In Ukraine, the OSCE has special possibilities to combat trafficking in cooperation with the IOM.

---

[43] Organization for Security and Cooperation in Europe, *Trafficking in Human Beings: Implications for the OSCE,* Review Conference, September 1999, ODIHR Background Paper, p. 21.

[44] Organization for Security and Cooperation in Europe, *Trafficking in Human Beings: Implications for the OSCE,* Review Conference, September 1999, ODIHR Background Paper, p. 26.

The ODIHR has set up a Proposed Action Plan 2000 for Activities to Combat Trafficking in Human Beings based on the background paper.[45] The plan aims to suggest specific actions for the OSCE and its participating states to address trafficking in human beings and to integrate anti-trafficking measures into their activities. In this action plan, trafficking in persons is considered one of the most pressing and complex human rights issues in the OSCE region. The proposed actions for the participating states are similar to those listed in the background paper although they are more detailed in the action plan. Trafficking in persons should be given a prominent place on the political agenda within the OSCE. Because of its extensive field presence in the participating states, the strength of the OSCE lies in the following activities.

- monitoring and reporting developments related to possible trafficking and forced prostitution, and specific aspects of trafficking.
- coordinating Core Mission Activities to assist victims, encourage and facilitate the prosecution of traffickers, and to promote law reform and governmental responsibility in cooperation with local NGOs.
- Coordinating mission activities with ODIHR and other national and international organisations and NGOs working on this issue, to avoid duplication.
- Initiating projects by the missions of the OSCE, addressing aspects of trafficking, depending on local circumstances and needs.

The role of the Advisor on Trafficking Issues is defined in the action plan. Special attention will be paid to the situation of trafficking in South Eastern Europe, according to the action plan. Some model projects to prevent and combat trafficking in persons are developed in an annex to the action plan. Furthermore, many other ODIHR activities contribute indirectly to the fight against trafficking as its mandate includes assisting states to build democratic institutions and to implement their human dimension obligations.

Another developed document on trafficking in persons in the framework of the OSCE is the Final Report of the Supplementary Human Dimension Meeting on Trafficking in Human Beings.[46] This topic was chosen because it is seen as one of the most urgent and complex human rights violations that takes place throughout the whole OSCE territory. This report states that the OSCE participating states should undertake a more active role to combat trafficking regardless of whether they are countries of origin, transit, or destination. The protection of and assistance to victims by legal protection and rehabilitation was one of the main issues during the meeting. The document is an elaboration of the proposed action plan and contains concrete recommendations on how this action plan can be implemented. Raising awareness, integrating the issue into the activities, strengthening the position of women in general, training law enforcement officers and judicial staff, intensifying

[45] Proposed Action Plan 2000 for Activities to Combat Trafficking in Human Beings, OSCE-ODIHR, Warsaw, November 1999.

[46] Supplementary Human Dimension Meeting on Trafficking in Human Beings, Final Report, OSCE, Vienna, 19 June 2000.

cooperation with NGOs, enacting legislation in the participating states to counteract trafficking and legislation on victim protection and prevention, increasing cooperation at the police and judicial levels seem to be the most important recommendations. Furthermore, Ministerial Council decision no. 1 of November 2000 and Ministerial Council decision no. 6 of December 2001 stress the importance of fighting trafficking in persons and reiterate the recommendations that were made in previous documents of the OSCE. Finally, the OSCE has adopted Anti-Trafficking Guidelines that include provisions on awareness and training, monitoring and reporting, and coordination. Furthermore, these guidelines suggest concrete actions for fieldworkers such as legal assistance to trafficking victims and the facilitation of shelter and translation services.

In conclusion it can be stated that, since 1999, trafficking in persons has received structural attention within the OSCE and has become one of the spearheads of its policy. Most of the activities and recommendations proposed do not contain new approaches or new methodologies as similar statements were made in other forums within Europe. However, the OSCE is in a unique position to combat trafficking in persons for two reasons. Firstly, the group of participating states encompasses states of origin, transit as well as destination. Many Central and Eastern European countries, which have been increasingly subject to trafficking in recent years, are included in the list of participating states. This gives the OSCE unique opportunities for effective remedies against trafficking because its policy covers many of the states involved in the whole trafficking process. Secondly, the OSCE has a long tradition of operational activities on subjects within their mandate. They have built a huge network with NGOs and on the political level. These existing structures can easily be used when activities to combat trafficking in persons have to be implemented.

4.2.5 **Conclusion**

The policy documents discussed above make up the most important ones on the European level to combat trafficking in persons. As was made clear in Section 4.2.1, many policy documents explicitly address the phenomenon of trafficking in persons and contain concrete steps to be taken in order to achieve the goal of the document. However, most of the documents mentioned above lack legally binding force and all lack direct effect. Consequently, the effect of these documents has so far remained limited as the phenomenon of trafficking to and within Europe is still growing. The lack of direct effect and legal binding force is one of the main problems with regard to the use of policy documents to combat trafficking in persons. On the one hand, there seems to be a missing link between the goals laid down in these documents and the achievement of these goals. There seems to be a lack of institutions and organisations with the power to transform the recommendations into concrete actions. On the other hand, states seem to be rather unwilling to act in accordance with their (non-binding) obligations as laid down in these documents. As we will see, when the document has a more binding nature, states become even more hesitant to adopt far-reaching provisions. In this regard, the protection of victims serves as a good example. In the non-binding policy documents, broad protection and assistance is recommended, including temporary residence status and witness protection programmes. However, in the legally binding Framework Decision on Combating Trafficking in Human Beings (which will be discussed below), none of these measures can be found. It can be said that the impact of non-binding policy documents is rather limited in combating trafficking in persons. Whether binding instruments result in the intended effect remains to be seen. Furthermore, it is remarkable that in many policy documents discussed above the lack of police and judicial cooperation between states is indicated as an important obstacle to an effective prosecution of trafficking in persons. This already supports the impression that the involvement of more states in trafficking aggravates the problems to involved in prosecuting the trafficking of persons.

4.3 OVERVIEW OF THE LEGAL INSTRUMENTS

4.3.1 **The concept of legal instruments**

The legal instruments that will be discussed in this study may be helpful to realise some of the goals and aims laid down in the policy documents discussed above. These legal instruments mainly focus on police and judicial cooperation in criminal matters. Criminal law is one of the fields that has, until now, remained almost completely within national sovereignty and cooperation between states at the EU level in this field is only in a preliminary stage. Many attempts have been made to improve cooperation in criminal matters, both within the EU and the Council of Europe. This has resulted, at least for Europe, in a tight web of rules, agreements, and treaties, often dealing with the same issues. The legal instruments are discussed in this section to the extent that they might facilitate the prosecution of trafficking cases. It follows from this characteristic that these instruments must be legally binding and grant rights to and impose duties on individuals.

Many of these legal instruments concern cooperation in criminal matters in general. The relevant instruments of both the EU and the Council of Europe will not be discussed in detail but the provisions in the instruments that might be relevant to prosecuting suspects of trafficking in persons will be outlined. Furthermore, formal procedures adopted in these instruments will be illustrated. The number of ratifications is also important to determine whether an instrument is relevant, as it makes no sense to discuss instruments that are only applicable to a few states.

However, before we are able to judge the value of the legal instruments within the EU, we have to understand the institutional framework of the EU with regard to police and judicial cooperation in criminal matters (the third pillar) in order to interpret the relevance of the legal instruments of the EU.[47]

---

[47] Also J.W. de Zwaan and A.J. Bultena, *Ruimte van vrijheid, veiligheid en rechtvaardigheid. De samenwerking op het gebied van Justitie en Binnenlandse Zaken in de Europese Unie*, Sdu publishers, The Hague, 2002, pp. 23-27, 75-85, 434-440.

4.3.2 The institutional framework for police and judicial cooperation in criminal matters in the EU

In this section, the establishment of the third pillar, its decision-making process, the Schengen acquis, Europol, Eurojust, the European Court of Justice (ECJ) and the proposals to set up a European Public Prosecutor (EPP) in the *Corpus Juris*, a Green Paper, and the European Convention will be consecutively discussed.

4.3.2.1 *The establishment of police and judicial cooperation in criminal matters*

Before the establishment of the EU in the Treaty of Maastricht,[48] there existed many working groups focusing on cooperation in criminal matters and the avoidance of negative effects of the abolishment of borders between some European states.[49] The member states of the European Community had established most of these groups. Hardly any form of coordination between these groups existed, resulting in an overlap of activities between the different groups. Furthermore, most of these groups lacked democratic legitimacy. The Treaty of Maastricht integrated many of these groups within the structure of the EU. The main aim for the institutionalisation of all these groups was to coordinate their activities. However, the inter-governmental way of policy making on an ad hoc basis, with a lack of democratic or judicial control used by these groups, could not be adopted in the framework of the European Community. Therefore, most of the elements regulated by these groups were placed in Title VI EU Treaty, which meant, at the time, in an intergovernmental framework.

With the Treaty of Maastricht, the three-pillar structure of the EU was introduced. The first pillar now consists of the two communities, namely the European Economic Community and the European Atomic Energy Community. The second pillar includes the Common Foreign and Security Policy (Title V EU Treaty), and the third pillar concerns Police and Judicial Cooperation in Criminal Matters (former Justice and Home Affairs, Title VI EU Treaty). In contrast to the first pillar, the powers of the institutions, except for the Council, are restricted in the second and third pillars. In the third pillar the Council of the EU as the representative of the member states is the authoritative organ, and the Commission, the EP, and the European Court of Justice play a subordinate role, as we will see below.

4.3.2.2 *The decision-making process on police and judicial cooperation in criminal matters*

At the moment the Single European Act (SEA)[50] was drafted, it was not possible to overcome the problems related to bringing some areas of Justice and Home Affairs

[48] The Treaty of Maastricht, signed in Maastricht, 7 February 1992, and in force since 1 November 1993, OJ C 224, 31.8.1992.

[49] Such as the Groupe d'Assistance Mutuelle '92, The Coordinators' Group on the Free Movement of Persons, CELAD (Comité Européen de la Lutte-Anti-Drogue), and the Ad Hoc Immigration Group.

[50] Single European Act, signed on 28 February 1986, and in force since 1 July 1987, OJ L 169, 29.6.1987.

under an EC heading, such as police cooperation and immigration. A special 'General Declaration' was attached to the SEA to emphasise that the competence concerning these issues should remain with the member states.[51] This means that the main decision-making organ within the third pillar remains the Council of the EU, the institution representing the member states. A whole army of experts and officials centralised in COREPER assists the Council in the preparation of its decisions.[52] A chart of this structure is attached to this study.[53] In the Treaty of Amsterdam, an effort was made to simplify the structure of COREPER. Generally, a decision is now prepared and taken in four steps. The first preparations take place in the technical groups, which send their advice to the Article 36 Committee, which then presents its opinions to COREPER who sends it to the Council for a final decision. The technical groups consist of working parties where the preparatory work is done. The Article 36 Committee has been set up to coordinate the activities in the field of police and judicial cooperation in criminal matters. Actually, the Article 36 Committee is assisted by the technical groups on Police and Customs Cooperation and on Judicial Cooperation in Criminal Matters.

The Council can take two different decisions, namely A and B decisions. A decision is considered an A decision when consensus exists on the issue in the Horizontal Group or in the Article 36 Committee. Normally, the Council follows the advice of the experts without discussion. For the B decisions, there is no consensus on the issue and the matter has to be further discussed in the COREPER and probably afterwards in the Council. The Council has to consult the EP in accordance with Article 39 EU Treaty before taking the decisions on the basis of Article 34, with the exception of common positions. In the third pillar, most of the decisions must be adopted unanimously; only measures implementing a decision are taken by qualified majority. The Commission has a shared right of initiative with the member states.

Following this decision-making structure it is not surprising that decisions made by the Council on third-pillar issues are not very accurate and often concern issues that have already been on the political agenda for some time. The efficiency of the Council's decision-making power could be improved if the decision-making structures were simplified.

According to the Treaty of Maastricht, the third-pillar instruments before the Treaty of Amsterdam were common positions, joint actions, and conventions. The instrument of joint action has no longer been used since the Treaty of Amsterdam.[54]

---

[51] General Declaration on Articles 13-19 SEA.

[52] The abbreviation COREPER stands for COmité REpresentatives PERmanente.

[53] Decision of the Council of the European Union Concerning the Responsibilities of Council Bodies in the Field of Justice and Home Affairs Following Entry into Force of the Treaty of Amsterdam, Brussels, 16 March 1999, CK4 12, Doc. 6166/2/99. Also 10336/01 JAI 66, 15515/01 HAI 184, and 5502/02 JAI 7. The organisation chart is enclosed in Appendix 1.

[54] Signed in Amsterdam, 2 October 1997, and in force since 1 May 1999, OJ C 340, 10.11.1997.

Whether this instrument was legally binding was and is subject to debate. For any binding force the heavy model of a convention had to be established. The disadvantage of adopting a convention to achieve legally binding effect is that the procedure is slow and inflexible because all the national parliaments have to ratify the convention. The current instruments that can be adopted in the third pillar can be found in Article 34 EU Treaty. The instruments in the third pillar after the Treaty of Amsterdam can be legally binding but lack direct effect except for conventions, which can have direct effect. Some of these new instruments have striking similarities with some Community law instruments. According to Article 34 paragraph 2 EU Treaty the current instruments within the third pillar are the following.

a. **Common positions** define 'the approach of the Union to a particular matter'. The Council adopts this instrument acting unanimously. The legal status of this instrument is not clear. Neither the Court nor the European Parliament plays any role in these common positions. Therefore, it is likely that it is more a political instrument than a legally binding one.
b. **Framework decisions** are similar to the directives of the first pillar, although the framework decision does not have direct effect but is binding as regards the result to be achieved for the member states. The member states are free to choose the form and measures used to achieve the result. Framework decisions are adopted for the purpose of approximating the laws and regulations of the member states on judicial and administrative issues. Framework decisions are taken unanimously, but a qualified majority may adopt implementing measures.
c. **Decisions** are binding on the member states but lack direct effect. The decisions are normally supplemented by implementing measures. For decisions, the same procedure must be applied as for framework decisions, which means that the decision is taken unanimously but that implementing measures may be adopted by a qualified majority.
d. **Conventions** are drafted by the Council and are presented to the member states for adoption by them. In contrast to the other instruments, conventions have to be ratified by the national parliaments of the member states. This makes the procedure for adopting conventions time-consuming and slow. Measures implementing the convention have to be adopted by two-thirds of the ratifying states.

The Council of the EU uses resolutions, recommendations, declarations, and other instruments to express its political will. None of these instruments are binding upon the Council or the member states. These instruments are more informal and therefore flexible, which means that they can be adopted and amended rather easily.

4.3.2.3 *The Schengen acquis*

In 1985, the Commission published a White Paper on the Completion of the Internal Market, which contained the aim of abolishing all internal borders between the member states of the European Community by the end of 1992. Compensatory measures were needed to remove the negative effects of this abolition. Such measures included stricter border control on the EC's outer border and harmonisation of the immigration and asylum policies. Increased cooperation between police authorities and between customs authorities was required. To realise these aims Germany, Belgium, France, Luxembourg, and the Netherlands established the first Schengen Agreement on 14 June 1985. It can be seen as the successor of the Franco-German Agreement of Saarbrücken of 13 July 1984.[55] Because this first Schengen Agreement was not workable, it was elaborated in the Schengen Convention applying the Agreement (The Schengen Convention) on 19 June 1990. The Schengen Convention contains provisions on the free movement of persons, exchange of information between police and customs authorities, provisions on cooperation in case of trafficking in narcotic drugs, firearms and ammunition, extradition, and judicial cooperation. The measures needed to compensate the abolition of the internal borders include checks at the external borders, partial harmonisation of legislation on visas, residence permits, and organised travel, and harmonisation of asylum procedures.[56] Owing to some delay, the Schengen Convention came into force on 26 March 1995 for Belgium, the Netherlands, Luxembourg, Germany, France, Portugal, and Spain. The Schengen Convention is now an important convention in the EU. Although its establishment was surrounded by silence, and democratic principles were set aside (the process of establishment was neither controlled by the EP nor by national parliaments), it became a guiding instrument in the 1990s in the field of police and judicial cooperation and this will be discussed in Section 4.3.3.5.

The Treaty of Amsterdam incorporated the Schengen acquis into the framework of the EU, partly in the third pillar and partly in the first pillar.[57] To facilitate the integration of the Schengen acquis in the EU two decisions were taken by the Council of the EU, namely, the decision defining the Schengen acquis, in which a definition decision was taken by the Council (the definition decision) and the decision determining the legal basis of these provisions (the allocation decision).[58] Surprisingly, the work for the allocation decision was completed before the work for the definition decision was ready.[59] Furthermore, the integration gave rise to problems, such as the lack of democratic and judicial control concerning the establishment and implementation of the Schengen acquis. The same level of democratic and judicial control as for Community law in general could not be guaranteed. Part of the provisions in the Schengen acquis are still confidential and not published. The confidentiality of the Schengen acquis will be reviewed and if it is necessary that these documents remain confidential, they will not be published. It is a very exceptional situation that provi-

[55] D. Cullen, J. Monar, and Ph. Myers, *Cooperation in Justice and Home Affairs. An Evaluation of the Third Pillar in Practice*, European Interuniversity Press, Brussels, 1996, pp. 23-24.

[56] E. Wagner, The Integration of Schengen into the Framework of the European Union, in: *Legal Issues of European Integration*, Volume 25, issue 2, 1998, pp. 5-6.

[57] Also J.W. de Zwaan and A.J. Bultena, *Ruimte van vrijheid, veiligheid en rechtvaardigheid. De samenwerking op het gebied van Justitie en Binnenlandse Zaken in de Europese Unie*, Sdu publishers, The Hague, 2002, pp. 54-64.

[58] Council Decision 1999/435 Defining the Acquis, OJ L 176, 10.7.1999, p. 1, and Council Decision 1999/436 Determining Legal Bases for the Acquis, OJ L 176, 10.7.1999, p. 17.

[59] M. den Boer and L. Corrado, For the Record or Off the Record: Comments about the Incorporation of Schengen into the EU, in: *European Journal of Migration and Law*, Volume 1, issue 4, 1999, p. 400.

sions within the EU are confidential and are not published. However, most of the documents have now been published in the Official Journal.[60]

The Schengen Protocol, an annex to the EU Treaty, describes the procedure of how the Schengen acquis has to be integrated into the EU framework. Pursuant to Article 2 of the Protocol the Schengen Executive Committee was replaced by the Council of the European Union, which has to determine the legal basis for all the separate provisions that constitute the Schengen acquis, by a unanimous vote. This means that the EP has no democratic control over the allocation of the Schengen provisions, and the commission has no role in this process either. Furthermore, Article 2 of the Protocol gives jurisdiction to the European Court of Justice (ECJ) over the allocation of the acquis. However, the ECJ has no jurisdiction regarding measures taken to secure public order or protection of internal safety. The provisions of the Schengen acquis (i.e., the Schengen acquis as it was defined by the Council's definition decision) that are not allocated will be located under the third pillar. In an annex to the Schengen Protocol, the content of the Schengen acquis is clarified: it includes the Schengen agreement, the Schengen Convention, the protocols and the agreements on the accession to these documents of Italy, Spain, Portugal, Greece, Austria, Denmark, Finland, and Sweden, the decisions and declarations adopted by the executive committee, and the decisions taken to implement the Convention taken by other bodies authorised by the Schengen Executive Committee. However, when the Treaty of Amsterdam was signed and ratified the Council was still debating the content of the Schengen acquis. The ratifying states did not exactly know what it consisted of.[61]

Articles 3, 4, and 6 of the Schengen Protocol concern the special relations with Denmark, Ireland, the United Kingdom, Iceland and Norway with regard to the Schengen provisions. [62]

The Schengen Convention does not directly refer to trafficking in persons and therefore the direct relevance of these provisions seems to be rather limited at first sight. However, the provisions on police cooperation are of major importance between the member states and therefore affect the enforcement of legal instruments on cooperation in criminal matters directly and thus the prosecution of trafficking in persons indirectly. Although much remained unclear with regard to the status and content of the Schengen acquis after the Treaty of Amsterdam, the impact of the provisions on police cooperation and mutual legal assistance cannot be denied and must be considered leading provisions in this field.

---

[60] The Schengen acquis as referred to in Article 1(2) of Council Decision 1999/435/EC of 20 May 1999, OJ L 239, 22.9.2000, pp. 1-473.

[61] S. Peers, Caveat Emptor? Integrating the Schengen Acquis into the European Union Legal Order, in: *Cambridge Yearbook of European Legal Studies,* Volume 2, 1999, pp. 98-100.

[62] S. Peers, Caveat Emptor? Integrating the Schengen Acquis into the European Union Legal Order, in: *Cambridge Yearbook of European Legal Studies,* Volume 2, 1999, pp. 93-94.

4.3.2.4 *Europol*[63]

The first efforts to establish some form of European police unit was launched in the TREVI[64] group.[65] During a meeting of the Council of the EU in December 1991, agreement was reached on the creation of a European Police Office. The Europol Drugs Unit (EDU), which became operational on 3 January 1994, preceded the establishment of Europol. The initial function of the EDU was to organise the exchange of information on narcotic drugs at the level of the Community's twelve member states. On 18 July 1995, the Council adopted the Convention on the establishment of Europol (the Europol Convention).[66] On 1 October 1998, the Europol Convention entered into force, which terminated the activities of the EDU in accordance with Article 45. Europol took up its full activities on 1 July 1999. The tasks of Europol are to facilitate the exchange of information among the member states; to obtain, collate, and analyse information; to notify the competent authorities of member states, without delay, of any investigation within the member states and to maintain a computerised system for collecting information. Its primary function is to gather and analyse information held by the different national police forces. Therefore, Europol has a Union-wide system for exchanging information. According to Article 2 of the Europol Convention, its aim is 'to improve [...] the effectiveness and cooperation of the competent authorities in the Member States in preventing and combating terrorism, unlawful drug trafficking and other serious forms of international crime where there are factual indications that an organised criminal structure is involved and two or more Member States are affected by the forms of crime in question'. This mandate was extended to trafficking in human beings with the joint action of 16 December 1996.[67]

The 1997 Action Plan to Combat Organised Crime gives Europol a central role in the battle against organised crime. In contrast to the national police forces, Europol does not have full operational authority. However, the EU Treaty includes some provisions which open the door for operational activities by Europol in the future. Article 30 EU Treaty confirms the future role of Europol, stating that the Council shall promote cooperation through Europol by

---

[63] Also J.W. de Zwaan and A.J. Bultena, *Ruimte van vrijheid, veiligheid en rechtvaardigheid. De samenwerking op het gebied van Justitie en Binnenlandse Zaken in de Europese Unie,* Sdu publishers, The Hague, 2002, pp. 268-285.

[64] TREVI stands for *Terrorisme, Radicalisme, Extrémisme et Violence Internationale.* Some claim that it is named after the fountain in Rome, where the first steps were taken to establish this group in 1976.

[65] J.S. Solomon, Forming a More Secure Union: The Growing Problem of Organized Crime in Europe as a Challenge to National Sovereignty, in: *Dickens Journal of International Law,* Volume 13, issue 3, 1995, p. 627.

[66] Convention Based on Article K.3 of the Treaty on European Union, on the Establishment of a European Police Office (Europol Convention), OJ C 316, 27.11.1995, p. 2.

[67] Joint Action of 16 December 1996 Adopted by the Council on the Basis of Article K.3 of the Treaty on European Union, Extending the Mandate Given to the Europol Drugs Unit, OJ L 342, 31.12.1996, p. 4.

- [enabling] Europol to facilitate and support the preparation, and to encourage the coordination and carrying out, of specific investigative actions by the competent authorities of the Member States, including operational actions of joint teams comprising representatives of Europol in a support capacity;
- [adopting] measures allowing Europol to ask the competent authorities of the Member States to conduct and coordinate their investigations in specific cases and to develop specific expertise which may be put at the disposal of Member States to assist them in investigating cases of organised crime;
- [promoting] liaison arrangements between prosecuting/investigating officials specialising in the fight against organised crime [...];
- [establishing] a research, documentation and statistical network on cross-border crime.

In the Tampere Conclusions, the key role of Europol in fighting international organised crime was strengthened. The relevant conclusions for Europol were the following.[68]

> 43. Maximum benefit should be derived from cooperation between Member States' authorities when investigating cross-border crime in any member state. The European Council calls for joint investigative teams as foreseen in the Treaty to be set up without delay, initially to combat terrorism, trafficking in drugs and human beings as well as terrorism. The rules to be set up in this respect should allow representatives of Europol to participate, as appropriate, in a support capacity.
> 44. The European Council calls for the establishment of European Police Chiefs Operational Task Force to exchange, in cooperation with Europol, experiences, best practice and information on current trends in cross-border crime and contribute to the planning of operative actions.
> 45. Europol has a key role in supporting Union-wide crime prevention, analysis and investigation. The European Council calls on the Council to provide Europol with the necessary support and resources. In the near future its role should be strengthened by means of receiving operational data from Member States [...].
> 46. To reinforce the fight against serious organised crime, the European Council has agreed that a unit (EUROJUST) should be set up composed of national prosecutors, magistrates, or police officers of equivalent competence, detached from each Member State according to its legal system. EUROJUST should have the task of facilitating the proper coordination of national prosecuting authorities and of supporting criminal investigations in organised crime cases, notably based on Europol's analysis as well as of cooperating closely with the European Judicial Network [...].
> 56. The European Council invites the Council to extend the competence of Europol to money laundering in general, regardless of the type of offence from which the laundered proceeds originate.

In conclusion, it can be stated that, from several perspectives, the role of Europol is strengthened and that its tasks are meant to be more operational in the future. How-

[68] Tampere European Council, 15 and 16 October 1999, Presidency Conclusions.

ever, so far, the member states have only formally agreed to the factual participation of Europol on the operational level. Although the mandate of Europol is extended to cover trafficking in persons as well, its operational field is limited to crimes committed by organised crime groups. Furthermore, the effective functioning of Europol is completely dependent on the willingness of member states to transfer relevant information. Following this limitation and the possibility granted, only recently, for operational activities by Europol, its power to improve the enforcement of legal instruments to facilitate the prosecution of traffickers must not be overestimated. Current developments with regard to Europol within the European Convention will be discussed in Chapter 7.

4.3.2.5 *Eurojust*

As stated above, it was proposed in Tampere to set up a European unit for the coordination of judicial cooperation in cases of organised crime. This unit, Eurojust, should be composed of national prosecutors, magistrates, or police officers of equivalent competence. Eurojust should have the task of facilitating the proper coordination of national prosecuting authorities and of supporting criminal investigations in organised crime cases. On 19 June 2000, a Council Decision on setting up an Eurojust team was taken[69] and Eurojust was finally established by the Council Decision of 28 February 2002.[70] According to Article 2 of this decision, the task of Eurojust is to provide support for investigations into major criminal offences in respect of which judicial legal assistance may be required for proceedings and into criminal offences against the financial interests of the EU. Trafficking in human beings is explicitly recognised as belonging to this group of crimes. The liaison officers seconded to Eurojust from each member state are the advisors and coordinators of questions on legal issues concerning their country for the investigating authorities of other member states, the European Commission, and Europol. In this sense, Eurojust will be equipped with similar facilities as Europol.

Article 31 EU Treaty strengthens the role of Eurojust. Paragraph 1(a) states that cooperation through Eurojust shall be conducted where appropriate. Furthermore, Eurojust is given a central role in paragraph 2 stating that the Council shall encourage cooperation through Eurojust by

(a) enabling Eurojust to facilitate proper coordination between member states' national prosecuting authorities;
(b) promoting support by Eurojust for criminal investigations in cases of serious cross-border crime, particularly in the case of organised crime, taking account, in particular, of analyses carried out by Europol;

[69] Initiative of the Federal Republic of Germany with a view to the adoption of a Council Decision on Setting up a Eurojust Team, OJ C 206, 19.7.2000.

[70] Council Decision of 28 February 2002, Setting up Eurojust with a View to Reinforcing the Fight against Serious Crimes, OJ L 63, 6.3.2002.

(c) facilitating close cooperation between Eurojust and the European Judicial Network, particularly, in order to facilitate the execution of letters rogatory and the implementation of extradition requests.

Unfortunately, Article 31 EU Treaty does not provide Eurojust with any operational powers and therefore its significance for the system of judicial cooperation in criminal matters still remains to be seen. Furthermore, and comparable to Europol, Eurojust will be dependent on the willingness of states to cooperate. The experiences of Europol with states transmitting relevant information are not very promising as states are reluctant to share operational information with Europol. In Chapter 7, the idea of granting operational powers to Eurojust and the current development in the European Convention with regard to Eurojust will be elaborated.

4.3.2.6 *The jurisdiction of the European Court of Justice*

Article 35 of Title VI EU Treaty determines the jurisdiction of the ECJ in the third pillar. In the first paragraph the possibility of preliminary rulings in the third pillar is provided for. It concerns an optional preliminary ruling with regard to the interpretation and applicability of framework decisions and decisions, the interpretation of agreements based on Title VI, and the interpretation and applicability of the execution measures of these agreements. States have to make a declaration if they accept this competence of the Court. They furthermore have to decide whether every national judicial authority has the competence to ask preliminary questions or whether this is the prerogative of the highest courts of appeal. Because of the voluntary option in the legal protection system of the preliminary procedure, nationals of participating and nationals of non-participating states will have a different level of legal protection and remedies.[71] This idea seems to encourage inequality in legal protection between European citizens.

By virtue of Article 35 paragraph 6 the ECJ is competent to review the legality of framework decisions and decisions in the third pillar. According to this paragraph, the Commission and each member state are authorised to initiate an annulment action before the ECJ. This procedure has a parallel link with Article 230 EC Treaty, especially because the grounds for initiating such a procedure are the same. The difference is that individuals, in contrast to Article 230 EC Treaty, have no access to this remedy because they are not supposed to be affected in third pillar issues by the decisions of the Council.

Furthermore, dispute settlement between member states about the interpretation and applicability of decisions taken by virtue of Article 34 paragraph 2 can be subject to

[71] J. Monar, Legitimacy of EU Action in Justice and Home Affairs: An assessment in the Light of the Reforms of the Treaty of Amsterdam, in: M. den Boer, et al., *Coping with Flexibility and Legitimacy after Amsterdam*, Current European Issues/EIPA, Maastricht, 1998, pp. 211-212.

the ECJ's decision (paragraph 7). This competence in dispute settlement between states concerning interpreting questions of decisions taken by the Council by virtue of Article 34 paragraph 2 is said to be the weaker little brother of Article 226 EC Treaty.[72] Article 35 EU Treaty does not provide the ECJ with a general interpreting competence for Title VI. However, the ECJ will have the authority to interpret Title VI EU Treaty to the extent necessary for the performance of its tasks under Article 35.

According to paragraph 5 of Article 35, the ECJ has no jurisdiction over the maintenance of law and order and the safeguarding of internal security. A second restriction on the ECJ's jurisdiction in the third pillar is the inability to review the validity or proportionality of operations carried out by the police or other law enforcement agencies. As the third pillar on police and judicial cooperation in criminal matters easily affects public order or internal security, the jurisdiction of the ECJ is considerably limited with these restrictions.

The ECJ is competent to review the allocation of the Schengen provisions by the Council.[73] This power through which the ECJ can check whether the Council does not allocate a provision under Title VI EU Treaty instead of Title IV EC Treaty and thus limits the competence of the Commission, is very important for attaining a balance between the organs.

In conclusion, Title VI EU Treaty now includes three procedures for legal protection. The first is the preliminary ruling, although it does not refer to Article 234 EC Treaty. Member states have to opt for the ECJ's jurisdiction in a special declaration in which they have to decide which national judges may initiate this procedure. This means that there is no obligation for the highest court to ask for preliminary questions. A preliminary ruling can be initiated for the validity and interpretation of framework decisions, decisions, implementing measures (Article 35 (1)) and the interpretation of third pillar conventions. The second procedure can be found in paragraph 6, which is comparable to Article 230 EC Treaty and can be initiated by the Commission and member states in case of decisions and framework decisions. It is generally accepted that the effect of the procedure under Article 35 paragraph 6 is the annulment of the decision. The third procedure can be found in paragraph 7 and concerns dispute settlement between member states concerning the interpretation and application of the acts adopted under Article 34 paragraph 2 EU Treaty.

---

[72] N. Fennelly, Preserving the Legal Coherence within the New Treaty, in: M. den Boer, et al., *Coping with Flexibility and Legitimacy after Amsterdam*, Current European Issues/EIPA, Maastricht, 1998, p. 77.

[73] M. den Boer and L. Corrado, For the Record or Off the Record: Comments about the Incorporation of Schengen into the EU, in: *European Journal of Migration and Law*, Volume 1, issue 4, 1999, p. 408.

4.3.2.7 *The idea of a European Public Prosecutor*

As stated in Chapter 1 and further elaborated in Chapter 2, the prosecution of transnational crime and thus the prosecution of trafficking in persons may be more effective when it is undertaken at the EU level. Some recent developments within the EU that may provide us with some starting points for such an approach will be focused upon below. These developments concern the proposals for the establishment of a European Public Prosecutor (EPP) for fraud against the financial interests of the EU.[74] Proposals to install an EPP, namely, in the *Corpus Juris,* in the Green Paper of the Commission, and in the Draft Convention of the European Convention, can be seen as initiatives reflecting the changing role of state sovereignty.[75] The proposed installation of an EPP is an idea with far-reaching consequences for both substantive and procedural criminal law. An analysis of whether the mechanism of an EPP will contribute to the improvement of the prosecution of trafficking cases will be made in Chapter 7 without elaborating on all the consequences of this concept for substantive and procedural criminal law in the member states. Before the question can be answered whether this concept can be used as a blueprint to facilitate the prosecution of traffickers in Chapter 7, the idea of the EPP will be explained in this section.

4.3.2.7.1 The idea of an EPP in the *Corpus Juris*

The idea of the *Corpus Juris* originates in an initiative by the European Commission for the protection of the financial interests of the EU and was elaborated by a group of experts under the direction of Mrs. M. Delmas-Marty.[76] The first draft of the text for a *Corpus Juris* was launched in 1997[77] and amended following criticism from many critics and experts in international and (European) criminal law. The *Corpus Juris* project was set up solely to fight fraud against the financial interests of the EU as described in Articles 1 to 8 of the *Corpus Juris*.[78] In essence, the proposed *Corpus*

[74] Also J.W. de Zwaan and A.J. Bultena, *Ruimte van vrijheid, veiligheid en rechtvaardigheid. De samenwerking op het gebied van Justitie en Binnenlandse Zaken in de Europese Unie,* Sdu publishers, The Hague, 2002, pp. 311-339.

[75] Reference is made to the text of the *Corpus Juris* as to how it was agreed in Florence in May 1999. Green Paper on Criminal-Law Protection of the Financial Interests of the Community and the Establishment of a European Prosecutor, COM(2001) 715 final, 11.12.2001 (Green Paper). The European Convention, Draft Constitution, Volume II, Brussels, 27 June 2003, CONV 836/03, Article III-170.

[76] An elaborate study on the feasibility of the *Corpus Juris* and the possible impact with regard to the present situation in national law when bringing the *Corpus Juris* into force has taken place under the direction of M. Delmas-Marty and J.A.E. Vervaele (eds.), The result is a document consisting of 4 volumes including the reports by the rapporteurs in each of the member states. M. Delmas-Marty and J.A.E. Vervaele, *The Implementation of the Corpus Juris in the Member States,* Intersentia, Antwerp, 2000.

[77] M. Delmas-Marty and Ch. van den Wyngaert, *Corpus Juris,* Intersentia Rechtswetensachppen, Antwerp, 1998.

[78] These offences are: fraud affecting the financial interests of the European Communities and assimilated offences, market-rigging, money laundering and receiving, conspiracy, corruption, misappropriation of funds, abuse of office, disclosure of secrets pertaining to one's office.

Juris concerns the establishment of an EPP[79] who may exercise its powers of investigation throughout the territory of the EU. The EPP consists of a European Director of Public Prosecutions (EDPP) and European Delegated Public Prosecutors (EDelPP) in each of the member states of the EU, who are appointed to this post.[80] The territory of the EU must be considered a European Judicial Space and concerns the whole territory of the EU. This means that the competence of the EPP and therefore of the EDPP and EDelPPs to issue warrants and judgements, to conduct investigations, and to render judgements by applying the *Corpus Juris* covers the whole territory of the EU.[81] The EDelPPs are bound by instructions from the EDPP. During the preparatory stage, 'judges of freedoms' at the European level decide on measures that restrict or deprive a person of his rights and fundamental freedoms, including coercive measures.[82] These judges of freedoms will be placed in a proposed pre-trial chamber. They will hold a hearing 'to confirm the charges upon which the European Public Prosecutor relies to bring the case to court'.[83] The judge of freedoms will take the final decision as to whether a case is ready to go to trial. Decisions by a judge of freedoms will be applicable in the whole territory of the EU.

The justification to set up an EPP is that the crimes described in Articles 1 to 8 cannot be efficiently suppressed with the current instruments. The national laws are too fragmented and diverse, and police and judicial authorities are authorised to operate only on their own territory. A centralised EPP would be the solution to these problems. This means that only when the crime is transnational in nature, i.e., when more states are involved in the crime, is the application of an EPP justified. When, for instance, fraud is taking place in one single state, the national law must be seen as the most convenient. However, the criterion that the crime concerned must be transnational is not mentioned as a prerequisite in the *Corpus Juris*. Furthermore, Article 19 paragraph 2 states that 'if an investigation conducted by a national authority reveals that one of the offences of Articles 1 to 8 has been committed, the file must be immediately submitted to the EPP'. Therefore, also those cases without a transnational link must be submitted to the EPP although a remedy at the national level may be more suitable. This means a violation of the principle of subsidiarity, as the application of Community law is only justified if national law is not sufficient.[84] Furthermore, Article 35 of the *Corpus Juris* seems to be in contradiction with the principle of subsidiarity and it states that national law supplements the provisions of the *Cor-*

[79] Articles 18 to 24 of the *Corpus Juris*.

[80] M. Delmas-Marty and J.A.E. Vervaele (eds.), *The Implementation of the Corpus Juris in the Member States*, Volume 1, Intersentia, Antwerp, 2000, foreword. Article 18 paragraph 3 of the *Corpus Juris*.

[81] M. Delmas-Marty and J.A.E. Vervaele (eds.), *The Implementation of the Corpus Juris in the Member States*, Volume 1, Intersentia, Antwerp, 2000, pp. 37-39.

[82] The judge of freedoms is independent and impartial, designated by each member state. Beside the competence to decide on coercive measures, he is also competent to order an expert opinion, Article 25bis paragraphs 1 and 2 of the *Corpus Juris*.

[83] M. Delmas-Marty and J.A.E. Vervaele (eds.), *The Implementation of the Corpus Juris in the Member States*, Volume 1, Intersentia, Antwerp, 2000, p. 91.

[84] Article 5 EC Treaty and Article 2 EU Treaty.

pus Juris. Besides, the remedy on the EU level must always meet the requirements of proportionality and the answer to the question of whether the proposed *Corpus Juris* is the most proportionate answer to crimes against the financial interests of the EU must be answered in the negative, for reasons mentioned previously.[85]

4.3.2.7.2 The idea of an EPP in the Green Paper

On the occasion of the Intergovernmental Conference in Nice at the end of 2000, the European Commission launched a proposal for the establishment of an EPP to remedy the fragmentation of the European law enforcement area as a response to fraud against the Community's finances. It included a revision of Article 280 of the EC Treaty to provide a legal basis for the establishment of the EPP. The proposal was not discussed in Nice by the heads of state because a more detailed study of the practical implications was needed. This was done by the Commission and resulted in the 'Green Paper on Criminal-Law Protection of the Financial Interests of the Community and the Establishment of a European Prosecutor'.[86] This document is clearly based on the *Corpus Juris* although one of the main starting points is the decentralised character of the concept. This is in contrast to the *Corpus Juris,* which chooses a centralised starting point. The Green Paper does not support the idea of establishing a pre-trial chamber, and the judge of freedoms is a national judge. The delegated European prosecutors remain subject to the national legal order although they are hierarchically subordinated to the European Prosecutor.

In contrast to the *Corpus Juris*, the Green Paper takes into account the principle of subsidiarity. It states that 'in accordance with the principles of subsidiarity and proportionality, this jurisdiction would remain limited to the minimum necessary in order to ensure effective and equivalent prosecution of unlawful conduct harmful to the Community's financial interests anywhere in the Community.'[87] Elsewhere, a clear reference is made to the transnational character of the cases in which the EPP might be involved.[88]

In the *Corpus Juris* as well as in the Green Paper, the absence of mutual recognition of evidence and the application of the principle of *locus regit actum* with regard to the use of evidence in court is considered problematic. This generates a related problem for the establishment of coercive measures such as search (of premises) and interception (of telecommunications). It is proposed in both drafts that the principle of

[85] The German report states that 'it is simply untrue that a single legal area requires the creation of an EPP,' M. Delmas-Marty and J.A.E. Vervaele (eds.), *The Implementation of the Corpus Juris in the Member States,* Volume 1, Intersentia, Antwerp, 2000, pp. 311-314. C. Fijnaut, De strafrechtelijke bescherming van de financiële belangen van de Gemeenschap tegen fraude, in: *Delikt en Delinkwent,* Volume 30, issue 10, 2000, pp. 972-978.

[86] Green Paper on Criminal-Law Protection of the Financial Interests of the Community and the Establishment of a European Prosecutor, COM(2001) 715 final, Brussels, 11.12.2001.

[87] Green Paper, para 3. Also paras 4.2.1, 6, 6.3.4.1, and 6.4.2.

[88] Green Paper, para 1.2.1.

mutual recognition of evidence must be introduced and that, in this regard, the principle of *forum regit actum* shall be applied.[89] Furthermore, the decisions of the judge of freedoms, even if he is situated in the legal order of a state, are binding in all member states. In a feasibility study on the constitution of the EU, the idea of an EPP was included, as well as in the Draft Constitution of the European Convention.[90] The latter will be discussed below.

4.3.2.7.3 The idea of an EPP in the Draft Constitution

It seems to be contradictory, but the concept of an EPP as proposed in the *Corpus Juris* and the Green Paper seems, on the one hand, to be too limited as it only concerns 'Eurofraud' and, on the other, it goes too far as it more or less requires the harmonisation of issues of procedural law. What might be more acceptable is a limitation of the harmonisation of procedural law aspects, leaving these powers as much as possible to the national states, and an extension of the 'European Prosecutor's' mandate to other forms of serious crimes. It can be said that the Praesidium of the European Convention has adopted such a system in its Draft Constitution. The European Convention was established in the Declaration of Laken in December 2001 with the aim being to improve democracy, transparency, and efficiency in the EU, taking into account the forthcoming enlargement. Furthermore, the Declaration of Laken created the possibility of proposing a Constitution for the EU. The European Convention has elaborated a Draft Treaty establishing a Constitution for Europe[91] in which the three pillars of the EU are merged and the co-decision procedure is adopted in all cases, with some exceptions for police and judicial cooperation in criminal matters, for instance. Article III-170 of the Draft Constitution, Volume II, proposes the establishment of an EPP. This article states:

1. In order to combat serious crime having a cross-border dimension, as well as crimes affecting the interests of the Union, a European law of the Council of Ministers may establish a European Public Prosecutor's Office from Eurojust. The Council shall acting unanimously after approval by the European Parliament.
2. The European Public Prosecutor's Office shall be responsible for investigating, prosecuting and bringing to judgement, where appropriate in liaison with Europol, the perpetrators of and accomplices in serious crimes affecting more than one Member States and of offences against the Union's financial interests, as determined by the law provided for in paragraph 1. It shall exercise the functions of prosecutor in the competent courts of the Member States in relation to such offences.
3. The European law referred to in paragraph 1 shall determine the general rules applicable to the European Public Prosecutor's Office, the conditions governing the performance of its functions, the rules of procedure applicable to its activities, as well

[89] *Corpus Juris* Article 32 and Green Paper para 6.3.4.1.

[90] The Feasibility Study, Contribution to a Preliminary Draft, Constitution of the European Union under the Responsibility of F. Lamoureux, European Commission, 4.12.2002, Article 73. The European Convention, Draft Constitution, Volume II, Brussels, 27 June 2003 CONV 836/03, Article III-170.

[91] The European Convention, Draft Treaty establishing a Constitution for Europe, Brussels, 30 June 2003, CONV 820/2/03 REV 2.

> as those governing the admissibility of evidence, and the rules applicable to the judicial review of procedural measures taken by it in the performance of its functions.

This means that the Draft Constitution creates the possibility to establish an EPP without elaborating on the way in which the EPP has to operate, what the requirements are for its establishment, and how it must cooperate with the member states. However, this article makes some important choices for the establishment of an EPP, namely, that its mandate will not be limited to offences against the Union's financial interests but will include serious crimes affecting several member states as well. This means that trafficking in persons will be included in the mandate of the EPP. Furthermore, this article states that an EPP must be set up within the framework of Eurojust. In Chapter 7, I will elaborate on how the EPP can operate within the framework of Eurojust to improve the prosecution of trafficking cases.

4.3.3 **Legal instruments within the EU**

Now that the framework of the EU with regard to police and judicial cooperation in criminal matters is clarified, we can concentrate on the legal instruments adopted within this framework. One of the most important legal instruments in which the intention to combat and prosecute trafficking in persons can be found is Article 29 EU Treaty. The creation of an area of freedom, security, and justice became the main objective of the third pillar, which will be realised by means of the prevention and the combating of crime, whether organised or not. Trafficking in human beings is listed in this article as one of the crimes that deserves particular attention. This article can be considered the basis for the legal instruments that will be discussed below. In this section, an overview will be given of the most important legal instruments developed within the EU to prosecute transnational (organised) crime, in general, and trafficking in persons, in particular. Except the Council Framework Decision on Combating Trafficking in Human Beings and the proposal for a Council Directive on the Short-Term Residence Permit, these instruments are not specifically set up to suppress trafficking in persons. Because of their general aim to improve police and judicial cooperation, these legal instruments affect trafficking in persons as well. When discussing these instruments we have to keep in mind that the majority of these instruments are based on the conventions enacted within the Council of Europe, which will be discussed in Section 4.3.4. These conventions of the Council of Europe often serve as the mother conventions of the EU instrument.

An overall overview of the instruments in the third pillar is beyond the scope of this section, so only the most relevant instruments will be discussed.[92] The framework

[92] For an overview, see J.W. de Zwaan and A.J. Bultena, *Ruimte van vrijheid, veiligheid en rechtvaardigheid. De samenwerking op het gebied van Justitie en Binnenlandse Zaken in de Europese Unie*, Sdu publishers, The Hague, 2002, pp. 344-355, 372-395. Because the authors do not distinguish between policy documents and legal instruments this overview contains both agreements. Also M. den Boer, Incorporation without Change? Police Cooperation from Schengen to the EU, paper presented at the Madrid Seminar on Immigration, Asylum, and Border Controls, February 2000, not published, pp. 21-25.

decision mentioned before, the EU Conventions on Extradition, the European Arrest Warrant, the EU Convention on Mutual Assistance and its protocol, the Schengen Convention, and the proposal for a Council Directive on the Short-Term Residence Permit will be discussed successively. In a separate section, the transformation in the use of current principles on cooperation in criminal matters that is adopted in some of these legal instruments will be reflected upon.

4.3.3.1 *The Council Framework Decision on Combating Trafficking in Human Beings*

The Framework Decision on Combating Trafficking in Human Beings[93] deserves special attention here. As we have seen, a framework decision is legally binding although it lacks direct effect in the member states. Because this instrument is legally binding, this particular framework decision may become an authoritative instrument to combat trafficking in persons at the European level.

The ratione materiae
The framework decision was set up in reply to the failure to implement the joint action of February 1997. According to the Commission, the main reason for this failure was the absence of commonly adopted definitions, incriminations, and sanctions in the member states. The definition of trafficking in human beings as used in this decision was already discussed in Chapter 3, Section 3.4.3. Articles 4 and 5 regulate the liability of and sanctions on legal persons. This is the first time that legal persons are addressed explicitly with regard to trafficking in persons. The explanatory memorandum does not indicate whether or not this is done to meet an increased involvement of legal persons. Article 6 reflects the current leading principles in international law to establish jurisdiction. It does not extend the possibilities to exercise jurisdiction, for instance, by granting the status of regional universality to the crime of trafficking in persons or an extensive use of the territoriality principle.

This framework decision is largely based on the Trafficking Protocol to the UNCTOC. However, the protection of and assistance to the victims is dealt with in detail in the Trafficking Protocol but is almost completely absent in the framework decision.[94] The framework decision only provides 'adequate legal protection and standing in judicial proceedings' although the proposals suggested some guarantees for the victims. This is a missed opportunity and has met with comment at the UN level.[95] The critics stated that 'aspects dealing with protection of victims and witnesses fall considerably short of established international standards'. Furthermore, it is regrettable that no reference was included on the prevention of trafficking by di-

[93] Council Framework Decision of 19 July 2002 on Combating Trafficking in Human Beings, OJ L 203, 1.8.2002, pp. 1-4.

[94] Compare Chapter II Trafficking Protocol and Article 8 Framework Decision.

[95] United Nations High Commissioner for Human Rights, *Observations by the UNHCHR and the UNHCR on the Proposal for a EU Council Framework Decision on Combating Trafficking in Human Beings.*

minishing the root causes of trafficking such as poverty, unemployment, and gender discrimination.

Procedural aspects
Article 9 in the first draft of the proposal contained a provision on cooperation between member states, which included a recommendation to use the existing applicable instruments. This article was simply skipped in the final text, which is highly regrettable, especially in view of the necessity for intensified cooperation. Unfortunately, no new provisions were proposed in this regard, except a provision on jurisdiction and prosecution. The role of Europol, which was included in earlier drafts of the framework decision, was also omitted.

Thus, the measures to be taken to prevent trafficking, to assist victims, and to cooperate with third countries, etc., were not dealt with or only vaguely referred to in the framework decision, which must, in my view, be considered as a missed opportunity. The possible reason could be that states may perhaps be more inclined to adopt this framework decision when they retain the authority to tackle these issues as they see fit.

4.3.3.2 *The EU conventions on Extradition*

Recently, two conventions on extradition have been drafted within the EU. *The Convention on Simplified Extradition Procedure between the Member States of the European Union* and the *Convention Relating to Extradition between the Member States of the European Union.*[96] The European Convention on Extradition of 13 December 1957 of the Council of Europe (the European Convention on Extradition) formed the basis of both conventions; it is 'the mother convention'. This means that extradition cannot solely be based on these two conventions but that the European Convention on Extradition is needed for issues not addressed in these two conventions. Both conventions aim to supplement and to facilitate the European Convention on Extradition.

4.3.3.2.1 The Convention on Simplified Extradition Procedure between Member States of the EU

The request for a simplified procedure on extradition emerged from the fact that, in many cases (more than 30 %), the suspect consents to extradition.[97] Since the procedure for extradition was rather long, irrespective of the suspect's consent, a more suitable legal framework was needed to allow quicker extradition. The principle contained in the convention is that, in case of consent by the suspect and agreement

[96] The Convention on Simplified Extradition Procedure between the Member States of the European Union, OJ C 78, 30.3.1995, p. 1. The Convention Relating to Extradition between the Member States of the European Union, OJ C 313, 23.10.1996, p.11.

[97] Convention on Simplified Extradition Procedure between the Member States of the European Union, Explanatory Report, OJ C 375, 12.12.1996, p. 4.

by the competent authority of the requested state, the person is surrendered without a prior request for extradition and without a formal procedure being applied.

The ratione materiae
This convention will generally be applied if the provisional arrest is requested for purposes of extradition, the arrested person consents to the extradition, and this person is not held in custody for another reason in the requested state. Extradition will take place on the basis of the information contained in the request for provisional arrest. Another situation in which this convention may be applied is that the person consents to extradition in the period after the 10-day period but before the expiration of the 40-day period of Article 16 of the European Convention on Extradition and before a request for extradition has been made. A third situation occurs if the person consents to extradition after the requesting state has filed a request. To this effect, the member state has to make a special declaration at the moment of ratification.

The aim of the Convention on Simplified Extradition Procedure is in accordance with the final clauses of the European Convention on Extradition, stating that participating states of the European Convention may only adopt agreements or conventions concerning extradition to facilitate and supplement the European Convention on Extradition. This aim is laid down in Article 1 of the Convention on Simplified Extradition. Article 2 of the convention contains the obligation for member states to surrender persons by applying the simplified procedure of the convention. Two requirements must be fulfilled before the simplified procedure can be applied. Firstly, the consent of the person to be extradited is required in accordance with Articles 6 and 7, and secondly, the requested state has to agree to the application of the simplified procedure in accordance with the rules applicable under national law. The consent of the person involved has to be given voluntarily and with full awareness of the consequences of his consent. The requested state must immediately notify the requesting state as to whether or not the person has consented.

Procedural aspects
The requested state must notify the requesting state within a period of 10 days after the provisional arrest as to whether the person has consented to extradition. The suspected person can also consent, where appropriate, to the renunciation of speciality (Articles 7 and 9). According to Article 9, states can make a declaration stating that the renunciation of speciality is not applicable in the case of a simplified procedure for extradition. This can have two meanings: 1) that the consent automatically includes a renunciation of speciality, or 2) that a renunciation of speciality is only included when the suspected person, when giving his consent, explicitly renounces the protection of the speciality rule. The consent will be recorded and is irrevocable. Extradition takes place as soon as possible but at the latest within 20 days after the decision has been taken. If the person is not extradited within this period, he must be released from custody in the requested state. If, pursuant to Article 9, the speciality principle is no longer applicable, the assent of the requesting state for re-extradition to another member state of the EU is no longer required. In the absence of the speciality principle, the requesting state has the authority to prosecute the person on any

grounds whether they were mentioned in the extradition request or not. Communication takes place between the competent authorities of the states involved.

Article 4 of the convention specifies the information that must be provided by the requesting state to both the person subject to extradition and the competent authorities of the requested state. The competent authorities of the requested state take the decision as to whether the simplified procedure will be applied and they inform the requesting state as soon as possible.

Article 14 simplifies the procedure of Article 21 of the European Convention on Extradition concerning the transit of the extradited person. The application for transit has to be accompanied by the information specified in Article 4. The member states shall indicate, in a statement when ratifying the convention, which authorities must be considered the competent authorities under this convention. The convention enters into force 90 days after all the states that were members at the time of signing have deposited their instruments of ratification. So far, only France and Italy have not ratified this convention.

4.3.3.2.2 The Convention Relating to Extradition between the Member States of the EU

The ratione materiae
A proper functioning of the national justice systems and the will to adjust these systems justified a revision of the most fundamental aspects of extradition between the member states. Therefore, this convention urges substantial changes to the principles of extradition and requires a review of national legislation and sometimes the constitution of member states. In the event of conflict between provisions in this convention with provisions in one of the conventions mentioned in Article 1, the provisions of this convention will prevail. Furthermore, the application of this convention will not affect the application of more favourable extradition agreements.[98] Article 2 reaffirms the requirement of double criminality. An offence is considered an extraditable offence when it is punished with deprivation of liberty for at least twelve months in the requesting state and at least six months in the requested state. The Benelux treaty on extradition allows extradition for acts punishable with a custodial sentence of at least six months in the requesting state. This means that this provision is more favourable for the contracting states of the Benelux treaty and therefore prevails over this convention. Article 3 forms an exception to the requirement of double criminality. When an act is classified in the requesting state as conspiracy or association to commit offences, punishment of these acts in the requested state is not a prerequisite for extradition. The differences in the criminal codes of the different member states relating to conspiracy and association have often resulted in the impossibility to extradite because of the requirement of double criminality. Article 3

[98] Convention Relating to Extradition between the Member States of the European Union, Explanatory Report, OJ C 191, 23.6.1997, p. 13.

tries to remedy this difficulty. There are two requirements for the application of Article 3, namely that the act must be punishable with a maximum custodial sentence of at least 12 months; the second is that the conspiracy or the association was related to one of the serious crimes belonging to the categories of terrorist offences, offences related to organised crime, including drug-trafficking offences, or violent offences. Paragraphs 3 and 4 of this article provide for a reservation to renounce the double criminality requirement.

According to Article 4, extradition may not be refused on the grounds that the deprivation of liberty will be executed in a place other than a penitentiary institution. Article 5 concerns the exception to refuse extradition in the case of political offences. Paragraph 1 of this article states that, when applying this convention, no offence may be regarded as a political offence. Paragraph 2 contains a reservation to paragraph 1 but it states that a reservation concerning an act of terrorism or offences of conspiracy or criminal association to commit serious crimes cannot be made. Article 6 states that extradition should also be granted if, in the requested state, fiscal offences are considered as similar offences as in the requesting state. Article 7 contains another major change to one of the foundations of extradition: it rejects the exception to extradite nationals. Paragraph 2 of this article allows the member states to make a reservation to this provision. Furthermore, this article provides a system that encourages states to review their reservations. According to Articles 8 and 9, extradition may not be refused on the ground of lapse of time or amnesty in the requested state. The second paragraph again contains a provision to make reservations to Article 8. Article 10 concerns the principle of speciality. This principle does not apply when the requesting state wants to prosecute or try the extradited person for an offence other than the one he was extradited for and this offence is not punishable with deprivation of liberty. Furthermore, the requesting state is allowed to prosecute and try the extradited person when he has expressly waived the benefit of the speciality rule after his extradition with regard to offences committed before his extradition even if the offence concerned is punished by deprivation of liberty. Consent has to be given with full respect for the rights of the person extradited. A general waiver of the rule of speciality is not valid but must be expressed with reference to specified offences.

Article 11 is a further mechanism for avoiding the speciality principle. It contains the presumption of consent on the part of the requested state for the exercise of criminal jurisdiction by the requesting state for offences other than the one for which the person is being extradited. In that case, Article 11 replaces the application of Article 10. Re-extradition to a third member state without the consent of the requested state is made possible in Article 12. However, a declaration can be made in which a state derogates from this rule unless the person has consented to the re-extradition or when he has waived the application of the rule of speciality.

Procedural aspects
Article 13 concerns some practical implications such as the indication of a central authority and the use of a facsimile for communication between the central authori-

ties. In a number of member states, the indicated central authority will be the Ministry of Justice. A request for additional information may be directly made to the competent authorities of the requested state by the competent authorities of the requesting state if a declaration is made to this effect. Article 15 contains a provision on the authentication of documents to improve the efficiency of the procedure. The information that has to be provided to a member state through which the transit takes place can be found in Article 16 together with some other formalities relating to transit. Article 17 states that no reservations other than those provided for in the convention itself are allowed. According to Article 18, this convention is to enter into force 90 days after the last ratification of the 15 member states that were members of the EU at the moment of adopting the act establishing the convention. So far, only France and Italy have not yet ratified this convention. Finally, Articles 19 and 20 concern the accession of new member states and the depositary of the convention, respectively.

In conclusion, it can be said that this convention contains far-reaching provisions aiming at mutual recognition and efficient extradition procedures. However, the possibility to make reservations is given to the most revolutionary provisions, and Article 17 states that reservations are also allowed with regard to the other provisions. Thus, the value of the new ideas and the withdrawal of formalities as adopted in this convention depend on how member states use their competence to make reservations to this convention.

4.3.3.3 *The European Arrest Warrant*

The European Arrest Warrant (EAW)[99] is the first serious and constructive attempt in realising the mutual recognition of judicial decisions and judgements that was agreed among the member states during the meeting in Tampere in 1998. However, the mechanism of the EAW reaches further, as it is also applicable in cases where the arrest and the extradition of a person is requested in a pre-trial stage. It further contributes to the realisation of an area of freedom, security, and justice as is laid down in Article 29 EU Treaty.

The ratione materiae

The EAW can be applied to the crimes listed in Article 2 paragraph 2 and includes trafficking in human beings. One of the innovative ideas adopted in the EAW is the abolishment of the double criminality requirement for these crimes. As in the EU the principle of double criminality did not cause major problems with regard to extradition nor with regard to mutual legal assistance in general, as we will see in the next two chapters, it is in line with current practice to abolish this requirement. Paragraph 4 of this article provides the opportunity to apply the double criminality principle for

[99] Council Framework Decision on the European Arrest Warrant and the Surrender Procedures between the Member States, 13 June 2002, OJ L 190, 18.7.2002, pp. 1-20. According to Article 32 the EAW will be fully operational on 1 January 2004.

crimes not included in the list of paragraph 2. The grounds for mandatory non-execution are limited to the case in which the crime is covered by an amnesty, in the case of a final judgement for the same acts for which the extradition is requested, and in case the requested person cannot be held criminally responsible due to his age under the law of the executing member state. Article 4 includes the grounds for the optional non-execution of the EAW which mainly concern the traditional grounds for refusal such as the exception not to extradite nationals, the application of *ne bis in idem,* and cases in which the offence (partly) took place on the territory of the executing state or criminal prosecution or punishment is statute-barred. Furthermore, states may notify the General Secretariat that consent is presumed for the waiver of the principle of speciality (Article 27 EAW). This principle entails that the extradited person can be prosecuted and tried for offences other than the offence for which he is extradited. The waiver of this principle is also presumed in cases described in paragraph 3 of this article. It also remains possible to make the execution of the EAW conditional upon the guarantee that life imprisonment will not be imposed and that a sentence containing the deprivation of liberty shall be executed in the executing state if the person extradited is a national or resident of the executing state.

Procedural aspects

The European Arrest Warrant aims at the arrest and extradition of persons within the EU at the request of a judicial authority of one of the member states with a minimum of formalities. This will be accomplished by avoiding the time-consuming channel for communication via the Ministry of Justice and by direct communication between the judicial authorities and by introducing an absolute time-limit of 90 days between the arrest and the decision to be taken on the extradition of the person when a person does not consent to extradition (Article 17 EAW). If a person does consent to his extradition, the judicial authority takes a decision within 10 days after his provisional arrest. It is not required under the EAW that this judicial authority is a judge and that his decision must be a formal court decision.[100] However, it is assumed that the term 'judicial authority' does not apply to the police authorities. Article 9 and Article 10 of the EAW state that direct communication between the judicial authorities shall take place, or authorities may request the arrest through an arrest warrant in the Schengen Information System. Such a procedure can only be successful when the member states have confidence in each other's legal systems and procedures. Although the member states have declared such confidence, not everyone is convinced of the quality and reliability of the legal systems of some member states.[101] In this regard, the Commission has also expressed its concern and has therefore issued a Green Paper on Procedural Safeguards referred to above.[102] It fol-

[100] For a different opinion, see R. Blekxtoon, Europees Arrestatiebevel, in: *NJB,* Volume 77, issue 22, 2002, pp. 1058-1061.

[101] See, for instance, R. Blekxtoon, Europees Arrestatiebevel, in: *NJB,* Volume 77, issue 22, 2002, pp. 1058-1061.

[102] Green Paper from the Commission on the Procedural Safeguards for Suspects in Criminal Proceedings throughout the European Union, COM(2003) 75 final, Brussels, 19.2.2003. Section 4.2.2.2 above.

lows from these concerns that, although reference is made in the EAW to the European Convention for the Protection of Human Rights and Fundamental Freedoms and the Charter of Fundamental Rights of the European Union, it may not necessarily be the case that all member states respect these rights.

The recently adopted EU Conventions on Extradition, discussed above (when they have entered into force), will still play a role under the EAW although the EAW will replace corresponding provisions of the conventions according to Article 31 EAW. However, the EAW only refers very briefly to extradition cases when the arrested person agrees to be extradited and, for these cases, the Convention on Simplified Extradition Procedure shall remain applicable. Article 17 paragraph 2 EAW states that if a person agrees to the extradition, the decision concerning the execution of the EAW must be taken within 10 days following his consent. Procedural safeguards for the consenting person are provided in Article 13.

This is only a brief overview of the content of the EAW to show how simplified procedures can be adopted and how cooperation in criminal matters on a European level can be facilitated. In Chapter 7, the potential of this mechanism for the improvement of the prosecution of trafficking cases will be specifically examined.

4.3.3.4 *The European Convention on Mutual Assistance in Criminal Matters between the Member States of the European Union and its protocol*

The EU Convention on Mutual Assistance in Criminal Matters[103] was signed on 22 May 2000 and must be considered as another effort to improve judicial cooperation in criminal matters within the EU.[104] This convention is linked to the European Convention on Mutual Assistance in Criminal Matters of the Council of Europe (the European Convention on Mutual Assistance),[105] in the same way as the EU Conventions on extradition with the European Convention on Extradition. This means that this convention supplements and facilitates the application of the European Convention on Mutual Assistance and its protocols and that matters not covered by this convention will be resolved in accordance with the European Convention on Mutual Assistance. Furthermore, it supplements and facilitates the application of the Convention of 19 June 1990 implementing the Schengen Agreement of 14 June 1985 (the Schengen Convention) and the Benelux Treaty on Extradition and Mutual Assistance in Criminal Matters. More favourable provisions always take precedence over the less favourable. The convention aims to find a balance between strengthen-

---

[103] Convention Established by the Council in Accordance with Article 34 of the Treaty on European Union, on Mutual Assistance in Criminal Matters between the Member States of the EU, Brussels, 22 May 2000, 7846/1/00 Rev 1, OJ C 197, 12.7.2000, p. 3.

[104] For an historical overview of the establishment of the Convention on Mutual Assistance, see G. Vermeulen, *Wederzijdse rechtshulp in strafzaken in de Europese Unie: naar een volwaardige eigen rechtshulpruimte voor de Lid-Staten?* Maklu, Antwerpen, 1999, pp. 35-53.

[105] The European Convention on Mutual Assistance in Criminal Matters of the Council of Europe will be discussed in Section 4.3.4.2.

ing judicial cooperation and the principle of proportionality. Under certain circumstances, proceedings brought before the administrative authorities will also profit from mutual assistance.

The ratione materiae
Controlled deliveries (Article 12) may be requested for and will be permitted in the framework of criminal investigations into extraditable offences. The competent authorities of the requested state will take decisions on these requests, which will be executed in accordance with the national law of the requested state. According to Article 13, joint investigation teams may be set up, by mutual agreement of the competent authorities of two or more member states, for a specific purpose and a limited period of time to carry out criminal investigations in one or more of the member states involved. This can be done when several member states have initiated investigations but a coordinated investigation will be more efficient because the acts being investigated are linked, or if a state has initiated an investigation but the criminal act clearly has links with other states, which is the case in many trafficking cases.

The joint teams will operate in the states setting up the team under the conditions stipulated in paragraph 3. The operations of the team will be carried out in accordance with the national law of the state on whose territory the operation takes place. Members of the joint team may ask the competent authorities of their state to take investigative measures. This state shall consider these measures as if they were requested as part of a national investigation. If assistance is required from a member state other than the member states that set up the joint team or from another third state, the competent authorities of the state of operation make the request to the competent authorities of the other state. Persons other than representatives of the competent authorities of the member states that set up the joint team can take part in the activities of the team as far as it is in accordance with their national law or the provisions of any legal instrument applicable between them. Member states may request assistance in undercover operations (Article 14). Specifications of the undercover operation will be subject to agreement between the requesting and the requested state. Article 10 provides that member states may also agree on the possibility of hearing an accused person by video conference. Hearings by video conference can only take place with the consent of the accused person (Article 10 paragraph 9). Article 11 provides for the hearing of witnesses and experts by telephone conference. The requested state as well as the witnesses or experts have to agree that this method can be used. According to Article 8, the restitution of articles obtained by illegal means may be subject to a request. If a person in custody has to be temporarily transferred (Article 9), for the purpose of the investigation, from the requested state to the requesting state, a request to this effect can be submitted. An agreement will be made including the practical implications of the temporary transfer. The consent of the person in custody is required if a member state has made a declaration to this effect.

Procedural aspects
Generally, the formalities and procedures indicated by the requesting state must be taken into account unless this convention contains provisions on this matter. This means the introduction of the principle of *forum regit actum*.[106] The requested state must execute the request as soon as possible. If the request cannot be complied with, the requested state contacts the requesting state immediately and they may subsequently agree on further action to be taken concerning the request (Article 4 paragraph 3). Procedural documents are normally send by post unless the address of the person is unknown, the law in the requesting member state requires proof of service other than the fact that it was posted, it has been impossible to serve the document by post, or the requesting member state has shown that sending the documents by post is ineffective or inappropriate. In these cases, the documents are sent through the competent authorities of the requested state. The document or the relevant passages must be served on the addressee in a language he understands. Requests must be made in writing and will be communicated between the judicial authorities with territorial competence for initiating and executing the request. This provision has no effect for the United Kingdom and Ireland when they make a declaration to this effect. In urgent cases, the request may be made via Interpol. Requests for the temporary transfer or transit of persons held in custody or notices of information from judicial records will be communicated via the central authorities of the member states involved. Spontaneous exchange of information may take place in accordance with the law of the providing state by the competent authorities. The providing authority may impose conditions on the use of this information, which are binding for the receiving authority.

The hearing of a witness or expert by the judicial authorities in another member state will take place by video conference if it is not desirable or possible for the person to be heard in person. If the technical equipment is not available in the requested state, the requesting state must make available the technical means by mutual agreement. Article 10 paragraphs 3-8 contain the rules of procedure for a video conference.

Judicial or equally competent authorities may make a request for interception, recording and immediate transmission of telecommunications in accordance with the national law of the requesting state. The requirements for such a request are stated in Article 18. According to Article 19, the interception of telecommunications by service providers can be subject to a request for mutual assistance to the state on whose territory the gateway is located. When interception takes place on the territory of another member state without the technical assistance of this member state, the intercepting state must notify this state prior to the interception or immediately after it is aware of the fact that it is operating on the territory of another state. The judicial or equivalent competent authorities of the notified state must immediately reply to the intercepting state after they have received the notification to allow or continue the

[106] See Chapter 5, Section 5.3.1.1.

interception. This reply shall contain a requirement not to carry out the interception or to terminate the interception, or a requirement that any intercepted material is not used or is used under certain conditions, or a requirement for a short extension before replying to the intercepting state. In the meantime, the intercepting state may generally continue its interception but may not use the material already intercepted. Personal data communicated between states or obtained in another way will only be used for the purpose of proceedings, in case of serious threat to public security, or for other purposes, with the consent of the providing state. The convention enters into force 90 days after eight member states, which were member states at the moment of adopting the act establishing this convention by the Council, have ratified this convention. So far, only Denmark, Portugal and Spain have ratified this convention. The provisions referred to in Article 2 paragraph 1 of this convention are also applicable to Iceland and Norway.

On 16 October 2001, a protocol to the EU Convention on Mutual Assistance was adopted in order to facilitate the search for and the tracing of bank accounts in other member states. It roughly concerns three obligations, namely to execute a request concerning bank account data, to execute a request concerning information on bank transfers, and to execute a request concerning bank transaction supervision. Double criminality as a ground for refusal remains, but national rules on banking secrecy or the fiscal offence exception are no longer accepted as grounds for refusal. This will be a great advantage since the fiscal offence exception may still be problematic in some cases, as we will see in Chapter 6.

The requirements pertaining to the request are included in the protocol and are rather elaborate, including, e.g., the grounds on the basis of which the requesting state may argue that banks in the requested state are involved. Furthermore, a provision on the confidential use of the provided information was adopted as well. However, it is a missed opportunity as rules concerning seizure and confiscation of bank accounts are not included in the protocol, as this is closely related to the subject of this protocol.

4.3.3.5 *Police and judicial cooperation under the Schengen Convention*

Title III of the Schengen Convention concerns police and security. Beside the provisions in the Schengen Convention, the issue of police and judicial cooperation is dealt with in many decisions and statements of the Schengen Executive Committee and the working groups and organisations authorised by this Executive Committee to take decisions. However, an exhaustive overview of these provisions, decisions, and statements is beyond the aim of this study and would be impossible because some of these documents are still considered to be confidential. Therefore, only the provisions in the Schengen Convention concerning police and judicial cooperation are discussed hereafter.

The ratione materiae

Article 39 of the Schengen Convention concerns mutual assistance and direct information exchange between police services. It is a simplification of the procedure for information exchange; the prior authorisation of another body is no longer required.[107] Article 40 of the Schengen Convention rules cross-border surveillance. Article 46 concerns spontaneous information exchange via a central organisation especially designed for this task. This form of information exchange normally takes place for the purpose of maintaining public order. According to Article 47, liaison officers, 'Schengen liaison officers', can be established on the basis of bilateral agreements. The task of the liaison officers is to improve cooperation between these states and to provide advice and assistance in the hosting state. Articles 48 to 53 of the Schengen Convention concern mutual assistance in criminal matters and supplement the 1959 European Convention on Mutual Assistance in Criminal Matters and the Benelux Treaty on Extradition and Mutual Assistance. The *non bis in idem* principle is set out in Articles 54 to 58. Article 54 deals with the applicability of this principle while Article 55 contains the exceptions. Chapter 4 of the Schengen Convention (Articles 59 to 66) contains the provisions on extradition and refers to the 1957 European Convention on Extradition and the Benelux Treaty on Extradition and Mutual Assistance. Its provisions are even binding upon states that are not party to the 1957 Convention. According to Article 62, amnesty granted by the requested state will not prevent extradition. Articles 67 to 69 concern the transfer of the execution of criminal judgements and supplement the European Convention on the Transfer of Sentenced Persons of 1983.

Procedural aspects

The procedure for trans-frontier observation and hot pursuit is rather complicated. If another Schengen state has authorised trans-frontier observation, police officers carrying out surveillance with respect to an extraditable offence are allowed to continue their action in this Schengen state. A prior request for such action is required except in the case of emergency. Further conditions for this continued action are elaborately dealt with in paragraph 3 of this article. Article 41 of the Schengen Convention concerns cross-border pursuit. In contrast to cross-border surveillance, the continued cross-border pursuit generally takes place without the prior authorisation of the other Schengen state. Each state is allowed to impose its own conditions on the penetration of its territory by police forces from other Schengen states.[108] All these different conditions in the different Schengen states lead to confusion during operations on foreign territory and obstruct a clear implementation and execution of this activity. Articles 42 and 43 contain some additional provisions to be taken into

[107] M. den Boer, Incorporation without Change? Police Cooperation from Schengen to the EU, paper presented at the Madrid Seminar on Immigration, Asylum and Border Controls, 21-25 February 2000, not published, p. 3.

[108] M. den Boer, Incorporation without Change? Police Cooperation from Schengen to the EU, paper presented at the Madrid Seminar on Immigration, Asylum and Border Controls, 21-25 February 2000, not published, p. 6.

account when executing cross-border surveillance or hot pursuit. Article 44 contains the obligation for the Schengen states to set up means for communication to facilitate police and customs cooperation. Article 49 concerns the applicability of the provisions on mutual assistance. According to Article 51, the conditions that may be imposed on the admissibility of letters rogatory for search or seizure are double criminality and consistency with national law. Procedural documents, such as a summons to appear before a court may be sent directly to the person by post. If the summons to appear addressed to a witness or expert contains a notice of penalty, this penalty cannot be imposed in the requested state (Article 52). According to Article 53, requests for assistance may be communicated directly between legal authorities, except for requests for the temporary transfer or transit of persons in custody, which must be communicated via the Ministries of Justice. The requests for extradition and for transit will be communicated between the Ministries of Justice or Foreign Affairs of the states involved. Article 66 can be seen as a predecessor of the new EU Convention on simplified extradition procedure. It states that no formal extradition procedures need to be applied when the person to be extradited consents to his extradition.

If we compare the Schengen Convention with the recently enacted conventions within the EU on extradition and mutual assistance and the EAW, discussed above, we see that the Schengen Convention is more conservative. Although it contains provisions that transform current principles in cooperation in criminal matters, they are not so revolutionary as the new documents. For instance, in some cases, direct communication between the competent authorities is adopted in the Schengen Convention but in case of extradition, the communication takes place via the Ministries of Justice or of Foreign Affairs. In the new EU documents, direct communication is the prescribed communication channel.

4.3.3.6 *Proposal for a Council Directive on the Short-Term Residence Permit*[109]

Since the Treaty of Amsterdam, visas, asylum, immigration, and other issues related to the free movement of persons have moved from the third to the first pillar. The provisions on visas, asylum, immigration, and other related areas of free movement of persons are Communautarised in Title IV of the EC Treaty. It is clear that Article 61, paragraphs a and b, and Article 63 open the way for a European immigration law.[110] The main aim of this title is the abolition of all internal border controls and to shift these controls to the external borders. In this sense, migration law is connected to trafficking in persons and it must be admitted that the free movement of persons can be counterproductive in the fight against trafficking in persons: it may

[109] Proposal for Council Directive on the Short-Term Residence Permit Issued to Victims of Action to Facilitate Illegal Immigration of Trafficking in Human Beings who Cooperate with the Competent Authorities, COM(2002) 71 final, Brussels, 11.02.2002.

[110] R. Barents, *Het Verdrag van Amsterdam in werking,* Europese Monografieën 62, Kluwer, Deventer, 1999, pp. 349-375.

be to the advantage of the traffickers that the persons being trafficked do not need to fulfil formalities when moving to another EU country once they have entered the EU. Another direct connection between trafficking in persons and the first pillar is the Proposal for a Council Directive on the Short-Term Residence Permit, which will be discussed below.

The proposed directive aims to strengthen the instruments for combating illegal immigration by introducing a residence permit for the victims of action, facilitating illegal immigration and trafficking in persons and to encourage them to cooperate with the competent authorities against those suspected of committing the crimes in question. It states explicitly and on several occasions that it is not aiming at the protection of the victims or witnesses of trafficking in persons, although the witness protection programmes of some of the EU member states and other documents concerning the protection of victims and witnesses are often referred to. Furthermore, the proposal includes many provisions that seem to be specifically drafted for the protection of victims. The most important is the introduction of a temporary residence permit for victims who cooperate with the judicial authorities in criminal matters. Witnesses who are not (yet) victims of the crime of trafficking seem to have been forgotten. The protection that can be obtained from this proposed directive is rather elaborate, apparently based on Article 6 of the Trafficking Protocol to the UNCTOC; it includes social, financial, legal, psychological, and medical aid. Furthermore, the victims are allowed to work and to receive education on the basis of their temporary residence permit. Special programmes must be set up for reintegration, either in the country of origin or the country of residence if the permit is extended. It is regrettable that it is not recognised in the proposed directive that these provisions are set up for the protection of victims and that witnesses cannot claim protection under this directive if they are not (yet) victims of trafficking. It would have been more in accordance with its content if the interest in criminal proceedings had been given greater perspective. Furthermore, trafficking in persons is seen, in the proposal, as part of illegal immigration. Therefore, the addressee of this directive always stays without a valid permit in one of the EU states. Consequently nationals of other EU member states cannot invoke this proposed directive, following the free movement of persons within the EU. This is a great obstacle and will even become greater when, in the near future, after the enlargement in 2004, many countries of origin will be members of the EU. Besides, when victims do cooperate, they can only be granted a temporary residence permit. This means that the victim will ultimately have to leave the country. This is not a very attractive perspective for the victim if she does not want to return to her home country. Therefore, under certain conditions, a permanent residence permit should be considered for such victims.

4.3.3.7 *Some new developments adopted in the legal instruments*

The legal instruments discussed above reflect the will to improve the cooperation in criminal matters within the EU. Some remarkable developments in the transformation of the use of current principles are codified in these conventions to facilitate cooperation in criminal matters and will be briefly discussed in this section. To what extent this transformation of the use of the current principles facilitates the prosecution of trafficking cases will be examined in Chapter 7.

Firstly, the principle of double criminality is not strictly upheld in the EAW, nor in Article 3 of the convention relating to extradition, although a reservation to this clause is possible.

Secondly, the strength of the traditional exceptions to the extradition principle has declined. The EAW and Article 7 of the convention relating to extradition allow the extradition of a state's own nationals. Furthermore, the use of the political and fiscal offence exceptions as grounds to refuse extradition is limited in Articles 5 and 6, respectively, of the convention relating to extradition. Although reservations to these provisions are allowed, the possibility to make a reservation to Article 5 is very limited.

A third major development is the transformation of the principle of speciality. Both EU conventions on extradition contain a provision that the person to be extradited can waive the application of this principle. Articles 7 and 9 of the Convention on Simplified Extradition Procedure and Article 10 of the Convention Relating to Extradition concern this issue. In the EAW, the application of this principle is also limited. A related issue is that re-extradition can take place without the consent of the requested state, which was normally required. The Convention Relating to Extradition even goes further by adopting the presumption of consent from the requesting state to prosecute the extradited person for offences other than the one for which he is extradited.

In addition, some major changes have also been codified in the EU Convention on Mutual Assistance. In general, these changes relate to simplifying the possibility to take operational measures on the territory of another state. This is, for example, the case for the joint investigation teams under Article 13 and the possibilities for intercepting service providers in another state as provided in Article 19. Furthermore, new possibilities are created to facilitate the hearing of experts, witnesses, victims, and accused persons by video conference or telephone conference.

Finally, the idea of the establishment of an EPP in the Draft Constitution of the European Convention can be seen as a first attempt to transfer some operational powers in criminal matters to the EU level. Therefore, the adoption of this idea in the Draft Constitution must be considered revolutionary. However, it remains to be seen whether this idea will be adopted in the final version of a new Convention that will be negotiated from the second half of 2003 to May 2004 by the Intergovernmental Conference.

When reviewing all these developments, the impression is given that the member states of the EU are really willing to improve cooperation in the area of freedom, security, and justice at the cost of their own control over cooperation in criminal matters on their own territory. These developments all facilitate the enforcement of legal instruments on cooperation in criminal matters directly and thus indirectly help the enforcement of the prosecution of trafficking in persons. However, for the moment, it is too early to be too optimistic because, so far, France and Italy have not ratified the two EU Conventions on Extradition, and the EU Convention on Mutual Assistance has so far only been ratified by Denmark, Spain, and Portugal, while its protocol has had no ratifications. Consequently, these conventions have not yet entered into force. Furthermore, the number of states party to these conventions can only be enlarged with the enlargement of the EU. This means that there are no possibilities for third states not belonging to the group of applicant countries to become party to these conventions. Moreover, states can always make reservations to the most far-reaching provisions in these conventions and thus invalidate the progressive developments discussed here. Besides, the idea for an EPP is currently in the draft stage and it is uncertain whether states will be inclined to adopt this provision in the final version.

4.3.4 **Legal instruments of the Council of Europe**

The central aim of the Council of Europe is to create greater unity among its member states. Therefore, it has adopted a whole list of conventions and numerous other documents. In this section, the conventions that facilitate police and judicial cooperation, and thus the prosecution of trafficking in persons, will be discussed.[111]

4.3.4.1 *The European Convention on Extradition*[112]

The ratione materiae
The total number of ratifications to the Convention is 45. One state did sign the Convention but did not ratify it.

According to Article 2, double criminality is one of the prerequisites for extradition. In both the requesting and the requested state, the act must be punishable by deprivation of liberty or under a detention order for a maximum period of at least one year or by a more severe penalty. Together with Article 1, it contains an obligation to extradite. This means that the requested state has no discretionary power to grant or refuse extradition as the exceptions to the obligation to extradite are listed exhaustively in the Convention.[113] According to Articles 3, 4, and 5, extradition may not be granted in the case of political offences, offences under military law, and if the requested state has substantial grounds to believe that extradition is being requested for the purpose of prosecuting a person on account of his race, religion, na-

---

[111] For an elaborate overview of the most important treaties established within the Council of Europe and the EU, see G. Corstens and J. Praedel, *European Criminal Law,* Kluwer Law International, The Hague, 2002, pp. 61-215.

[112] European Convention on Extradition, Paris, 13 December 1957, ETS no. 024.

[113] Explanatory Report to the European Convention on Extradition, <http://conventions.coe.int/Treaty/EN/cadreprincipal.htm>.

tionality, or political opinion. An attempt on the life of a head of state or a member of his family is not considered to be a political offence and, in such a case, extradition is compulsory. Furthermore, the requested state may refuse the extradition of its own nationals but then the requested state must submit the case to its competent authorities at the request of the requesting state (Article 6). This can be considered a form of *aut dedere aut judicare.* A state may also refuse the extradition of a person if the *locus delicti* is wholly or partly within its territory. In some countries, extradition is not allowed when the offence has been committed outside the territory of the requesting state. According to the convention, this exception cannot be made unless the laws of the requested state do not authorise prosecution for a similar offence committed outside its territory or for the offence which is the subject of the request. It has to be avoided that different states commence actions for the same offence. Therefore, extradition may be refused if the requested state has already begun a procedure against the person whose extradition is requested. Another exception clause is *non bis in idem,* which means that extradition cannot be granted if a final judgement has been delivered against the person claimed in respect of the offences for which extradition is requested (Article 9). Furthermore, the time for prosecution or punishment may not have lapsed. The possibility that the death penalty may be implemented after extradition is another reason to refuse extradition, even if the death penalty is not provided for or normally not carried out for the extraditable offence in the requested state.

Procedural aspects
As a rule, a request for extradition is communicated via diplomatic channels, accompanied by the necessary documents. In most states, a judicial authority must take the decision. The extradited person can only be prosecuted for the acts for which he is extradited unless the extraditing state has given its consent to prosecution for other offences as well. The extradited person may not be re-extradited to a third state without the consent of the requested state (Article 15). The principle of speciality fully applies in this convention. A request for provisional arrest can be made to any other contracting state in the case of urgency. This provisional arrest shall terminate after 18 days if no request for extradition is received (Article 16). Property that can serve as evidence can be handed over to the requesting state as well. Other conditions and rules of procedure are provided in the convention but it is beyond the scope of this section to discuss them in depth.[114] This convention can be seen as a minimum standard for extradition. Participating states are free to conclude bilateral or other multilateral agreements concerning extradition as long as they supplement or facilitate the application of the principles in this convention. The member states of the European Union have recently concluded such agreements.

Two additional protocols were added to the convention.[115] The first protocol concerns Articles 3 and 9, on political offences and the principle of *non bis in idem,* re-

[114] This concerns, among other things, the way of transit, the language to be used, and expenses.

[115] Additional Protocol to the European Convention on Extradition, 15 October 1975, ETS no. 086

spectively. In the first Chapter of this protocol, some exceptions to the concept of political offences are provided. Violations of the laws of war were excluded from the definition of a political offence. Article 9 was amended with 3 paragraphs extending the possibilities to refuse extradition on the basis of earlier judgements. When the person has been convicted for the same acts in another contracting state, extradition must not be granted. The second protocol mainly concerns Article 5 of the convention, i.e., fiscal offences. It contains a limitation to the fiscal offence exception. Besides, some minor changes to the convention were adopted in the protocol. An amendment was made to Article 12, which states that the request must be in writing and must be addressed by the Ministry of Justice of the requesting state to the Ministry of Justice of the requested state. However, the use of diplomatic channels is not excluded.

4.3.4.2 *The European Convention on Mutual Assistance in Criminal Matters*[116]

The ratione materiae

This Convention has had 42 ratifications and 2 signatures not followed by ratification.

Mutual assistance in this convention pertains to both letters rogatory and to other requests for mutual assistance.[117] The convention is not limited to the forms of mutual assistance mentioned in the convention, but it covers all forms of mutual legal assistance. The contracting states undertake to afford the widest measure of mutual assistance. This may be refused in case of political or fiscal offences or if the requested state is of the opinion that assistance will violate its sovereignty, public order, or other essential interests. Letters rogatory contain requests relating to a criminal matter for the purpose of procuring evidence or transmitting articles to be produced in evidence, records or documents. These requests are dealt with by the requested state in accordance with its law. Letters rogatory in this article means a mandate given by a judicial authority of one country to a foreign judicial authority to perform in its place one or more specified actions, for instance, the hearing of witnesses, experts, or accused persons. Article 4 gives the authorities of the requesting state the possibility to be present when the requested activities are carried out in the requested state. According to Article 5, special conditions may be specified for a request to search or to seize property. Mutual assistance also includes the service of writs, and records of judicial verdicts. Service has to be understood in a broad sense as referring to both simple transmission and official notification. The document need not be personally handed to the person to be served. Furthermore, it includes the appearance of witnesses, experts, and prosecuted persons. If a person fails to respond to a

---

and Second Additional Protocol to the European Convention on Extradition, 17 March 1978, ETS no. 098, respectively

[116] European Convention on Mutual Assistance in Criminal Matters, Strasbourg, 20 April 1959, ETS no. 030.

[117] Explanatory Report to the European Convention on Mutual Assistance in Criminal Matters, <http://conventions.coe.int/Treaty/EN/cadreprincipal.htm>.

summons to appear, the possible penalty or fine that follows cannot be enforced in the requested state. Furthermore, some procedural issues are addressed in the convention such as the expenses and allowances to be refunded, the content of the summonses or requests, the hearing of a person in custody, the transfer, and the content of a letter rogatory. A witness or expert visiting the requesting state appearing before the judicial authorities may not be prosecuted or detained for acts anterior to his departure from the requested state. Information relating to judicial records (of the civil courts or administrative authorities) must be communicated, if so requested by the state concerned, upon the same conditions as they would be communicated to its own judicial authorities.

Procedural aspects
Chapter V contains the procedural conditions for mutual assistance in general. Letters rogatory and requests for the personal appearance of a person in custody are generally communicated between the Ministries of Justice of the states involved. In urgent cases the letters may be addressed directly to the judicial authorities, as is the case for requests for extracts from, and information relating to, judicial records. However, after the execution of letters rogatory, the Ministry of Justice of the requested state must return rogatory documents to the Ministry of Justice of the requesting state. Requests for mutual assistance other than letters rogatory, such as, requests for investigations preliminary to prosecution made by the public prosecutor and the service of writs, can be communicated directly between the judicial authorities. However, regardless of the channel adopted to communicate the requests, states can always use diplomatic channels if they think it is necessary or freely to choose the channel they think most appropriate in that case (Article 15 paragraph 6). Article 22 introduces the rule of automatic communication of information from judicial criminal records of nationals of other contracting states. The contracting states may conclude multilateral and bilateral agreements on matters of mutual assistance as far as they supplement the convention or facilitate the application of the provisions of the convention, as we have seen in Section 4.3.3.4. The member states of the EU have recently concluded a Convention on Mutual Assistance between the Member States of the EU, supplementing and facilitating this convention.

In 1978, an additional protocol to the European Convention on Mutual Assistance in Criminal Matters was adopted.[118] The protocol mainly concerns fiscal offences and states that mutual assistance may not be refused solely on the ground that something is considered to be a fiscal offence. If double criminality is required for the search and seizure of property in the case of fiscal offences, this requirement is fulfilled when the legislation of the states involved contain similar provisions.

---

[118] Additional Protocol to the European Convention on Mutual Assistance in Criminal Matters, Strasbourg, 17 March 1978, concerning fiscal offences and certain other aspects, ETS no. 099.

In November 2001, an important second additional protocol to the European Convention on Mutual Assistance in Criminal Matters was adopted.[119] So far, only Albania and Denmark have ratified this protocol and since three ratifications are required, the protocol has not yet entered into force. According to the summary of the protocol, it is intended to:[120]

> improve States' ability to react to cross-border crime in the light of political and social developments in Europe and technological developments throughout the world. It will therefore serve to improve and supplement the 1959 Convention on Mutual Assistance and the 1978 Additional Protocol to it, in particular by broadening the range of situations in which mutual assistance may be requested and making the provision of assistance easier, quicker and more flexible. It also takes account of the need to protect individual rights in the processing of personal data.

To this end, the protocol has adopted provisions that are largely based on (and sometimes duplicates of) instruments on mutual assistance that were adopted within the EU, in particular the EU Convention on Mutual Assistance and the Schengen Convention. The most important provisions included in the protocol are those on the use of direct communication (Article 4), hearing by video conference (Article 9), hearing by telephone conference (Article 10), cross-border observations (Article 17), controlled delivery (Article 18), covert investigations (Article 19), and joint investigation teams (Article 20). When this protocol enters into force, the far-reaching provisions that have just been adopted within the EU can also be applied in relations with member states of the Council of Europe, which is a significant advantage.

4.3.4.3 *The Convention on the Transfer of Sentenced Persons*[121]

The ratione materiae

This convention has been signed by one state that did not ratify the convention and it has 53 ratifications. Twelve non-member states of the Council of Europe, including Australia, the United States, Canada, and Israel, have ratified it.

The convention applies only to a punishment or measure, which involves deprivation of liberty. According to Article 2, the sentenced person must be transferred to another state in order to serve the sentence imposed on him. The main aim of the convention is to facilitate the transfer of foreign prisoners to their home countries so that they can serve the sentence there.[122] Sentenced persons may express their interest to the effect that it might facilitate the social rehabilitation of perpetrators if they can serve their sentence in their own country. Absence of language barriers, contacts

---

[119] Second Additional Protocol to the European Convention on Mutual Assistance in Criminal Matters, Strasbourg, 8 November 2001, ETS no.182.

[120] <http://conventions.coe.int/Treaty/en/Summaries/Html/182.htm>.

[121] Convention on the Transfer of Sentenced Persons, Strasbourg, 21 March 1983, ETS no. 112.

[122] Explanatory Report to the Convention on the Transfer of Sentenced Persons, <http://conventions.coe.int/Treaty/EN/cadreprincipal.htm>.

with relatives, and being subject to their own culture and customs may contribute to rehabilitation. According to Article 3 the transfer may only take place

- if the sentenced person is a national of the country he is transferred to;
- if the judgement is final;
- if the sentence is indeterminate or more than six months is left of the sentence at the moment the request is received;
- if the transfer is consented to by the sentenced person;
- if the requirement of double criminality is met, and
- if both states agree to the transfer.

The consent of the person concerned is necessary because otherwise the effect of rehabilitation is nil. The consent has to be given freely and voluntarily with full knowledge of the legal consequences of the decision. For the requirement of double criminality, it is not necessary that the act is punishable in exactly the same way and that it constitutes the same criminal offence. In case of continued enforcement, the administering state is bound by the legal nature and duration of the sentence as determined by the sentencing state. Nevertheless, the sanction may be adapted by a court or administrative order if the duration or nature of the sentence is incompatible with the law of the administering state. If the sentence is converted, the administering state is bound by the findings of the facts from the judgement in the sentencing state. A sanction involving deprivation of liberty may not be converted to a pecuniary sanction. In both procedures, the punishment may not be aggravated and the procedure is subject to the law of the administering state. Review of the judgement can only take place in the sentencing state.

Procedural aspects

The initiative to transfer has to be taken by the sentencing state, which informs the administering state (the state to which the sentenced person is transferred), if the sentenced person wishes to be transferred, although the transfer can also take place at the request of the administering state. The sentenced person is informed about the progress of the procedure. Unless otherwise agreed, all communication takes place from the Ministry of Justice of the administering state to the Ministry of Justice of the sentencing state. If so requested by the sentencing state, the administering state includes documents that indicate to what extent the requirements of Article 3 paragraph 1 are fulfilled. The sentencing state provides the administering state with a certified copy of the judgement and the law on which it is based, a statement indicating how much of the sentence has already been served, a declaration containing the consent of the person to be transferred, and medical or social reports on the sentenced person. Pursuant to Article 9, the administering state either continues the enforcement of the sentence or converts the sentence, through a judicial or administrative procedure, into a decision of that state. It informs the sentencing state in advance as to which of the two procedures should be taken. Contracting states can exclude the application of one of these procedures in a general way in accordance with Article 3. After the transfer, the administering state is obliged to inform the sentencing state about the expected termination of the sentence, if the person has escaped custody or if the sentencing state asks for a report (Article 15). The permission of the states of transit is required to transport the person. A special request to that effect has to be sent to the states of transit. Transit through the airspace of a state does not require the permission of that state unless a landing in its territory is scheduled. Formalities concerning language and costs are dealt with in Article 17.

An additional protocol to the Convention on the Transfer of Sentenced Persons concerns the transfer of nationals.[123] Under certain circumstances, a state may be requested to transfer its own nationals, for example, when the sentenced person has fled to his own state and has to serve a penalty in the sentencing state. In these cases, the consent of the sentenced person is not required. Furthermore, the protocol contains provisions for a sentenced person who is released from prison and is afterwards expelled or deported from the sentencing state.

4.3.4.4 *The Convention on Laundering, Search, Seizure and Confiscation of the Proceeds from Crime*[124]

The ratione materiae

This convention has been signed by 4 states that have not ratified the convention. The total number of ratifications is 41. Australia and Monaco are the only non-member states of the Council of Europe who have signed and ratified the convention.

According to the explanatory text, the aim of the convention is 'to facilitate international cooperation as regards investigative assistance, search, seizure and confiscation of the proceeds from all types of criminality, especially serious crimes, and in particular drug offences, arms dealing, terrorist offences, trafficking in children and young women and other offences which generate large profits'.[125] The national laws of the states differ widely and sometimes legal measures on confiscation or proceeds are absent. Criminals use this situation to avoid punishment. The convention starts with the definitions of the terms used in this document. The obligation of the participating states is to adopt legislative and other measures necessary to enable the confiscation of instrumentalities and proceeds or property of which the value corresponds to such proceeds. The contracting states can adopt a list of offences that are subject to this obligation. The tracing of property that is liable to confiscation must be facilitated. Legislative and other measures must create the possibility that bank, financial, or commercial records must be made available or can be seized. Bank secrecy may not be invoked to refuse the application of these rules. According to Article 4 paragraph 2, special investigative techniques may be used to facilitate the identification and tracing of proceeds and the gathering of evidence related

[123] Additional Protocol to the Convention on the Transfer of Sentenced Persons, Strasbourg, 18 December 1997, ETS no. 167.

[124] Convention on Laundering, Search, Seizure and Confiscation of the Proceeds from Crime, Strasbourg, 8 December 1990, ETS no. 141.

[125] Explanatory Report to the Convention on Laundering, Search, Seizure and Confiscation of the Proceeds from Crime, <http://conventions.coe.int/Treaty/EN/cadreprincipal.htm>.

thereto. Special investigative techniques such as monitoring orders (judicial orders to a financial institution to provide information about transactions), observation, interception of telecommunications, access to computer systems, and orders to produce specific documents are mentioned here. Article 6 paragraph 1 describes four cases that must be considered as laundering offences and which must be punishable by law. The subjective element in some of the cases, namely that the person must know that the property constitutes proceeds of a criminal offence, will be inferred from objective, factual circumstances. It is not necessary that the state where the laundering offence took place has jurisdiction over the predicate offence.

International cooperation is considered essential to combat laundering offences and is mainly dealt with in Chapter III of the convention. The contracting states have to cooperate with each other to the widest extent possible. Legislative and other measures in the contracting states must contribute to the realisation of investigative assistance and confiscation of property and other proceeds of crime. Assistance is also required for the identification and tracing of instrumentalities, proceeds and other property liable to confiscation (Article 8). The assistance must be rendered in accordance with the national law of the requested state. This means that differences in the rendering of assistance remain. Spontaneous information exchange, without a prior request, is introduced in this convention. A state must take the necessary provisional measures, such as freezing or seizing, which are needed to facilitate confiscation or seizure by another state at a later stage even if the state has not yet received a request from another state.

A state can make a request for the confiscation of instruments or proceeds from offences to another state. This request has to be ordered by the court of the requesting state or the requested state has to forward it to its own appropriate authorities in order to obtain such an order to confiscate (Article 13). In some cases, the requested state must pay a sum equivalent to the value of the property confiscated; this is a second system of confiscation. Confiscation must take place in accordance with the law in the requested state that is bound by the findings as to the facts insofar as they are provided by the requesting state (Article 14 (2)). Article 18 gives the grounds by which to refuse cooperation with other states. Refusal is allowed if assistance would be a violation of the fundamental principles of the legal system, the sovereignty, security, public order, or other essential interests of the requested state. Furthermore, refusal is allowed if the requested state thinks that the action is not proportional, is in contradiction with the principle of *ne bis in idem,* does not fulfil the requirement of double criminality, or is related to a political or fiscal offence. Article 18 paragraph 4 lists some additional grounds for refusal. The enactment of a requested action may be postponed if such action would prejudice investigations or proceedings by the authorities of the requested state. Consequently, the requested state, in some cases, has to conduct a supplementary investigation to find out whether refusal or postponement is allowed. The requested state is always bound to consider whether the request may be granted partially or subject to conditions, before refusing cooperation. For cooperation with third parties, special provisions are set out in Articles 21, 22, and 23. Any person affected by the enforcement of a confiscation order or involved in confiscation proceedings under Article 13 paragraph 1.b, but who is not the offender, may be considered as a third party. A central authority, responsible for the execution of the requests, must be established in each of the contracting states.

Procedural aspects

Normally, communication between the requesting and the requested state takes place between the central authorities except in urgent cases, when the judicial authorities of the requesting state may communicate directly to the central authorities of the requested state. A request may also be made through Interpol. Only in exceptional cases may communication take place between the competent authorities of the requesting and the requested state directly. In Article 27 and Article 28, the formalities for a request are listed, which mainly concern data which are necessary for an efficient and smooth execution of the request. A decision other than compliance with the request has to be justified by the requested state and the grounds therefore have to be given. Any effort made towards the execution of the request has to be reported by the requested state to the requesting state. The requesting state must inform the requested state of any changes in the enforceability of the confiscation. The requested state may impose conditions on the execution of the request. Both states can propose suggestions on the confidentiality of the request and the results of the execution of the request but the degree of confidentiality in international cooperation is similar to the degree of confidentiality in national cases. The condition that the conclusion of bilateral and multilateral agreements on this subject may only take place to supplement and strengthen this convention or to facilitate its application is laid down in Article 39.

4.3.4.5 *The European Convention on the Transfer of Proceedings in Criminal Matters*[126]

The ratione materiae

Fourteen states have signed but not ratified this convention. The number of ratifications is 18.

One of the aims of this convention is to avoid the disadvantages that may arise in case of conflict of jurisdiction. The most leading principle to impose jurisdiction is the territoriality principle.[127] In case of conflict of jurisdiction, the general rule is that the state in which the act was committed should have priority to prosecute the offender.[128] Article 8 lists the reasons for a request to take over proceedings. However, reasons of rehabilitation of the offender are increasingly important to determine the most appropriate state to claim jurisdiction. The transfer of proceedings is

[126] European Convention on the Transfer of Proceedings in Criminal Matters, Strasbourg, 15 May 1972, ETS no. 073.

[127] See also Chapter 2, Section 2.3.2.2.

[128] Explanatory Report to the European Convention on the Transfer of Proceedings in Criminal Matters, <http://conventions.coe.int/treaty/en/Reports/Html/073.htm>.

not limited to certain offences but can take place for any offence as long as it contributes to a proper administration of justice. Article 2 gives a very broad interpretation of the jurisdiction of the contracting states. It states that: '...any contracting state shall have competence to prosecute under its own criminal law any offence to which the law of another contracting state is applicable'. This includes that the prosecution after the transfer takes place in accordance with the criminal law of the requested state (i.e., the state which takes over the proceedings). Furthermore, the transfer of proceedings can only take place when both states involved have jurisdiction. The decision as to whether or not to make a request is taken by the competent authority which is empowered by the state to take the decision. A state is never obliged to transfer proceedings but is allowed to request the transfer up to the enforcement of the judgement. In case of a jurisdiction conflict, a state may, on request, end the proceedings it had imposed on the suspected person and accordingly facilitate a final decision in the other state. To grant the request, double criminality *in concreto* is required. This means that the requested state would have had jurisdiction if the crime had taken place on its territory. The fact that an offence is committed against a person of public status cannot be considered a reason to refuse the transfer of proceedings.

The requested state takes the decision to transfer proceedings in accordance with its national law. Proceedings may not be transferred when the time-limit to commence proceedings has expired. Reasons by which to refuse a request (Article 11) are the following.

- The grounds on which the request is based are not justified.
- The suspect does not normally reside in the requested state or does not have the nationality of the requested state.
- The offence is of a political, military, or fiscal nature.
- There are grounds to believe that the request was motivated by considerations of race, religion, nationality, or political opinion.
- Prosecution for this offence is time-barred in the requested state.
- The *locus delicti* is outside the requested state.
- Proceedings would be contrary to international undertakings or fundamental principles of the legal system of the requested state.
- The requesting state has violated a rule of procedure of this convention.

In all these cases, the requested state may withdraw its acceptance of the request and also if the appearance of the suspect during the hearing cannot be guaranteed or a possible sentence cannot be enforced. The special regime of Article 24 applies if a complaint is required to take proceedings.

Procedural aspects

In general, communication between the states involved will take place between the Ministries of Justice unless otherwise agreed or in urgent cases, when communication takes place via Interpol. All relevant documents, such as the criminal file and procedural actions already taken in the requesting state, must be sent together with the request. The decisions taken by the requested state are to be promptly forwarded to the requesting state. In some cases, the suspect will be heard by the requested state before a decision is taken (Article 17). Provisions on language and costs can be found in Articles 18, 19, and 20. Following the request, the requesting state must refrain from instituting proceedings or discontinue any proceedings already instituted but it retains the right to prosecute. This means that the requesting state, pending the request, may take any steps in respect of prosecution, short of bringing the matter before the trial court. The right to prosecute the suspect reverts to the requesting state if a negative answer is received from the requested state. Such a negative answer may include decisions by the requested state to the effect that it will not take any action on the request, that it refuses the acceptance of the request, that it withdraws the acceptance of the request, or that it will not institute proceedings or will discontinue them. The right to prosecute also reverts if the requesting state withdraws its request. The sanction pronounced in the requested state may not exceed the sanction of the requesting state if the competence of the requested state is based on Article 2. The prosecuting activities already undertaken in the requesting state will have the same value in the requested state after the transfer of proceedings. Under certain conditions, the requested state may arrest the suspect in anticipation of the request. The conditions and formalities for this provisional arrest can be found in Article 27. Other provisional activities may be taken by the requested state, such as remanding the suspect in custody or seizure of property, as long as they are taken in accordance with its national law. The period during which the suspect can be held in custody after a provisional arrest must be limited in accordance with Article 29. In case of plurality of criminal proceedings, states must endeavour to determine which of them will continue to conduct proceedings. Meanwhile, judgements on the merits will be postponed. This form of consultation between states involved is also recommended if the suspect has committed several offences on which all the states involved have jurisdiction or if one offence has been committed by several persons together and all states involved have jurisdiction. The transfer of proceedings may never be a violation of the principle of *ne bis in idem*, but a contracting state is not always bound by the judgement of another state. The state taking new proceedings must take into consideration the earlier conviction for the same act. The final clauses are the same as in the other conventions and are based on the final clauses of agreements and conventions that were approved by the Committee of Ministers of the Council of Europe during its 113th meeting. Appendix 1 to the convention contains some reservations that can be made by the contracting states.

4.3.4.6 *The European Agreement on Travel by Young Persons on Collective Passports between the Member Countries of the Council of Europe*[129]

The ratione materiae

One state has signed the agreement without ratifying it, while 19 states have ratified or acceded to the agreement. Beside 12 member states of the EU (i.e., except Aus-

[129] European Agreement on Travel by Young Persons on Collective Passports between the Member Countries of the Council of Europe, Paris, 16 December 1961, ETS no. 037.

tria, Finland, and Germany), Iceland, Liechtenstein, Malta, Norway, Switzerland, the Former Yugoslav Republic of Macedonia, and Turkey have ratified the agreement.

The reason for including this instrument in this overview is that this instrument might easily be abused by traffickers who act, in the terminology of the agreement, as 'a leader' to traffic young persons to other states. As we will see, this agreement creates the opportunity to cross the border with a group of young persons on one document. It could be attractive for traffickers to use such a document when they want to traffic young persons from one country to another.

This agreement facilitates travelling between the contracting states by young persons by initiating the possibility for them to travel on collective documents. Young persons are persons who have not yet reached the age of 21. A person older than 21 years of age has to accompany the group of young persons. This leader retains possession of the collective travel document and ensures that the members of the party remain together. A collective document may include a minimum of five and a maximum of fifty young persons (excluding the leader). The leader must report any missing person to the local authorities. A young person who has become separated from the group may in some cases obtain an individual travel document. The maximum period of stay on a collective travel document is three months.

Procedural aspects
The formalities for issuing the collective document are described in Article 9. The persons who are travelling on a collective document must be able to present some form of identity if so requested.

4.3.4.7 *The European Convention on the International Validity of Criminal Judgements*[130]

The ratione materiae
Although this convention could be of great importance for judicial cooperation in criminal matters, it was only signed but not ratified by 10 states while 15 states have ratified the convention.

This convention addresses the validity of final decisions delivered by a criminal court of a contracting state. The convention concerns sanctions involving deprivation of liberty, fines or confiscation, and disqualifications. These sanctions are defined in Article 1. The convention facilitates the enforcement of a sanction imposed in one of the contracting states in another contracting state, at the request of the sentencing state. Double criminality is required for enforcement by another state. According to Article 5, the request may only be sent to another contracting state if

[130] European Convention on the International Validity of Criminal Judgements, The Hague, 28 May 1970, ETS no. 070.

- the sentenced person normally has residence in the requested state;
- the social rehabilitation of the sentenced person benefits from it;
- the sanction could be enforced following the enforcement of another sanction which the sentenced person is undergoing at that moment (in both cases it must concern deprivation of liberty);
- the requested state is the state of origin of the sentenced person;
- the sentencing state is not able to enforce the sanction.

In the following cases, the request to enforce the sanction may be refused (Article 6).

- Enforcement is contradictory to the fundamental principles of the legal system of the requested state.
- The offence underlying the request is of a political or military nature according to the requested state.
- The requested state has substantial grounds to believe that the request is motivated by considerations of race, religion, nationality, or political opinion.
- Enforcement would be contrary to the international undertakings of the requested state.
- The requested state has taken or intends to take proceedings in respect of the act or when it has decided not to take proceedings or when it has dropped proceedings already started.
- The act was committed outside the territory of the requesting state.
- The requested state is unable to enforce the sanction.
- The request is solely based on the fact that the requesting state is not able to enforce the sanction.
- It must be considered that the requesting state is able to enforce the sanction.
- The age of the sentenced person is an exclusive ground in the requested state for prosecution.
- In the requested state, the sanction can no longer be enforced because of the lapse of time.
- The sanction imposed is a disqualification.

Article 9 of the convention contains the speciality principle, which means that only the sanction mentioned in the request may be enforced in the requested state unless the convicted person has consented to the enforcement of other sanctions. The sanctions are to be enforced in accordance with the national law of the requested state. The transfer of the enforcement ends the competence of the requesting state to enforce the sanction itself. If the request is withdrawn by the requesting state or if the requested state refuses to enforce the sanction the right to enforce reverts to the requesting state. The consent of the state through which a sentenced person has to be transported is required and the same applies in the case of a scheduled landing when the transport is by air.

Procedural aspects
Communication will normally take place via the Ministries of Justice unless otherwise agreed. In urgent cases, the request may be sent through the channels of In-

terpol. Communication must be accompanied by the relevant documents. The requested state keeps the requesting state informed about the progress made in the enforcement of the sanction. Under certain conditions (Article 32), the requested state may arrest the sentenced person as a provisional measure even if the request has not yet been received by the requested state. He may only be held in custody for a certain period of time (Article 33). Before a sanction can be enforced in the requested state, a decision of one of its courts is required. Other authorities in the requested state may be endowed with decision-making power if the sanction is a fine or confiscation. Before such a decision is taken, the sentenced person must be given the opportunity to be heard. The requested state is bound by the findings of fact as stated in the decision of the requesting state. In the case of deprivation of liberty, the court of the requested state will substitute, in accordance with its own national law, the sanction imposed by the requesting state. The penal situation of the sentenced person may not be aggravated. In all cases, the principle of *ne bis in idem* has to be taken into consideration. The final provisions of this convention are also based on the final clauses of agreements and conventions that were approved by the Committee of Ministers of the Council of Europe during its 113th meeting.

4.3.4.8 *Final remarks*

This is only a brief selection of the instruments within the Council of Europe by which to improve cooperation in criminal matters between European states. Only those instruments most relevant for cooperation in criminal matters and thus for combating trafficking in persons have been discussed in this section. This overview already indicates that police and judicial cooperation is a difficult task with many pitfalls. Double criminality is often required before cooperation can take place. The formalities that have to be fulfilled can be an obstacle to efficient cooperation. Even though the procedural aspects were not discussed exhaustively, it is clear that they create a complex system of rules, exceptions, and agreements, which needs a separate study before it can be applied, even without referring to the declarations which states might have made to the different conventions.

With these remarks in mind, it is not surprising that the complexity of the *ratione materiae* and the procedural implications are an obstacle to the enforcement of instruments to prosecute traffickers.

4.4 CONCLUSION

As was shown in this chapter, many policy documents and legal instruments are adopted to combat and prosecute trafficking in persons. As a rule, policy documents directly focus on the fight against trafficking in persons while legal instruments focus more on police and judicial cooperation in general and in this way address trafficking in persons indirectly. In general, the policy documents cannot be legally enforced because most of the policy documents lack binding effect. Especially within the EU, many documents are adopted that reflect the good intentions of the states and institutions involved without a strong obligation to comply with these good intentions. Before the legal instruments of the EU were discussed, the framework of police and judicial cooperation in criminal matters within the EU was described for a better understanding of the legal instruments adopted within the EU. The legal instruments are needed and must be used to achieve some of the goals in the policies. With regard to the prosecution of those suspected of trafficking in persons in Europe, it must be said that the effect of these legal instruments has, until now, been rather limited as the prosecution of traffickers is still problematic. However, as analysed in this chapter, the transformation of the use of current principles in cooperation in criminal matters adopted in several instruments recently enacted within the EU, seems to indicate a willingness on the part of states to intensify cooperation in criminal matters. The proposals to establish an EPP go even further, as this requires the transmission of some of the powers of the member states in criminal matters to the EU level. In Chapter 7, I will examine to what extent and how this transformation of the use of current principles and the establishment of an EPP will contribute to the more effective prosecution of those suspected of trafficking in persons.

The question underlying this chapter was whether the involvement of more than one state in trafficking in persons aggravates the problems involved in prosecuting trafficking in persons. An answer to this question is necessary in order to find out whether the solution to prosecute trafficking must be sought beyond national borders. In many policy documents, the lack of cooperation and coordination with other member states and with third countries is explicitly mentioned as one of the problems with regard to trafficking in persons. Consequently, it is likely that the problems involved in prosecuting trafficking in persons with regard to cooperation in criminal matters are aggravated by the involvement of more than one state. In the next two chapters, the effectiveness of the cooperation in criminal matters will be examined and obstacles to an effective prosecution will be identified. Only then can a final answer be given to the question of whether prosecution problems are aggravated by the involvement of more than one state, and thus whether a solution must be sought beyond national borders. Besides, only when the content and the dimensions of these problems are known, can the development of strategies to improve the prosecution of trafficking in persons be realised.

CHAPTER 5
THE EFFECTIVENESS OF POLICY DOCUMENTS TO COMBAT TRAFFICKING IN PERSONS AND LEGAL INSTRUMENTS TO PROSECUTE THIS PRACTICE

5.1 INTRODUCTION

One of the concerns put forward in Chapter 1 was that, in spite of the many policy documents and legal instruments at the European level dealing with trafficking in persons, the ability or willingness of states to use them efficiently or to transform them into concrete actions in national law to suppress and prosecute trafficking in persons is often lacking. In the previous chapter, these policies and instruments were discussed. In this chapter, the effectiveness of these policy documents and instruments will be evaluated and obstacles to efficiently use them will be identified.

In Section 5.2, some general analytical remarks will be made on the reasons contributing to the absence of the intended effect. Section 5.2.1 and Section 5.2.2 will deal with both the policy documents and legal instruments. As this study mainly focuses on the prosecution of those suspected of trafficking in persons, the obstacles to an effective use of the legal instruments will be the subject of research in Sections 5.2.3, 5.2.4, 5.3, and 5.4. In Section 5.3, the problems with regard to the application of legal instruments indicated in the legal literature will be discussed and the most important views will be analysed. These problems will be categorised as substantive, procedural, and organisational problems. This categorisation will also be used in Section 5.4. In a joint action of 5 December 1997, it was agreed by the Council that 'a mechanism for evaluating the application and implementation at national level of international undertakings in the fight against organised crime' should be set up.[1] In this context, an evaluation of the mutual legal assistance systems in all member states of the EU was carried out. The evaluation reports on mutual legal assistance and urgent requests for the tracing and restraint of property are the major source of information for the analysis in Section 5.4 of this chapter.

[1] Joint Action of 5 December 1997 adopted by the Council on the basis of Article K.3 of the Treaty on European Union, Establishing a Mechanism for Evaluating the Application and Implementation at National Level of International Undertakings in the Fight against Organised Crime, OJ L 344, 15.12.1997, pp. 7-9.

5.2 GENERAL REMARKS ON THE EFFECTIVENESS OF THE POLICY DOCUMENTS AND LEGAL INSTRUMENTS TO COMBAT AND PROSECUTE TRAFFICKING IN PERSONS

5.2.1 The legal basis of the policy documents and legal instruments

A first reason why the policy documents and legal instruments discussed in Chapter 4 have not had the intended effect is the legal basis of these documents. This legal basis varies considerably and is also dependent on the organisation that has established it, as we will see in Sections 5.2.1.1 to 5.2.1.3.

It is important to determine the legal basis of documents and instruments, as it is decisive for the question of whether the documents and instruments are binding or not. Furthermore, it is important to distinguish between the various ways in which a document or instrument can have binding force.[2] A document or instrument can be legally binding *stricto sensu,* which means that the document or instrument can grant rights and obligations to states and individuals without any interference. When a document or instrument is politically binding, it can be said that states that have signed or established it are obliged vis-à-vis each other to act in accordance with the provisions in the document or instrument, but it does not create direct rights and obligations for the citizens of the states parties.[3] A last form of binding status is that a document or instrument is morally binding, which means that the parties that have established it are morally obliged to act in accordance with the document or instrument.

The binding status of documents and instruments is easily confused with, but also related to, their enforceability. Both concepts have their own specific characteristics and problems, as will be shown in this section and in Section 5.2.2.

5.2.1.1 *The legal basis of policy documents and legal instruments within the EU*

The situation with regard to the legal basis of EU documents and instruments and, consequently, their binding status is rather complex. Firstly, it is relevant whether the decision is made under the first or the third pillar. Secondly, it depends on the type of decision whether or not binding force can be attributed to the document or instrument. As was outlined in Chapter 4, the types of decision that can be taken within the framework of the third pillar have changed substantively with the Treaty of Amsterdam.[4] Because the documents and instruments discussed in Chapter 4 concern documents and instruments from before and after the Treaty of Amsterdam,

---

[2] H. Lauterpacht and L. Oppenheim, *International Law, A Treatise, Volume I, Peace*, Longmans, London, 1961, pp. 7-15.

[3] M.N. Shaw, *International Law,* third edition, Grotius publications, Cambridge University Press, Cambridge, 1995, pp. 11-12.

[4] Chapter 4, Section 4.3.2.2.

both the regimes from before and after the Treaty of Amsterdam are relevant when determining the legal status of the decisions discussed in Chapter 4.

Before the Treaty of Amsterdam, the Council of the EU, as the decision-making body in the third pillar, could adopt common positions, joint actions, and conventions.[5] Legally binding force was often denied to these instruments that were established within the third pillar prior to the Treaty of Amsterdam, except for the conventions.[6] To deny any binding status to the other instruments would be going too far, as these are adopted unanimously, often after long negotiations. Although it was not clear whether or not a joint action was legally binding it had a certain status and it was recognised in practice as potentially having legally binding force.[7] The legally binding effect of a joint action was dependent on the content and the wording.[8] Furthermore, the measure implementing the joint action was also relevant.[9] It is without doubt that joint actions were more legally binding than soft law instruments in the third pillar, for instance resolutions.[10] It was recognised that individuals could not claim rights or obligations following a joint action without the interference of the national legislator and that national authorities were obliged to act in accordance with the joint action as far as possible within their competences.[11] Common positions lacked legally binding force in the pre-Amsterdam period.

Since the Treaty of Amsterdam, the Council can adopt common positions, framework decisions, decisions, and conventions, which were discussed in Chapter 4, Section 4.3.2.2.[12] Both framework decisions and decisions lack direct effect. This means that individuals cannot derive rights and obligations from these instruments without the interference of a national legislative authority.[13] It is not clear whether

---

[5] Article K.3. (2) Treaty of Maastricht.

[6] J. Monar and R. Morgan, *The Third Pillar of the European Union. Cooperation in the Fields of Justice and Home Affairs,* European Interuniversity Press, Brussels, 1994, pp. 34-36 and pp. 182-183.

[7] R. Barents and L.J. Brinkhorst, *Grondlijnen van Europees Recht,* W.E.J. Tjeenk Willink, Deventer 2001, p. 539.

[8] E. Pouw, Het gemeenschappelijk optreden in de 'Derde Pijler' van de EU, in: *Regelmaat,* Volume 12, issue 3, 1997, pp. 109-114.

[9] J. Monar and R. Morgan, *The Third Pillar of the European Union. Cooperation in the Fields of Justice and Home Affairs,* European Interuniversity Press, Brussels, 1994, p. 36.

[10] D. Cullen, J. Monar, and Ph. Myers, *Cooperation in Justice and Home Affairs. An Evaluation of the Third Pillar in Practice,* European Interuniversity Press, Brussels, 1996, p. 43.

[11] E. Pouw, Het gemeenschappelijk optreden in de 'Derde Pijler' van de EU, in: *Regelmaat,* Volume 12, issue 3, 1997, pp. 113-114.

[12] Article 34(2) EU Treaty. Arguments supporting the statement that this article is the main legal basis for the adoption of instruments can be found in R.H. van Ooik, *De keuze der rechtsgrondslag voor besluiten van de Europese Unie,* Europese Monografieën no. 63, Kluwer, Deventer, 1999, pp. 379-380. For a description of these instruments see, for instance, J. Monar, Justice and Home Affairs in the Treaty of Amsterdam: Reform at the Price of Fragmentation, in: *European Law Review,* Volume 23, issue 4, 1998, pp. 326-327. A.H. Klip, Amsterdams Uniestrafrecht, in: *NJB,* Volume 73, issue 18, 1998, pp. 811-816. Chapter 4, Section 4.3.2.2.

[13] E. Pouw, Het gemeenschappelijk optreden in de 'Derde Pijler' van de EU, in: *Regelmaat,* Volume 12, issue 3, 1997, pp. 112-113. E. Manunza, *EG-aanbestedingsrechtelijke problemen bij privatiseringen*

common positions adopted after the Treaty of Amsterdam have binding force. They could be considered as a sort of 'collective negotiating mandate' and therefore as more compelling than the pre-Amsterdam common positions.[14] In that regard, it can be defended that common positions are politically binding.

The conventions remained after the Treaty of Amsterdam. This treaty contains provisions to speed up the entry into force of conventions, as the long ratification processes in the different member states often frustrated the effect of conventions in the pre-Amsterdam period. Now the ratification process has to commence within a period determined by the Council and a convention enters into force after ratification by a minimum of half of the member states.[15] These conventions are binding on the basis of Public International Law. In general, this means that they are binding for the states party to the convention and not for the citizens of these states.[16] However, this does not mean that the provisions of these conventions do not apply directly to individuals. It is recognised that treaties can expressly grant direct rights to individuals. These rights need not be transformed into national law but are directly applicable and enforceable.[17] This is only the case if provisions are intended to grant rights to individuals and are detailed enough to be applied. In these cases, a treaty or a provision of a treaty can become self-executory and the authorities of the states do not have to take any steps to make these provisions applicable. This means that the national courts have jurisdiction to enforce these provisions. However, most of the provisions adopted in treaties do not grant rights directly to individuals. For those provisions, it often completely depends on the willingness of the states whether they implement them in their national law.

The role of the European Parliament (EP) in the pre-Amsterdam period was threefold.[18]

- The Presidency and the Commission had to inform the EP regularly on the activities undertaken in the third pillar.
- The Presidency had to consult the EP and these views had to be duly taken into account.
- The EP had the possibility to ask questions.

The weak position of the EP in this period was characterised by the absence of any real influence and by vague norms. The role of the EP remained limited after the

en bij de bestrijding van corruptie en georganiseerde criminaliteit, Kluwer, Deventer, 2001, pp. 273-277.

[14] R. Barents and L.J. Brinkhorst, *Grondlijnen van Europees Recht,* W.E.J. Tjeenk Willink, Deventer 2001, p. 539.

[15] R. Barents and L.J. Brinkhorst, *Grondlijnen van Europees Recht,* W.E.J. Tjeenk Willink, Deventer 2001, p. 540.

[16] H. Lauterpacht and L. Oppenheim, *International Law, A Treatise, Volume I, Peace*, Longmans, London, 1961, pp. 923-929 and pp. 19-22.

[17] *Jurisdiction of the Courts of Danzig* case, Advisory Opinion, PCIJ, Series B, no. 15, p. 17.

[18] Article K.6. Treaty of Maastricht.

Treaty of Amsterdam. The EP must be consulted before (framework) decisions and conventions can be adopted but its advice is not binding on the Council.

The role of national parliaments is formally limited to the establishment of conventions, as these must be ratified in accordance with national procedures. The Council prefers to adopt other instruments. No criteria exist as to what sort of decision must be taken in a certain case. Consequently, the Council can opt to exclude the national parliaments from participation, namely, by not choosing the concept of a convention.[19]

Beside these pre- and post-Amsterdam instruments, the more traditional instruments such as resolutions, recommendations, declarations, and conclusions are more often used in the third pillar. It is clear that these are not legally binding but provide a political declaration of intent, which may lead to a certain moral obligation.[20] These instruments of soft law are often used as they leave the sovereignty of member states untouched.[21] The Council is the only institution that can formally adopt binding instruments within the third pillar in accordance with Article 34 EU Treaty, which means that agreements enacted by the Commission or the EP can never have binding force. Most of the policy documents on trafficking in persons within the EU discussed in Chapter 4 lack legally binding force as they are adopted within the third pillar and often not by the Council of the EU but by the Parliament or the Commission. Other reasons for the lack of legally binding instruments within the third pillar are the requirement of unanimity, the confusion on the binding status of documents, long negotiation and ratification procedures for legally binding conventions, and an opaque decision-making process.[22]

5.2.1.2 *The legal basis of policy documents and legal instruments within the Council of Europe*

From the policy documents discussed in Section 4.2.3 in Chapter 4, the Recommendation on Action against Trafficking in Human Beings for the Purpose of Sexual Exploitation of 2000 and the Recommendation on Traffic in Women and Forced

[19] R.H. van Ooik, *De keuze der rechtsgrondslag voor besluiten van de Europese Unie,* Europese Monografieën no. 63, Kluwer, Deventer, 1999, pp. 399-401.

[20] D. Cullen, J. Monar, and Ph. Myers, *Cooperation in Justice and Home Affairs. An Evaluation of the Third Pillar in Practice,* European Interuniversity Press, Brussels, 1996, p. 48.

[21] R.H. van Ooik, *De keuze der rechtsgrondslag voor besluiten van de Europese Unie,* Europese Monografieën no. 63, Kluwer, Deventer, 1999, pp. 405-407. For an analysis of the erosion of the principle of sovereignty of states after the Treaty of Amsterdam, see E.M.H. Hirsch Ballin, Soevereiniteit in de Europese Unie, in: *NJB,* Volume 72, issue 44, 1997, pp. 2005-2010.

[22] D.M. Curtin and J.F.M. Pouw, Samenwerking op het gebied van justitie en binnenlandse zaken in de Europese Unie: pre-Maastricht-nostalgie? in: *SEW,* Volume 43, issue 9, 1995, pp. 599-602. N. Walker, Current Developments: EC Law; Justice and Home Affairs, in: *International and Comparative Law Quarterly,* Volume 47, issue 1, 1998, pp. 234-236. J. Monar, Justice and Home Affairs in the Treaty of Amsterdam: Reform at the Price of Fragmentation, in: *European Law Review,* Volume 23, issue 4, 1998, pp. 320-321. See Chapter 4, Section 4.3.2.2.

Prostitution are the most important. A convention dealing with this issue was never drafted. The term recommendation already implies the non-binding status of the document. Recommendations must be considered soft law and lack legally binding force *stricto sensu*, but are politically and morally binding.[23]

The legal instruments within the Council of Europe discussed in Chapter 4 are conventions that were drafted by a committee of experts appointed by the governments of the member states of the Council of Europe. The conventions were drafted on the basis of unanimity. However, the experts are not necessarily guided by statements from their governments.[24] The consent to be bound by the treaty is expressed by ratification, acceptance, or approval of the treaty by an authorised representative of the state concerned. Sometimes a clause is included in the treaty to the effect that only the signature of a state expresses the consent of a state to be bound. Further ratification, acceptance, or approval is not then required. This is an increasing practice. These conventions are treaties of Public International Law.[25]

These conventions are only binding for the states that have ratified them, but as far as they include provisions that grant rights to individuals and that are sufficiently detailed, these provisions can have direct effect and individuals can invoke these provisions before national courts. Most of these conventions, however, are broadly formulated and require implementation before they can have effect at the national level. The addressees of the conventions are the states party to the conventions and it is unusual for these conventions to have direct effect in the state parties. However, many member states of the Council of Europe recognise the self-executing status of the Treaty on Extradition and the Convention for the Protection of Human Rights and Fundamental Freedoms. Furthermore, the Federal Constitutional Court of Germany did not accept a declaration by Germany intended to prevent individuals from claiming direct rights on the basis of the Convention on the Transfer of Sentenced Persons.[26]

5.2.1.3 *The legal basis of policy documents within the OSCE*

Agreements and decisions taken within the framework of the OSCE can be regarded as political agreements. Although often adopted by the permanent council by ambassadors of the member states, in the ministerial council by the ministers of foreign affairs of the member states, or during summits by representatives of governments, they lack the status of Public International Law. No national procedures of ratifica-

[23] J.F. Nijboer, Recommendations. Over het 'zachte' (straf)recht van de Raad van Europa, in: *Justitiële Verkenningen,* Volume 27, issue 2, 2001, pp. 81-87.

[24] J. Polakiewicz, *Treaty-Making in the Council of Europe,* Council of Europe Publishing, Strasbourg, 1999, pp. 19-22.

[25] J. Polakiewicz, *Treaty-Making in the Council of Europe,* Council of Europe Publishing, Strasbourg, 1999, pp. 153-160.

[26] Federal Constitutional Court of Germany, 18 June 1997, GER-1997-2-009 in the Codices database, <http://www.venice.coe.int/codices>.

tion will be commenced after the adoption of such documents. These documents are politically and morally binding, but they lack legally binding force *stricto sensu,* as they do not create rights for or impose obligations upon individuals.

The main documents discussed in Chapter 4, Section 4.2.4, concluded within the OSCE include a decision of the ministerial council, the final report of the supplementary human dimension meeting on trafficking in human beings, and an action plan. The latter two are not legally binding as they were adopted by the Office for Democratic Institutions and Human Rights (ODIHR), which has no authority to adopt binding decisions.[27] This does not take away the fact that they have their influence on the activities of the OSCE. Because the action plan and the final report are rather detailed, for instance, with specific reference to the role of the advisor on trafficking issues and an annex with some model projects to prevent and combat trafficking in persons, they are already determinative for OSCE policy.

Although the OSCE has no binding documents *stricto sensu* at its disposal to combat trafficking in persons, it seems that this does not prevent the organisation from undertaking concrete actions and steps to achieve the goals named in its policies. This practice is not exceptional within the OSCE framework and it is said that soft law within the OSCE can create 'a new source of valuable reference for policy- and law-makers'.[28]

5.2.2 Lack of legal enforcement of policies and legal instruments

Besides the legal basis of the policy documents and legal instruments, a second, and very important, cause of their lack of effectiveness to suppress and prosecute trafficking in persons is the absence of enforcement mechanisms. Since the policies are not legally binding, they cannot be enforced by legal means. Nevertheless, the OSCE, has adopted some mechanisms to enforce compliance with non-binding OSCE commitments, as we will see below.

5.2.2.1 *Legal enforcement within the EU*

Within the EU, the ECJ did not have competence in third pillar issues before the Treaty of Amsterdam. As was discussed in Chapter 4, Section 4.3.2.6, the competence of the ECJ in third pillar issues is now adopted under certain conditions in Article 35 EU Treaty, but its competence is weak in comparison to its competence

---

[27] The ODIHR is an important body to execute the policy of the OSCE that is outlined primarily by the Permanent Council in Vienna. The ODIHR is responsible for the promotion of human rights and democracy, <www.osce.org/structures_institutions/>.

[28] The Lund Recommendations on the Effective Participation of National Minorities in Public Life of September 1999 is a good example of a document that, despite the fact that it is not legally or politically binding, has proved its relevance in practice and gained some authority by its application. See J. Packer, The Origin and Nature of the Lund Recommendations on the Effective Participation of National Minorities in Public Life, in: *Helsinki Monitor,* Volume 11, issue 4, 2000, pp. 29-45.

under the first pillar.[29] First of all, its competence to give preliminary rulings on decisions and framework decisions is facultative and states can choose whether they grant the possibility to ask preliminary questions to all national courts or only to the national courts against whose decisions there is no judicial remedy under national law. Within the third pillar, no options are open to commence proceedings at the ECJ for individuals. Therefore, the legally binding conventions, framework decisions, and decisions can hardly be enforced on the EU level. The competence of the Commission under Article 226 EC Treaty to file a complaint at the ECJ if a state has acted negligently does not exist in the third pillar. However, Article 35 paragraph 7 EU Treaty provides for dispute settlement if disagreement exists between states on the interpretation and application of decisions taken on the basis of Article 34 paragraph 2 EU Treaty. In the first pillar, the Commission regularly uses its competence on the basis of Article 226 EC Treaty if states do not implement directives in time. Although it is said that framework decisions are similar instruments to directives, the absence of a similar competence to Article 226 EC Treaty in the third pillar must be regretted. This may result in the situation that member states can postpone acting in accordance with the framework decisions while legal measures cannot be invoked in such cases. As a consequence of the fact that neither these framework decisions nor the decisions taken on the basis of Article 34 (2)(c) EU Treaty have direct effect, individuals cannot file a complaint with the (national) court.[30] The conventions adopted on the basis of Article 34 (2)(d) EU Treaty must be considered conventions of Public International Law and are therefore binding for the states party to the conventions. Provisions on dispute settlement by an independent court are absent in these conventions. Although some of the documents adopted on the basis of Article 34 EU Treaty are legally binding, when these documents cannot be enforced, the added value of these instruments must not be overestimated.

5.2.2.2 *Legal enforcement within the Council of Europe*

Conventions that are adopted within the framework of the Council of Europe are binding on the same basis as the conventions within the EU on the basis of Article 34 (2)(d) EU Treaty, as these conventions are conventions of Public International Law. States parties are obliged vis-à-vis one another to implement the provisions of the treaty. So far, all the efforts of the Parliamentary Assembly to establish a judicial organ for at least uniform interpretation of treaties have failed.[31] Another effort to establish such an organ was made by the Czech Republic, but its proposal was not adopted. Within the Council of Europe disputes have arisen as to whether disputes concerning these treaties can be brought before the ICJ, provided that the states involved have recognised the jurisdiction of the ICJ. Furthermore, there is a tendency

---

[29] See also Chapter 4, Section 4.3.2.6. J. Monar, Justice and Home Affairs in the Treaty of Amsterdam: Reform at the Price of Fragmentation, in: *European Law Review*, Volume 23, issue 4, 1998, pp. 330-332.

[30] For the result of direct effect for individuals, see *Van Gend en Loos* 26/62, 1963, 3.

[31] J. Polakiewicz, *Treaty-Making in the Council of Europe*, Council of Europe Publishing, Strasbourg, 1999, p. 119.

to confer judicial functions on the European Court of Human Rights rather than on the International Court of Justice. Besides, the Convention on Laundering, Search, Seizure and Confiscation of the Proceeds from Crime is the only relevant treaty that provides for arbitration procedures. In the other conventions discussed in Chapter 4, no specific provisions on dispute settlement can be found.

In 1993, the Committee of Ministers and the Parliamentary Assembly both established procedures for political control to monitor whether member states act in accordance with their commitments. The European Committee on Crime Problems is endowed with the monitoring of all the legal instruments discussed in Section 4.3.4, Chapter 4, except for the European Agreement on Travel by Young Persons on Collective Passports.[32] The Committee has enacted a number of resolutions to facilitate the application of the treaties falling within its competence. In case of dispute, the Committee 'shall do whatever is necessary to facilitate a friendly settlement of any difficulty which may arise out of its application'. So far, the Committee has used this competence only once.

5.2.2.3 *Legal enforcement within the OSCE*

Within the Human Dimension, the OSCE introduced, in 1989 and 1991, two supervisory mechanisms to encourage its member states to act in accordance with their obligations within the OSCE, the Vienna mechanism and the Moscow mechanism, respectively.[33] Furthermore, there is the possibility to conduct fact-finding missions. All these mechanisms have a more or less diplomatic character and start with consultations.

Beside these mechanisms the OSCE also has a Court of Conciliation and Arbitration, which must be convened if a dispute is not settled within a reasonable period of time or at any agreed time.[34] The Court of Conciliation and Arbitration is based on a Convention that is legally binding and subject to national ratification procedures. Some 32 member states have ratified the convention. According to Article 31 of the Convention on Conciliation and Arbitration, the award of the arbitral tribunal has binding force for the parties to the dispute and is not subject to appeal. According to Article 14 of the Rules of the Court, the purpose of conciliation is to assist the parties to a dispute in finding a settlement in accordance with international law and

---

[32] J. Polakiewicz, *Treaty-Making in the Council of Europe,* Council of Europe Publishing, Strasbourg, 1999, pp. 126-129.

[33] The Vienna mechanism consists of four phases, namely, requesting information on a particular situation, discussing the human dimension situation in a bilateral meeting, bringing the human dimension situation to the attention of the other OSCE states, and providing information at follow-up meetings. The Moscow mechanism provides for the addition of the system of expert missions or OSCE rapporteurs, even against the will of the state involved. In contradiction to the Vienna mechanism, the Moscow mechanism has only been used a few times. See W.J.M. van Genugten (ed.), *Human Rights Reference Handbook,* Netherlands Ministry of Foreign Affairs, The Hague, 1999, pp. 151-153.

[34] Articles 18 and 26 of the Convention on Conciliation and Arbitration within the OSCE.

their OSCE commitments.[35] The purpose of the arbitral tribunal is to settle such disputes as are submitted to it.[36] When states have not reached an agreement following the procedure of the conciliation commission, the report of this commission is forwarded to the arbitral tribunal.

5.2.3 The complexity caused by the multiplicity of applicable legal instruments

A third reason for the lack of effect of the legal instruments discussed in Chapter 4 is that many overlaps exist with regard to instruments on cooperation in criminal matters in general and on mutual legal assistance in particular.[37] This multiplicity leads to confusion regarding what instruments can be applied in a certain situation and to the application of more than one instrument at the same time. As these instruments have different provisions on the same matter, the application of several instruments at the same time might be problematic. The problems originating from the application of different instruments can be illustrated by the practice of the use of communication channels for mutual legal assistance as most of the conventions on mutual legal assistance provide their own system with regard to communication channels.

The 1959 Convention on Mutual Assistance provides for the communication of requests via the Ministries of Justice, except in urgent cases when requests may be transmitted directly or via Interpol.[38] When direct channels are used, the authorities referred to in Article 24 of this convention are competent. In many European countries, the Interpol channel is used for urgent and speedy transmission. The Schengen Convention provides for direct communication under Articles 52 and 53. Furthermore, some regional conventions and agreements are operational within the EU, e.g., the Benelux Convention on Extradition and Mutual Assistance in Criminal Matters and the conventions on mutual assistance within the Nordic countries. These provide a more flexible form of mutual assistance with less formalities. Then, in most of the EU countries, national legislation applies with regard to mutual legal assistance, in some cases with specific rules on the use of communication channels. The EU Convention on Mutual Assistance in criminal matters, signed on 29 May 2000, prescribes the use of direct communication channels. Finally, the Europol channel can be used for the transmission of requests as well. Besides, it has to be taken into account that a request can be based on

[35] Article 14, Rules of the Court of Conciliation and Arbitration within the OSCE, 1 February 1997.

[36] Article 22, Rules of the Court of Conciliation and Arbitration within the OSCE, 1 February 1997.

[37] Also M. Rantala, A Treaty Labyrinth of Legal Cooperation in Criminal Matters: Can Europe Find Ariadne's Thread? in: V. Kronenberger, *The European Union and the International Legal Order: Discord or Harmony?* T.M.C. Asser Press, The Hague, 2001, pp. 519-552. For an overview of the legislation on different levels see, Ch. van den Wyngaert and G. Stessens, Mutual Legal Assistance in Criminal Matters in the European Union, in: J. Dugard and Ch. van den Wyngaert, *International Criminal Law and Procedure,* Dartmouth, Aldershot, 1996, pp. 283-325. F. Thomas, *Internationale Rechtshulp in Strafzaken. Algemene praktische rechstverzameling,* Story-Scientia, Brussels, 1998, pp. 5-40.

[38] Article 15, European Convention on Mutual Assistance.

- the European Convention on the Suppression of Terrorism of 27 January 1977
- the United Nations Convention of 20 December 1988, against Illicit Traffic in Narcotic Drugs, or
- the Convention on Laundering, Search, Seizure and Confiscation of the Proceeds of Crime of 8 November 1990.

Finally, if no treaty or other agreement exists, states can always use the diplomatic channel for the transmission of requests.

These are the main channels and instruments that are applicable in the case of mutual legal assistance in a nutshell. With this example in mind it is easy to imagine that, by applying the different instruments on cooperation in criminal matters which are available, confusion may easily arise. It is easy to imagine that all these different channels prescribed in the various documents cause confusion as to what channel must be used and which instrument must be applied and thereby lead to opaque practices on mutual legal assistance.[39] As we will see, practitioners often use more than one means of communication at the same time, which contains the risk of duplication of efforts, both in the requesting and the requested state.

5.2.4 The limited number of ratifications of treaties and the reservations to treaties

The number of ratifications and the various reservations to treaties on cooperation in criminal matters can be seen as a fourth and last reason for the absence of the intended effect of the legal instruments discussed in Chapter 4. For an efficient system of cooperation in criminal matters it is important that relevant instruments are ratified and adequately implemented.[40] This was already recommended in the Action Plan of 28 April 1997 to Combat Organised Crime,[41] and again in the plan for 'The Prevention and Control of Organised Crime: A European Union Strategy for the Beginning of the New Millennium'.[42]

The first requirement for a treaty to have any standing is that it is ratified by a considerable number of states. It is conducive to efficient cooperation in criminal matters if the states involved are party to the same convention so that they can use the

[39] P.C. Kortenhorst and P.A.M. Verrest, De *magistrat de liaison*. Een pionier in de internationale samenwerking, in: *Justitiële Verkenningen,* Volume 27, issue 2, 2001, pp. 56-67. For an elaborate overview of applicable instruments, see J. Koers, *Nederland als verzoekende staat bij de wederzijdse rechtshulp in strafzaken. Achtergronden, grenzen en mogelijkheden,* Wolf Legal Publishers, Nijmegen, 2001, pp. 11-48. We will see in Chapter 6 that the practitioners involved in the file study did not experience the existence of parallel procedures as an obstacle but rather as an advantage.

[40] Final Report on the First Evaluation Exercise – Mutual Legal Assistance in Criminal Matters, OJ C 216, 1.8.2001, p. 17.

[41] Action Plan to Combat Organised Crime, Adopted by the Council on 28 April 1997, OJ C 251, 15.8.1997, recommendations 13 and 14.

[42] The Prevention and Control of Organised Crime: A European Union Strategy for the Beginning of the New Millennium, OJ C 124, 3.5.2000, recommendation 27.

system developed in that particular convention. Therefore, states must be encouraged to sign and ratify relevant treaties. In Chapter 4, we have seen that the number of ratifications to the relevant treaties within the Council of Europe varies although a large number of states have ratified the main conventions on extradition (45 ratifications), mutual legal assistance (42 ratifications), and transfer of sentenced persons (53 ratifications). The convention on money laundering has been ratified by 41 states. The number of ratifications to the convention on transfer of proceedings is 18, a number which should be increased. The process of ratification of instruments from the Council of Europe often takes a very long time, even up to twenty years. This frustrates the quick establishment of an efficient system of cooperation in criminal matters within the Council of Europe. The situation in the EU is not much better. For instance, the lack of ratifications is an obstacle to the entry into force of the EU conventions on extradition and the EU Convention on Mutual Assistance that were discussed in Chapter 4. A transparent system for cooperation in criminal matters is further thwarted by various reservations that are made by states to the conventions of the Council of Europe, in particular. Consequently, every time the relevant treaty is applied, the reservations must be looked at in order to determine the applicability of the provision of that treaty for that particular state.

5.3 OBSTACLES TO THE APPLICATION OF LEGAL INSTRUMENTS INDICATED IN LEGAL LITERATURE

In this section, the problems with regard to cooperation in criminal matters as they are described in legal literature will be discussed. These problems will be divided into substantive, procedural, and organisational problems. The same categorisation will be used in the next section when an analysis is made of the evaluation reports on mutual legal assistance in the EU.

- Substantive problems are those problems that are related to the content of the different legal systems of the member states and the interpretation given by the member states to certain terms used with regard to cooperation in criminal matters.
- Procedural problems concern obstacles that are experienced by the member states when following the procedures for cooperation in criminal matters laid down in the legal instruments.
- Organisational problems are the practical problems experienced by practitioners when engaging in cooperation in criminal matters. These problems do not follow directly from the legal system itself.

5.3.1 **Substantive problems**

5.3.1.1 *Locus regit actum or forum regit actum?*

The principle of *locus regit actum* still prevails with regard to mutual legal assistance.[43] This means that a request must be executed in accordance with the law of

[43] F. Thomas, *Internationale rechtshulp in strafzaken. Algemene praktische rechtsverzameling,*

the requested state. However, this may cause problems when evidence is used in criminal proceedings. The tendency to increasingly use some form of the principle of *forum regit actum* can be observed.[44]

Legal literature has recognised the problems originating from the fact that requests are executed in accordance with the law of the requested state.[45] For instance, problems may arise with regard to the checking of evidence obtained in another state following a request. Koers indicates that, if another state is party to the European Convention on Human Rights (ECHR), it is not allowed to check whether the information provided by this state meets the requirements of Dutch law. This is a consequence of the application of the *locus regit actum* principle. The only possible check is a superficial review of whether the evidence is obtained in accordance with provisions in the law of the requested state and of whether there are strong indications that the evidence or information was obtained illegally.[46] If the information is used as direct evidence, a stronger check of the provisions of the ECHR is allowed. If it concerns only start information, then the only check that may take place is whether the suspect's rights of defence have been violated.[47] It is rather striking that the court of the requesting state, pursuant to the law of the requesting state, must carry out the examination of the evidence collected in another country. Thorough examination as to whether evidence has been obtained in accordance with the law of the requested state is normally not required and judges are not equipped to carry out this examination. Thus the execution of a request takes place in accordance with the law of the requested state while the examination of whether the evidence was legally obtained and can be used in a criminal procedure is examined in accordance with the law of the requesting state.[48]

The EU Convention on Mutual Assistance will tackle this problem by introducing the execution of the request in accordance with the law of the requesting state as the main principle.[49] An example of the application of the principle of *forum regit*

Story-Scientia, Brussels, 1998, pp. 184-185. Ch. van den Wyngaert and G. Stessens, Mutual Legal Assistance in Criminal Matters in the European Union, in: J. Dugard and Ch. van den Wyngaert, *International Criminal Law and Procedure,* Dartmouth, Aldershot, 1996, pp. 296-298.

[44] G. Vermeulen, *Wederzijdse rechtshulp in strafzaken in de Europese Unie: naar een volwaardige eigen rechtshulpruimte voor de Lid-Staten?* Maklu, Antwerpen, 1999, pp. 134-143.

[45] G. Vermeulen, *Wederzijdse rechtshulp in strafzaken in de Europese Unie: naar een volwaardige eigen rechtshulpruimte voor de Lid-Staten?* Maklu, Antwerpen, 1999, pp. 132-148.

[46] J. Koers, *Nederland als verzoekende staat bij de wederzijdse rechtshulp in strafzaken. Achtergronden, grenzen en mogelijkheden,* Wolf Legal Publishers, Nijmegen, 2001, pp. 554-562.

[47] Start information must be seen as the information given to authorities to make them aware of the possibility that a criminal act has taken place, often by laying an information with the police, see Ch. van den Wyngaert, *Strafrecht en strafprocesrecht in hoofdlijnen,* Bruylant, Brussels, 1998, pp. 926-928.

[48] J. Koers, *Nederland als verzoekende staat bij de wederzijdse rechtshulp in strafzaken. Achtergronden, grenzen en mogelijkheden,* Wolf Legal Publishers, Nijmegen, 2001, pp. 557-558.

[49] EU Convention on Mutual Legal Assistance, Article 4. G. Vermeulen, *Wederzijdse rechtshulp in strafzaken in de Europese Unie: naar een volwaardige eigen rechtshulpruimte voor de Lid-Staten?* Maklu, Antwerpen, 1999, pp. 143-148.

actum can also be found, for instance, in Articles 9, 12, and 27, paragraph 1, of the Convention on Money Laundering.

5.3.1.2 *The principle of double criminality*

The tendency within the EU to reduce the application of double criminality is celebrated by contributors to the relaxation of mutual legal assistance.[50] Vermeulen presumes that reservations to mutual legal assistance such as double criminality are made to frustrate international mutual legal assistance.[51] Several authors are of the opinion that the importance of the double criminality requirement is vanishing within Europe.[52] In the early 1990s, Swart already stated that it was no longer possible to apply the traditional principles (or obstacles) of cooperation in criminal matters, such as double criminality, because of the increased emphasis on the protection of human rights.[53] He further argued that the reasons underlying the non-internationalisation of certain acts must be taken into account when the abolishment of double criminality is considered. Instead of abolishing the double criminality requirement, he pleaded for introducing the *ordre public* clause which could be applied instead of the double criminality principle, although he admits that this is a rather vague term.[54]

The idea has become accepted that the requirement of double criminality is not such a major obstacle as was previously thought and that, especially within the EU, double criminality does not frustrate mutual legal assistance so much. The question of whether and to what extent double criminality causes problems with regard to mutual legal assistance was posed during the evaluations that will be discussed below. The tendency that the requirement of double criminality is vanishing is also perceptible in recent documents such as the Treaty on Money Laundering and the European Arrest Warrant. It also follows from other documents that the requirement of double criminality is no longer obvious.[55]

---

[50] G. Vermeulen, *Wederzijdse rechtshulp in strafzaken in de Europese Unie: naar een volwaardige eigen rechtshulpruimte voor de Lid-Staten?* Maklu, Antwerpen, 1999, pp. 93-94. J. Koers, *Nederland als verzoekende staat bij de wederzijdse rechtshulp in strafzaken. Achtergronden, grenzen en mogelijkheden,* Wolf Legal Publishers, Nijmegen, 2001, p. 489.

[51] G. Vermeulen, *Wederzijdse rechtshulp in strafzaken in de Europese Unie: naar een volwaardige eigen rechtshulpruimte voor de Lid-Staten?* Maklu, Antwerpen, 1999, pp. 93-94.

[52] J. Koers, *Nederland als verzoekende staat bij de wederzijdse rechtshulp in strafzaken. Achtergronden, grenzen en mogelijkheden,* Wolf Legal Publishers, Nijmegen, 2001, p. 490. G. Vermeulen, *Wederzijdse rechtshulp in strafzaken in de Europese Unie: naar een volwaardige eigen rechtshulpruimte voor de Lid-Staten?* Maklu, Antwerpen, 1999, pp. 93-94. Indirectly; F. Thomas, *Internationale rechtshulp in strafzaken. Algemene praktische rechtsverzameling*, Story-Scientia, Brussels, 1998, p. 141.

[53] A.H.J. Swart, Human Rights and the Abolition of Traditional Principles, in: A. Eser and O. Lagodny (eds.), *Principles and Procedures for a New Transnational Criminal Law,* Max Planck Institute, Freiburg im Breisgau, 1992, pp. 505-534.

[54] A.H.J. Swart, Human Rights and the Abolition of Traditional Principles, in: A. Eser and O. Lagodny (eds.), *Principles and Procedures for a New Transnational Criminal Law,* Max Planck Institute, Freiburg im Breisgau, 1992, pp. 520-525.

[55] See, for instance, Joint Action of 24 February to Combating Trafficking in Human Beings and

5.3.1.3 *The relation between cooperation in criminal matters and the principle of confidentiality*

Legal literature recognises that a special relation exists between the application of the principle of double criminality and the principle of confidentiality. The principle of confidentiality applies in relation to other EU states and states with which bilateral treaties have been concluded.[56] In these relations, the necessity to invoke the principle of double criminality is low because the states involved have confidence in each other's legal system. Vermeulen states that it is a missed opportunity that the tendency of not applying double criminality has not been incorporated in the EU Convention on Mutual Assistance as the systems of the member states are similar and it may be assumed that the member states have confidence in each other's systems.[57] When states are party to the main human rights conventions, the International Convention on Civil and Political Rights, the International Convention on Economic, Social and Cultural Rights, and, for European countries, the European Convention on Human Rights, it is a first indication that human rights are respected in criminal procedures. However, the mere fact that a state has ratified these conventions does not automatically mean that the principle of confidentiality applies. Furthermore, it is believed that confidence is presumed to be present if a convention on mutual legal assistance or extradition exists between states.[58] However, this leaves untouched the power of the requested state to investigate the fairness and legitimacy of procedures conducted in the requesting state.

The problems indicated by Gully-Hart with regard to cooperation in criminal matters are clearly expressed in the following statement.[59]

> Many obstacles and delays in the process of international cooperation are caused by the contracting parties' inability or unwillingness to relinquish a certain number of rules and requirements which are intended to safeguard the rights of the persons who are the targets of criminal investigations. Multilateral treaties have recognized this situation by allowing contracting States to opt out of certain treaty commitments by making reservations.

From this statement, it can be concluded that the lack of confidence in each other's systems is a major obstacle for cooperation in criminal matters, otherwise states

---

Sexual Exploitation of Children, OJ L 63, 4.3.1997, title II, B and C. Action Plan to Combat Organised Crime, OJ C 251, 15.8.1997, point 4, p. 7 and point 16a, p. 11.

[56] J. Koers, *Nederland als verzoekende staat bij de wederzijdse rechtshulp in strafzaken. Achtergronden, grenzen en mogelijkheden,* Wolf Legal Publishers, Nijmegen, 2001, pp. 458-480.

[57] G. Vermeulen, *Wederzijdse rechtshulp in strafzaken in de Europese Unie: naar een volwaardige eigen rechtshulpruimte voor de Lid-Staten?* Maklu, Antwerpen, 1999, pp. 93-95.

[58] J. Sjöcrona and A. Orie, *Internationaal strafrecht,* Kluwer, Deventer, 2002, pp. 112-114. A.H.J. Swart, Human Rights and the Abolition of Traditional Principles, in: A. Eser and O. Lagodny (eds.), *Principles and Procedures for a New Transnational Criminal Law,* Max Planck Institute, Freiburg im Breisgau, 1992, p. 517.

[59] P. Gully-Hart, Loss of Time through Formal and Procedural Requirements in International Co-Operation, in: A. Eser and O. Lagodny (eds.), *Principles and Procedures for a New Transnational Criminal Law,* Max Planck Institute, Freiburg im Breisgau, 1992, p. 248.

would be more willing to relinquish these safeguards. He further argues that human rights violations are a specific ground to refuse extradition or mutual assistance.[60]

5.3.2 **Procedural problems**

5.3.2.1 *Means of communication*

With regard to the means of communication, Thomas states that the use of diplomatic channels causes delays in mutual legal assistance and therefore communication more often takes place via the Ministries of Justice. However, to improve efficient communication, more recent agreements impose the use of direct communication as the standard.[61] Thomas states that it is not always clear that the participating authorities are sufficiently qualified and he regrets that central control is absent when direct communication is practiced.[62] Vermeulen also has reservations about the proposed direct communication under the EU Convention on Mutual Assistance. He states that the abolishment of the power of a central authority to decide on the grounds for exception goes too far and that the role of a central authority with regard to coordination and uniform application of mutual legal assistance provisions must not be underestimated.[63] Without frustrating the possibility for direct communication, he proposes a parallel transmission of certain requests to the Ministry of Justice instead of the current opt-out provision. When the request concerned raises questions or doubts for the Ministry, it can, for instance, demand that the request is not immediately executed.[64] He furthermore regrets that the transmission of requests via fax or e-mail is not laid down in the EU Convention on Mutual Assistance. Notwithstanding these comments, the advantages of direct communication are nowadays generally accepted.[65]

It is explicitly recognised that direct communication can only take place if professional support is available to the competent authorities that will help them to dis-

[60] P. Gully-Hart, Loss of Time through Formal and Procedural Requirements in International Co-Operation, in: A. Eser and O. Lagodny (eds.), *Principles and Procedures for a New Transnational Criminal Law,* Max Planck Institute, Freiburg im Breisgau, 1992, pp. 249-250.

[61] F. Thomas, *Internationale rechtshulp in strafzaken. Algemene praktische rechtsverzameling*, Story-Scientia, 1998, Brussels, pp. 262-264.

[62] F. Thomas, *Internationale rechtshulp in strafzaken. Algemene praktische rechtsverzameling*, Story-Scientia, 1998, Brussels, pp. 257-266.

[63] G. Vermeulen, *Wederzijdse rechtshulp in strafzaken in de Europese Unie: naar een volwaardige eigen rechtshulpruimte voor de Lid-Staten?* Maklu, Antwerpen, 1999, p. 469.

[64] G. Vermeulen, *Wederzijdse rechtshulp in strafzaken in de Europese Unie: naar een volwaardige eigen rechtshulpruimte voor de Lid-Staten?* Maklu, Antwerpen, 1999, pp. 495-499.

[65] G. Vermeulen, *Wederzijdse rechtshulp in strafzaken in de Europese Unie: naar een volwaardige eigen rechtshulpruimte voor de Lid-Staten?* Maklu, Antwerpen, 1999, pp. 469-482. J. Koers, *Nederland als verzoekende staat bij de wederzijdse rechtshulp in strafzaken. Achtergronden, grenzen en mogelijkheden,* Wolf Legal Publishers, Nijmegen, 2001, pp. 300-301, 312-316. F. Thomas *Internationale rechtshulp in strafzaken. Algemene praktische rechtsverzameling*, Story-Scientia, Brussels, 1998, pp. 257-265.

cover to whom the request has to be sent. Besides, they need a network of (personal) contact points in several countries. Earlier initiatives to set up such logistic support have failed. The European Judicial Network[66] can play an important role in establishing such a system.[67]

5.3.2.2 *Lack of knowledge concerning the legal systems of other states and problems in identifying the competent authorities*

With regard to mutual legal assistance, familiarity with the legal systems of other states is necessary. This knowledge becomes even more important when the principle of *forum regit actum* is applied because then the request must be executed in accordance with foreign law, namely the law of the requesting state. As was already indicated above, the knowledge of other legal systems is also important when the principle of *locus regit actum* is applied in order to determine whether the request was executed in accordance with the law of the requested state. Furthermore, the differences between the common law system and the civil law system are sources of misunderstanding, and authorities are often not sufficiently informed of the differences between these systems.[68]

The need for knowledge of the legal systems of other states also follows from the different initiatives that were taken to formalise the gathering of information from a foreign state and the establishment of the European Judicial Network. Several authors argue that the competent authorities do not possess this knowledge.[69] So far, none of these initiatives have had a substantive influence on the need for information. The European Judicial Network has a great potential for the future, although the tasks of the Network are not bound by obligations.

---

[66] For general remarks on the EJN, see J. Koers, *Nederland als verzoekende staat bij de wederzijdse rechtshulp in strafzaken. Achtergronden, grenzen en mogelijkheden,* Wolf Legal Publishers, Nijmegen, 2001, pp. 64-70. C.J.C.F. Fijnaut, Europol en Eurojust, in: *Justitiële Verkenningen,* Volume 27, issue 2, 2001, pp. 11-23.

[67] G. Vermeulen, *Wederzijdse rechtshulp in strafzaken in de Europese Unie: naar een volwaardige eigen rechtshulpruimte voor de Lid-Staten?* Maklu, Antwerpen, 1999, pp. 482-485. Also J. Koers, *Nederland als verzoekende staat bij de wederzijdse rechtshulp in strafzaken. Achtergronden, grenzen en mogelijkheden,* Wolf Legal Publishers, Nijmegen, 2001, pp. 332, 64-70.

[68] For an overview of the pitfalls following from the differences between civil and common law systems, see B. de Smet, *Internationale samenwerking in strafzaken tussen Angelsaksische en continentale landen,* Intersentia, Antwerp, 1999, pp. 45-99.

[69] G. Vermeulen, *Wederzijdse rechtshulp in strafzaken in de Europese Unie: naar een volwaardige eigen rechtshulpruimte voor de Lid-Staten?* Maklu, Antwerpen, 1999, pp. 173-178. J. Koers, *Nederland als verzoekende staat bij de wederzijdse rechtshulp in strafzaken. Achtergronden, grenzen en mogelijkheden,* Wolf Legal Publishers, Nijmegen, 2001, pp. 64-65. P. Gully-Hart, Loss of Time through Formal and Procedural Requirements in International Co-Operation, in: A. Eser and O. Lagodny (eds.), *Principles and Procedures for a New Transnational Criminal Law,* Max Planck Institute, Freiburg im Breisgau, 1992, pp. 253-254.

5.3.2.3 *Waste of time, money, and human resources*

The problem of a waste of resources cannot be seen separately from the problems mentioned before as this problem (partly) follows from the problems indicated above. The problem of a waste of resources exists in the fact that procedures for co-operation in criminal matters are generally too long and complicated with too many authorities involved. Gully-Hart recognises the examination of the request by the requested state as 'the main cause of delay since the requested state will usually submit the request for international cooperation to judicial review.'[70] The lack of relevant information in a request is seen as another reason for inefficiency in cooperation in criminal matters.[71] Bassiouni states that 'Probably the most serious of all problems is bureaucratic divisions which burden the administration of criminal justice and sometimes paralyse the system'.[72] Some of the problems mentioned above follow from a lack of priority being given to the proper functioning of the mutual legal assistance system and a lack of financial resources.

5.3.3 **Organisational problems; language problems**

A request for mutual legal assistance is made in the language of the requesting state or that of the requested state, although the requesting state often attaches a translation into the language of the requested state in order to avoid delays.[73] Apart from this reference made by Thomas with regard to this subject, other authors remain silent on this practical issue and consequently do not mention possible problems in this regard.

5.4 OBSTACLES TO THE APPLICATION OF LEGAL INSTRUMENTS ON MUTUAL LEGAL ASSISTANCE IN THE EU

In this section, the effect of legal instruments discussed in Chapter 4, particularly those concerning mutual legal assistance, will be addressed. In 1998, the Multi-Disciplinary Group (MDG) of the Council of the EU started to collect information on the application and implementation of EU and other instruments on cooperation in criminal matters between the member states of the EU for the purpose of evaluation.

---

[70] P. Gully-Hart, Loss of Time through Formal and Procedural Requirements in International Co-Operation, in: A. Eser and O. Lagodny (eds.), *Principles and Procedures for a New Transnational Criminal Law*, Max Planck Institute, Freiburg im Breisgau, 1992, p. 254.

[71] F. Thomas, *Internationale rechtshulp in strafzaken. Algemene praktische rechtsverzameling*, Story-Scientia, Brussels, 1998, p. 253

[72] M.C. Bassiouni, Policy Considerations in Inter-State Cooperation in Criminal Matters, in: A. Eser and O. Lagodny (eds.), *Principles and Procedures for a New Transnational Criminal Law,* Max Planck Institute, Freiburg im Breisgau, 1992, p. 825.

[73] F. Thomas, *Internationale rechtshulp in strafzaken. Algemene praktische rechtsverzameling*, Story-Scientia, Brussels, 1998, pp. 266-271 and pp. 276-279.

For this collection, firstly, a questionnaire was sent to all the member states in order to obtain an impression of the existing situation. Secondly, various authorities involved in mutual legal assistance in the member states were interviewed by a group of experts. These evaluating groups consisted of different practitioners from several member states and were constituted differently on each occasion. The interviews took place between June 1998 (Luxembourg was visited first) and March 2000 (the United Kingdom was visited last). The results of the answers to the questionnaire and the information received by the experts during their visits were collected in 15 separate country reports.[74] Never before had such an elaborate examination of the system of mutual legal assistance in all the member states of the EU been embarked upon. The separate evaluation reports are a major source of information on the practice and problems concerning cooperation in criminal matters in the EU. Since the persons involved in this project concerned almost exclusively practitioners in the various member states, the results of this inquiry give a good impression of the problems that are met in daily practice, although a more theoretical discussion must not be sought in this study. Furthermore, the study was limited to the EU.

In this section, I will focus on the main problems identified when analysing the reports. The parts of the reports on mutual legal assistance will be analysed in detail whereas the parts on the search and seizure of property will be dealt with only superficially. The problems are divided into three categories, namely, substantive problems, procedural problems, and organisational problems.[75] Furthermore, a remainder category, called ‘other problems’, contains problems that are signalled in the reports but fall outside the other three categories. Per category, the most pressing problems will be focused upon, by using the comments and examples discussed in the reports. It was not always possible to give a complete overview of the practices with regard to these problems in all the member states. A matrix is compiled for a quick and compact overview of the most important problematic areas. Some recommendations will subsequently be discussed.

In general, the reports show that the way in which mutual legal assistance takes place in the EU member states is not as bad as is often claimed. In many countries, the system is adequate, but a clear trend can be perceived in that the number of requests is on the increase.[76] The enlargement of the EU will certainly have its conse-

[74] Austria, 22 December 2000, 14911/00 crimorg 170, Belgium, 16 May 2000, 7704/00, crimorg 60, Denmark, 09 September 1999, 10860/99, crimorg 128, Finland, 07 July 2000, 9392/00 crimorg 94, France, 10 October 2000, 12000/00 crimorg 131, Germany, 11 December 2000, 13365/00 crimorg 153, Greece, 23 August 1999, 10596/99, crimorg 125, Ireland 18 August 1999, 9079/99 crimorg 70, Italy, 22 March 2000, 7254/00, crimorg 52,Luxembourg, 15 February 1999, 5932/99, crimorg 21, The Netherlands, 18 August 1999, 10595/99, crimorg 124, Portugal, 02 April 2001, 7251/01, crimorg 33, Spain, 22 March 2000, 5819/00, crimorg 16, Sweden, 27 March 2001, 7250/01, crimorg 32, United Kingdom, 26 March 2001, 7249/01, crimorg 31.

[75] For a description of these categories, see Section 5.3.

[76] Final Report on the First Evaluation Exercise – Mutual Legal Assistance in Criminal Matters, OJ C 216, 1.8.2001, p. 17.

quences in this regard. For many EU member states, the experts openly expressed their concern as to whether the current systems of mutual legal assistance will be sufficient in the future if the number of requests increases further.

5.4.1 Substantive problems

In this section the substantive problems following from the evaluation reports will be discussed. Successively, the execution of requests in accordance with the law of the requested state (the principle of *locus regit actum*), the double criminality requirement, and the different use of terms will be reviewed. We will see that some of the problems originate in the fact that legal systems are based on different traditions i.e., the common law and civil law systems.

5.4.1.1 *Execution of requests by applying the national law of the requested state*

So far, a request for mutual legal assistance must be executed in accordance with the law of the requested state. If the EU Convention on Mutual Assistance enters into force, this will change. It must be admitted that the precondition that requests are executed in accordance with the law of the requesting state causes problems as requirements for criminal procedures differ between states, as do the guarantees for witnesses and suspects. This problem is closely related to the lack of knowledge concerning each other's legal system, as follows from the problems that will be focused upon below.

Belgium, for instance, expressed some comments on the practice in the Netherlands with regard to the execution of requests made by Belgium. It stated that the Netherlands assessed the appropriate action to be taken on a request for assistance in the light of its own requirements.[77]

In the UK, it was not allowed, until recently, to intercept telecommunications upon a request from another state. However, since October 2000, new legislation on the interception of telecommunications is in force, which also permits the fulfilment of a foreign request. Furthermore, in the UK, fingerprints and DNA samples cannot be obtained following a request.[78]

Another example is the problem which exists between the Netherlands and Luxembourg with regard to requests to restrain bank accounts. In the Netherlands, the public prosecutor is authorised to make such a request, but, in Luxembourg, such a request must be made by an examining magistrate.[79]

Austria experienced some problems when an authority other than a court made a request. As mutual legal assistance in Austria is almost the sole competence of the

[77] Belgian report, Section 2.11, p. 23.
[78] Report of the United Kingdom, Section 2.1.7, p. 10.
[79] Dutch report, Section 4.4.3, p. 46.

judges, practitioners were cautious when they received requests from, for instance, a prosecutor. Austria solved this problem by requesting additional information and convincing itself that a competent authority had made the request.[80]

An exceptional situation exists in Italy, where it is possible for the Italian authorities to provide assistance on the basis of a foreign request, even if assistance would not be granted in a domestic case, as long as such a measure is not prohibited by Italian law.[81]

It is indicated in several reports that delays are often caused by the fact that some additional information to the request is required by the requested state. Delays caused by the necessity for additional information is often a result of the lack of sound knowledge concerning the legislation of the requested state. Only when the differences between the system of the requested state and the system of the requesting state are known, can the correct questions be asked.

For instance, requests from France and Belgium to the UK are not detailed enough and therefore cannot be executed.[82] Similar problems concerning unspecified requests are reported by Ireland.[83]

Additional specific and detailed information is also required when the requested state wants to take into account the requirements in the requesting state, for instance, if it is not clear who has to execute the request according to the legislation of the requesting state, whether it is necessary that the evidence should be taken on oath, or whether it is required that the hearing should take place in the presence of counsel. Thorough knowledge of the law of the requesting state is then required.

Some developments to challenge this problem are already emerging in the EU. France, for instance, has adopted new legislation in June 1999 to increase the effectiveness of criminal procedures. It requires that the law of the requesting state, indicated in a request, must be taken into account as far as possible when executing the request. For instance, if Italy asks for the hearing of a witness, the witness will be heard in the presence of counsel when this is indicated in the request, although this is not required according to French domestic law.[84] In Portugal, the principle of *forum regit actum* is applied under certain conditions, which means that it is progressive in this regard.

[80] Austrian report, Section 2.8.4, p. 28.
[81] Italian report, Section 2.4.4, p. 8.
[82] Report of the United Kingdom, Section 2.12.5, p. 29.
[83] Irish report, Section 4.15, p. 29.
[84] French report, Section 2.1.4, p. 6, and Section 4.1.6, pp. 42-43.

5.4.1.2 *Double criminality*

Contrary to what is often presumed, the reports indicate that the requirement of double criminality is not a major restraint on mutual legal assistance. In the majority of cases, the crimes for which mutual legal assistance is requested are criminalised in all the member states. Furthermore, it can be stated that the requirement of double criminality is envisaged with flexibility, in the sense that it is more a requirement of double punishability.[85] Nevertheless, where the double criminality requirement is applied, for instance with regard to coercive measures, it remains a potential obstacle to and a time-consuming element within mutual assistance. The question of double criminality may become less acute as the harmonisation of substantive criminal law develops within the EU. The different practices in the member states where the application of double criminality still plays a role will now be reviewed.

Denmark is one of the countries in which double criminality is required in all cases of mutual legal assistance. However, the Danish report mentioned some contradictory practices concerning the use of the principle of double criminality. It said that double criminality is officially applied only in cases of search and seizure. But as a result of the lack of Danish national legislation on international mutual legal assistance, the Danish authorities apply their own domestic legislation by analogy. It seems that this practice includes some form of double criminality.[86]

In Luxembourg, the principle of double criminality applies as well. However, it was said that a request is very rarely refused as a result of the absence of double criminality.[87]

In Italy, it is stated that double criminality is not a ground for refusal, although the execution of a request will be denied if the facts for which mutual legal assistance is required do not constitute an offence under Italian law unless the defendant has consented to the request.[88]

While the application of double criminality in Greece is formally denied, its practitioners do apply it.[89]

---

[85] Final Report on the First Evaluation Exercise – Mutual Legal Assistance in Criminal Matters, OJ C 216, 1.8.2001, p. 19.

[86] Danish report, Section 2.1, p. 4.

[87] Luxembourg report, Section 2.2, p. 8.

[88] Italian report, Section 2.2, p. 5, and Section 2.4.3, p. 8.

[89] The experts of the evaluation team had some problems in uncovering the practice on the application of double criminality as this varied considerably between the authorities. This was very confusing for the evaluators. The Greek authorities therefore made a statement on double criminality saying that the confusion was not caused by a contradiction between the provisions of Greek legislation but was derived from the actual application of the 1959 Convention, the Schengen Agreement, and the 1990 Schengen Convention, and the Convention on Laundering, Search, Seizure and Confiscation of the Proceeds from Crime. They saw this as a problem that concerns all the member states of the EU. Greek report, Annex D.

In Spain, double criminality is required in all cases of mutual legal assistance.[90]

In Portugal, the principle of double criminality is only applied to coercive measures. However, the term coercive measure is used so broadly that it can be said that this principle also plays a role in other situations. It includes 'any measure which imposes a restriction or deprivation of personal freedom or which generally involves recourse to law enforcement agencies' including, for instance, a summons for someone to appear in court or to make someone the subject of an investigation.[91]

In the UK, the principle of double criminality is applied to search and seizure as well as for the use of investigative powers of the Serious Fraud Office or the Crown Office. Furthermore, it is applied 'in respect of requests from Belgium and Luxembourg seeking sworn evidence or authenticated documentary evidence for use in fiscal cases.'[92] Furthermore, the UK has refused assistance on the ground of the absence of double criminality.

In Sweden, the principle of double criminality is a ground for refusing assistance although it is not applied in cases of service of documents. However, the new law, in force since October 2000, has abolished this requirement in relation to requests made by public prosecutors, the taking of evidence by courts, the transfer of persons in custody, and the hearing of witnesses by telephone or video conference. This means that the principle of double criminality only remains applicable to coercive measures.[93]

In Austria, the principle of double criminality applies as a rule and in a broad way in mutual legal assistance cases, except in cases of service of documents.[94]

5.4.1.3 *The different use of terms by different states and different authorities*

Problems concerning mutual legal assistance may occur when legal terms and instruments are interpreted and implemented differently by different states and by different authorities within one state.

A clear example in this regard is Greece, where a great discrepancy exists between the practitioners and the central authorities with regard to the use of the principle of double criminality. Although it was said that double criminality was only required in case 'an onerous measure is to be taken in Greece',[95] the practitioners believed that the principle of double criminality had to be applied in all cases.

---

[90] Spanish report, Section 2.2, p. 9.

[91] Portuguese report, Section 2.2.2, p. 15.

[92] Report of the United Kingdom, Section 2.1.6.1, p. 10.

[93] Swedish report, Section 2.2.5, pp. 12-13.

[94] Austrian report, Section 2.2.2, pp. 9-10.

[95] Greek report, Section 2.2.2, p. 27.

Furthermore, the UK considers that the greatest problems with regard to mutual legal assistance between the UK and other EU countries concern differences in legal terminology.[96] Germany admitted that problems existed with the UK as a consequence of the different legal systems.

Another observation is that the interpretation of the term 'urgent' is problematic and leads to great differences. The different interpretation of the term 'urgent' was regarded as problematic in several reports. Italy, for instance, issues relatively many urgent requests as a consequence of limited time for the conclusion of preliminary investigations and for prosecutions. Whether urgent requests sent to Italy are dealt with urgently depends primarily on the workload of the specific Court of Appeal. In the UK, no differentiation is made at all between urgent and non-urgent requests.

In most countries, the need is felt to define the term 'urgent' in order to bring some harmonisation among the member states in the use of the term and that the real urgent cases be dealt with first. Therefore, the statements on good practices, following the Joint Action on Good Practices on Mutual Legal Assistance in Criminal Cases, of all the member states include some phrases on the use of the term.[97] All the member states except Sweden have made the statement that incoming urgent requests are given priority as far as this is not inconsistent with their national law. Furthermore, all states have declared that urgent foreign requests will not be treated less favourably than national requests. With regard to outgoing requests, all member states have made the declaration that the reasons why a request is urgent will be included in the request and that an urgent request will only be made if an urgent reply is required.[98]

5.4.2 **Procedural problems**

The procedural problems that were raised in the evaluation reports will be discussed below. The most important problem in this category is the use of direct communication channels. Closely related to this item, and therefore adopted under this heading, is the use of the European Judicial Network (EJN). Furthermore, the wasting of resources, the internal communication between and among competent authorities, the instructions and guidelines, the confusion with regard to the formalities to be fulfilled, and, finally, the appeals as a delaying strategy will be discussed.

[96] Report of the United Kingdom, Sections 2.12.1 and 2.12.2, p. 28.

[97] Joint Action of 29 June 1998 on Good Practices on Mutual Legal Assistance in Criminal Cases, OJ L 191, 7.7.98, p. 1.

[98] Good Practices on Mutual Legal Assistance in Criminal Cases. Statements of the Member States of the EU, Secretary General of the Council of the EU, February 2000.

5.4.2.1 *The use of direct communication channels*

The final report indicates that direct communication between judicial authorities is a practice that is on the increase.[99] However, it is difficult to prove this with statistics as requests are not made regularly in most of the member states and if statistics have been compiled at all, they mostly concern requests that are communicated via the central authorities and not the requests that are communicated directly.

In many states, direct channels are not commonly used because practitioners are not familiar with the use of these channels.[100] However, it is recognised that the use of direct communication channels can considerably reduce the time necessary for mutual legal assistance.

The way in which communication between states takes place divides itself into two directions.
1. Formal communication channels are used in nearly all cases.
2. Direct communication takes place whenever this opportunity is available.

With this division, the member states can be allotted into two groups, although it is not always crystal clear to which group a certain state belongs.

In the first group, we find the states that seem to be persistent in using the formal communication channels instead of direct channels.

In Greece, communication is always conducted via the central unit at the Ministry of Justice. Although the competent authority may execute requests directly communicated to Greece, replies to such requests are transmitted via the central authority at the Ministry of Justice. Furthermore, Greece still occasionally receives requests from Denmark, France, and Spain via diplomatic channels. For outgoing requests in Greece, the channels for direct communication are not commonly used also because translations have to be obtained via the Ministry of Foreign Affairs after permission from the Ministry of Justice. Furthermore, practitioners in Greece do not know that requests can be submitted directly under Article 15(2) of the 1959 Convention and under the Schengen Convention.

A similar practice exists in Ireland were the judicial authorities are not competent to execute requests that are directly communicated to them; they have to forward these requests to the central authority at the Ministry of Justice, Equality, and Law Reform.[101] In the case of police-to-police communication, the Irish police can transmit

[99] Final Report on the First Evaluation Exercise – Mutual Legal Assistance in Criminal Matters, OJ C 216, 1.8.2001, p. 16.

[100] Final Report on the First Evaluation Exercise – Mutual Legal Assistance in Criminal Matters, OJ C 216, 1.8.2001, p. 23. Dutch report, Section 4.3.5, p. 42.

[101] Irish report, Section 4.7, p. 26.

cooperation replies to a request, but not before having obtained the advice of the central authority. Therefore, in practice, the materials are normally transmitted via the central authority. Furthermore, advice from the Chief State Solicitor's Office is also required and causes further unnecessary delays. In Ireland, judges have the authority to issue requests although they have to be informed by the Public Prosecutor's Office who, at the instigation of the Garda Siochana, makes drafts for requests.

France must be allocated to this group as well. Communication between France and Sweden takes place via diplomatic channels, and between France and Ireland and France and the UK via the Ministry of Justice, which causes serious delays. Furthermore, Austria reported problems with France as the latter returned requests that were sent directly to the competent authorities.[102]

In Luxembourg, communication takes place via the Ministry of Justice or via diplomatic channels, although the authorities involved recognise the advantages of efficiency, speed, and flexibility by direct contacts between judicial authorities.

In Belgium, the execution of directly submitted requests is only possible after authorisation from the Minister of Justice, except in cases in which a request is made within the framework of the Benelux Convention.[103]

In the UK, requests are to be sent via the International Branch of the National Criminal Intelligence Service (NCIS) or the UK central authority (the Home Office), even if the transmission of requests on a police-to-police basis is allowed. The NCIS is also the competent authority when urgent requests are sent via the Interpol channel. Authorities that have received requests directly have to refer to the UK central authority in order to obtain a direction from the Secretary of State. Currently, the UK is reviewing its practice with regard to direct transmission in order to make the application of the Schengen provisions possible in the future.

In general, the German report indicated that direct communication channels, within the Schengen framework, were not used although this is provided for.[104] They admitted that the German authorities also often failed to use this channel, which was said to be one of the causes of delays.

In Spain, requests are communicated via the Ministry of Justice as a rule, except requests that are made pursuant to the Schengen Convention and Article 15 of the 1959 Convention. Furthermore, judges and courts can respond to a request that is

---

102 Austrian report, Section 4.2.3, p. 44.

103 This will change when the new law on criminal procedure enters into force. It is proposed that requests sent to Belgian authorities are sent to the Ministry of Justice but if no reaction is received from the Ministry within 24 hours, the authority may execute the request.

104 German report, Section 2.12.2, p. 20.

sent directly to them. Although this is a practice which is on the increase, it was not commonly used until recently.[105]

In Italy, a similar pattern exists although, even in the case of direct communication, the request is always transmitted via the Prosecutor's General Office to the Court of Appeal as well. Furthermore, only 61% of the requests were sent directly by Italy and only 50% of the received Schengen requests were transmitted directly.

Portugal must also be accommodated in this group of states.

Within the second group, those states can be found that use direct communication channels whenever possible.

In Sweden, urgent requests to and from non-Nordic countries had to be communicated via the Ministry of Justice but this practice has changed following new legislation which entered into force October 2000. Direct communication is now the rule.

In Austria, most requests come from and go to other states party to the Schengen Convention and consequently most of these requests are communicated directly. The general practice in Austria is that the courts deal with requests without the involvement of another authority. Only if a request is rejected and if foreign officers would like to attend the execution of a request must the Ministry of Justice be notified. However, mutual legal assistance is exclusively dealt with on the federal level.

In Denmark, Finland, and the Netherlands, direct communication channels are standardly used as a rule as well.

Although the use of direct communication channels, if available, must be encouraged, the role of the central authority, in most cases the Ministry of Justice, must not be eliminated. It still plays an important role in cases of mutual legal assistance with countries outside the EU. Furthermore, it could play an important role in guiding member states and applicant countries in the web of mutual legal assistance in Europe. Its role with regard to data collection, registration of requests, and detecting problems, must not be underestimated. Finally, it can be important that guidelines are adopted by the central authorities, namely, to underline the importance of these guidelines and to ensure a homogeneous interpretation and application of the relevant provisions.

5.4.2.1.1 The use of the European Judicial Network

Because the European Judicial Network (EJN) is discussed in relation to the use of direct communication channels, it is placed within the category of procedural prob-

[105] Spanish report, Section 2.4, pp. 13-15.

lems as part of the issue on the use of direct communication channels. The institution of the EJN was discussed in Chapter 4.

The positive effects of direct contacts between judicial authorities are repeatedly reported. A first statement made by the member states in this regard is that the use of direct contacts in general must be considered as facilitating mutual legal assistance. For instance, the Danish authorities are convinced that direct contacts between the authorities involved in the requesting and the requested state facilitate the effectiveness of assistance and shortens the delays in executing requests.

A second statement is that the use of liaison magistrates must be considered a valuable possibility to facilitate mutual legal assistance. It is recognised by France that the presence of foreign liaison magistrates in France or French liaisons abroad contribute to an effective and speedy procedure in the case of mutual legal assistance. For urgent requests, Sweden makes intensive use of the Nordic liaisons that are seconded to several states. By using these contacts, it tries to get in touch with the competent authorities in the requested state. It also makes use of the Interpol channels.

A third statement with regard to the use of direct contacts is that the advantages of the 'old boys network' must not be underestimated as it is extremely important to establish direct contacts. Swedish officers, for instance, admit that informal contacts with officials from other member states established during various meetings are very helpful to facilitate proceedings on mutual legal assistance. In Finland, an oral request can be executed as long as the person making the request is known to the Finnish authorities.

Direct contacts with the requesting state, for instance when more information with regard to the request is needed, are facilitated by the EJN. Most of the countries note the advantages of the EJN or indicate that they expect a positive impulse in the future once this Network is operational in their country. Italy has great expectations for the EJN and it has positive experiences with the exchange of liaison officers with France. Similar expectations are nourished by Greece and Belgium, especially with regard to diminishing delays.

Belgium reported that it experienced a high number of EJN contact points in France, Germany, and Italy. However, it also admitted that delays in the execution of requests in Italy are very common.

Because the EJN was installed in September 1998,[106] the effects reported in the evaluation reports are limited. Some reports, like the Danish,[107] the Swedish, and the

[106] Following the Joint Action of 29 June 1998 on Good Practices on Mutual Legal Assistance in Criminal Cases, OJ L 191, 7.7.1998, p. 4.

[107] Danish report, Section 2.3.11, p. 11.

Austrian, indicated that it was too early to include the experiences with the EJN. In France, the EJN was not known to most of the examining magistrates.

Germany is the only country that explicitly expressed its positive experiences with the EJN, which has led to prompter action in respect of requested measures. In each of the *Länder*, contact points for the EJN were established and four of them were assigned to serve as regional coordination points.

It is believed that, in the future, the EJN will play an important role in facilitating direct contacts for mutual legal assistance within the EU.

5.4.2.2 *Waste of time, money, and human resources*

In many countries, the procedure from the moment a request enters the country to the moment the request is executed and afterwards returned to the requesting country is too long and involves too many authorities. This may lead to duplication of efforts, and a waste of human resources. This duplication is often justified by the need for verification.[108]

In Sweden, for instance, an incoming request is registered first at the Ministry of Justice and afterwards at the Prosecutor General's Office and its legality is checked at the Ministry of Justice as well as at the local prosecutor's office.

In the Netherlands, a request that has been sent directly to the examining magistrate has to be sent first to a public prosecutor for registration before execution can commence.

If a request to Finland is sent via the Ministry of Justice, it can occur that its legality is examined on three occasions, first by the Ministry of Justice, then by the National Bureau of Investigation, and finally by the executing police office.

In Spain, a similar system exists where the request is first examined by the head of the section for international mutual assistance in criminal matters and by the Section staff, both at the Ministry of Justice, and then by the competent judicial authority.[109]

In Denmark, non-urgent cases sent via the Ministry of Justice can take one month before they are sent to the competent authorities for execution and it can take another month before they are returned to the requesting country.[110]

France is also struggling with the problem of multiple checks as formal and legal checks take place by all authorities that are involved in the mutual legal assistance,

---

[108] Final Report on the First Evaluation Exercise – Mutual Legal Assistance in Criminal Matters, OJ C 216, 1.8.2001, p. 20.

[109] Spanish report, Section 2.4(a), p. 13.

[110] Danish report, Section 2.4.2, p. 12.

so both the authorities which forward the request and the authorities which execute it. Furthermore, the mutual legal assistance system in France is very fragmented with many special commissions and bureaus for various aims. Among other things, there are the drugs units, the money laundering units, the financial units, the mutual assistance office in Paris, the Financial unit in Paris, the principal state counsel's offices, the central office for combating major financial crime, the central office of the crime squad, etc. This makes the system very complicated.

In Greece, at first sight, there seems to be a clear division of controlling competence between the central authority which checks the formalities of a request and the prosecutor of the Court of Appeal who carries out the checks as to the substance of the request. However, an overlap between these proceedings is unavoidable, for instance, when the reasons for the request are checked by the central authority, it also touches on the grounds for refusal, which is checked by the public prosecutor. Furthermore, when the prosecutor forwards a request to an examining magistrate, its substance is again checked. For outgoing requests, the same duplication in checking the request takes place. In general, the system for mutual legal assistance in Greece can be considered too long, with several authorities with overlapping competences that are not aware of each other's responsibilities.

In Ireland, all requests have to be forwarded first to the central authority, including urgent requests. Especially time-consuming are the procedures in which witnesses must be heard on oath before a court. In these procedures, the advice of the Attorney General's Office and the Chief State Solicitor's Office are required and the Minister has to appoint a judge of the District Court. If enquiries are necessary before a request can be executed, for instance to find out the identity of a witness, delays may occur as well.

In Belgium, the prior authorisation of the Minister of Justice for the execution of a request is necessary, even for urgent and directly transmitted requests. Only requests made within the framework of the Benelux Treaty are treated on the same conditions as national requests, i.e., without prior authorisation. The minister checks whether it concerns one of the offences listed in Article 1 of the Extradition Act and whether it fulfils the requirements of Article 2(b) of the 1959 Convention.[111] The system of mutual legal assistance in Belgium is very complicated and approximately 20 steps must be taken before an ordinary request is executed and returned.[112] Some indicate that it takes at least two months before all these steps have been taken. In this chain, the legality of a request is checked several times and coordination between the various authorities is absent.

In Portugal, various steps must be taken before an outgoing request can be sent although it is said that this process takes between 10 and 18 days for untranslated re-

[111] These requirements are that the execution of the request does not prejudice the sovereignty, security, public order, or other essential interests of the country.

[112] Belgian report, Section 4.1b, pp. 32-33.

quests. The numerous checks on the legality of incoming requests lead to pointless duplication. Because the different authorities are not aware of the nature of each other's checks there is a risk that, in the end, a proper check has still not taken place.

In general, one or more links in the chain are often only formalities but do not add any substantial advantages. For instance, in France and Austria, the approval by the Ministry of Justice for the presence of foreign officials at the execution of a request and for magistrates travelling abroad is required, although this is not a substantial check.[113]

Although it is often said that these formalities do not cause any delays, it is preferable that these steps are excluded from the chain in order to streamline the channels and to make the channels more transparent. This has been done in Austria, for instance, where the communication lines are now rather short.[114]

In conclusion, it must be admitted that the national procedures with regard to mutual legal assistance are very long, complicated, and opaque. This easily results in delays in the execution and transmission of requests. Furthermore, it leads to duplication of efforts and thus to a waste of resources. Those steps in the procedure that are superfluous or a repetition of earlier actions should be eliminated from the procedure.

5.4.2.3 *Communication between judicial and police authorities and within the judiciary*

The effectiveness of mutual legal assistance is also dependent on the relation between the judicial authority and police forces in a country and the way in which the police force is organised. In most of the states, the execution of a request, or a part thereof, is the task of the police. If the division of competence between the judiciary and the police is not clear, if they are not cooperative with each other, or if the police lack resources, problems may occur.

The latter was the case in the Netherlands where, in 1997, only an estimated 50% of the requests sent to the district court of Amsterdam could be sent for execution to the police as a result of the lack of personnel within the regional police teams.[115]

Denmark has positive experiences in this regard because, for requests made by the police, the confirmation of the Court is sometimes required. Because the police and the judiciary (especially the public prosecutor) work closely together, this will not cause any problems. In many states, the police set the priorities in cases of mutual legal assistance.

---

[113] French report, Section 4.2.1(e) and (f), p. 49. Austrian report, Section 4.2.17, p. 51.

[114] Austrian report, Section 4.1.1, p. 41, and Section 2.4.3, p. 14.

[115] Dutch report, Section 4.3.3, p. 41.

In Sweden, as in most other countries, the prosecutors rely to a large degree on the police for the execution of requests, as prosecutors do not have their own investigative resources. Furthermore, the competence of the prosecutors with regard to sending requests was not clear and was a source of confusion.[116]

Another related observation is that the power of the police varies considerably between countries, which may lead to problems. For instance, in Finland, the police are authorised to execute requests on their own account. The police both issue and execute the majority of requests in Finland without the involvement of a prosecutor, court, or Ministry of Justice.[117] However, it was recommended by the evaluating experts that the police should receive specific training in drawing requests and that the Ministry of Justice should be more involved in order to coordinate and guide the whole process.

In Germany, the police forces also have a broad competence and the judicial authorities are strongly dependent on the information, know-how, and cooperation of the police forces. A more active role for the judicial authorities was recommended.

Communication within the judiciary and especially between judges and prosecutors can be problematic as well. The French report gives the impression that the Ministry of Justice has problems with controlling the execution of requests for mutual legal assistance. The report states that 'the examining magistrates enjoy a great independence in comparison to the prosecutors' and that 'it is almost impossible to measure the performance of the Principal 'State Counsels' Offices and the examining magistrates'.[118]

Furthermore, there are enormous differences between the countries with regard to the competence of the different disciplines. For instance, in Portugal, the public prosecutor has extensive power in dealing with incoming and outgoing requests and the role of the examining judge is superfluous, whereas, in other states, notably Austria, mutual legal assistance is almost the sole competence of the judges.

5.4.2.4 *Instructions and guidelines*

In most of the countries, guidelines and circulars do contribute to a univocal application of provisions on mutual legal assistance. The Ministry of Justice or another central authority normally plays an important role in issuing these documents. However, as a consequence of the division of powers between the administrative authorities and the judiciary, and the independent status of the judiciary in general, the latter cannot be bound by these documents that are issued by the administrative authorities. This practice was reported by Greece, for instance.

[116] Swedish report, Section 2.3.5, p. 16.

[117] Finnish report, Section 4.1.4, p. 32.

[118] French report, Section 4.2.2.1(b), pp. 52-53, and Section 4.2.4, pp. 61-62.

In Portugal, the Ministry of Justice is not allowed to issue guidelines or instructions to the public prosecutors because of their independence. Only the Chief Public Prosecutor has the power to instruct public prosecutors; instructions and guidelines issued by the Chief Public Prosecutor are binding. Furthermore, court judges are independent and cannot receive instructions from anybody.

In Sweden, court judges as well as public prosecutors cannot receive binding instructions from any ministry as they operate independently in the exercise of their duties.

The Belgian authorities are flooded with instruction manuals and some of the documents in use were very old or even outdated, which frustrates an efficient process of mutual legal assistance.

In the UK, various authorities, for instance the Home Office and the international division of the NCIS, issue guidelines, some of them having binding status.

In Germany, the federal government and the government of the *Länder* have issued directives dealing with foreign countries in criminal matters. These directives are binding and, as regards matters falling within the competence of the courts, they contain advice on these matters.

5.4.2.5 *Confusion as to what formalities must be fulfilled and which channels must be used*

In all EU member states, international law (both multilateral and bilateral agreements) and national law is applicable with regard to mutual legal assistance. Consequently, it is not immediately clear what laws regarding mutual legal assistance apply in a certain case. This leads to a great variety of channels that can be used for the transmission of requests and of the formalities to be fulfilled.[119] When persons have no clear picture of the particular system in a state, this may lead to uncertainty as to what rules can be applied. Practitioners do not have enough knowledge on many aspects of the judicial systems of other states and do not know how these systems work in practice. Some examples may illustrate these confusing practices.

In Italy, the channel of Interpol is used for urgent requests in compliance with Article 15(2) of the 1959 Convention. Pursuant to Articles 52 and 53 of the Schengen Convention, the Italian judicial authorities are encouraged to transmit requests directly.

The confusing practice as to what channels must be used is apparently present in the United Kingdom. First of all, for this purpose the United Kingdom of Great Britain and Northern Ireland also includes the independent offshore jurisdictions of the

[119] See, for instance, Dutch report, Section 4.4.1, p. 45.

Channel Islands and the Isle of Man, as well as the Self-Governing Dependent Territory of Gibraltar and so it is divided into seven jurisdictions, namely England and Wales, Northern Ireland, Scotland, two in the Channel Islands (Jersey and Guernsey), the Isle of Man, and Gibraltar. Requests regarding the Channel Islands, the Isle of Man, or Gibraltar must be forwarded via the relevant Attorney General. Furthermore, many authorities and agencies are involved in mutual legal assistance, all with their own defined competence and internal procedures. Some of them are competent for the whole territory of the UK, others only for parts of it. Then the system in the UK differs considerably from the other systems in the EU (except the Irish system) as it concerns a common law system and most of the practitioners in other countries involved in mutual legal assistance are not familiar with this system. For instance, foreign authorities do not always understand that, in the UK, courts do not have independent jurisdiction to execute letters of request. Conversely, law enforcement officers from the UK, who have broad competence in the UK, are not familiar with the fact that, in civil law countries, the powers of the police are often more limited. It is understandable that, in this jungle of rules and procedures, foreign authorities become confused when they try to understand the system. The complexity of the system is further aggravated by the fact that many officials and authorities are designated as judicial authorities pursuant to Article 24 of the 1959 Convention. Most of these authorities are competent to write letters of request but not to receive these requests directly.

5.4.2.6 *Appeals as a delaying strategy*

Most of the states indicate that appeals in the requested state may cause serious delays but that the number of appeals is so low that this causes no serious problems, except in the case of Luxembourg, where it is reported that the appeals procedure is being abused as a delaying tactic. In Ireland, it was reported that appeals procedures were causing serious delays.

5.4.3 **Organisational problems**

The organisational problems that will be discussed below originate in the actual execution of mutual legal assistance requests. These problems consist of the identification of the competent authorities abroad, practical problems in contacting these authorities, and language problems.

5.4.3.1 *Identification of competent judicial authorities*

The competences of the various authorities involved in mutual legal assistance differ considerably between the member states and are consequently a source of misunderstandings. The identification of the competent judicial authorities is important when a request is to be sent directly or when a state wants to know the actual state of affairs with regard to a request that has been previously sent. Problems regarding identification can be traced to the lack of knowledge of each other's legal system.

In general, it can be said that the competence of the police in the Nordic countries is broader than in other EU countries. Problems are reported in the Danish evaluation report, which states that the position of the police commissioners may cause problems abroad as it is required in some countries that requests are signed or made by a judge or another legal authority.[120] Similar problems are encountered by Finland with Luxembourg, as the latter refused to execute requests that were made by Finnish police officers because the Luxembourg authorities did not recognise them as judicial authorities competent to make requests.

Austria experienced problems in identifying the competent authority abroad when sending direct requests.[121]

Often the specific competences are divided among various (judicial) authorities. For instance, in Denmark, the police commissioners, in their function of local chief prosecutor, are the competent local judicial authority to deal with requests to obtain evidence. Requests which are purely for the service of documents must be sent to the local police.[122]

The requesting state often needs some background information on the system of the requested state in order to be able to identify the competent authority, but this background information is often absent.

In France, the police do not belong to the judicial authorities, which include (senior) presidents, appeal court judges, criminal court judges, examining magistrates and members of the State Counsels' Office. However, only judges of the ordinary courts are authorised to receive urgent requests pursuant to Article 15 of the 1959 Convention while the principal State Counsels' Office is competent in the context of Article 53 of the Schengen Convention. Furthermore, the urgent requests are returned to the requesting state via the Ministry of Justice while other requests are returned directly. Although the French police have executing power, the requests remain under the control of the judicial authorities.

In Austria, the role of the prosecution service with regard to mutual legal assistance is very limited since the courts have to complete the procedures. Logically, the courts have been cautious when they receive requests made by an authority other than a court, for instance, a prosecutor.

In Germany, the opposite situation exists, namely, with a central role for the prosecution departments and a very limited role for the courts. The German report indicated that foreign requesting authorities often did not make any effort to identify the appropriate public prosecutor's department or court in Germany for the execution of

[120] Danish report, Section 2.2.17, p. 8.

[121] Austrian report, Section 2.8.5, p. 28.

[122] Danish report, Section 2.4.3, p. 12.

the request. This often led to considerable delays. Germany has therefore developed a document with local directories, available on diskette, which has been distributed in the EU member states. In Germany, the *Länder* are primarily responsible for issuing letters of request. These powers may be delegated to other authorities. This means that differences exist among the *Länder* in the organisation of the mutual legal assistance system, which is rather confusing for foreign requesting authorities. The German authorities themselves also experienced problems with identifying the competent authorities abroad when sending requests.

In general, the execution of the request must take place in the district or the part of a country that is relevant in that particular case, often the district that has geographical connections to the case. The request, if not sent directly to the competent authority, has to be forwarded to the competent local authority. Problems may also arise when more than one district is relevant and the request must be executed in different parts of a state.

This regularly occurs in Italy and Germany. In Italy, in such a case, all appeal courts (which, in Italy, are responsible for the execution of requests) have autonomous jurisdiction and the Ministry of Justice is the coordinating authority. In Germany there is never a central authority to coordinate such cases, and the request has to be forwarded from one *Land* to the other. This requires at least some knowledge of the prosecuting system and the geographical division in these states. The UK has experienced some coordinating problems, especially with Spain and Italy when evidence had to be obtained from different parts of a country. In those cases, each part of the request was executed separately. A similar system exists in Austria, except when the request is transmitted via the Ministry of Justice, in which case the Ministry coordinates the execution. The system in Sweden to challenge this problem seems to be more efficient as one single prosecutor can coordinate the execution of a request that has to take place in different parts of the country.

Austria has adopted the system that, if a request is sent to the wrong authority, this authority is obliged to forward the request to the competent one and to inform the requesting authority to this effect.[123] This system could be helpful in solving the problems experienced in finding the competent authority. It could be efficient, because the authority that has received the request is familiar with its own legal system and can therefore identify the competent authority more easily. Furthermore, it is acquainted with the practice on mutual legal assistance so that the request can be forwarded via the most efficient channel in that particular case.

Another improvement for the identification of authorities could be that each member state and all applicant countries should develop a web page explaining their system and providing details concerning the competent authorities, as was suggested in one of the reports.

[123] Austrian report, Section 2.4.16, p. 21.

In conclusion, it can be said that problems with regard to the procedure of mutual assistance often consist of the fact that states have different, and sometimes several, law enforcement services with different competences. Furthermore, police officers have different competences in different countries and the position of the examining magistrate is different from one state to another or does not exist at all in some countries, which may have consequences for the position of the public prosecutor. In the common law countries, the police generally have broader competences and the public prosecutor fewer. Furthermore, an examining magistrate is often non-existent. The position of the public prosecutor in the Netherlands is different from that, for instance, in Germany, Belgium, Luxembourg, or France. To be able to identify the competent authority in the requested state, some knowledge of the judicial system of the requested state is required. This knowledge is often lacking.

5.4.3.2 *Practical problems in contacting the authorities involved*

In many reports, the absence of personal details concerning the authority responsible for the sending of the request is seen as an obstacle for direct communication and a major obstacle to an efficient mutual legal assistance procedure, especially when the requested authority feels the need for additional information.[124]

Greece and Luxembourg both stressed that the most common practical obstacle to direct contacts is the lack of telephone details and other data on letters of request.

The Dutch practitioners regularly had problems getting into contact with their responsible counterparts from Spain, Portugal, and Greece.[125] This problem is also identified in Finland although no specific states are mentioned.[126]

Belgium has experienced problems with France in this regard, as requests from France often lack addresses, telephone and fax numbers of the authority making the request. Germany indicated that France and Spain continue to send requests without any information on the requesting authority, which frustrates the establishment of direct contacts. However, it was admitted that the German authorities themselves could play a more active role by using phone, fax, and e-mail, when they consider direct contacts to be advisable. Ireland also indicated that delays arise if an appropriate contact point is not specified in the request or cannot be identified.

5.4.3.3 *Language problems*

In almost all EU member states, language problems are recognised as a major obstacle to mutual legal assistance, in general, and to the establishment of direct contacts that facilitate an efficient exchange of information and requests, in par-

[124] See, for instance, the Dutch report, Section 4.4.3, p. 46. Austrian report, Section 3.14, p. 31.
[125] Dutch report, Section 4.4.3, p. 46.
[126] Finnish report, Section 2.5.7, p. 15.

ticular.[127] Two main problems are identified by the member states with regard to language.

1. It must be recognised that a vast majority of the authorities involved in mutual legal assistance cannot express themselves properly in legal terms in a language other than their own.
2. The need for translations is often a cause of delay and a source of miscommunication.

With regard to the first problem, the following statements were made.

The Italian report states that there is currently a lack of officials who speak foreign languages. In Greece, most officers involved in mutual legal assistance speak only Greek, although language training is considered important. Access to language training in Portugal is now often limited to the central authority. It might be more profitable if local authorities receive language training as this might directly contribute to the use of direct communication. In Sweden, the need is felt to improve language training. In Austria, the language skills of the practitioners involved in mutual legal assistance should be improved, but they seem to be reluctant to receive language training.

Language problems causing delays and miscommunication due to (a lack of) translations can be illustrated by the following experiences.

In the Netherlands, due to an error in the translation, 'death penalty' had been translated as 'life time imprisonment'.[128] Finland, Portugal, Spain, Greece, and Ireland indicated that delays often result from the need to translate requests and related documents. The delays are often dependent on the length of the document that has to be translated and varies from a couple of days to at least one month. Germany indicated that delays occurred as a consequence of untranslated incoming requests and poor translations into German by Spain and Italy.[129] The Belgian report states that translations of requests are time-consuming but that this way is sometimes preferred to translations made by the requesting state as they can be very inaccurate, for instance, translations made by Turkey.[130] The UK indicated that the quality of translations from Turkey, Spain, and sometimes from France and Portugal are poor.[131]

In conclusion, it can be said that an improvement in the language skills of practitioners involved in mutual legal assistance could considerably facilitate mutual legal assistance.

---

[127] Final Report on the First Evaluation Exercise – Mutual Legal Assistance in Criminal Matters, OJ C 216, 1.8.2001, p. 17.

[128] Dutch report, Section 4.4.2, p. 45.

[129] German report, Section 2.12.4, p. 22.

[130] Belgian report, Section 4.2b, p. 37.

[131] Report of the United Kingdom, Section 2.12.2, p. 28.

5.4.4 Other problems

This is a category of miscellaneous problems and includes all relevant other commonly experienced problems indicated in the evaluation reports that have not yet been discussed.

5.4.4.1 *Problems with regard to search and seizure*

Although the problems with regard to search and seizure are not thoroughly dealt with in this study, some remarks on this topic will be made here. Specific problems exist with regard to tracing and confiscating of bank accounts. In some member states, assistance can only be granted if the account is conclusively identified. However, this is often difficult as identification is frequently incomplete. Some states considered the requests with incomplete data to be inadmissible 'fishing expeditions', which are forbidden in most of the countries in the EU, except in France and Italy. With regard to investigations concerning bank accounts, the lack of a centralised register of all bank accounts on the national level is often seen as a complicating factor for an adequate reply to a request. Only in Portugal and France does a centralised system for the identification of bank accounts exist. However, in Portugal, this does not really contribute to the speedy handling of requests in this country as it can take two or three months before a reply to a request is received.

In all countries, double criminality is required with regard to search and seizure and in the majority of the states also for other coercive measures. However, in Sweden, the principle of double criminality with regard to search and seizure carried out to obtain evidence is not applied when requests are made by other EU member states.

5.4.4.2 *Lack of adequate records*

It is generally observed that in most of the member states the adequate keeping of records is lacking. This is considered to be important because it can give an indication of whether the current system is sufficient to cope with the number of requests and for the allocation of resources. Only Germany is not in favour of such a centralised system as it thinks that the benefits will not compensate the effort and the costs involved in setting up such a system.[132]

5.4.4.3 *Presence of requesting authorities in the requested state*

It is recognised that the presence of an authority from the requesting state at the execution of the request abroad contributes to a speedy and more relevant execution of the request, particularly if it concerns searching for and hearing witnesses.[133] Some reports indicated that a request to be present caused problems and is often refused.

[132] German report, Section 2.6, pp. 14-15.

For instance, Belgium reported that, in some drugs and tax cases, the presence of their officials was refused in the Netherlands.

It is recommended for the EU that the possibility of direct questioning by the requesting authority in the presence of the authorities of the requested state should be promoted, in order to reduce duplication of work.[134] In Italy, the consent of the central authority is needed before local competent judges can authorise the presence of foreign authorities during the execution of a request.[135]

5.4.4.4 *Frustrating the mutual legal assistance system by sending requests in minor cases*

Some states indicated that the sending of requests in relatively minor cases frustrated an efficient system for mutual legal assistance by clogging the system.[136] It is reported that Portugal, Spain, and France often send minor requests. Furthermore, the quality of requests that are sent by states with little experience in international judicial cooperation is often poor and the time-limit for reaction is often too short.

The UK made a distinction in the traditions with regard to mutual legal assistance in this regard. It said that the Nordic countries, the Netherlands, and the UK are aware of the fact that the use of mutual legal assistance is rather expensive and therefore only use the system in more serious cases. France, Spain, Belgium, and Germany, on the other hand, are of the opinion that the system must not only be used for serious cases but for all types of crime. Consequently, they more frequently send requests for minor cases, which can sometimes dominate those requests involving serious crime.[137]

5.4.4.5 *Lack of resources*

It was noticed in several reports that there is a lack of resources especially in modern technological facilities, for instance, computer networks, e-mail services, up to date software, mobile phones, access to internet facilities, and portable computers, in several states. Especially if the expected increase in the number of requests becomes a reality, the call for these facilities will grow.

The shortage of resources was reported quite often and included, besides technical facilities mentioned above, a lack of human resources as well. Belgium, for instance, reported that the execution of requests made to Luxembourg was often problematic

[133] Final Report on the First Evaluation Exercise – Mutual Legal Assistance in Criminal Matters, OJ C 216, 1.8.2001, p. 24.

[134] Dutch report, Section 5.3, p. 48.

[135] Italian report, Section 4.2.1, p. 37.

[136] See, for instance, Dutch report, Section 4.4.3, p. 46.

[137] Report of the United Kingdom, Section 2.12.4, p. 29.

due to the fact that Luxembourg 'has too few resources for handling requests and that the magistrates were overworked.'[138]

5.4.5 A matrix

For a quick overview of the most characteristic observations in the reports and to make the problematic areas visible, a matrix has been compiled on the basis of the analysis of the reports, (see p. 194). Although the structure of the reports is very similar, not all the points that are included in the matrix are dealt with in all the reports. For instance, no remarks on the EJN were made in the Luxembourg and Dutch reports as, at the time of visiting, this network had not yet been implemented. Thus, in some exceptional cases, the fact that no cross has been placed against a state does not reflect a positive practice to the concerned item in that particular state. In general, the more crosses a state has collected, the more problematic the system on mutual legal assistance. Furthermore, only the items causing serious problems for mutual legal assistance or the items that considerably facilitate mutual legal assistance when adequately incorporated into the system are included in the matrix.

5.4.6 Recommendations

A considerable number of recommendations for both the individual states and for the EU were made in each report. In this section, recommendations and new developments not mentioned before are discussed, most of them originating from the recommendations in the reports.

5.4.6.1 *Informal procedures for the service of documents*

It was recommended that the requests concerning the service of documents be dealt with more informally as they do not require the same complex measures as other requests for mutual legal assistance.[139] The cooperation between the Nordic states in this regard could serve as an example.[140]

In Ireland, the requests for the service of judicial documents are generally sent directly to the Garda Siochana for execution. This means that these requests are not first transmitted to the Chief State Solicitor's Office and the Attorney General's Office and this way of communication is therefore very effective. Although it is allowed by law that the service of documents is executed by post, this practice is not commonly used, but probably will be used more frequently in future. In Austria, the principle of double criminality does not apply to the service of documents. These in-

---

[138] Belgian report, Section 2.11, p. 24.

[139] Final Report on the First Evaluation Exercise – Mutual Legal Assistance in Criminal Matters, OJ C 216, 1.8.2001, p. 20.

[140] Also Section 5.4.6.3. below.

	Austria	Belgium	Denmark	Finland	France	Germany	Greece	Ireland	Italy	Luxembourg	The Netherlands	Portugal	Spain	Sweden	United Kingdom
Double criminality is applied for non-coercive measures	X	X	X				X			X		X	X		X
Other states reported problems with regard to the application of national law	X									X	X		X		X
Urgent requests are not automatically treated as such				X	X						X		X		X
Direct communication channels are not standard used for outgoing requests		X			X	X	X	X	X	X		X	X		X
The EJN is not yet fully operational	X		X	X			X	X	X			X	X	X	X
Duplication of efforts is reported		X	X	X	X		X	X		X	X	X	X	X	X
Other states reported problems to contact competent authorities			X		X	X	X	X	X	X		X	X		X
Language problems are reported	X	X			X	X	X	X	X			X	X	X	X
Minor requests are often send		X			X	X			X			X	X		
Absence of adequate computer facilities	X	X				X	X		X	X		X	X	X	X
Presence of foreign authorities is problematic					X				X		X	X			

formal practices with regard to the service of documents should be further elaborated and extended to other forms of mutual legal assistance.

5.4.6.2 *Development of a standard form for mutual legal assistance*

A standard form for requests is now being developed for the establishment of a uniform method for of requesting mutual legal assistance abroad.[141] A special heading gives the requesting state the opportunity to describe the specific requirements of its national law that have to be taken into account when executing the request. Furthermore, it includes a specific question on which persons have to be present upon execution. Under the first heading, information on the person and the authority making the request (telephone and fax numbers, e-mail address, etc.) has to be filled in. The conventions that are applied must be stated as well. What would have been helpful is the question of whether the requesting authority must be recognised as a judicial authority following Article 24 of the 1959 Convention. It would have been helpful for requested states to find out whether the requesting authority is competent. The use of this standardised form will certainly lead to a more efficient system of mutual legal assistance because the authorities involved can see at once what precisely is requested when they become more familiar with these forms. Furthermore, the EJN has developed a standardised form for mutual legal assistance as well, which can be accessed via the Internet.[142]

Besides, the KRIS system used in the Netherlands can serve as a helpful tool to improve the standard of drafting requests. This computerised system, available on diskette, includes an overview of the treaties that are in force for each country and what particular requirements by treaty and by legislation are to be met for each step. Furthermore, it includes the Dutch legislation on the issues addressed in the several steps, and it is possible to extract translations of those provisions in English, French, German, and Spanish.[143]

5.4.6.3 *Cooperation between the Nordic countries*

The way in which police cooperation and judicial cooperation is organised between the Nordic countries (Denmark, Finland, Iceland, Norway, and Sweden) can serve as an example for the rest of the EU.[144] A special treaty was concluded with regard to the service of documents and production of evidence.[145] This treaty contains the obligation of persons summoned in one of the state parties to be heard as a witness to

---

[141] 'Request for mutual legal assistance in criminal matters', Brussels, 23 February 2001, 5873/01.

[142] <http://ue.eu.int/ejn2/default.asp?lang=EN>.

[143] Dutch report, Section 2.9.1, p. 17.

[144] For positive remarks, see, for instance, Swedish report, Section 4.1.2, p. 49. R. Lahti, Sub-Regional Co-Operation in Criminal Matters: The Experience of the Nordic Countries, in: A. Eser and O. Lagodny (eds.), *Principles and Procedures for a New Transnational Criminal Law,* Max Planck Institute, Freiburg im Breisgau, 1992, pp. 305-310.

[145] Nordic agreement of 26 April 1974 between Finland, Iceland, Norway, Sweden, and Denmark.

appear, an obligation which is also codified in the Benelux Treaty. Police cooperation between the Nordic countries is based on established practice, which has become customary law. They have adopted similar criminal codes, which facilitates the provision of assistance. This cooperation is very informal and operates solely via direct contacts. Specific provisions are made with regard to language issues, for instance, that Sweden accepts requests made in one of the Nordic languages. Procedural obstacles are almost absent between these states due to the fact that joint procedures were agreed upon at an earlier stage. Furthermore, the principle of extraterritoriality is applicable between these Nordic countries following the agreement of 6 February 1970.[146]

5.4.7 Cooperation with states outside the European Union

Most of the requests made and received by the member states concern requests between EU member states. It is estimated that this concerns between 75% and 95% of the total number requests. Most of the requests seem to originate from neighbouring states. For instance, in Finland, more than half of all the requests come from other Nordic countries.[147] Almost all the remaining ones concern requests from and to EU candidate states.[148] The conclusion can be drawn that mutual legal assistance within the EU shows a positive picture. The question is: what does this say about cooperation with third states?

a. Mutual legal assistance with non(-candidate) EU states does not frequently occur or,
b. mutual legal assistance with third states is not used very often because it is problematic.

To decide what remedy can be best applied to improve mutual legal assistance, it must be determined whether the first or the second situation applies. In the first case, the improvement must be sought in EU documents; in the second case, the cooperation with third states must be improved.

Because the 1959 Convention is the major basis for mutual legal assistance, it is plausible that mutual legal assistance with states not party to this convention is more complicated and is more formal. However, mutual legal assistance on the sole basis of the 1959 Convention is also rather formal and mutual legal assistance only becomes more efficient when the Schengen Convention, the Benelux Treaty, or the Nordic Convention can be applied.

Some reports made remarks on cooperation with applicant countries. As all the applicant countries are party to the 1959 Convention, this convention is often the basis

---

[146] Agreement on cooperation between the Nordic prosecution services of 6 February 1970.

[147] Finnish report, Section 2.6, pp. 15-19.

[148] Final Report on the First Evaluation Exercise – Mutual Legal Assistance in Criminal Matters, OJ C 216, 1.8.2001, p. 16

for cooperation. Some countries indicated that cooperation with Eastern European Countries was in some ways problematic. For instance, Denmark reported difficulties in identifying the competent authority to which the request had to be sent. For incoming requests, problems existed as to whether the request was made by the competent body in the form required and with a sufficiently clear description of the crime and the relevant provisions. Furthermore, information on the requesting authority was often absent, which made it difficult to find out whom to contact when additional information is needed.[149] Sweden experienced some problems with applicant countries as the time taken to respond to a request was rather long, the requests sent to Sweden by these countries were sometimes difficult to understand, and competent and responsible authorities were difficult to contact.

Austria is rather experienced in mutual legal assistance with applicant countries and it has hardly had any problems in this regard. With some countries, direct communication is possible on the basis of bilateral agreements. This is the case with the Czech Republic and Slovakia.[150] Germany has positive experiences with Poland, the Czech Republic, and Hungary with regard to mutual legal assistance as they show a particular willingness to cooperate and execute requests properly and in good time, which is not Germany's experience with some of the EU member states.

As the experiences on mutual legal assistance with the applicant countries are very diverse, it is not (yet) possible to make some general remarks on the reasons why cooperation with third states does not frequently take place. However, it is plausible that the absence of treaties on mutual legal assistance with countries outside the EU and outside the Council of Europe causes problems in practice.[151]

5.4.8 Concluding observations

Following the analysis of the reports, some concluding remarks can be made.

First of all, it is striking that the substantive problems discussed in this section seem to have a lesser impact on the practice of mutual legal assistance than the procedural and organisational problems. Direct communication is recognised by the member states as a practice that can easily reduce delays and considerably improve cooperation in criminal matters. Therefore, it is rather surprising that the member states have so far, had only little experience with the EJN, even though it has been established very recently, and that, in many states, the use of direct communication channels was not standardised in cases where this opportunity is available.

A related problem is that many states have difficulties in identifying the competent authority in the requested state. The practice in Austria, namely, that a request is for-

[149] Danish report, Sections 2.12 and 2.12.4, p. 20.

[150] Austrian report, Section 2.8.6, p. 28, and Section 4.2.3, p. 44.

[151] J. Koers, *Nederland als verzoekende staat bij de wederzijdse rechtshulp in strafzaken. Achtergronden, grenzen en mogelijkheden,* Wolf Legal Publishers, Nijmegen, 2001, pp. 143-145.

warded to the competent authority if it is not addressed to the correct authority, is a practical solution which merits adoption by other states.

Another cause of the problems with regard to cooperation in criminal matters is the fact that the practitioners involved are not sufficiently and specifically educated and trained in mutual legal assistance. This lack of specified personnel has resulted in problems in other areas as well. Often training in mutual legal assistance is absent in the education programmes for practitioners, and if it is available, it is not compulsory. As the use of direct communication channels will be extended in the future, more and more officials will be involved in mutual legal assistance, and, consequently, it will be necessary to educate more and more practitioners. In the EU Convention on Mutual Assistance, the requested state must execute the request in accordance with the requirements and modalities as indicated in the request by the requesting state as far as they are not inconsistent with the law of the requested state. Therefore, it will even become more important that practitioners have at least basic knowledge of countries' legal system.

The waste of money, time, and human resources was elaborately discussed in this chapter as it is another important obstacle to an efficient and effective mutual legal assistance system. As we have seen, the waste of resources is often caused by too lengthy and complex procedures for the execution of mutual assistance requests by too many different authorities.

Another main area of concern is that language problems are reported by most of the states and that the absence of sufficient language skills causes serious delays in the settlement of requests. Furthermore, inadequate translations entail the risk of miscommunication and confusion.

5.5 CONCLUSION

In this chapter, an evaluation was made of the effectiveness of the policy documents and legal instruments discussed in Chapter 4 in order to answer the question of what problems exist with regard to the prosecution of transnational crime in general and trafficking in persons in particular.

First of all, some general remarks were made on the effectiveness of the policy documents and legal instruments discussed in Chapter 4. The documents and instruments of the EU, the Council of Europe, and the OSCE were examined as to their binding status. As policies are not legally binding, they add very little to the achievement of the goals in the policy documents. However, for the OSCE, this conclusion seems to be less valid. Although this organisation has not adopted documents that are legally binding *stricto sensu* for trafficking in persons, it is rather successful in the enforcement of the non-binding instruments it has adopted. This is due to the fact that the organisation has a balanced network of fieldworkers and projects, in contrast to the EU or the Council of Europe, which are more dependent on the willingness of their member states and states party to the conventions for the enforcement of the indicated documents. However, the EU also has specialists to execute the programmes it has adopted such as the STOP and DAPHNE programmes. After the problems related to the lack of legal enforcement mechanisms were identified, the analyses focused on the effectiveness of legal instruments. Successively, the multiplicity of applicable legal instruments and the number of ratifications of and reservations to treaties were discussed.

As this study focuses on the problems related to cooperation in criminal matters in order to improve the prosecution of trafficking in persons, the problems with regard to cooperation in criminal matters identified in the legal literature were discussed in Section 5.3. These problems were divided into substantive, procedural, and organisational problems. This categorisation was also used in Section 5.4 (where a fourth category of additional problems was added to this categorisation, and) where an analysis was made of the procedure and practice on mutual legal assistance within the member states of the EU on the basis of the evaluation reports that were made following a Joint Action for Setting Up a Mechanism for Evaluating the Application and Implementation of International Undertakings in the Fight against Organised Crime. With regard to the substantive problems, it can be said that their impact in general is less serious than is often thought. The procedural problems mainly consist of the absence of transparency as regards the channels to be used and whom to contact, often as a result of differences in competences between the relevant authorities of the member states and a lack of knowledge of each other's system. The organisational problems mainly concern the identification of the competent authorities abroad and practical problems in contacting the authorities involved, either due to the absence of telephone or fax numbers and personal details concerning the competent person, on the one hand, and language problems, on the other. Within the category of other problems, the lack of resources seems to be the main obstacle. Finally, a matrix was compiled for a quick impression of the cooperation in criminal matters problems in the EU. Recommendations that were given following these problems concern the cooperation between the Nordic Countries as an exemplification of intensified cooperation, the setting up of an 'old boys network' for the judiciary, the automatic transfer of requests to the competent authority in a state if the request is not correctly sent, and language training. As follows from the problems indicated in Sections 5.3 and 5.4, the main problems indicated in the legal literature are also recognised in the reports. However, there are also significant differences. For instance, the lack of confidentiality discussed in legal literature is not dealt with explicitly in the reports and the problem of *locus regit actum* is addressed more directly by legal writers. Furthermore, the reports indicate language problems as an obstacle to mutual assistance while most of the legal authors are silent on this problem.

In the next chapter, the extent to which the problems indicated in this chapter actually form an obstacle to the prosecution of traffickers will be explored. To that end, a file study of trafficking cases with a transnational feature was conducted. The problems indicated in this chapter served as a starting point for the analysis of these cases.

CHAPTER 6
OBSTACLES TO THE APPLICATION OF LEGAL INSTRUMENTS TO PROSECUTE TRAFFICKING IN PERSONS IN THE NETHERLANDS

6.1 INTRODUCTION

To what extent do the problems concerning cooperation in criminal matters identified in Sections 5.3 and 5.4 of Chapter 5 exist with regard to the prosecution of those suspected of trafficking in the Netherlands? Can the same problems be detected or are trafficking cases so exceptional that other problems play a decisive role in the prosecution of the perpetrators of this crime? These are the main questions in this chapter. All the legal instruments that have been adopted to combat trafficking in persons directly or indirectly by facilitating cooperation in criminal matters that were discussed in Chapter 4 have so far had a limited effect on the prosecution of trafficking in persons. The hypothesis underlying this part of the study is that if police and judicial cooperation between different countries becomes a necessity for the prosecution of trafficking cases, problems on the substantive, procedural, and organisational level may arise.[1] This hypothesis is based on the presumption that the involvement of more than one state aggravates the problems involved in prosecuting those suspected of trafficking in persons.[2] However, the frequency and the scope of these problems in trafficking cases have never been studied. Before conclusions can be drawn and recommendations can be made on the improvement of the prosecution of those suspected of trafficking in persons, the content of these problems has to be clarified.

In Chapter 5, I analysed the problems with regard to the application of legal instruments on cooperation in criminal matters in general. In Chapter 6 the problems resulting from the use of instruments discussed in Chapter 4 with regard to trafficking in persons will be identified in order to find out whether the problems involved in prosecuting trafficking in persons are aggravated by the involvement of more than one state. Only when these problems are identified can the question be answered of whether solutions must be sought on an EU level. Then the two additional criteria must be considered to be fulfilled as well. Until now, no overall empirical research has taken place that indicates and analyses the problems that impede the application of these instruments in trafficking cases in the Netherlands and thus form an obstacle to improving the prosecution of trafficking in persons. The empirical study described in this chapter will fill this gap.

[1] For a clarification of the terms 'substantive', 'procedural', and 'organisational' in this regard see Chapter 5, Section 5.3.

The empirical study took place at several district courts in the Netherlands and consisted of three phases. Firstly, preliminary interviews were conducted with five prosecutors specialised and experienced in trafficking cases. Secondly, a study of relevant files in three courts in the Netherlands took place and, thirdly, concluding interviews with the prosecutors of the cases studied were conducted in order to answer questions that had arisen following the file study.

The research method used in this empirical study will be discussed in Section 6.2, followed by the results of the preliminary interviews in Section 6.3. In Section 6.4, the results of the file study will be outlined and the answers following from the concluding interviews will be discussed in this section as well. Section 6.5 contains the conclusions.

6.2 METHOD OF RESEARCH

Following the above, the aim of the analysis of the files is to identify the substantive, procedural, and organisational problems in the field of cooperation in criminal matters that occur in the prosecution of trafficking cases in the Netherlands, in order to formulate recommendations for the improvement of this prosecution. To achieve this aim, an inquiry took place that consisted of the following three phases.

In the first phase, preliminary interviews were conducted with five prosecutors from different courts specialised and experienced in international cooperation in criminal matters in trafficking cases. The aim of these interviews was to obtain a first impression of the nature of the problems that play a role in the prosecution of traffickers. Furthermore, it was a first step towards answering the question of what role the problems identified in Chapter 5 play with regard to the prosecution of trafficking cases. The information from these interviews was used to formulate additional questions for the analysis of the files. The problems identified in these preliminary interviews, discussed in Section 6.3 below, were subsequently transformed into questions that were used for the analysis of the files.

The second phase consisted of the analysis of files in trafficking cases in the three courts in the Netherlands that had the largest number of trafficking cases in the period 1995-2000. The selected courts were the District Court in Amsterdam, the District Court in The Hague, and the District Court in Rotterdam.[3] Two criteria had to be fulfilled for a file to be relevant for this analysis. The first criterion was that prosecution took place on the basis of Article 250ter or Article 250a of the Dutch Criminal Code in which trafficking in persons is penalised.[4] The analysis covered the

---

[2] See Chapters 2 and 3, Sections 2.5.5 and 3.10, respectively, on this criterion for transnational crime.

[3] In the 1995-2000 period, Amsterdam registered 121, The Hague 118, and Rotterdam 94 trafficking cases. Bureau Nationaal Rapporteur Mensenhandel, *Mensenhandel. Eerste rapportage van de Nationaal Rapporteur,* Bureau NRM, The Hague, 2002, p. 131.

[4] Article 250ter of the Dutch Penal Code was amended and renamed Article 250a in 2000, i.e., in the

cases that were registered on the basis of Article 250ter or 250a in the three above-mentioned courts in the years 1999 and 2000. According to the figures in the report of the Dutch National Rapporteur on Trafficking in Human Beings, these included 29 cases in Amsterdam, 32 in The Hague, and 8 in Rotterdam, i.e., a total of 69 cases.[5] Some of these are individual cases and some relate to a group of suspects. The total number of cases that were registered in this way in the Netherlands in 1999 was 103 and in 2000 134. This means that 69 of the 237 cases (almost 30%) were part of the file study following the first criterion.

The second criterion was that all the cases had to be transnational in nature.[6] This meant that this criterion is not fulfilled if the trafficking took place in the Netherlands and the suspects as well as the victims all resided in the Netherlands. Furthermore, the studied cases in the district of The Hague that had led to an appeal were analysed as well, in order to obtain an impression of the specific problems that arise on appeal.

Before the analysis was carried out, a screening list was filled in of all the 69 cases in the courts where the research took place in order to obtain an indication of whether the crime was transnational.[7] The actual analysis was carried out on the basis of a questionnaire that reflected the problems identified in Chapter 5 and the problems identified in the preliminary interviews.[8] The questions based on the analysis of the evaluation reports discussed in Chapter 5 were again divided into substantive, procedural, and organisational questions. The additional questions based on the preliminary interviews constituted a fourth category of questions. By answering all these questions on the basis of the information gathered from the files, a picture could be obtained of the problems that arise in the prosecution of trafficking in persons. As a result of the fact that all the cases studied were brought before the Dutch courts, co-operation in these cases only concerned requests to other states and not the execution of requests from other states.

The third and last phase of this study consisted of further interviews with the practitioners responsible for the cases that had been studied, in order to answer questions that had arisen during the analysis of the files with the ultimate aim to obtain full answers to the questions raised in the questionnaire.

---

period under review. Therefore, it was necessary to select cases based on the old article 250ter as well as those on the new article 250a.

[5] Bureau Nationaal Rapporteur Mensenhandel, *Mensenhandel. Eerste rapportage van de Nationaal Rapporteur,* Bureau NRM, The Hague, 2002, p. 131.

[6] See also Chapter 2, Section 2.5.3.

[7] The screening list used in this study is included in Appendix 2 to this study.

[8] This questionnaire is included in Appendix 3 to this study.

6.3 PROBLEMS INDICATED IN THE PRELIMINARY INTERVIEWS

To obtain a first impression of the problems that play a role in the prosecution of trafficking cases, five prosecutors who are the contact persons for trafficking in persons at the District Courts of Amsterdam, Groningen, Roermond, Rotterdam, and The Hague were interviewed. These visits took place during the months of November and December 2001. Some problems that were discussed were characteristic of a particular district, but most of the problems were experienced by more than one prosecutor. When three or more prosecutors indicate the same problem, this problem can, in my view, be qualified as a problem that appears regularly in trafficking cases in general. By comparing the different problems indicated by the five prosecutors and listing the problems that were mentioned by three or more prosecutors, a picture can be drawn of the primary problems that arise in the prosecution of trafficking cases in the Netherlands. Not in all the interviews were the same subjects discussed, as the interviews did not take place on the basis of a questionnaire that had been prepared in advance but had the form of an open interview. However, during the interviews, there was ample opportunity for the prosecutors to put forward the obstacles they experienced in the prosecution of those suspected of trafficking in persons in the Netherlands. Therefore, it may be presumed that all the relevant items were discussed.

In this section on the preliminary interviews, the problems that were mentioned by three or more prosecutors and therefore can be considered as primary problems that regularly arise in trafficking cases will be discussed first in Section 6.3.1. Afterwards, in Section 6.3.2, the secondary problems that were mentioned by fewer than three prosecutors but are relevant in order to obtain a complete picture of the mutual legal assistance in trafficking cases will be discussed. Finally, some additional experiences of the prosecutors that were discussed during the interviews, not necessarily related to cooperation in criminal matters but which might affect the prosecution of trafficking cases, will be dealt with in Section 6.3.3.

6.3.1 **Primary problems of cooperation in criminal matters in trafficking cases in the Netherlands**

1. What was indicated by all prosecutors as one of the main problems in trafficking cases is the absence of victims and witnesses as a result of their return to their country of origin, often as a consequence of the policy of the immigration police. Expulsion takes place because victims of trafficking are in the Netherlands without a legal permit.[9] In some cases, the police or the examining magistrate had had the opportunity to hear victims or witnesses before they were expelled but in most cases they

[9] This practice was also confirmed by the national prosecutor on smuggling, trafficking and child pornography in J.C.F. van Gelder, *De keten op de keeper beschouwd, Rapportage Project intensivering strafrechtelijke aanpak mensensmokkel, mensenhandel en ama's,* Landelijk Parket Openbaar Ministerie [National Public Prosecutor's Office], Rotterdam, 30 April 2002, not published, pp. 17, 32.

had not. As the testimonies of victims and witnesses are usually of crucial importance for the burden of proof in trafficking cases as a consequence of the absence of other hard evidence, it is clear that this problem is a major one.[10] When victims and/or witnesses are sent back to their country of origin without being properly heard and the defence asks to hear these persons or if hearing them is necessary for the collection of evidence, the hearing normally has to take place in the country where the victim or witness resides. The first problem to be dealt with is to trace the victim or witness. In most cases, the Dutch authorities do not have sufficient data on these persons and the cooperation of the local authorities is necessary to discover the address of the victim or witness. Only one prosecutor had positive experiences with some Eastern European countries in tracing the victims and she said that their administration was well-organised. Then permission for the hearing of the victim or witness must be obtained from the local authorities, the person must be summoned to the hearing, in some cases taken into detention, and an appointment must be made as to when and where the person will be heard. In general, this process takes a long time and because of dependency on the cooperation of the authorities in the country of residence, control over the progress of the criminal proceedings is lost.

An extra stimulus for victims and witnesses to testify in trafficking cases is the use of the B9 procedure, which is laid down in Chapter B of the immigration circular.[11] Some prosecutors felt limited regarding the possibility to apply coercive measures to retain the person who uses the B9 procedure if she wants to leave the country. A related problem is that, in quite a number of cases, victims who stayed in safe houses disappeared and consequently were not available for criminal proceedings. The defence often argues that the testimony of the victims or witnesses using the B9 procedure is unreliable because they are promised a temporary residence permit. It is the experience of most prosecutors that the defence asks to hear a victim or witness more often if the victim or witness has been sent back or has travelled back to her home country or another country than if the victim or witness has remained in the Netherlands, under the B9 procedure or not, and is therefore available to be heard.

Furthermore, the summons, hearing, and possibly the detention of the victim or witness take place in accordance with the law and practices of the requested countries. It is not precluded that this law or these practices are not in concordance with the law in the Netherlands, for instance, when other rules are applied with regard to the

[10] 'Hard evidence' is evidence that, in court, can directly lead to the conviction of an accused.

[11] According to this rule, a victim of trafficking can, after a reflection period of three months, obtain a temporary residence permit for the period during which the case is pending before the court. However, her permit will be withdrawn after the proceedings in the fact-finding instance and she must leave the country after all. According to the B9 procedure, a witness is eligible for a temporary residence permit for the time that her presence is considered necessary by the Public Prosecutions Department. See, in this context, the proposed Council Directive on the Short-Term Residence Permit Issued to Victims of Action to Facilitate Illegal Immigration or Trafficking in Human Beings Who Cooperate With the Competent Authorities, COM(2002) 71 final, Brussels, 11.02.2002, which was discussed in Chapter 4, Section 4.3.3.6.

use of coercive measures to make a person testify or the length of the detention that is allowed in such cases. However, the prosecutors interviewed did not see any problems in this regard. One of them said: 'What they don't tell, we don't know' and 'it is their business to determine if and how long they want to keep a person detained'. The recently held raids on houses where illegal aliens were accommodated in Amsterdam and The Hague and at the streetwalkers' district in Amsterdam and where a number of Bulgarians and Romanian citizens without a valid residence permit were expelled from Dutch territory are a good example that illustrates the practices that may frustrate criminal proceedings. It is likely that victims or potential victims of trafficking were among the group of expelled persons

2. The second problem which is in some way related to the first problem and was observed by four of the five prosecutors, is that victims and witnesses who have returned to their country of origin, voluntarily or otherwise, are often reluctant to testify. Several reasons can explain this. Victims and witnesses are often controlled by the persons or organisations that have trafficked them, even after their return. These traffickers have contacts to easily find out what the witnesses have declared to the police, either in the Netherlands or in the country of origin, and they force victims and witnesses to cease cooperation with the authorities or to withdraw earlier testimonies. The families of victims and witnesses are often also subject to threats in order to cease cooperation or to withdraw testimonies. Another reason for the reluctant attitude of victims and witnesses is their primarily negative experiences with the authorities in the countries of origin and the contacts these authorities have with the organisation or persons that have trafficked the victim or witness. Therefore, they do not want to testify in the presence of these authorities.

Another problem arises when the 'boyfriend' of the victim or witness wants to be present during the hearing in the country of origin, firstly, because it is difficult to determine whether the boyfriend has any connections with the persons who have previously trafficked the victim and wants to attend the hearing as a spy for the organisation, secondly, because the Dutch officers present in the requested country are dependent on their colleagues abroad, which means that the Dutch officers cannot themselves decide whether to allow the presence of the 'boyfriend' or not.

Furthermore, if the victims have succeeded in starting a new life in their country of origin, they often do not want to be reminded of the forced exploitation in prostitution and therefore they are not cooperative with the Dutch authorities. Sometimes, the family and the immediate surroundings of the victims do not know what has happened to the victim, nor that she has worked in prostitution, and the victim wants to keep this a secret. The victim is afraid that her relatives will find out about her activities and that she will be expelled and isolated by her surroundings, notwithstanding the fact that she was forced to work in prostitution. In this regard, we have to keep in mind that the perception of prostitution and prostitutes in the countries of origin is often less tolerant than it is in the Netherlands.

The hearing of victims and witnesses is essential in trafficking cases because there is in general a lack of hard evidence. As stated previously, evidence often only consists of testimonies and sometimes also telephone taps. Therefore, every effort must be made to make the hearing of victims and witnesses possible.

3. Not only when the victims are sent back to their country of origin is it difficult to receive testimonies from them, but also when they remain in the Netherlands, whether or not in detention. Problems exist in establishing a relationship of confidence with the victims by the police, often as a result of threats by the traffickers, because of their illegal status in the Netherlands that places them in a vulnerable position, or their bad experiences with the police in their home country. It takes a while before victims have confidence in the Dutch police and it depends on the cooperation with the immigration police whether or not this time is given.[12] Despite the directives of the Board of Prosecutors General, stating that the prosecutor appointed as the contact person in trafficking cases has to be contacted if suspicions have arisen that a person is a victim of trafficking, this is not done in many cases.[13] Furthermore, the B9 procedure provides for a reflection period of a maximum of three months to give the victim the opportunity to decide for herself whether she wants to report to the police or not. During this period, expulsion is suspended and a relationship based on mutual trust could be established, which increases the possibility that the victim will testify. However, it is common practice that the terms of expulsion for illegal aliens are strictly observed regardless of the fact that a person might be a victim of trafficking. Furthermore, it may be problematic when the immigration authorities make a strict distinction between control and investigative activities, because, in the case of investigative activities, the suspect has the right to know what the suspicion against him is when he is arrested.[14] Therefore, the immigration police are sometimes not willing to control the prostitutes, as the underlying aim of such control may be investigative purposes, for instance, to find out whether these persons may be victims of trafficking. In this preliminary stage of the case, the police and prosecutors prefer to keep the available information secret from the suspect. Only one of the prosecutors said that the cooperation with the immigration authorities was good and, in her view, satisfactory.

4. Language was indicated as an obstacle which causes delays in cooperation in criminal matters, by all interviewees. Texts, documents, and conversations have to be translated, hearings can only take place when an interpreter is available and

[12] This practice was also confirmed by the national prosecutor on smuggling, trafficking and child pornography in J.C.F. van Gelder, *De keten op de keeper beschouwd, Rapportage Project intensivering strafrechtelijke aanpak mensensmokkel, mensenhandel en ama's,* Landelijk Parket Openbaar Ministerie [National Public Prosecutor's Office], Rotterdam, 30 April 2002, not published, pp. 5-6, 17.

[13] College van Procureurs-Generaal, Aanwijzing aanpak mensenhandel en andere vormen van uitbuiting in de prostitutie, [Directives of the Board of Prosecutors General on the strategy in trafficking in persons cases], Staatscourant, no. 188, 28 September 2000, p. 20, in force since 1 October 2000, especially point 4, and Annex 4, section 2.2.1.

[14] According to Article 5(2) ECHR and Article 9(2) ICCPR. See also G.J.M Corstens, *Het Nederlandse strafprocesrecht,* Gouda Quint, Arnhem, 1993, pp. 348-249.

sometimes a language is so rare that there are no or only few reliable interpreters available, for instance, for some West African dialects. In general, officers in the Southern part of Europe and in Eastern European countries do not speak English, although there were also some positive experiences in this regard with some Central and Eastern European countries.

5. Four of the five prosecutors interviewed indicated that the reliability of officials on the local level in Eastern European countries such as Poland, Bulgaria, the Czech Republic, and Slovakia is questionable and the reliability of the evidence obtained from them is difficult to verify.[15] Cooperation with them is therefore avoided. Experiences with officials at the central level of these countries are more promising.

6. Four prosecutors mentioned that cooperation with Spain was problematic in general. It often takes a long time before an answer is received, it is difficult to retrieve the responsible person, and many formalities have to be fulfilled before a request is taken into consideration. Besides, two prosecutors had doubts about the reliability of the Spanish officials.

7. The practice on the use of communication channels gives a variable picture with some generalities. In general, it can be said that if the police have direct contacts with officials in the requested country, either with the police or the judiciary, these contacts are used for the transmission of a request or for the collection of information on how to proceed and who to contact. In general, the Dutch police have more contacts with their colleagues from other EU countries than with colleagues from outside the EU. Even if direct contacts exist, the request will normally also be sent via the Ministry of Justice. This is also the case when liaison officers are used for communication. Furthermore, it has to be borne in mind that the choice of what means of communication will be used is very much dependent on the urgency of the case.

It seems that most prosecutors do not have a general standard on how to act if a request has to be made. It depends on the case, the requested country, and the existence of contacts with officials in the requested state. Liaison officers are a welcome substitute for or a supplement to police contacts as the liaison officers normally have direct contacts with the relevant officials in the countries falling under their responsibility. Four of the prosecutors qualified their experiences with liaison officers as positive. The experiences with the Office for International Legal Assistance in Criminal Matters (BIRS) at the Ministry of Justice vary. Two of the prosecutors stated that it normally takes a very long time before an answer is received, if at all, and three prosecutors said they have good contacts with the department and trust it im-

[15] This practice was also confirmed by the national prosecutor on smuggling, trafficking and child pornography in J.C.F. van Gelder, *De keten op de keeper beschouwd, Rapportage Project intensiveringstrafrechtelijke aanpak mensensmokkel, mensenhandel en ama's,* Landelijk Parket Openbaar Ministerie, [National Public Prosecutor's Office], Rotterdam, 30 April 2002, not published, pp. 15-16.

plicitly. A frequently heard comment is that, when contact is established via informal channels and information is obtained in this way (for instance, via the police), it often takes a very long time before this information is formalised and can be used in criminal proceedings. Four prosecutors interviewed recognised the problem of finding the competent person in another country willing to take the request into consideration. This is also due to the fact that responsibilities in other countries often differ from those in the Netherlands and therefore it is difficult to determine on which level contacts have to be established. Language may also form an obstacle for direct communication. Furthermore, it is difficult to trace the person responsible for the execution of the request or to find out the actual state of affairs in the requested state when a request is accepted.

8. Most of the prosecutors did not experience concurrent jurisdiction as a problem in the cooperation with other countries. They said that there is a lack of recognition of the phenomenon of trafficking and prioritising the fight against trafficking rather than a concurrent jurisdiction problem. Furthermore, in the exceptional cases in which concurrent jurisdiction existed, agreement was reached on how to proceed. The problem of lack of priority in other countries is a more significant problem that may lead to delays in cooperation in criminal matters. However, also within the Netherlands, differences exist between districts on the recognition of the importance of prosecuting those suspected of trafficking in persons.

9. Three prosecutors experienced problems when they wanted to commence an investigation on the financial situation and assets of the suspect in the requested state. They experienced a lack of cooperation with Morocco, Spain, Poland, and Bulgaria.

10. The absence of cooperation with African States in general and with Nigeria in particular is experienced by three prosecutors as problematic and an obstacle to the prosecution of trafficking cases in the Netherlands.

6.3.2 Secondary problems of cooperation in criminal matters in trafficking cases in The Netherlands

1. Some prosecutors have problems with common law countries as the regime in these countries differs significantly from the system in the Netherlands and these countries have a different concept of some legal terms.[16] This complicates cooperation with these countries and forms an extra obstacle to making a request.

2. Two prosecutors indicated that there are significant differences between the various countries as concerns the formalities to be fulfilled before the requested authorities accept a request. In some countries, namely France and Spain, the number of formalities to be fulfilled is considerably higher than in other countries and, in many cases, it is not clear what formalities must be fulfilled. Furthermore, the required formalities also differ per district and are sometimes dependent on the competent authority.

3. Contacts on the judicial level are in many cases absent. In general, the police have many contacts with their counterparts in many countries. Some of the prosecutors regretted that these contacts do not exist on the judicial level, although they were rather satisfied with the existing police contacts. However, all five prosecutors were in favour of increasing the number of liaison officers with judicial liaison officers with specific expertise in the judicial procedures and requirements in a particular country and preferably with some expertise in trafficking. They thought that this possibility was feasible as the majority of trafficking victims originate from a limited number of countries, namely, Central and Eastern European and some Eastern African countries.

4. In general, the experience is that mutual assistance with regard to trafficking in persons takes a long time and progress is very slow. The main factors indicated by the prosecutors as contributing to this situation are the lack of priority and bureaucratic obstacles in the requested countries.

5. The testimonies of the victims relating to the recruitment phase are difficult to verify. Therefore, some prosecutors find it necessary to investigate on the spot in the country of origin, if the recruitment practices are included in the indictment. Some of the prosecutors interviewed stated that the added value of including the recruitment practices in the indictment is negligible because it does not allow for harsher sentences to be demanded. One prosecutor even stated that it was general policy in his district not to include in the indictment activities of the suspect that took place outside the Schengen territory and, if possible, to limit the indictment to acts that took place in the Netherlands.

6.3.3 Problems not specifically related to cooperation in criminal matters

1. The prosecution policy on trafficking varies between the different regions of the interviewed prosecutors with regard to the application of the element of force. In some districts, the practice is that only the cases in which there is an element of force are prosecuted, either as a consequence of actual policy or due to lack of capacity to prosecute other cases. Some regions make intensive use of Article 250a paragraph 1 sub 2° Dutch Penal Code, which states that: a person who recruits, takes with him or kidnaps another person with the object of causing that person to become involved in prostitution in a foreign country, is guilty of trafficking in persons. This means that when the victim of trafficking originates from a different country, the element of force is not an element in the definition. Despite this difference in the requirement of force, all districts interpret the concept of force in a broad way in accordance with the explanation given by the Board of Prosecutors General in their guidelines.[17]

---

[16] For instance, the term 'intelligence' is normally translated as information in civil law countries, whereas in common law countries it is used in relation to telephone taps and other clandestine operations.

[17] College van Procureurs-Generaal, Aanwijzing aanpak mensenhandel en andere vormen van uit-

2. Prior to the interviews in this empirical study, the hypothesis was raised on the use, in trafficking cases, of Article 197a of the Dutch Penal Code on smuggling of persons, as the burden of proof for Article 197a seems to be lighter. It was presumed that, in some cases, the suspect was charged with the crime of smuggling of persons although it concerned trafficking cases. The prosecutors were questioned on this issue and the answers reflect the variety in the use of this article. Some of the prosecutors always used Article 197a in trafficking cases as the subsidiary crime. In some cases, the indictment contained both crimes cumulatively. The prosecutors who only used Article 250a in their indictments had thought about using Article 197a as the subsidiary crime in trafficking cases in their indictments in the future. It is observed that there is a tendency to structurally base a charge on Article 197a as the subsidiary or cumulative crime in trafficking cases.

3. The opinions on the 'Rouvoet Motion'[18] which entails that controlled deliveries with regard to trafficking in persons or the continuance of the trafficking are not allowed, differed between the prosecutors. Some prosecutors interpreted the motion as stating that it urges immediate action to stop the presumed trafficking as it is not allowed to let the trafficking practice subsist or the presumed victims to continue crossing the Dutch border.[19] Other prosecutors said that it is disputable when one is certain that a woman will be exploited against her will in prostitution as traffickers generally do not use blatant force. These prosecutors interpreted the motion as stating that action on the basis of the 'Rouvoet Motion' is necessary only if force is explicitly present. In this regard, one prosecutor said that there is a constant tension between the juridical, ethical, and practical interests of a case.

4. As a result of the Jany case,[20] citizens of applicant countries are, under certain conditions, allowed to work as self-employed prostitutes in the Netherlands on the basis of association agreements concluded with these countries. The prosecutors were asked what they expected with regard to the burden of proof following this decision. In general, they expected more difficulties in proving the existence of a dependent relationship between the victim and the trafficker as the trafficker will try to conceal the exploitative relationship. The defence may argue that there is no relation between the alleged trafficker and the alleged victim and that the woman is working as a self-employed person. Furthermore, some feared that the possibilities for criminal action against the traffickers will be reduced and thus the possibility to establish

buiting in de prostitutie, [Directives of the Board of Prosecutors General on the strategy in trafficking in persons cases], Staatscourant, no. 188, 28 September 2000, in force since 1 October 2000, Annex 1 section 4.

18 Rouvoet Motion, *Kamerstukken II*, 1998-1999, 25403, no. 30.

19 This practice was also confirmed by the national prosecutor on smuggling, trafficking and child pornography in J.C.F. van Gelder, *De keten op de keeper beschouwd, Rapportage Project intensiveringstrafrechtelijke aanpak mensensmokkel, mensenhandel en ama's,* Landelijk Parket Openbaar Ministerie, [National Public Prosecutor's Office], Rotterdam, 30 April 2002, not published, p. 17.

20 C-268/99, *Jany case* 20 November 2001.

a relationship of confidence, as these women now have a legal justification to work on a legal basis as a prostitute in the Netherlands.

6.3.4 Additional questions in the questionnaire

On the basis of the outcome of the preliminary interviews, additional questions were developed for the questionnaire. These additional questions, resulting from the preliminary interviews, are the fourth category of questions, besides the categories of questions on the substantive, procedural, and organisational level. In contrast to the evaluation reports analysed in Chapter 5, which concerned mutual legal assistance in general, the interviews were specifically focused on mutual legal assistance with regard to trafficking in persons. Although some problems that were raised during the interviews can also be categorised as substantive, procedural, and organisational problems, it was more appropriate to introduce a fourth category because the problems that emerged in the interviews are specifically related to the crime of trafficking. Based on the problems indicated in the interviews, the questions in the fourth category were:

a. What problems occur as a result of the fact that victims and/or witnesses have returned to their country of origin
   i. with regard to their willingness to testify?
   ii. with regard to the cooperation of the authorities in tracing the victims and/or witnesses?
   iii. with regard to the application of local law on criminal procedure when the victim and/or witness is heard in her country of origin?
   iv. How is the cooperation with the immigration police?

b. What problems cast doubts on the reliability of the authorities on the local level in the requested country?

c. What are the obstacles to the establishment of a relationship based on mutual trust with victims and/or witnesses? To what extent are victims and/or witnesses influenced in this matter by the perpetrators?

d. What is the added value when insight is provided with regard to the recruitment practices in the countries of origin?

e. What problems are experienced as a consequence of the absence of cooperation with African countries in general and with Nigeria in particular (for instance, with regard to falsification of passports, look-alikes, the application of different identities)?

f. What problems are experienced in the cooperation in criminal matters with Spain?

g. What problems are experienced with regard to the investigation of financial data and assets in the requested country?

6.4 RESULTS OF THE ANALYSIS OF THE FILES

6.4.1 **Introduction and figures**

In the second phase of the empirical study, the files of the trafficking cases registered with the District Courts of Amsterdam, Rotterdam, and The Hague in 1999 and 2000 were analysed. Registration of these cases took place on the basis of the fact that the suspects were prosecuted on the grounds of Article 250ter or Article 250a of the Dutch Penal Code. Thus the first criterion for the subject of research was automatically fulfilled. Therefore, the cases only had to be judged on the transnational criterion. The criterion was also considered to be fulfilled if the transnational aspect was only minimal. In The Hague and Amsterdam, some of the cases could not be traced, because numbers were incorrect or because files had been lost in the process of distribution. In most cases, the responsible prosecutor had his own duplicate file that was made available instead. Each trafficking case corresponds with one suspect, but that does not mean that the case must be considered as being isolated from other cases. For instance, in The Hague, a wide investigation into trafficking resulted in 9 suspects, thus 9 cases. Some of them were later dismissed or a former suspect turned out to be a victim. However, these cases were also included in the file study because it might be relevant to find out on what grounds a case was dismissed and it might reflect the complexity of a case. An overview of the relevant cases studied in the different districts yields the following figures.

In Amsterdam, 29 cases were registered on the basis of Article 250ter or Article 250a Dutch Penal Code in 1999 and 2000. From these cases, 1 was joined to another case but concerned the same suspect, 3 cases were untraceable and from 2 cases the numbers were incorrect in the sense that the cases did not exist. Furthermore, 1 case was closely related to 4 cases that were registered in 1998 and, because of their connection, these were studied as well. This means that, in Amsterdam, a total number of 27 cases could be traced. Of these 27 cases, 18 cases had a more or less transnational aspect.

In The Hague, 32 cases were registered and 27 of them could be traced. As an adequate list of all the registered cases was not available, it was unclear whether the other 5 cases had been lost or whether there were other reasons as to why they could not be traced. A total of 25 of these cases had a transnational aspect and were thus relevant for the study.

In Rotterdam, all 8 cases were traced plus one extra case appeared that had not been previously registered. 6 of the 9 cases had a transnational aspect. Furthermore, I was given the opportunity to study the documents in a big transnational investigation in Rotterdam that was registered in 2001. When referring in this chapter to the results of this investigation, which contained 3 cases, it will be clearly indicated that it concerns these particular cases.

The same holds true for the results of a study of an investigation in a trafficking case executed in the district of Roermond. Specific reference will be made to this case when the results of this investigation are used in this chapter.

This means that, of all the cases traced, 49 were relevant for this study as they had a more or less transnational element. Therefore, 49 cases out of the total number of 237 cases that were registered in the Netherlands in the years 1999 and 2000 were studied in-depth in this file study. This means a percentage of 20.7.

6.4.2 **Results of the file study**

As stated previously, the questionnaire used for the analysis of the files was based on the problems identified in the analysis of the evaluation reports as described in Chapter 5 and the additional questions that emerged in preliminary interviews. The same subdivision in categories was used in the questionnaire, with the difference that a fourth category was added to the three categories of questions on the substantive, procedural, and organisational levels. This fourth category contained the additional questions based on the interviews. In the course of the analysis of the files, it became clear that not all the questions in the questionnaire could be answered on the basis of the information in the files. For instance, the question of whether practical problems exist in finding the right person to send a request to is one of the questions to which indications for an answer could be found in only a few cases. However, to assume that, in the majority of the cases, there was no problem in contacting the relevant authorities shows an unrealistic picture of the situation. Therefore, I will indicate when the impression arose that the question could not be adequately answered on the basis of the information given in the files. If these items were not discussed during the preliminary interviews, they were subjects for the additional interviews with the prosecutors and other authorities involved.

The system used in this section to discuss the results of the file study corresponds as much as possible to the division used in Chapter 5, but three changes to the system were necessary. One problem that was indicated in Chapter 5 does not occur in the questionnaire, namely, 'instructions and guidelines'. This problem is so much a policy item that it was not expected that any information on this subject could be found in the files. Furthermore, two additional headings were needed to discus all the relevant problems, namely, the use of Article 197a Dutch Penal Code in trafficking cases and the analysis of the penalties imposed when the defendants were convicted of trafficking in persons.

The third phase of the study concerned additional interviews with the prosecutors or officials involved in the trafficking cases studied. Many of the questions that arose in the analysis of the files were closely related to the case and the questions in the questionnaire. The information from the additional interviews with the responsible prosecutors that was directly related to the files will be given while discussing the outcome of the file study. When information on the discussed item comes from the additional interviews, this will be indicated in the analysis. In Section 6.4.3, I will focus on two elements discussed with the prosecutors in the additional interviews that did not necessarily relate to specific cases but influenced the practice on mutual legal assistance. This means that phase three of the empirical study will be partly discussed in the section at hand and partly in Section 6.4.3.

6.4.2.1 *Substantive problems*

6.4.2.1.1 Execution of requests by applying the national law of the requested state

In this section, the answers to question I b of the questionnaire will be discussed. In Chapter 5, it was stated that the application of domestic law following a request from another state can cause problems in cases in which the requirements of the applicable law differs from the requirements of the relevant law in the requesting state. Furthermore, we have seen that cautious steps have been taken to neutralise these differences.

In two cases studied, this item complicated the cooperation in criminal matters. In one case, Spain was asked by the prosecutor to trace bank accounts. However, in Spain a court decision is required before bank accounts may be traced, which led to extra delays. In another case, a request to Luxembourg and to Switzerland for search and seizure of bank accounts led to some extra correspondence. Luxembourg was asked to block and confiscate the bank accounts of a suspect in Luxembourg. The relevant information on the accounts was obtained in the Netherlands via a search of premises of the suspect by the prosecutor. In Luxembourg, only the examining magistrate can order search and seizure. Therefore, Luxembourg asked what the normal procedure was in the Netherlands in this regard, and asked for the signing of the relevant documents by the examining magistrate if the prosecutor was not competent. The prosecutor answered this question and following this answer the request was executed. In conclusion, it can be said that the application of national law did not cause any great problems in the cases studied. However, it is remarkable that in both cases in which this item raised problems it concerned requests related to the search and seizure of bank accounts.

6.4.2.1.2 Double criminality

In this section, the answers to question I c of the questionnaire will be discussed. The conclusion on this subject following the analysis of the reports in Chapter 5 is that double criminality is not a major constraint on mutual legal assistance. It is applied more often and may cause some obstacles only with regard to coercive measures.

The cases studied did not give much information on the application of the double criminality principle. In a number of cases, no answer was received on a request but there were no indications that this was caused by the absence of double criminality. When no answer was received to a request, it was quite often in cases in which the tracing of telephone numbers was requested. According to one of the prosecutors, this could be due to the fact that, in some countries, providers are not obliged to co-operate with the authorities in criminal investigations, also in some EU countries.

6.4.2.1.3 Different use of terms by different states and different authorities

In this section, the answers to question I d of the questionnaire will be discussed. The problems indicated following the analysis of the evaluation reports in Chapter 5 on this item concerned the use of the term 'double criminality' and the term 'urgent', and the differences that exist between civil law and common law countries.

In the file study, the only cases in which this item caused problems was with regard to the trafficking of Western African (mainly Nigerian) women to the Netherlands. In these cases, the traffickers (when they are women, they are often called 'Madam') used Voodoo rites to intimidate the victims and to make them obey the traffickers.[21] The execution of these Voodoo rites normally commenced in Nigeria and continued in the Netherlands. During house searches, some Voodoo packages were found with attributes that did not look suspicious at first sight, such as soap, oil, and underwear.[22] Furthermore these voodoo packages generally consisted of a piece of hair or nail of the victim or a piece of textile with the blood of the victim. Following telephone taps and testimonies by victims, it became clear that these packages frightened the victims especially when these packages were in the possession of the Madam or when they were lost or could not be traced. For a good understanding of the meaning of these packages and the preceding rites, the African Study Centre in Leyden was asked to study this phenomenon and to report to the prosecutor. Another complicating factor in these cases was the use of the term 'sister'. Women from Western African countries address each other with the term sister if they have a similar hierarchical position, whether they are relatives or not. This caused some confusion in determining the identity of these women.

With regard to the term 'urgent' it is remarkable that most of the requests included in the cases studied were indicated as urgent. However, this did not seem to have any accelerating effect in obtaining an answer to a request. Only in some requests was it indicated why the case was typified as urgent. Despite the references to the use of the term urgent in the statements on good practices, following the Joint Action on Good Practices on Mutual Legal Assistance in Criminal Cases,[23] the prosecutors in the Netherlands were not selective in the use of the term urgent. Nor did they consequently indicate why an answer to a request was urgently needed. Besides, the replying countries did not pay much attention to this indication either.

---

[21] For more information on the use of voodoo in this regard, see R. van Dijk, et al., Een schijn van voodoo; Culturele achtergronden van de handel in Nigeriaanse meisjes voor de Nederlandse prostitutie: een verkenning, African Study Centre, Leyden, 2000. C. Rijken, Van asielzoekster tot prostituee, in: *Nemesis,* Volume 16, issue 1, 2000, p. 5.

[22] See on the Voodoo packages also Section 6.4.2.4.3 below.

[23] See Chapter 5, Section 5.4.1.3.

In the subsequent interviews, one prosecutor indicated that he had experienced problems in this regard with the UK, a country that is not at all familiar with a prosecutor or examining magistrate as they exist in civil law countries. He stated that, because of the problems originating from the difference between the common law and civil law countries and consequently the differences in the use of terminology, the liaison officer seconded to the embassy in the Netherlands was frequently contacted in cases of mutual legal assistance with the UK.

6.4.2.1.4 The use of Article 197a Dutch Penal Code in trafficking cases

In this section, the answers to question I a of the questionnaire will be discussed. This item is directly related to the prosecution of trafficking in persons in the Netherlands and therefore it was not discussed during the analysis of the evaluation reports in Chapter 5. It was stated, in Section 6.3.3 under 3 above, that the use of Article 197a in some trafficking cases was expected. This practice was confirmed by several of the prosecutors interviewed.

The cases studied also confirmed this practice but also showed the differences between the districts in the application of this article. In The Hague, it was almost standard practice in trafficking cases to base the charge on Article 197a Dutch Penal Code cumulatively, which was not the practice in Rotterdam and Amsterdam. In a total of eight cases, there were indications that it could have led to a successful prosecution of the suspect if the charge had been based on Article 197a together with Article 250ter or 250a Dutch Penal Code while the case had been withdrawn or dismissed because the charge was only based on Article 250ter or 250a. Some of the suspects in these cases had helped to accommodate persons they knew were staying in the Netherlands illegally. In one case, the suspect ran a brothel in which prostitutes without a valid residence and working permit in the Netherlands were working while the suspects were aware of the illegal position of the prostitutes. In such cases, it may be difficult to prove that the person running the brothel is involved in the trafficking and it is probably easier to prove Article 197b and 197c Dutch Penal Code.

Article 197b states that a person who allows another person to do work either under a contract or by public appointment, where he knows or has serious reasons to suspect that that person's gaining entry or remaining is unlawful, is punishable. Article 197c states that the commission of this offence by profession or custom is an aggravating circumstance. If the consequence of the sole use of Article 250ter or 250a would be that a case has to be withdrawn or will be dismissed, it is preferable to make the consideration to base the charge on Article 197a or 197b or 197c either subsidiary or cumulatively if this increases the possibility of successful prosecution.

6.4.2.2 *Procedural problems*

6.4.2.2.1 The use of direct communication channels and the European Judicial Network

In this section, the answers to question II a of the questionnaire will be discussed. In Chapter 5, Section 5.4.2.1, it was stated that direct communication channels were seldom used in cases of mutual legal assistance and that these requests were often sent via the central authorities, mostly the Ministry of Justice.

In the cases studied, reports were made on a total of 57 requests. Some of these were made for more than one suspect, in some cases more requests were made and in some cases no request was made at all. Some files mentioned, for instance, that fingerprints had been sent to a country in Europe but it was not reported by whom, whether an answer was received, and within what time. Only the requests that were completely reported were included in this analysis. The picture that can be drawn of the use of communication channels gives a more variable picture than the analysis of the evaluation reports in Chapter 5. Many different channels were used, sometimes simultaneously, such as police to police, or police to other authorities, Europol, Interpol, liaison officers, prosecutor to prosecutor, or prosecutor to other authorities, the Ministry of Justice, the Ministry of the Interior, or the Ministry of Foreign Affairs, and from the Ministry of Justice to other ministries.

By quantifying the different channels, the following overview can be made. Police to police contact was reported 18 times, a request was sent by Europol 3 times and via Interpol 19 times. Liaison officers were contacted 9 times for the transmission of requests, the Ministry of Justice 19 times, and the prosecutors sent 14 requests directly to the authorities abroad. The Ministry of the Interior and the Ministry of Foreign Affairs were involved in mutual legal assistance 3 and 4 times, respectively.

Even when the police took the responsibility for making a request, in the majority of the cases the prosecutor was contacted in advance for consultation. It is highly exceptional that the prosecutor is not involved at all, which is actually only the case when the police have complete control over the request. A request was never sent solely via the Ministry of Justice but always in combination with another channel of communication, for instance direct communication between the prosecutors of the requesting and requested states.

If we distinguish between requests made within the EU and outside the EU, only in one case was there contact between the Dutch police and the police from a country outside the EU. The Ministry of Justice contacted the foreign authorities outside the EU in 12 cases, Interpol also in 12 cases, Europol in 2 cases, the Ministry of the Interior in 1 case, the Ministry of Foreign Affairs in 2 cases, and the prosecutor in 3 cases. On the basis of these figures, it can be said that police authorities, i.e., a more informal way of communication, is preferred in contacts with other EU countries. With regard to the use of direct communication channels by the prosecutors, the same practice exists. The Ministry of Justice and the Interpol channel are used relatively more often when cooperation takes place with countries outside the EU.

Requests are in general not often sent via Europol, and in the cases where the Europol channel was used, an answer was received in only one case. This may be due to the fact that two requests also concerned requests to countries outside the EU of which no liaison officers were seconded to Europol. Furthermore, it was only the District Court of The Hague that made use of the Europol channel.

In none of the cases studied was specific reference made to the European Judicial Network. This raised the impression that practitioners are not aware of the existence of the EJN and do not know where to find the contact points in other EU states.

6.4.2.2.2 Wasting of time, money, and human resources (duplication of efforts)

In this section, the answers to question II b of the questionnaire will be discussed. As stated in Chapter 5, Section 5.4.2.2, the time period necessary for answering a request is often very long and it is not exceptional that some activities are executed more than once, such as checking the legality of a request. The lack of coordination in the requested state often causes these duplications.

Relevant information to answer this question could not easily be obtained from the files. Only in a small number of cases, did the steps taken in the requested country become visible from the files. However, as we have seen in Section 6.4.2.2.1, a request is often sent via more than one channel and this practice already increased the risk of duplication of efforts. In some countries, a request has to go through many formalities before an answer can be given. For instance, in France, with regard to the tracing of telephone numbers, a request had to be sent to many persons before the actual execution could take place and, after the execution, the same steps had to be taken again. The request concerned was sent on 6 June 2000 via Interpol and an answer was received on 5 February 2001. Another example concerned Spain, where the answer to a request that was sent via the Ministry of Justice was returned via the Ministry of the Interior.

Furthermore, it is actual practice that documents informally obtained by the police have to be formalised by a subsequent official request. This formalisation often takes a long time and sometimes does not arrive until after the trial. Documents also have to be formalised even when a prosecutor, the examining magistrate, or both were present in another country during the execution of a request. For instance, in the case where the visiting Dutch authorities immediately received the reports of testimonies from witnesses via the police of Estonia. However, they had to wait for the official documents that were transmitted via official channels. In my view, it is a justified question to ask why this subsequent formalisation is required when the examining magistrate was present.

Some prosecutors confirmed the practice, in some countries, that many formalities must be fulfilled by various authorities before a request finally reaches the person who is going to execute the request. Especially with regard to France and Spain, they reported the vagueness of the formalities to be fulfilled, and the impression was given that this also depended on the person or district handling the request. The liaison magistrate, seconded to France, with specific expertise in judicial matters, was very helpful in finding the appropriate way in which to send a request.

The prosecutors involved said that problems did occur as a consequence of the lack of priority given to the fight against trafficking in persons in some countries inside as well as outside the EU. One prosecutor said that requests for assistance in drug cases or cases of terrorism were dealt with more accurately and seriously. Furthermore, they experienced a lack of adequate financial resources in their own working department as an obstacle to effective prosecution. Some of them had to admit that this lack was often a reason not to undertake action on mutual legal assistance and that they always had to balance the costs and the benefits before undertaking action on mutual legal assistance.

6.4.2.2.3 Communication between judicial and police authorities and within the judiciary

In this section, the answers to question II c of the questionnaire will be discussed. In Chapter 5, Section 5.4.2.3, it was indicated that the prioritisation at the police level and the capacity of the police is, in many countries, mainly decisive for the execution of requests for mutual legal assistance.

The answer to this question hardly becomes apparent in the files and can only be answered by giving the examples deduced from the relevant cases. In Spain, in one case, the coordination between the police and the judiciary seemed to fail since on the same day that an answer to a request was written stating that a decision of the court was needed for the tracing of bank accounts, the court had actually taken the decision on the tracing of bank accounts. If there had been more coordination between the judicial and police authorities, the latter could have delayed their answer until the court had taken its decision. The coordination between judicial and police authorities in Estonia with regard to the extradition of a suspect seemed remarkably good. An answer from the judiciary indicated what was the best time for the Estonian police to transfer the suspect, and which police officer had to be contacted for further arrangements.

With regard to the tracing of telephone numbers in France, the many steps that had to be taken concerned both the police and the judiciary. It is not clear from the file whether the communication between these two was problematic in this case and resulted in the delay of the request.

An additional answer to this question was not received from the prosecutors involved as they did not have a good picture of the communication between the authorities in other countries.

6.4.2.2.4 Confusion as to what formalities must be fulfilled and which channels must be used

In this section, the answers to question II d of the questionnaire will be discussed. In Chapter 5, this item was discussed on the basis of the problem of how to identify the competent person to whom the request should be sent.

With regard to the analysis of the files, the question of what channel was used was already discussed in Section 6.4.2.2.1. The prosecutors stated in the concluding interviews that one of the main practical problems with regard to the sending of a request was identifying the competent person to whom the request should be sent.[24] The availability of different channels for the transmission of a request is generally not experienced as being problematic, but rather as an advantage.

With regard to the formalities to be taken into account, the file study showed that a request is very detailed. Normally, it includes the offence for which the suspect was remanded, and the relevant provisions of the law are attached to the request. The identity of the suspect and possibly fellow suspects are given as well. Furthermore, the content of the request is explicated and some relevant information in this regard is given. For example, when the hearing of victims was requested, an indication of the preferred time period for the hearings and the names and telephone numbers of the persons who would visit the requested country were stated. Reference was made to the relevant international agreements that formed the basis of the request. However, these agreements were referred to in general terms and the applicable articles of these agreements were not specified. Remarkable in this respect is that the Benelux Convention on Extradition and Mutual Legal Assistance was not referred to in the case of mutual legal assistance with Belgium or Luxembourg. One prosecutor stated that he did not realise that this convention was applicable.

Normally, the request is signed by the prosecutor, and his address, telephone and fax number were included. The use of e-mail is not yet common practice, at least not among the judiciary; at the police level, communication with their counterparts abroad by e-mail takes place more often. In some cases, some background information is given on the investigation as well. Sometimes, the sender's preferred way of responding to the request is indicated. The request, including the enclosures, is normally already translated into the language of the requested state before it is sent, unless there are indications that a common language is understood by the requesting and requested authorities. If a request is indicated as urgent, it is rarely explicated why a request must be treated as such. Standardised forms are only used in exceptional cases. From all the requests studied, only one request was filled in on a standardised form. The standard request of the European Judicial Network, which is also available on the Internet,[25] had not been used by the prosecutors because they were

[24] See Section 6.4.2.3.1 below.

[25] <http://ue.eu.int/ejn2/default.asp?lang=EN>.

unaware of its existence. A standardised form will contribute to conformity in the requests although this does not seem to be a problematic issue. The added value of the use of standardised forms was not recognised by all the prosecutors.

6.4.2.2.5 Appeals as a delaying strategy

The answers to question II e will be discussed here.

'Appeals as a delaying strategy' seemed to be a problem in a minor number of cases and, in general, this information is not easily extracted from the files. However, in one case, concerning the confiscation of bank accounts in Switzerland and Luxembourg, the appeals against the decisions of the courts in Switzerland and Luxembourg caused serious delays in the whole procedure. In Switzerland, the account holder has the opportunity to appeal twice against a decision that information concerning his account will be provided to investigative authorities. In this case, the suspect appealed twice, causing substantial delays. However, pending the appeals, it was possible to block the bank accounts. A similar procedure for the account holder exists in Luxembourg.

6.4.2.2.6 Penalties

In this section, the answers to the last question on the screening list will be discussed. To get a good impression of the penalties that are imposed and to discover possible differences between the three courts, the exact penalties will be given below, subdivided by the court. When considering the average numbers in this section we have to keep in mind the limited number of cases, the various other crimes for which the offenders were punished, and the limited time period in which the research took place.

In The Hague, 4 cases out of the total number of 25 were dismissed, 3 because the facts could not be proved and 1 case because the suspect turned out to be a victim. In 3 cases the suspect was not brought before the court and in 4 cases the suspect was acquitted of trafficking in persons. In 1 case the indictment was declared invalid, as it could not be served on the suspect. In 1 case the accused was convicted on the basis of Article 197a but not 250ter. Thus, in 12 cases, almost 50%, conviction took place on the basis of the crime of trafficking in persons. In only 2 cases was the penalty imposed solely on the basis of Article 250ter or 250a. In all the other cases, the accused was guilty of trafficking in persons together with other crimes. In some cases, these were crimes related to trafficking such as forgery, deprivation of liberty, smuggling, interfering with witnesses, or participation in a criminal organisation. In a minor number of cases, crimes not related to the crime of trafficking, such as trafficking in firearms and drugs trafficking, were also proved. The harshest penalty imposed was 6 years and the lowest penalty was 1 year imprisonment. The other sentences that were imposed were 5 years once, 3 years 3 times, 2½ years once, 2 years once, 20 months once (of which 5 months were suspended), 15 months twice and 18 months once (of which 6 months were suspended). In 1 case, a fine was imposed in addition to the prison term. In some cases, probation was imposed as well. This means that, dismissals and acquittals included, the average term of imprisonment in the relevant cases in The Hague was almost 15 (14.96) months.

If we make a similar overview for the cases studied in the District Court of Amsterdam, we see that 2 cases were dismissed, and in 7 cases out of a total of 18 cases, the suspect was acquitted. In 1 case, the investigation was considerably delayed because of letters rogatory, and a judgement had not yet been delivered. This means that in 8 out of 18 cases, a penalty was given on the basis of the crime of trafficking. In 4 cases, related crimes were committed, namely, on 3 occasions, participation in a criminal organisation and, in one case, participation in a criminal organisation plus forgery. In 3 cases the criminals were also found guilty of other crimes, namely, trafficking in firearms, theft, and arson besides trafficking in persons. The harshest penalty imposed was 7½ years imprisonment. The lowest penalty was 2 years imprisonment (of which 6 months were suspended). Other terms of imprisonment imposed were 3½ years for trafficking in persons and firearms, 2½ years twice, 27 months once, 26 months once (of which 7 months were suspended), and 2 years once. In 2 cases, a financial penalty of € 5,000 was imposed in addition to imprisonment and, in the same cases, the traffickers had to pay € 3,000 in immaterial compensation to the victims. The average penalty at the Court in Amsterdam in trafficking cases was 16.3 months. If we compare the averages of The Hague and Amsterdam, then the conclusion must be drawn that the difference between the average custodial sentences is small. However, if we calculate the average of the cases in which the accused was convicted of trafficking, leaving out the cases in which the suspect was acquitted or the case was dismissed or judgement was still pending, then we see that the average sentence in The Hague is 31 months imprisonment and in Amsterdam 36.6 months imprisonment. This means that there are no great differences between Amsterdam and The Hague with regard to the percentage of trafficking cases that may lead to a conviction, but that the sentence imposed in Amsterdam is in general higher. Remarkable differences between the districts with regard to the indictment of other crimes, either related to trafficking or not, do not exist. However, participation in a criminal organisation is found relatively often in Amsterdam. There are indications that this is due to the fact that The Hague limits its indictments as much as possible to activities that have taken place in the Netherlands.[26]

Finally, the situation in the District Court of Rotterdam will be described. As the number of relevant cases in Rotterdam is very small, far-reaching conclusions cannot be drawn. One suspect was acquitted for trafficking in persons, 3½ years imprisonment was imposed once, 12 months imprisonment was imposed once for trafficking in persons and for the abuse of minors for pornography, an alternative sanction of 120 hours community service was imposed once for trafficking together with smuggling and the employment of illegal aliens. In 1 case a judgement was still pending and in 1 case a penalty was imposed on the basis of the employment of ille-

[26] See Sections 6.4.2.4.4 and 6.4.3.1 below.

gal aliens but not on the basis of trafficking in persons. The calculation of an average penalty will not have any added value with these small numbers.

6.4.2.3 *Organisational problems*

6.4.2.3.1 Identification of the competent judicial authorities

In this section, the answers to question III a of the questionnaire will be discussed. The main point following from the evaluation reports in Chapter 5 on this item was that judicial practitioners do not always have sufficient knowledge to identify the competent authorities in other countries with regard to mutual legal assistance. Besides, the competence of police and judicial authorities varies between countries, which may cause problems in answering and sending requests.

The problem of identifying the competent authority in the requested state also emerged in the file study. If contacts with foreign authorities already exist, mainly on the police level, these contacts will be addressed either to ask for the relevant information or to ask who is competent in that country to receive the request. If these contacts do not exist, a liaison officer or the Ministry of Justice will be approached to forward the request. Often, at a later stage of the correspondence with the requested country, when the responsible persons or department are known, they will be addressed directly. In one case, in Amsterdam, in which neither the liaison magistrate nor the Office for International Legal Assistance in Criminal Matters at the Ministry of Justice had succeeded in finding a reliable contact in Bulgaria within a reasonable time, the prosecutor together with the police were very active in establishing contacts with this country themselves. They sent a fax to the Head of the International Cooperation Department of the Ministry of the Interior in Sofia, referring to the efforts already made and asking him to help in identifying the competent person for handling the request. Finally, they were successful in establishing direct contact on the central and on the local levels for the execution of the request.

The police often attempt to establish the first contacts with the authorities in the requested state if they have direct contacts. However, they generally do so in close cooperation with the prosecutor and official letters are always signed by the prosecutor. Therefore, the problem that the police are found not to be competent by the authorities in the requested state is bypassed. Only in one case, already referred to before, did a country (Luxembourg) ask additional questions on the competence of the prosecutor to execute a warrant to search premises of the suspect.[27]

In the interviews, the prosecutors involved admitted that it is often difficult to determine on what level to establish contacts with the authorities in other countries. As stated before, some of them had doubts as to the reliability of the authorities in countries both inside and outside the EU.

[27] See Section 6.4.2.1.1 above.

With these problems in mind it was remarkable that, if an answer to a request was urgently needed within a certain period of time, the authorities involved were successful in establishing the necessary contacts and obtaining the required information within that time-limit. This was, for instance, necessary in cases in which surveillance was requested concerning a person who would arrive in the requested country at a certain time. Thus, when the pressure to obtain an answer is great, the authorities were able to find the responsible person to fulfil the request, sometimes even within one day.

6.4.2.3.2 Practical problems in contacting the authorities involved

In this section, the answers to question III b of the questionnaire will be discussed. In Chapter 5, it was indicated that a major obstacle for direct communication was the absence of personal details of the requesting authority.

The practical problems in contacting the competent authorities in the requested country hardly appear from the files, for three reasons. Firstly, in the Netherlands, the police normally take care to contact the foreign authorities as they have an executive role in the request, for instance, when surveillance, hearings, or the transfer of suspects have to take place. Secondly, the police in general have a broader spectrum of contacts abroad at their disposal, so it seems obvious that they directly address their contacts. And thirdly, these problems, if they arise at all, are not reported in the files.

However, a general impression that could be obtained from the files is that a request is often addressed to the judicial authorities via the Ministry of Justice or Interpol and is returned directly to the competent prosecutor if he has stated his complete name and address in the request. Furthermore, it is remarkable that communication in the majority of cases takes place via fax, but that the use of e-mail is not yet common practice. In one request to Spain, direct communication with the competent authorities could only be established after a judge had taken note of the request.

In the concluding interviews, it was indicated by several authorities involved that practical problems also existed with regard to the accessibility of authorities in other countries. The responsible person was often not available when contact was sought, problems existed with regard to the language, and sometimes limited and different office hours abroad caused problems in this regard.

6.4.2.3.3 Language problems

In this section, the answers to question III c of the questionnaire will be discussed. The language problems indicated in the evaluation reports in Chapter 5 concern the establishment of contacts and delays and miscommunication due to the need for translations.

These problems are also current in the cases studied. In a large case, in which the suspects originated from West Africa, telephone conversations that were tapped and communication with the suspects mainly took place in the Edo language. This language is spoken in a small part of Nigeria and only a few qualified and reliable interpreters in this language are available in the Netherlands. The interpreters used were afraid of retaliation by the suspects and therefore precautions to protect them had to be taken such as to ensure the anonymity of the interpreters. In another case, the interpreters also felt intimidated by the suspects. This case also concerned suspects from Western Africa. In the former case, the suspects had expressed their doubts as to the quality of the translations and stated that the translations were incorrect. Therefore, some parts of the translations had to be done a second time, causing delays and difficulties in finding another interpreter. In a case in Rotterdam, there were also problems in finding enough translators in the Romanian language. Furthermore, in that case, another problem existed, namely that the suspects used several languages at the same time so more interpreters were necessary. This caused logistical problems. Furthermore, some doubt arose as to the reliability of some of the interpreters, as they, for instance, did not keep appointment.[28] As stated before, requests are normally translated into the language of the requested state unless it is clear that both parties can express themselves in a common language.

The translations of the requests and the replies take some time and cause delays, varying from a couple of days to one month. The establishment of direct contacts between law enforcement authorities is problematic when there is not a common language. Only with the help of an interpreter can the competent persons be addressed in the requested state. This is a time-consuming process and a process that must be carefully coordinated. After all, the interpreter has to come to the office of the prosecutor and, at that moment, the prosecutor must be available to make the contact. The competent person in the requested state must be present as well and, at that same time, be prepared to answer some relevant questions. This way of contacting counterparts abroad entails many risks and was, in the cases studied, only used in one case where an interpreter happened to be available at the court for other duties.

The files also identified another problem with respect to the use of foreign languages, namely, communication with the victims and the suspect. In one case, language was a manipulative means for the suspect to provoke confusion about his nationality. Communication with suspects and victims from abroad can often only take place with the use of a translator. It is easy to imagine that this is a complicating factor in establishing a relationship of trust with victims and in persuading them to tell their experiences.[29]

[28] This practice was also confirmed by the national prosecutor on smuggling, trafficking and child pornography in J.C.F. van Gelder, *De keten op de keeper beschouwd, Rapportage Project intensiveringstrafrechtelijke aanpak mensensmokkel, mensenhandel en ama's,* Landelijk Parket Openbaar Ministerie, [National Public Prosecutor's Office], Rotterdam, 30 April 2002, not published, pp. 17, 23.

[29] See Section 6.4.2.4.3 below.

6.4.2.4 *Additional problems following the questions based on the preliminary interviews*

6.4.2.4.1 Residence of the victim and/or witness outside the territory of the Netherlands

In this section, the answers to question IV a of the questionnaire will be discussed. It appears from the file study that this is one of the most characteristic problems for the prosecution of those suspected of trafficking in persons in the Netherlands. The fact that victims and witnesses have returned to their country of origin, either by an order of the immigration officers or voluntarily, causes difficulties when they have to be heard at a later stage of the proceedings. Difficulties exist in discovering where the victims live. This problem was more serious when the victims were expelled by the immigration service before the police or the examining magistrate had an opportunity to hear them. It is observed that the defence asks more often to hear the victims and witnesses when these have been sent back to their country of origin and are therefore not directly available. However, neither the Court in The Hague nor the Court in Amsterdam were inclined to agree with such a request if it was obvious that it was impossible to trace the victims or if the victims had already been heard and the defence had had the opportunity to be present at the hearing. If victims request the B9 procedure, the defence objects that they use this procedure to obtain a residence permit in the Netherlands and that the statements of the victims must therefore be considered unreliable. In a number of cases, the victims who used the B9 procedure disappeared from their safe houses to an unknown destination. This practice has undermined the purpose of the B9 procedure. Although some victims were given the opportunity to make use of the B9 procedure, they preferred to travel back to their home country. In these cases, the authorities tried to hear the victims before they returned. In some cases, this was not possible because the immigration service had already expelled them from Dutch territory, even before the prosecutor knew that (possible) victims had been arrested. This is a violation of the B9 procedure, which gives the victim a period of three months of reflection to consider to file a complaint against the trafficker. The immigration police have to offer this opportunity when there are indications that the person is a victim of trafficking. There are no legal possibilities to retain the victims for the criminal procedure in the Netherlands if the person wants to return immediately. In some cases, this was problematic as the victims had to be traced in their country of origin at a later stage at the request of the defence. This caused serious delays in the criminal proceedings. Furthermore, it is a point of contention between the prosecutor and the defence, for instance, in the case in which the defence accused the prosecutor of not making sufficient efforts to trace the victims while the prosecutor was completely dependent on the cooperation of the authorities abroad.

With regard to victims from Western African countries, another problem exists. The Hague had quite a number of cases with victims from these countries, and although the immigration police wanted to return these women to their country of origin immediately, this could not be done as much confusion existed with regard to the question of what their country of origin and their identity was. The victims further confused this matter by not using their real names. A complicating factor in this regard was that many victims looked like one another (look-alikes). In one case, the consequence was that the wrong victim, detained because of her illegal stay, was brought before the court, resulting in a release from detention. The embassies of the countries involved were asked to help with identifying these persons. This tour along several embassies was a time-consuming activity and while the identities of the supposed victims was investigated, they were kept in detention, which gave the police the opportunity to establish a relationship of trust with them. In some cases, the police were successful in this regard as, after a while, the supposed victims were prepared to tell of their experiences, to make use of the B9 procedure, and to file a complaint against the traffickers. In these cases, a problematic situation turned out to be a profitable one.

In this regard, it is important that the immigration police have close contacts with the prosecutor and the police as they must report when they suspect the existence of trafficking in a certain case. Although the interviewed prosecutor in The Hague stated that the cooperation with the immigration police was far from optimal, this did not appear from the cases studied. This may be due to the fact that, in many cases studied, the victims could not be expelled immediately as the country of origin of the victims was not clear and it took a while before this was sorted out. In another case in The Hague, the victim was heard twice before she was sent back to her country of origin, and in another case the victim was also heard by the examining magistrate before she was expelled. The inadequate cooperative relations with the immigration police in Rotterdam was confirmed in a case where the victims were expelled immediately, causing serious problems when the defence successfully requested on two occasions to hear the victims at a later stage.

In Amsterdam it was reported in the preliminary interview that the cooperation with the immigration police was satisfactory. The problems in this regard in Amsterdam existed in the fact that many victims who used the B9 procedure disappeared from the safe houses. In one specific case, the victims were directly sent back to their country of origin, but not by the immigration police of Amsterdam but by the immigration police of Utrecht. In other cases, the victims were offered the opportunity to use the B9 procedure and were heard by the police; in some cases, they were heard by the examining magistrate when they waived this opportunity.

6.4.2.4.2 The reliability of local authorities in the requested state

In this section, the answers to question IV b of the questionnaire will be discussed. In some files, there are indications that contacts between the suspect and the authorities in other countries exist and that these authorities cooperate with the perpetrators. For instance, in a case in Amsterdam, it followed from telephone taps that the perpetrators had contacts with Turkey on a high level, and that the persons in Turkey were financed by the criminal group in the Netherlands. However, no requests for legal assistance were sent to Turkey. It is not clear to what extent the knowledge of the existence of these contacts was a reason not to send requests to Turkey. In another case in Amsterdam, the suspect had contacts with a person at the Dutch embassy in Romania who was helpful in obtaining a visa.

With regard to a request to Spain in a case in Rotterdam, it is remarkable that it was explicated in the request that the information from the request would only be used by the police and the judiciary. Furthermore, the request was not so elaborate as in other cases and the names of the victims and witnesses were not given. However, when the responsible prosecutor was questioned on this observation, he denied that this had been done for the reason that the Spanish authorities were not reliable.

In a case in The Hague, relations existed between a criminal group and the director of the airport in Burgas, Bulgaria, who seemed to be helpful in the transport of women. Contacts also existed with a person who was almost elected as Mayor of Sofia, who could help with obtaining visas. Furthermore, contacts existed with a border control officer at the Czech-German border who passed on information on the patrols of the German border control officers. The prosecutor involved said that, for these reasons, he was cautious in making requests, especially to Bulgaria.

In one case in Amsterdam, the lawyer of the suspect received letters from authorities in Bulgaria and the family of the victims. The letters from the authorities included, for instance, the former convictions of the victims and statements that they had worked as prostitutes before and that they had been addicted to drugs. The letters from the family of the victims also included statements that they had previously worked in prostitution. The defence used these documents to adduce the unreliability of the victims, but the victims disputed the authenticity of these documents.

Apart from the remark made earlier with regard to Spain, no indications as to the reliability of authorities from EU countries appeared from the files studied.

In the Roermond case studied, the reliability of authorities abroad was not the problem, but the integrity of the lawyer representing one of the suspects was. In this case, telephone taps made during the detention of the suspect, revealed that the lawyer transmitted orders from the suspect to other persons in a criminal organisation in the Ukraine. Following these orders, the victims and their families were intimidated by the organisation.

When discussing the reliability of the authorities in non-EU countries with the prosecutors, they confirmed their restraint in establishing direct contacts themselves in these countries because they had no guarantees as to the reliability of these contacts. This is regularly a reason not to send a request to these countries, even at the expense of the production of evidence. When other colleagues have positive experiences with contacts in these countries or when a liaison officer or the Ministry of Justice has contacts in these countries, the prosecutors are more inclined to use these contacts.

6.4.2.4.3 The establishment of a relationship based on trust with the victim by the police and the role of the trafficker

In this section, the answers to question IV c of the questionnaire will be discussed. As stated in section 6.4.2.3.3, language problems are an obstacle for the police to establish a relationship of trust with the victims. This is further complicated by the influence that the suspects have on the victims. In most cases, the suspects succeeded in remaining in contact with the victims even when the victims were accommodated at secret addresses or when they had returned to their country of origin. Furthermore, the suspects used violence and other means to intimidate the victims not to testify to the police or to withdraw earlier testimonies. This influence consisted of physical violence, including rape, but also the threat that a child of the victim would be taken from those taking care of it in the home country or that it would be made public that the victim worked in prostitution. In several cases, the suspect had made pornographic images of the victims, usually against their will, and threatened to send this material to the family of the victim. In a case with Nigerian victims, photographs were taken of the victims in humiliating circumstances, namely, they had to empty the rubbish bin naked. What the suspect did not realise was that her address was shown on a piece of paper in the bin so that this picture could be used as direct evidence against her.

The suspects are usually adequately and quickly informed of the testimonies made by the victims, often via their lawyers, which, in some cases, was a reason for victims no longer testifying. One suspect threatened the victims after they had testified against him. Violence against the family of the victim was also frequently used as a way of controlling the victim. Victims were told by their traffickers not to contact the police in the Netherlands because they are not reliable and they only expel the victims from the country as they have no legal residence permit for the Netherlands. This also complicated the establishment of a relationship of trust with the victim. In the 'lover-boy' cases, victims were made completely dependent on the suspect by means of false promises and pretending that the victim was the love of the suspect's life and that he would build a future with her. Finally, the 'lover-boys' persuade or force the girls into prostitution. It is difficult to convince these victims of the wicked intentions of their 'boyfriend', and strong persuasion is needed to open the eyes of the victims. Another means of controlling the victims is to take their passports in order to prevent them from escaping.

In the case of Nigerian victims, Voodoo was used as a way of subduing the victims. The victims often attach great significance to these rituals and strongly believe that their trafficker (the Madam) has influence over them as long as she has possession of their voodoo package.[30] Therefore, the victims are often very loyal to their Mad-

[30] For more information on the use of voodoo in this regard, see R. van Dijk, et al., Een schijn van voodoo; Culturele achtergronden van de handel in Nigeriaanse meisjes voor de Nederlandse prostitutie: een verkenning, African Study Centre, Leyden, 2000. C. Rijken, Van asielzoekster tot prostituee, in: *Nemesis,* Volume 16, issue 1, 2000, p. 5.

am and are not willing to testify as long as they do not have the voodoo package in their own possession. As long as the Madam has possession of these materials, the victim is under influence of the Madam. In a case in The Hague, some victims became really anxious because the voodoo packages could not be found. Furthermore, the Nigerian victims feared being sent back to Nigeria as they feared for their lives; they did not rely on the protection of the Nigerian police as they thought the police to be corrupt. Because the final consequence of the use of the B9 procedure was that the victims would be sent back to their country of origin, this procedure was not an attractive option for them. This, of course, also holds true for victims from other countries who fear for their lives if they return to their country of origin, for instance, in the case of victims originating from Bulgaria. It was confirmed by the prosecutors that the above-mentioned circumstances of the Nigerian victims complicated the establishment of a relationship based on trust with this category of victims. In some cases, there were strong indications that the traffickers had threatened the victims and that the victims were therefore afraid to testify, although they denied that the traffickers had threatened them.

When discussing the vulnerable situation of the victims with the prosecutors, they said that the normal protection measures were granted to the victims if they were threatened by the traffickers. In these cases, the victims received a police telephone number that could be used in urgent cases. The B9 procedure is also supposed to protect victims, by providing a safe address, for instance, but as stated before, the traffickers succeed in contacting the victims even if they are accommodated at secret addresses. The use of witness protection programmes is not common practice in trafficking cases.

Finally, it is remarkable that the hearings of the victims in The Hague were often executed by two male police officers and in Amsterdam by one male police officer. It would be preferable for testimonies to be taken by a male and a female police officer in order to make the victim feel more comfortable when talking about her experiences.[31] However, one prosecutor stated that it was more important to look at the qualifications of the police officers and not at their sex. Furthermore, he stated that it was more important to have a female interpreter because direct communication takes place with the interpreter. It was stated, furthermore, that the requirement to conduct a hearing with one male and one female police officer would cause practical personnel problems.

[31] Each district should have enough female specialised investigators according to the directive on the treatment of victims of indecent offences. College van Procureurs-Generaal, Aanwijzing bejegening slachtoffers van zedendelicten, [Directive of the Board of Prosecutors General on the treatment of victims of indecent offences], Staatscourant, no. 64, 2 April 2001, in force since 1 April 2001.

6.4.2.4.4 The possibility to chart the recruitment practices in the country of origin and its added value

In this section, the answers to question IV d of the questionnaire will be discussed. The absence of cooperation in criminal matters with African countries as described in Chapter 5 also appeared from the files of several cases in The Hague and Amsterdam. Only if the identity and nationality of the victims is not known, is contact sought with the embassies of African countries in the Netherlands for help in clarifying these issues. Even if there are strong indications, for instance, from telephone taps and testimonies, that certain persons, e.g., in Nigeria, are involved in criminal practices, cooperation is not sought with these countries because of the absence of reliable contacts in these countries. Consequently, it is impossible to obtain a true picture of the complete organisation including those persons operating in the countries of origin. Furthermore, in some cases, it appeared from telephone taps that violence was used or would be used against potential victims or against the family of the victims but as cooperation with Nigeria and other African countries was absent, this information could not be passed on to the competent authorities in these countries or could not be verified. In one case in The Hague, it could not be excluded that the suspect had contacts with the Dutch embassies in Nigeria and Ghana to obtain visas, as he could easily obtain false documents. In a case in Amsterdam in which connections with Turkey, the Czech Republic, and Slovakia existed, these connections were not verified so that the role of the organisation in these countries could not be cleared up.

In another case in The Hague, the trafficker had close relations with persons in the Czech Republic who were said to form part of the Bulgarian mafia in this country. These persons were suspected of involvement in the trafficking as well. However, no investigation was carried out to clarify the role of these persons and therefore a picture of the whole organisation could not be obtained. Consequently, a charge could not be based on Article 140 Dutch Penal Code on participation in criminal organisations.[32] In The Hague, and to a lesser extent also in Amsterdam, this problem also arose in other cases. In that regard, cooperation with other countries to trace the complete organisation behind a suspect in the Netherlands was important but was consciously avoided as it was too complicated and involved too many risks of failure. In The Hague, it was standard practice to limit the indictment as much as possible to activities that occurred in the Netherlands and otherwise to limit it as much as possible to countries within the EU, even if the consequence was that some related crimes, such as participation in a criminal organisation, could not be punished or that co-offenders remained unpunished.

---

[32] See Section 6.4.3.1 below.

6.4.2.4.5 Absence of cooperation with African countries in general and Nigeria in particular

In this section, the answers to question IV e of the questionnaire will be discussed. Besides the consequences indicated in the previous section, the absence of cooperation with African countries in general, and Nigeria in particular, cause some specific obstacles. In many cases with Western African victims, there was confusion as to the identity and nationality of the persons, and people often used the passports of look-alikes to enter the country. However, it was not possible to check the identity and nationality of the victims via a request to the specific countries. If financial transactions to Nigeria or other Western African countries had taken place, the beneficiaries in these countries and their possible involvement in the trafficking could not be verified. The practices with regard to Voodoo could not be clarified in Nigeria and information on these practices had to be obtained from external experts. Finally, traffickers send a substantive part of their earnings back to Nigeria and invest it there, and live a rather sober life in the Netherlands. They often have debts with telephone companies or are in arrears with rent, for instance. An action by the victims for illegally obtained money, compensation, or lost income either during the criminal proceedings or in separate civil proceedings before a Dutch court is therefore destined to fail, as it is not possible to seize the assets in Nigeria.

6.4.2.4.6 Cooperation in criminal matters with Spain

In this section, the answers to question IV f of the questionnaire will be discussed. This question was adopted in the questionnaire following the outcome of the analysis of the evaluation reports in Chapter 5 and the doubts of the prosecutors with regard to the efficiency of cooperation in criminal matters with Spain.

In the cases studied, a request was only sent to Spain for cooperation in criminal matters on three occasions. In one case, the suspect was arrested in Spain on 7 August 1998 following an international arrest warrant followed by a request by the Netherlands to extradite the person. The person was finally extradited on 8 October 1999, after a repeated request and frequent correspondence with the Spanish authorities. Communication from Spain took place via diplomatic channels and the procedure for extradition was surrounded by a number of formalities to be fulfilled. In another case where information concerning the suspects was requested, it was stated that direct contact with the competent authorities was only possible after the Spanish court had received the request. In this case, the answers that were received following the request were of no value to the case and the impression arose that the Spanish authorities had made little effort to handle the request properly. The request to trace bank accounts had to be decided by the court and it took one month before the accounts were identified. The answer stating that a court decision was necessary was issued on the same day that the court decision was delivered, but the answer itself did not include the decision of the court. However, the request also concerned the seizing of assets, the hearing of witnesses, and the tracing of telephone numbers. The request was made on 11 September 2000 and, on 28 May 2001, Spain requested additional information. The authorities did not precisely indicate what information they needed for the execution of the request. In June 2001, the Dutch authorities made an additional request. Finally, the Spanish authorities reported that some of the telephone numbers could not be traced because one figure was missing and no further efforts were made to resolve the matter. According to the documents in the files it took from 27 November 2000 until 9 May 2001 to send the request from the Tribunal Superior to a Court of First Instance and Preliminary Investigations (Juzgado de Primera Instancia e Instrucción). In another case, a request was made to the Spanish consulate to verify whether passports that had been seized were false. Within one week, the answer confirming that this was the case was received. In two other cases, a request to Spain was not made although the case had strong connections with Spain and an investigation of these connections could have clarified the case. The prosecutor said that he had acted with reservations with regard to making requests to Spain because his experiences with Spain had not been satisfactory.

6.4.2.4.7 Investigation of the suspect's financial situation and assets in other countries

In this section, the answers to question IV g of the questionnaire will be discussed. In Section 6.4.2.4.5, the problems with regard to the financial situation and the assets of suspects in African countries were mentioned. In one case in Rotterdam, there was intensive contact with Switzerland and Luxembourg with regard to tracing and seizing a suspect's bank accounts. On the basis of the information received from Switzerland and Luxembourg, an action for the forfeiture of illegally obtained money could be commenced. With regard to Switzerland, it took around eight months before a final decision was taken on the possibility to inform the Dutch authorities concerning details of the suspect's bank accounts and to seize these accounts. Meanwhile, the accounts were frozen. The delay was mainly caused by the legal proceedings granting the account owner the opportunity to appeal against the decision to provide information with regard to bank accounts to foreign officials and the seizure of his bank accounts. In this particular case, the suspect exhausted all the remedies to prevent the execution of the Dutch request. In Luxembourg, it took even longer, almost fifteen months, to answer the request with regard to the bank accounts of the suspect, for the same reasons as in Switzerland. An extra delaying factor was the additional request of Luxembourg concerning the procedures and competences in the Netherlands with regard to the searching of premises. There was direct communication with both countries. In Switzerland, the police established the contacts and they discovered whom the prosecutor had to contact. The competent person in Switzerland had already been informed beforehand that the prosecutor would contact him. With Luxembourg, direct communication took place after formal contacts were established via the Ministry of Justice. After a while, an additional request was sent to the competent persons in both countries asking to be informed of the actual state of affairs.

In three other cases, a request was sent to Estonia enquiring into the financial position of the suspects but no answers were received. In one case, a request was made to Bulgaria asking the authorities to investigate the financial position of traffickers who were detained in the Netherlands. However, no answer was received. The prosecutor in The Hague who led a separate case against a perpetrator for the forfeiture of illegally obtained profits from one of the trafficking cases studied had experienced a lack of cooperation with the Moroccan authorities in this regard.

In the case in Roermond, a rogatory commission to Poland had planned searches but the mission had to be cancelled prematurely. The suspects involved in the trafficking who thought that the commission had come to search and seize their assets, had planned an attack on the members of the commission.

Although far-reaching conclusions cannot be drawn from these findings, it can be said that there are indications that information with regard to bank accounts in other countries is not easily obtained and that the execution of requests to search and seize these accounts can take a long time, also as a consequence of the appeal procedures against decisions taken in this regard.

6.4.2.5 *Other problems*

In this section, the answers to question V a of the questionnaire will be discussed. In quite a number of cases, the suspect had relations with or was known in other countries but these relations were generally not investigated. For instance, in two cases, it was known that the suspects had been convicted in another country but no inquiry was made as to the nature of the crime. The role of the possible co-offender is often not investigated if this person resides in another country, although it could provide some useful information, for instance, on the modus operandi of the suspect and investigations in different countries to avoid any duplication of efforts. Furthermore, it is important to prosecute all the persons involved in the trafficking, in order to put a successful end to trafficking in persons.

In one large investigation in Amsterdam, no victims of trafficking could be traced. However, the trafficking in that case only played a minor role in the range of criminal activities of the organisation. Therefore, the trafficking was less of a priority and not much effort was taken to trace the victims. Consequently, the case was destined to fail: without the testimonies of the victims, it is very difficult to prove the existence of trafficking in persons. Another complicating factor in these cases was that the employment of the victims took place in a different district, causing extra coordination efforts. In another investigation in Amsterdam, the crime of trafficking also formed a minor part of the activities of the organisation and specific questioning of the prostitutes with regard to their relationship with the suspect and with regard to trafficking did not taken place.

6.4.2.6 *Specific problems in appeal cases*

In this section, the cases that were prosecuted in The Hague in which an appeal was lodged will be discussed. In 9 cases an appeal was lodged but 4 of them were withdrawn. In 4 cases, the judgement of the district court was confirmed on appeal and, in one case, part of the non-suspended prison sentence was converted into a suspended one.

In two of the cases of which the judgement was confirmed, the perpetrators were sentenced in absentia by the district court and again by the court of appeal. Therefore, the facts as they had been established at first instance were not disputed on appeal and thus an additional investigation by the court of appeal was not necessary.

In the third case in which the judgement was confirmed, there were no new facts in the appeal case and no additional investigation by the court of appeal was necessary.

In the fourth case in which the judgement was confirmed on appeal, tape recordings were again translated, which raised some problems in finding qualified and reliable interpreters who were willing to translate. In this case, a witness was heard during the trial but she did not give any new information on the case. She was not feeling very well during the hearing and she had forgotten all that had happened and that she had declared in earlier testimonies. The fact that the defence persisted in its request to hear this witness led to some delay in the process as she was residing in Ghana. Furthermore, the defence stated that for the crimes in the indictment that took place in Ghana and Nigeria, the prosecution had to be barred because of the absence of double criminality.

In the case where the sentence was amended on appeal, the judge acquitted the accused of one of the facts in the indictment, namely, intimidating witnesses, because the identity of the relevant witness was incorrect. At the trial, another person was heard. It could not be established whether this confusion arose due to the fact that the witness came from another country.

Although the number of appeal cases is limited and far-reaching conclusions cannot therefore be draw, we can say that the fact that more states are involved in the trafficking does not seem to generate specific problems. Generally, the court of appeal is bound by the indictment adopted at first instance and therefore an in-depth investigation of the facts of the case is often not required on appeal. Some of the problems that were raised in the district courts also occurred in the appeal cases, for instance, language problems during the trial and the problem of finding qualified and reliable interpreters.

6.4.3 **Other issues raised in the concluding interviews**

In this section, the issues raised in the concluding interviews, which were not discussed exhaustively in the former sections, will be focused upon. These are matters that are not necessarily related to the cases themselves. First of all, the use of Article 140 Dutch Penal Code will be discussed and thereafter the influence of the policy choices on the prosecution of trafficking cases will be elaborated.

6.4.3.1 *Trafficking in persons and participation in a criminal organisation*

In this part, the outcome of the interviews with the prosecutors on the importance of basing the charge on Article 140 Dutch Penal Code, participation in a criminal organisation, will be discussed. Questions on this issue were raised during the study of the files because, in a number of cases in The Hague and Rotterdam, Article 140 was not included in the indictment, although there were strong ties between the co-offenders and, in some cases, a more or less hierarchical relationship between those criminals also existed. Furthermore, the impression arose, which was later confirmed by the prosecutors, that in these cases, the choice was made not to commence investigations in foreign states by sending requests, which was an important reason why the existence of, or participation in, a criminal organisation could not be proved and the suspects were not charged with this crime. In some concluding interviews, the question was raised what the added value would be of adding Article 140 to the indictment, as Article 250a Dutch Penal Code already includes the committing of the crime by two or more persons jointly as an aggravating circumstance. Some prosecutors thought that the added value was negligible as it would not lead to higher sanctions. Others said that the charge was based on Article 140 when it was clear that the suspect had participated in a criminal organisation but when trafficking in persons was not so obvious or difficult to prove. An Attorney General stated that the practice with regard to the punishment of trafficking in persons committed by a criminal organisation was not consistent. In some cases, the judge saw this as a reason to increase the term of imprisonment whereas, in other cases, no extra sanction was imposed.

In my view, the added value of basing the charge on Article 140 in trafficking cases must be sought in the term of imprisonment that can be imposed according to the rules of coincidence of crimes, notwithstanding the existence of the possibility of including in the charge the aggravating circumstance that the trafficking took place by two or more persons jointly under Article 250a. With regard to coincidence of crimes, Article 57 of the Dutch Penal Code states that in the case of coincidence of crimes with the same sort of punishment (in this case imprisonment) only one punishment can be imposed. In the case of imprisonment, the term may not exceed the maximum of the severest penalty by more than one third. If trafficking in persons has been committed by two or more persons jointly the maximum penalty is ten years. The maximum penalty for participating in a criminal organisation is six years imprisonment. This means that, pursuant to Article 57, the maximum penalty will be ten years plus 40 months, i.e., 13 years and three months. This means that an indictment based on Article 140 in conjunction with Article 250a has its added value in the sense that a higher penalty could be imposed, but subject to the condition, of course, that Article 140 can be proved, if necessary with the use of mutual legal assistance.

6.4.3.2 *The consequences of policy choices with regard to the prosecution of trafficking in persons*

Policy differences among the courts where the file study took place in prosecuting trafficking cases were sometimes raised as an argument when the question was discussed whether, in some cases, it would have been advantageous if more effort had been taken to obtain information from other countries. In The Hague and in Rotterdam the prosecution of trafficking cases forms part of the Serious Crimes Department, while in Amsterdam, it is part of the Indecency Offences Department. In general, more attention and thus more money is paid to the Serious Crimes Departments. The prosecution of serious crimes is managed in a project-structured approach, which means that the budget is divided among the crimes categorised under serious crimes. This means that trafficking in persons, when it is part of this department, always receives a just share of the pie. On the other hand, a calculation is made of the estimated costs, which also means that if, in the course of an investigation, extra money is needed, for instance to travel abroad to hear witnesses, this may cause problems. It is impossible to foresee what implications a trafficking case will have and therefore choices must be made on the basis of a cost/benefit analysis during investigations. In some cases, this was also a reason not to exhaust all the possibilities in the field of mutual legal assistance. Furthermore, when, during an investigation, the Serious Crimes Department in Amsterdam found indications that the suspects were also active in the field of trafficking, the solving of the trafficking case was less important. In some cases in Amsterdam, this was a reason why not all the possibilities were exhausted, including mutual legal assistance, to solve the trafficking case. Because the approach in Amsterdam was not project-based, the activities took place on an ad hoc basis, depending on the results of police investigations. It was true of all courts that because of the heavy workload, legal action was taken only in the cases that, at first sight, could lead to a successful prosecution of the suspect.[33] Some practical explanations were given by the prosecutors as to why the possibilities of mutual legal assistance which were available to obtain information from abroad were not used exhaustively.

6.5 CONCLUSIONS

In this section, the conclusions of the empirical research will be given and the question will be discussed whether trafficking in persons must be considered as a transnational crime.

[33] This practice was also confirmed by the national prosecutor on smuggling, trafficking and child pornography in J.C.F. van Gelder, *De keten op de keeper beschouwd, Rapportage Project intensiveringstrafrechtelijke aanpak mensensmokkel, mensenhandel en ama's*, Landelijk Parket Openbaar Ministerie, [National Public Prosecutor's Office], Rotterdam, 30 April 2002, not published, pp. 26, 31-32.

6.5.1 Conclusions from the empirical study

The most remarkable outcome of the analysis of the files and the interviews was that, in general, the practitioners consider the need for mutual legal assistance to be an obstacle in a criminal case and is avoided as much as possible, even if this is at the cost of the indictment of one or more related offences.

One of the main obstacles to the prosecution of those suspected of trafficking in persons is the absence of victims and witnesses, often due to the fact that immigration officers have expelled them from the country. A considerable reduction in the problems associated with the prosecution of transnational trafficking in persons can be achieved by closer cooperation between the immigration police and the police and the judiciary. This reduces the risk that victims who are relevant to the case are returned to their country of origin before they have been heard by the police or, even more importantly, by the examining magistrate. Some initiatives for such cooperation have already been taken in Amsterdam and are proposed in The Hague. For instance, in Amsterdam, when a person from one of the applicant countries applies to work as a self-employed prostitute, the police and immigration officers work closely together. Yet, it is too early to draw far-reaching conclusions on the effect of this cooperation, although the experiences in Amsterdam have been encouraging. Closer cooperation between these two disciplines would also be in line with the directive of the Board of Prosecutors General on the strategy on trafficking in persons cases referred to previously.[34] However, recent practices in the Netherlands where illegal immigrants at the streetwalkers' district were caught by the immigration police and expelled from the country are not very promising.

It must be concluded that formal communication lines are normally used for the transmission of requests and that, even if direct communication is allowed, these lines are used. The existence of parallel procedures is not considered problematic by the practitioners, but rather as an advantage. The officials involved persist in following the formalities needed for the transmission of information, unless the requesting person is known to the provider of the information. This latter factor is more often the case on the police level than on the judicial level. In Finland, it is even official policy that all kinds of information can be provided as long as the requesting authority is known. The formalities surrounding the practice of mutual legal assistance are regularly an obstacle in the process. For instance, it is a pity that documents that are directly obtained from counterparts abroad cannot be used in a criminal procedure because the documents in question have not (yet) been formalised via the official channels.

---

[34] College van Procureurs-Generaal, Aanwijzing aanpak mensenhandel en andere vormen van uitbuiting in de prostitutie, [Directives of the Board of Prosecutors General on the strategy in trafficking in persons cases], Staatscourant, no. 188, 28 September 2000, in force since 1 October 2000, point 1-5, and annex 4 Section 2.2.1.

Another outcome of the file study is that if an answer to a request is urgently needed within a certain time period, the competent authorities succeed in obtaining the answer within that time period. In these cases, the formalisation of the request and the answers also have to be subsequently obtained. This situation shows that the added value of the formalisation for the content of the answers is limited, as the formalisation process in these cases only takes place after the request has been executed.

The prosecutors interviewed described the role of the Office for International Legal Assistance in Criminal Matters at the Ministry of Justice in very different ways and this different practice also follows from the files studied. In Rotterdam, the interviewees said that this department only intervened if a request was made outside the EU and that they had to handle the requests made within the EU themselves. In The Hague, all requests were systematically sent via the Ministry of Justice irrespective of the requested country. In Amsterdam, a division was made between requests to EU countries, which were not systematically sent via the Ministry of Justice, and requests to non-EU countries, which were sent via the Ministry of Justice.

In general, the absence of double criminality was often considered as an obstacle to mutual legal assistance, although it was already concluded in Chapter 5 that this did not appear from the evaluation reports analysed in that chapter. The problem of absence of double criminality with regard to trafficking in persons was neither observed by the prosecutors in the interviews, nor does it follow from the trafficking cases analysed in the file study. What is recognised as problematic by the prosecutors is the lack of priority and the absence of attention for the phenomenon of trafficking in persons, both in the Netherlands and in other countries. They stated that this absence caused serious difficulties and delays with regard to mutual legal assistance in trafficking cases.

One last conclusion based on the interviews and the file study is that requests sent to other countries are, in general, very elaborate with reference to the suspects, co-suspects, information on the investigation of the case, personal details of the sender and reference to applicable international agreements. In a minor number of cases information on this final item was not complete and in one exceptional case was completely absent.

6.5.2 Is trafficking in persons a transnational crime?

Now that the problems relating to cooperation in criminal matters in general and the prosecution of trafficking in persons in particular have been elaborated in Chapter 5 and Chapter 6, respectively, the final answer can be given to the question of whether trafficking in persons must be considered to be a transnational crime. Following the criteria developed in Chapter 2 and the analysis made in Chapter 3, this question must be answered in the affirmative when the two additional criteria are met.[35] This

[35] See Chapter 2, Section 2.5.5, and Chapter 3, Section 3.10.

means that problems involved in prosecuting trafficking in persons are aggravated by the involvement of more than one state and therefore the solution must be sought beyond national borders. Most of the problems indicated and analysed in this chapter originate from the fact that more states are involved in the prosecution of a trafficking case. For instance, major problems exist when victims have returned to their home country, whether or not voluntarily, because these victims are often needed for successful prosecution. Problems exist in identifying the competent authorities and in understanding the legal system of other countries.

As we have seen in this chapter, prosecutors try to avoid cooperation in criminal matters as much as possible because it normally takes a long time and includes many risks of failure. They avoid mutual legal assistance even at the cost of being able to charge the suspects with related crimes. Consequently, the recruitment and transport phase is often not investigated because such an investigation requires intensive cooperation with other states and therefore other persons within the organisation or accomplices escape with impunity. This situation cannot be considered satisfactory. When activities in the recruitment phase are not investigated and are not included in the charge, the accomplices and organisers behind the trafficking remain free. These persons will continue their practices and the trafficking will continue. Therefore, the current practice on the prosecution of traffickers must be considered to be not effective and problematic. These examples, together with the analysis in this chapter, make it clear that problems involved in prosecuting trafficking in persons are aggravated by the involvement of more than one state and thus that a solution to these problems must be sought beyond national borders. This means that the two additional criteria are also met.

However, this does not mean that all problems originate in the involvement of more than one state. As we have seen in this chapter, part of the problems involved in prosecuting those suspected of trafficking in persons originate in the failure to prioritise the prosecution of this crime in the Netherlands as well as in other countries and the lack of adequate financial resources. But as the major problems originate in the fact that more than one state are involved in trafficking in persons, the solution to these problems must be sought beyond the national level, in this case at the EU level. In the next chapter, starting points for such an approach at the EU level will be elaborated.

CHAPTER 7 CONCLUSIONS

7.1 SUMMARY

7.1.1 Introduction

In this study the conclusion was drawn that trafficking in persons must be considered a transnational crime and that the fact that more states are involved in the crime of trafficking aggravates the problems of prosecuting trafficking in persons.[1] The content of the problems with regard to the prosecution of trafficking in persons was elaborated in Chapter 6. In this chapter, the problems of prosecuting those suspected of trafficking in persons will be summarised first by focusing on the three main disparities that were important in this study. The first two disparities were already described in Chapter 1 and the third follows from the file study in Chapter 6.

The first disparity follows from the fact that the involvement of more than one state in the crime of trafficking in persons is an obstacle to an effective prosecution of this crime. The underlying disparity is between the fact that the crime of trafficking in persons is, as we have seen, a transnational crime with a transnational element and the fact that strategies to combat it are largely based on national competences, i.e., the disparity of *transnational crime versus national competence.*

The second disparity that was important in this study and was referred to in the first chapter is between the juridical recognition of the phenomenon of trafficking in persons that is reflected in many policy documents and legal instruments although the willingness or ability of states to efficiently use them or to transform them into concrete actions in national law is often lacking, i.e., the disparity of *juridical recognition versus the unwillingness or inability of states.*

The third disparity was elaborated especially in the file study described in Chapter 6. It concerns the position of the victim of trafficking in persons, namely, the disparity between the practice often used to expel victims of trafficking once it is discovered that the victims are staying in the Netherlands without the necessary permits, on the one hand, and the importance of the testimonies of the victims for criminal proceedings and the protection of victims of trafficking that is laid down in various documents and instruments on national and non-national levels, on the other. The disparity that will be discussed is that of *the application of migration law versus the importance for prosecution and the protection of the victims.*

[1] The requirements before criminal conduct can be qualified as a transnational crime were developed in Chapter 2, Section 2.5.5.

In the following sections, these three disparities will be further analysed on the basis of the outcome of this study. Afterwards, recommendations for the improvement of the prosecution of trafficking in persons will be elaborated in Section 7.2, before the final conclusion will be drawn in Section 7.3.

7.1.2 **Transnational crime versus national competence**

Now that it has been determined that trafficking in persons must be considered a transnational crime, the characteristics that were provided in Chapter 2 for this type of crime are applicable. In Chapter 2, it was said that one of the main problems in the suppression of transnational crime in general is that the borders between states are easily crossed by criminals and criminal groups that commit transnational crime. Conversely, states are bound, for the application of their national criminal laws, to the territory of the state because the sovereignty of states and the territoriality principle currently still prevail in criminal law and each state has its own criminal legal system. However, for an effective prosecution of trafficking cases, states are obliged to establish an effective system of cooperation in criminal matters with other states. The questions that arose in this regard and were reflected upon in Chapter 1 will be discussed below on the basis of the outcome of this study. In this section, the changing concept of state sovereignty will be discussed first of all. Secondly, current developments in the granting of jurisdiction will be discussed since they might facilitate cooperation in criminal matters. Thirdly, reference will be made to confidence between states, which is an absolute condition before states will be able to realise an effective form of cooperation.

7.1.2.1 *The changing concept of state sovereignty*

The changing role of the state as a sovereign entity was already described in Chapter 1. States cannot continue to insist that they have an exclusive right to enact criminal law within their own territory. Recently developed instruments on the European level, such as the European Arrest Warrant, the EU Convention on Mutual Assistance between the Member States of the EU, with the introduction of the principle of *forum regit actum* in Article 4, and the introduction of joint teams in Article 13, the EU conventions on extradition, and the proposed EPP have adopted a transformation of the use of current principles such as *double criminality, the rule of speciality, and grounds to refuse extradition* in order to facilitate cooperation in criminal matters.[2] Consequently, a state should, for instance, accept that investigative actions with law enforcement officers from other EU member states have to take place on its territory and that evidence gathered in another country can be used in its courts. At first sight, this transformation of the use of current principles indicates an erosion of the concept of state sovereignty. However, these actions can only take place in accordance with the law of that state and after a state has explicitly consented to these opera-

[2] Chapter 4, Section 4.3.3.8.

tions, either by ratifying a convention or in another, less formal, way. The execution of these forms of cooperation is the primary responsibility of the member states.[3] Therefore, it is questionable whether the concept of state sovereignty is being eroded or that it has the appearance of erosion. Maybe state sovereignty has actually become stronger as many steps in closer cooperation with and the granting of competence to authorities on a non-national level require the explicit consent of the state.

The developments concerning cooperation in criminal matters in recently adopted instruments referred to above and discussed in Chapter 4, Section 4.3.3.8, can be summarised by stating that cooperation in criminal matters, in particular extradition and mutual legal assistance, must be simplified and extended. Diminishing the formalities and extending possibilities for this cooperation, often at the cost of the control of states over this cooperation, will achieve this. It can be said that it has gradually become accepted that some decisions with regard to criminal law are made at the EU level and not solely at the national level. However, we have to take into account that the general policy with regard to procedural criminal law has so far been aimed at closer cooperation by retaining the differences existing in the criminal law systems of the EU member states, i.e., there has been no harmonisation in this area. With regard to substantive criminal law, the developments in the EU are already more far-reaching. Following Article 31(1) sub. e EU Treaty, the Council has adopted common definitions for some crimes in several framework decisions. Undoubtedly the most important for this study is the Framework Decision on Combating Trafficking in Human Beings.

The practice that decisions are increasingly made at the EU level will probably be strengthened in the future when the forthcoming Intergovernmental Conference in 2003/2004 will decide on the constitutional reform of the EU. Within the forum of the European Convention, various persons and working groups have made known their ideas with regard to the future of the EU.[4] The common denominator in these documents is the wish for one constitutional treaty by merging the three pillars of the EU, the abolishment of the right to veto and the introduction of the majority vote for police and judicial cooperation in criminal matters. The co-decision procedure should become the general procedure for taking decisions unless indicated otherwise. Consequently, decisions on police and judicial cooperation in criminal matters will be taken within the normal structures of the European Community with some exceptions, for instance, a shared right of initiative for the European Commission

[3] This also follows from the analysis of the reports in Chapter 5.

[4] Feasibility Study, Contribution to a Preliminary Draft, Constitution of the European Union under the responsibility of F. Lamoureux, European Commission, 4.12.2002. Final report of Working group X, Freedom, Security and Justice, Brussels, 2.12.2002, CONV 426/02. A Project for the European Union, Brussels, 22.5.2002, COM(2002)247 final. For the European Union, Peace, Freedom, Solidarity, Brussels, 4.12.2002, COM(2002)728 final. For a description of the relevant documents, see C.J.F.J. Fijnaut and M.S. Groenhuijsen, De toekomst van de Europese Unie en de lidstatelijke samenwerking in strafzaken, in: *Delikt en Delinkwent*, Volume 33, issue 5, 2003, pp. 462-492.

with a quarter of the member states. As a result, states will lose the right to veto and the right of initiative for each state in police and judicial cooperation in criminal matters and can be bound by decisions taken against their will. Thus the real Communautarisation of police and judicial cooperation in criminal matters then starts. This would mean, for instance, a transmission of sovereign powers in third pillar issues as part of the Communautarisation process. I wonder if all states realise these consequences of the Communautarisation of police and judicial cooperation in criminal matters and do in fact want this change. As we have seen in this study, states are only inclined to accept decisions taken on the EU level in a limited number of cases and hold on to their competence in criminal law matters.

Although I support the initiatives of the Convention, in my view the member states are not yet prepared to adopt such a system with regard to police and judicial cooperation in criminal matters and the proposals do not reflect the reserved attitude of states in this regard.[5] This reserved attitude follows from the fact that police and judicial cooperation in criminal matters within the EU has just started and that, so far, the strategy of mutual recognition of each other's criminal law system has been chosen to achieve an area of freedom, security, and justice, but, unfortunately, not always with the desired result. We can say that state sovereignty has so far remained largely untouched but that the globalisation of criminal activity and criminal relations forces states to cooperate with other states and to share responsibilities in this regard.

7.1.2.2 *Jurisdiction: The territoriality principle, the principle of universal jurisdiction, and regional jurisdiction*

The concept of jurisdiction is inextricably bound to the concept of sovereignty with regard to criminal law. As various principles can be and are applied to claim jurisdiction, it is in some cases unclear which state has jurisdiction.[6] Furthermore, the extent of a crime, especially when such a crime has transnational features, is often not clear from the onset, which complicates the process to determine the most appropriate state to exercise jurisdiction. For instance, it can turn out that the state that seemed most appropriate in the beginning is not the most appropriate when more details of the case and its extent emerge. Besides, the problem of concurrent jurisdiction may exist and then the question is what rules can be applied for the granting of jurisdiction, although a total absence of states claiming jurisdiction is more frequently observed with regard to trafficking cases.

The territoriality principle is still the leading principle when questions of jurisdiction are at stake, but several authors describe the erosion of the strict territoriality

[5] See, for instance, the interview with the Dutch Minister of Justice in a Dutch newspaper in which the Minister aired his concerns on the transmission of national powers to the EU level in justice and home affairs issues. 'Samenwerken ja, uniformeren nee', Minister Donner over Europese justitie, *NRC Handelsblad*, 10 May 2003.

[6] These various principles were elaborated in Chapter 2, Section 2.3.2.2.

principle.[7] Especially with regard to transnational crimes such as trafficking in persons, the territoriality principle, for reasons mentioned above, is not very helpful in answering the question of what state has jurisdiction and does not guarantee that jurisdiction is granted to the most appropriate state. Therefore, a strict application of the territoriality principle must be abandoned. As was already described in Chapter 2, Section 2.3.2.2, the territoriality principle has met some changes during the last decades and different views exist on the interpretation of this principle.[8] Furthermore, states adopt a flexible use of this principle and address the question of jurisdiction from a pragmatic point of view.

Although the universality principle has recently met with increased attention, as was described in Chapter 2, universal jurisdiction is not easily granted and it can be said that a certain link with the crime, the offender, or the victims is necessary before a state may claim jurisdiction.[9] The question here is whether the concept of universal jurisdiction can be applied in the case of trafficking in persons. As was stated in Chapter 2, Section 2.3.2.2, this concept only applies to crimes that threaten the international community as a whole in such a grave way that it is justified that each state of the international community may claim jurisdiction. It is clear that reference is made here to the international crimes defined in Chapter 2, Section 2.3.1.2. This means that the universality principle will not be applied in the case of trafficking in persons, as this crime must be considered a transnational crime in this study.[10] However, the EU member states proclaimed on several occasions that the crime of trafficking must be considered a grave violation of fundamental human rights and that the eradication of this crime is not the sole concern of each member state but a shared responsibility. A clear expression of this shared responsibility was the adoption of the Framework Decision on Trafficking in Human Beings, in July 2002, discussed in Chapter 3 and again in Chapter 4. Thus, it is recognised by all member states of the EU that trafficking in persons is a serious crime that must be combated. Therefore, it can be stated that, within the EU the crime of trafficking in persons should be seen as a crime for which all states may claim jurisdiction regardless of whether it was committed on their territory or not.[11] Such a new form of jurisdiction,

[7] Chapter 2, Section 2.3.2.2. A.H.J. Swart, *Goede rechtsbedeling en internationale rechtshulp in strafzaken*, Kluwer, Deventer 1983, p. 13.

[8] The different views on the interpretation of the territoriality principle are the following: the subjective and the objective territoriality doctrines, the doctrine of the instrument, and the doctrine of ubiquity. By applying these four interpretations, states try to extend the application of the territoriality principle.

[9] *Separate opinion* of the President of the ICJ, G. Guillaume, in *the Democratic Republic of Congo* v. *Belgium* case (Yerodia case), 14 February 2002, point 16. Explanatory text to the proposed International Crimes Act in the Netherlands, TK 2001-2002, 28 337, no. 3, p. 18. M. Boot-Matthijssen and R. van Elst, Wetsvoorstel internationale misdrijven, in: *NJB,* Volume 77, issue 35, 2002, pp. 1748-1750.

[10] The conditions before trafficking in persons can be considered as the international crime of slavery were discussed in Chapter 3, Section 3.6.

[11] A similar provision was adopted in Article 9, paragraph 1 (a) of the Council Framework Decision of 13 June 2002 on Combating Terrorism, OJ L164, 22.6.2002, pp. 3-7. This article states that 'each Member State may extend its jurisdiction if the offence is committed in the territory of a Member State'.

where the concept of 'universal jurisdiction' is only applied in a certain region, may be called 'regional jurisdiction'. In this way, the current universality principle can be transformed into a more flexible concept to facilitate the prosecution of trafficking in persons. The system with regard to cooperation in criminal matters in the Nordic countries may be considered as an elaboration of this concept. The Treaty of Helsinki (1962), on cooperation between the Nordic countries, includes provisions such as the creation of uniform provisions concerning crime and the penalties to be imposed, investigation and prosecution in one of the countries to be pursued in another Nordic country, and mutual recognition of court decisions and decisions from other judicial authorities. Furthermore, it contains simplified extradition provisions, double criminality is not required, and the extradition of nationals is allowed within the Nordic sub-region.[12]

7.1.2.3 *Confidence among states in each other's systems*

For the simplification and facilitation of cooperation in criminal matters by mutual recognition, it is essential that states have confidence in each other's systems. This is even more important when an approach to prosecuting traffickers originates at the EU level. As we have seen in Chapters 5 and 6, this confidence is not always present and is even completely absent with regard to the criminal law systems of some EU countries and some Central and Eastern European countries that will become members of the EU in the near future. As the applicant countries must adopt the documents and legal instruments on police and judicial cooperation in criminal matters[13] before they can accede to the EU, an efficient application of these documents and instruments is not to be expected, as confidence in these countries with regard to cooperation in criminal matters does not automatically materialise once they join the EU. However, it will be an advantage that, after accession, the applicant countries will have to apply the conventions and other EU instruments on cooperation in criminal matters and trafficking in persons as well. It remains to be seen whether this advantage will neutralise the effect of the lack of confidence. Especially for trafficking cases, it is important that cooperation with these countries is intensified and op-

---

[12] R. Lahti, Sub-Regional Co-Operation in Criminal Matters: The Experience of the Nordic Countries, in: A. Eser and O. Lagodny (eds.), *Principles and Procedures for a New Transnational Criminal Law,* Max Planck Institute, Freiburg im Breisgau, 1992, pp. 305-310.

[13] The Council Presidency has stated 'that the joint actions, joint positions and conventions arrived at under the heading of cooperation in the area of justice and home affairs are part of the Community "*acquis*" which must be accepted in full by the applicant countries. Furthermore, the new Member States had to undertake to adapt their institutions and administrative systems and arrangements to the standards prevailing in the EU so as to allow efficient implementation of the Community "*acquis*" in this area.' M. den Boer and G. de Kerchove, A Hurdled Admission: The Integration of the Candidate Countries into the Area of Freedom, Security and Justice, in: V. Kronenberger (ed.), *The European Union and the International Legal Order: Discord or Harmony?* T.M.C. Asser Press, The Hague, 2001, p. 319. Pre-Accession Pact on Organised Crime between the Member States of the EU and the Applicant Countries of Central and Eastern Europe and Cyprus, OJ C 220, 15.7.1998, pp. 1-5. Article 8 of the Schengen Protocol to the EU Treaty.

timised as many victims and traffickers originate from applicant countries and traffickers from Western European countries often have criminal connections in Central and Eastern European countries. In some of the courts in the file study, the reluctance to cooperate with countries outside the EU originated from preconceptions that were not based on personal experiences. However, it cannot be denied that, in other cases, the prosecutors had to be very tenacious before positive results in the field of mutual legal assistance could be established.

7.1.2.4 *Conclusion*

Summarising the above, the conclusion with regard to the first disparity must be that, on the one hand, an approach to prosecuting suspects of trafficking in persons on the EU level based on the concept of regional jurisdiction seems to be the most appropriate and effective. On the other hand, some interesting developments have emerged at the EU level for closer cooperation between states on police and judicial cooperation in criminal matters that are based on national competences but seem to indicate an erosion of state sovereignty as well. In general, there is a tendency that the role of the nation state is changing but that states are reluctant to leave criminal matters to the EU. One of the main reasons for this reluctance is the lack of confidence in other (EU) states' legal systems. Furthermore, a distinction must be made between criminal procedure where closer cooperation with the retention of existing powers is the tendency, and substantive criminal law, with regard to which states are more inclined to adopt a form of harmonisation. The new proposals in the forum of the European Convention aimed at merging the three pillars are proposals with far-reaching consequences, which do not reflect the current cautious practices of the member states on third pillar issues. A consequence of these proposals might be the transmission of sovereign powers in police and judicial cooperation in criminal matters to the EU. This dichotomy between intentions and initiatives for cooperation in criminal matters originating at the EU level and state practices that reflect the resistance to transmit competences to the EU level is characteristic of the subject of this study. This dichotomy will be further elaborated in Section 7.3 below.

7.1.3 **Juridical recognition of the phenomenon of trafficking in persons versus the unwillingness or inability of states**

This disparity was already described in Chapter 1, Section 1.4, and was further analysed in Chapters 4, 5, and 6. As we have seen in Chapters 5 and 6, there are several reasons why all the efforts to establish these policies and instruments have not so far contributed to diminishing the phenomenon of trafficking. These reasons originate in the absence of the binding force of the policy documents, an inefficient application of the legal instruments, and the lack of priority given to the suppression of trafficking in persons by the states. As stated in Chapter 1, to achieve the main aim of this study, the reasons for the failure of an efficient prosecution of traffickers must be identified. It was concluded in Chapters 5 and 6 that such substantive problems as the requirement of double criminality are not so problematic as is often thought,[14] but, according to Chapter 3 of this study, the problem of the lack of an overall definition did, until recently, pose a real problem. Other problems are generated by procedural and organisational problems. In the category of procedural problems, the absence of the use of direct communication channels, even if this possibility exists, is seen as a missed opportunity. Furthermore, the identification of the competent authority abroad is seen as a major obstacle to efficient cooperation in mutual legal assistance. Besides, the absence of adequate education concerning the criminal law systems of other countries, the wasting of money, time, and human resources, and language problems frustrate efficient cooperation as well. Consequently, as follows from the file study, criminal law practitioners experience the involvement of other states in the crime of trafficking as a complicating factor and in general try to avoid cooperation with other countries as this is considered troublesome and time-consuming. These main problems, identified in Chapters 3, 5, and 6 will be focused upon below.

7.1.3.1 *Difficulties in defining trafficking in persons*

As follows from Chapter 3, no generally accepted definition of trafficking in persons existed until recently. In December 2000, the UN Convention on Transnational Organised Crime was adopted together with a protocol on trafficking in persons, including a definition of the phenomenon. The two main items that were, and continue to be, problematic in establishing this definition were the element of consent and the question of whether the crossing of a border is an element in the crime of trafficking in persons. With regard to the element of consent, those who believe that prostitution cannot be consented to and automatically implies a form of coercion oppose those who believe that persons can freely consent to work as a prostitute. This problem was solved by the adoption of a paragraph stating that the existence of consent is irrelevant when a form of coercion as described in the definition is used. Both groups could agree on this paragraph. The question of whether the crossing of a border must take place was solved by referring to the Convention on Transnational Organised Crime itself, where the term transnational was further elaborated. Within the EU, a commonly accepted definition was adopted in the Framework Decision of Trafficking in Persons in July 2002. This definition is clearly based on the definition in the Trafficking Protocol to the UNCTOC.

However, we have seen in Chapter 3 that many different definitions of the phenomenon exist. Organisations prefer to adopt a definition that is inspired by the aims or goals of the organisation. I do not believe that all problems that existed regarding the absence of a commonly accepted definition are solved with the acceptance of the two definitions referred to above, although these definitions can be expected to become the leading ones in the future.

---

[14] Chapter 5, Sections 5.3.1.2 and 5.4.1.2, and Chapter 6, Section 6.4.2.1.2.

7.1.3.2 *Many formalities and opaque procedures for mutual legal assistance*

One of the main outcomes of the analysis of the evaluation reports on mutual legal assistance in Chapter 5 and the file study in Chapter 6 is that mutual legal assistance is time-consuming, costly, and surrounded by uncertainties and many formalities. These are the main reasons why practitioners often try to avoid cooperation in criminal matters with other states. It would make them dependent on authorities abroad, the value of the outcome of cooperation in criminal matters is uncertain and they have no influence on the time-limits. Furthermore, as all states have, until now, applied their own national laws for mutual legal assistance, it has to be continually discovered who is the responsible person in the requested country, whether evidence collected in the requested state can be used without further formalities, which channel can be used for sending a request, etc. Besides, the time between the request and a final answer to the request differs considerably between states and the reason for this is not always clear. Therefore, it was most remarkable that when an answer was needed within a very short period of time, for instance for the surveillance of a suspect who would be leaving the country the next day, the answer was received in time. The formalities were then fulfilled afterwards, which, in some cases, took quite a while. The problem that many formalities must be fulfilled exists in many countries, often because of a need for verification, especially in France, where formal and legal checks take place by each authority involved in answering the request. Another example of the large number of formalities to be fulfilled concerned Belgium, as around 20 steps had to be taken before a request was executed and returned. It would be advisable for each country to review its legislation in this regard and to eliminate all formalities that are superfluous and frustrate an efficient system of mutual legal assistance.[15]

7.1.3.3 *Lack of direct contacts within the judiciary and problems in identifying the competent person*

In Chapter 5, Sections 5.3.2.1 and 5.4.2.1, it was stated that, in many states, direct communication channels are not commonly used, as practitioners are not familiar with the use of these channels. However, the use of direct communication is a practice that is on the increase and the positive effect of contacts between judicial authorities is repeatedly reported. However, the evaluators often mentioned their concern about the capacity of the mutual legal assistance system in the future when the applicant countries join the EU and direct communication will be extended to these countries as well. Direct contacts can only be used when the competent judicial authority can be identified and this remains one of the crucial problems with regard to mutual legal assistance. This problem mainly originates in the fact that states have different law enforcement services with different competences. Furthermore, the position of the examining magistrate is not the same in all states and is non-existent in some countries, which may have consequences for the position of the prosecutors or

[15] See Section 7.2.2.1.3 below.

law enforcement officers.[16] Practitioners often have no up to date and sufficient knowledge of the criminal law system in other states, which is absolutely essential to identify the competent authority. The practice demonstrated in the file study is that a large number of requests are sent via direct communication channels, i.e., via the informal way.[17] In the majority of cases, such a request is simultaneously sent via the Ministry of Justice as well. Informal and personal contacts exist more at police level and not as much at the level of the judiciary. Most of the prosecutors interviewed confirm the advantage of direct contacts when available. Often police contacts are used to discover to whom the request should be sent. In Finland, it is even common policy that information can be given orally when the requesting person is known. The 'old boys network', establishing contacts between police officers in several countries, is very useful and must also be established for the judiciary. An example of a formalised network for the judiciary is the European Judicial Network (EJN). It is remarkable that the EJN was not used in any of the cases studied, which gave rise to the impression that practitioners (prosecutors and examining magistrates) are not familiar with the existence of the EJN. The limited role of the EJN is also observed in the analysis of the evaluation reports on mutual legal assistance.[18] Direct contacts to facilitate mutual legal assistance are further facilitated by Eurojust, which will be discussed below in Section 7.2.3.1. Furthermore, it would be helpful if the judiciary could use the contacts that have already been established by colleagues in their state. Therefore, positive experiences by practitioners have to be shared with their colleagues. In general, the practitioners in the Netherlands are positive on the use of liaison officers abroad for transmission and guidance in mutual legal assistance. As the same countries often have to be contacted with regard to mutual assistance in trafficking cases, it would be advisable to second liaison officers in these countries.

7.1.3.4 *Absence of global sociality and adequate (financial) resources*

The absence of global sociality[19] follows from the lack of prioritising the fight against trafficking in persons in other states, and within the Netherlands in some districts as well. An important reason for the absence of global sociality can be found in the limited damage which the crime of trafficking inflicts on society. For instance, in the Netherlands, the majority of the victims originate from other countries and although the damage to these persons is in general extensive and grave, the damage to Dutch society is less visible. Furthermore, the traffickers try to prevent that the victims establish contacts with other persons in and outside their place of work with the effect that society is only very rarely confronted with the consequences of trafficking. This means that only a small part of society becomes shocked by these practices, as they remain unknown to the public at large.

[16] Chapter 5, Section 5.4.3.1.

[17] Chapter 6, Section 6.4.2.2.1 and Section 6.4.2.3.1.

[18] Chapter 5, Section 5.4.2.1.1.

The common responsibility of states to suppress and prosecute trafficking in persons is set out in many policies and instruments. However, the absence of global sociality forms an obstacle to effectuating this common responsibility and states only seem to be interested in those cases that affect their own state and, even then, states are not always prepared to make the necessary resources available. This study indicates that, in the domain of mutual legal assistance, the lack of resources is generally an obstacle to an effective system of cooperation in criminal matters. This lack can only exist because the importance of mutual legal assistance is underestimated. Many obstacles to mutual legal assistance in general, as indicated in Chapter 5, can be attributed to the absence in providing resources for mutual legal assistance. For example, language problems can be reduced when investments are made in language education. Furthermore, practitioners need to be well-educated on mutual assistance matters; when they are aware of the importance of mutual legal assistance, they will be more inclined to cooperate efficiently. Due to the lack of priority and financial resources for prosecuting traffickers in the Netherlands and other countries both within and outside the EU, the prosecution of trafficking cases is problematic. All prosecutors experienced this problem and one of them stated that, for instance, cooperation with Spain was not so problematic when it concerned a case on drug trafficking or terrorism. The prosecutors in the file study experienced a lack of resources in general as well. Complex cases with many uncertainties, such as trafficking cases, are not popular in an environment of scarcity. Within the Public Prosecutions Department in Rotterdam and The Hague, trafficking in persons forms part of the Serious Crimes Department, which means that resources are allocated to trafficking in persons. In other districts, such a clear choice is not made and trafficking cases have to compete for priority with drug trafficking and cases on terrorism. For these reasons, trafficking cases often lose this competition.

7.1.3.5 *Absence of cooperation in criminal matters with some countries*

The victims of trafficking in persons in EU countries mainly originate from a limited number of countries, namely, Central and Eastern European countries and Western African countries. Especially with the countries outside the EU that are non-applicant countries, cooperation in criminal matters can be a considerable obstacle to the prosecution of this crime. This is even more problematic when these countries are not a member of the Council of Europe either. This is, for instance, the case with African and East Asian countries. Following the absence of bilateral or multilateral agreements on cooperation in criminal matters with these countries, the cooperation in criminal matters is dependent on (non-binding) international agreements. The recently adopted UN Convention on Transnational Organised Crime includes elaborate provisions on cooperation in criminal matters and is therefore of great importance for cooperation with countries outside the EU which are non-applicant

[19] In this study, the term 'global sociality' is used to refer to the solidarity of governments and societies on a particular cause, in this case, trafficking in persons.

countries,[20] especially in trafficking cases, as a protocol on trafficking is added to this convention. Currently, some 29 states have ratified the Trafficking Protocol so it has not yet entered into force, as, according to Article 17 of the protocol, 40 ratifications are needed before it enters into force. With states that are not members of the Council of Europe and which have ratified the protocol and the convention, the mutual legal assistance provisions adopted in the Trafficking Protocol may be applied in trafficking cases in the future.[21] Nevertheless, it would be a great advantage if the non-applicant states would become parties to the conventions facilitating cooperation in criminal matters that have been adopted by both the Council of Europe and the EU. If this is not possible, states that actively combat trafficking in persons must be encouraged to conclude agreements with these countries using the existing conventions on mutual legal assistance as a framework.

7.1.3.6 *Conclusion*

The main obstacles with regard to the prosecution of trafficking in persons originate partly in the fact that states continue to hold on to their own criminal law systems and partly in the lack of priority and available (financial) resources to prosecute this crime. Therefore, the causes for ineffective prosecution must partly be sought in the impossibility for states as the current regime based on national laws contains limitations on cooperation in criminal matters and partly in the unwillingness of states to provide sufficient resources.

7.1.4 **Application of migration law versus the importance for prosecution and the protection of victims**

This third disparity originates in the practice revealed in the file study that the prosecution of suspects of trafficking in persons is often delayed and frustrated by the absence of witnesses. Although this disparity does not, in contrast to the other two disparities, originate in (the lack of) cooperation in criminal matters, this problem was so evident in the files studied in Chapter 6 that this summary would not give a realistic picture without mentioning this problem. Furthermore, an effective prosecution of trafficking in persons cannot be achieved as long as this disparity continues to exist. The problem exists in the fact that the actions of immigration and law enforcement officers are not properly coordinated and the consequences of their non-coordinated actions for victims of trafficking and for compiling cases against traffickers are not taken into account. These problems will be discussed below and some recommendations will be given.

[20] In particular, Articles 16-21 and Articles 24-28.

[21] However, these instruments can only be directly applied when they are meant to impose rights and obligations on individuals. Besides, the direct effect of international instruments also depends on whether the relevant state has adopted a monistic or dualistic system. Although a number of the provisions in the Trafficking Protocol seem to confer rights upon individuals, it remains to be seen whether individuals can invoke these provisions.

7.1.4.1 *Consequences of the application of migration law for criminal proceedings and for victims*

The victims of trafficking often have three different roles, namely, they are victims, witnesses, and illegal immigrants. Combining these three roles at one and the same time seems to be contradictory. The role of the illegal immigrant is often seen as contradictory to the other two roles.[22] Immigration officers do not recognise victims of trafficking as such and see these persons only as illegal immigrants who must be expelled from the country because they have no valid residence permit. Consequently, these victims are not given the opportunity to invoke rules which protect victims and which facilitate the criminal proceedings, such as the B9 procedure in the Netherlands. This means that migration laws are often strictly applied whereas the application of victim or witness protection rules would be more justified and more advantageous to criminal proceedings. Consequently, these victims are not easily available to testify in court.

That the absence of victims and thus the absence of the best witnesses frustrates criminal proceedings against the traffickers is not taken into account at the moment of expulsion. When states mean business when they say that trafficking in persons is a serious crime that has to be eradicated, they have to treat the victims as victims and not as criminals. They must stop the expulsion of these persons in all cases and especially when they are willing to testify. This problem is not new and was already signalled at the beginning of the 1990s. However, it is now time for states to take action and to start carrying out their promises in this regard. Protection of both victims and witnesses must be guaranteed in the relevant instruments. States must give victims and witnesses the opportunity to apply for a (temporary) residence permit such as in Belgium, Italy, the Netherlands, and Spain for example. A strategy must be explicitly set up for victims and witnesses of trafficking. The aim of such a measure must be twofold. It must stimulate the victims and witnesses to file charges against their traffickers and it must be used to rehabilitate the victims and witnesses. Therefore, schooling and working opportunities must be included in such a mechanism. Furthermore, immigration officers must be stimulated to transmit alleged victims to the police for further hearing instead of expelling illegal persons as much and as quickly as possible, regardless of the motive which the person in question may have. However, the recently held raids on houses where illegal immigrants were accommodated and in the streetwalkers' district in several cities in the Netherlands and where a number of aliens without the required permits were taken and immediately expelled from Dutch territory are not very encouraging and may frustrate criminal proceedings against traffickers.

[22] Recommendations by the OSCE, Chapter 4, Section 4.2.4.

7.1.4.2 *Victim protection in the EU*

Although policy makers had a good opportunity to provide victims with the necessary safeguards when they adopted the Council Framework Decision on Trafficking in Human Beings in July 2002, no provisions on witness protection were included, despite earlier drafts of this decision. This must be considered to be a missed opportunity. For the protection of victims, we have to refer to the Council Framework Decision on the Status of the Victim in Criminal Procedures although no specific reference was made to this document in the Framework Decision on Trafficking.[23] Although most of the witnesses in trafficking cases are victims of trafficking as well, it is not a general rule and, therefore, witnesses who are not (yet) victims are not protected by the provisions of this decision. Furthermore, this framework decision has not been specifically drafted for victims of trafficking, but rather for victims of all kinds of crime and is therefore not very specific. This instrument mainly concerns assistance to victims during criminal procedures, such as the right to be informed, safeguards on communication, and the right to be protected, including the use of video conferencing.

A second instrument that might be valuable for victims and witnesses of trafficking in persons is the proposal for a Council Directive on the Short-Term Residence Permit that was discussed in Chapter 4, Section 4.3.3.7.[24] One of the three main objections to this proposal is that it states explicitly and on several occasions that this directive is not aimed at the protection of witnesses or victims, although the provisions in the proposal include many provisions that seem to be specifically drafted for the protection of victims. It is a pity that the objective of criminal procedures is the only aim and that it is not recognised in the proposed directive that these provisions have been determined for the protection of victims and that witnesses cannot claim protection under this directive when they are not victims of trafficking. Therefore, it would have been more in accordance with the content of the directive if the protection of illegal immigrants and witnesses and victims of trafficking was recognised as the main aim of this directive. The second objection to the proposal is that trafficking in persons is seen in the proposal as forming a part of illegal immigration. Consequently, the addressee of this directive always stays without a valid permit in one of the EU states, which means that the proposed directive does not apply to nationals of other EU member states because of the free movement of persons within the EU. This is a great obstacle that will become even greater when, after the enlargement in 2004, many countries of origin will become member states of the EU. Consequently, many victims and witnesses of trafficking will be left empty-handed, as other mechanisms for witness and victim protection on the EU level are very sober. There-

[23] Council Framework Decision on the Status of the Victim in Criminal Procedure, OJ L 82, 22.3.2001, pp. 1-4.

[24] Proposal for a Council Directive on the Short-Term Residence Permit Issued to Victims of Action to Facilitate Illegal Immigration or Trafficking in Human Beings Who Cooperate with the Competent Authorities, COM(2002) 71 final, Brussels, 11.2.2002. Following this proposal, the European Parliament made amendments on 5.12.2002 that were taken into account by the Commission.

fore, the two crimes of trafficking in persons and the smuggling of persons must be distinguished, although it cannot be denied that they are interrelated in some way as we have seen in Chapter 3, Section 3.5; however, trafficking in persons cannot be considered as part of illegal immigration. A strict distinction between these crimes will solve the problem that only persons without the required valid residence permit can invoke the proposed directive and that EU citizens are excluded. A third objection made to this proposal is that it only provides for a temporary residence permit, which means that, in the end, the victim will be expelled from the country. This is not a very attractive perspective and therefore the stimulus for victims to cooperate with the authorities will be limited. It would have been more encouraging for the victims if a permanent residence permit was provided for in the proposal.

7.1.4.3 *Conclusion*

This third disparity forms an important practical obstacle to the prosecution of trafficking cases, which can best be tackled with practical solutions such as contacting judicial authorities before any victims are expelled. However, this will not have the intended effect as long as immigration officers are encouraged to expel illegal immigrants as much as possible. Furthermore, victims must be treated as such and not as criminals. It is therefore a missed opportunity that provisions on victim protection have not been adopted in the Council Framework Decision on Trafficking in Human Beings and that the proposed Council Directive on the Short-Term Residence Permit does not explicitly adopt victim and witness protection as its aim. In conclusion, it must be said that the system of the protection of witnesses and victims of trafficking in persons within the EU is fragmented, complex, and with important lacunas.

7.2 SUGGESTIONS TO IMPROVE THE PROSECUTION OF TRAFFICKING IN PERSONS

7.2.1 **Introduction**

As stated in Chapter 1, the aim of this study is to help to improve the prosecution of trafficking in persons and to indicate whether remedies for improvement must originate on a national or an EU level. Achieving this aim concerns both the first and second disparity as both disparities concern criminal law on the national and the EU levels. They both visualise the hybrid character of efforts so far taken to prosecute those suspected of trafficking in persons more effectively. Therefore, the remedies for the improvement of the prosecution of trafficking in persons will not be discussed on the basis of these two disparities but on the aim of this study, namely, to answer the question of whether these remedies must originate on a national or an EU level. The suggestions for improvement that will be discussed below take into account the obstacles identified in this study. In the recommendations, it will be indicated which obstacles will be removed by the suggested improvements.

It follows from this study that the prosecution of trafficking in persons is problematic as a result of the involvement of more than one state in this crime. As we have seen, the greater part of these problems originate in the fact that all states have their own legal system with regard to cooperation in criminal matters and their own substantive law and criminal procedure, and that states are not easily persuaded to give up their sovereignty on these issues. This frustrates an effective system of cooperation in criminal matters. When states stick to their sovereignty in the sense that they reject the interference of other states in criminal matters on their territory, the concept of state sovereignty must be seen as an obstacle to intensified cooperation in criminal matters. Therefore, the question is legitimate as to whether a system for intensified cooperation should originate on the EU level and not on the national level, as is the current practice. Before this question can be answered, the pros and cons that follow from this study of the two approaches will be given as regards the desirability and the feasibility of these approaches.

7.2.2 The approach to improve the prosecution of trafficking in persons on a national level

7.2.2.1 *The desirability of an approach on the national level*

As we have seen in Chapters 5 and 6 and again in Section 7.1.2 above, many problems exist with regard to the current system of cooperation in criminal matters that is largely based on preserving national competence and the equality of states. Given these problems and their impact, the conclusion must be that a national approach based on national competences in the criminal law field is not desirable at first sight. As we have seen, some new instruments have already generated a transformation of the use of some principles in order to facilitate the system of cooperation in criminal matters. These instruments were discussed in Chapter 4[25] and must be further elaborated here and their potential to prosecute trafficking in persons must be examined in order to give a complete picture and a detailed answer to the question of desirability. These instruments are the European Arrest Warrant, the EU Convention on Simplified Extradition Procedure, and the EU Convention on Mutual Assistance.

7.2.2.1.1 The value of the European Arrest Warrant and the EU Convention on Simplified Extradition Procedure for the prosecution of trafficking in persons

In the European Arrest Warrant (EAW) and the EU Convention on Simplified Extradition Procedure, the many formalities that have to be fulfilled for extradition are reduced and the procedures are simplified as much as possible. The main characteristic of the EAW is the mutual recognition of judicial decisions, the abolishment of the exception not to extradite nationals and the abolishment of the double criminality requirement for some crimes. In the EU Convention on Simplified Extradition Procedure, the non-requirement of a request for extradition and the replacement of the formal procedure by an informal procedure if a person consents to his extradi-

[25] See Chapter 4, Sections 4.3.3.2.1, 4.3.3.3, and 4.3.3.4.

tion are the main issues. In these cases, the request for the arrest of a person is enough to extradite the suspect after his arrest. In contrast to the extradition procedure in the EAW, the simplified extradition procedure is only applicable if the suspect consents to his extradition. The time-limit adopted in the Convention is that the arresting state must, at least within a period of 10 days after the provisional arrest, notify the requesting state of whether the person has consented to the extradition. Pursuant to the EAW, the judicial authority must take a decision within 60 days, possibly to be extended by 30 days.

In the file study, we have seen that, in two cases, a request for extradition was followed by the extradition of the suspects, one from Spain and one from Estonia. In the Spanish case, the delay was caused in particular by the absence of action by the Spanish authorities. After an international arrest warrant was sent, the Spanish authorities responded that they had arrested the suspect on 7 August 1998, only 4 days after the issuing of the arrest warrant. After the arrest, the Dutch authorities had to send a request for extradition. In October 1998, the Ministerial Council in Spain had decided to continue the extradition procedure. The Court in Spain decided on the request to extradite on 10 February 1999, probably following a second request to extradite from the Netherlands. In March 1999, the Dutch authorities received the message that the decision was final but that the Spanish government had to take a final decision on this case. This decision was communicated on 5 July 1999. Then, finally, the Ministerial Council gave its consent to the actual transfer of the suspect. This decision was taken on 10 September 1999 and was communicated on 8 October 1999. The suspect was then transported to the Netherlands on the same day.

In the other case, the requested person was arrested on 14 February 2001 in Estonia and the Court decided on the request to extradite on 27 February 2001. The government of Estonia decided on 28 March 2001 to extradite the suspect and communicated this decision to the Dutch authorities on 4 April 2001. On 15 May, they sent a request to the Netherlands to contact the responsible persons to make arrangements for the transportation of the suspect. On 29 May 2001, the suspect was handed over to the Dutch authorities. In this case, there was frequent contact with the competent persons in Estonia. The authorities in the Netherlands knew what steps had to be taken and they were promptly informed by the Estonian authorities when new information had become available.

Although, in these two cases, a similar procedure had to be followed the procedure in Spain took much longer than the procedure in Estonia, namely, fourteen months and three and a half months, respectively. In the cases discussed above, the suspect in Spain did not consent while the suspect in Estonia did consent to the extradition. Following the time-limits given in the EAW and the Convention on Simplified Extradition Procedure, this means that, in both cases, time could have been saved if Spain and Estonia had been bound by the provisions of the EAW. Furthermore, if Estonia had been a party to the Convention on Simplified Extradition and if this convention had been in force, extradition could have taken place without the formal decision of the government. These two cases show that the EAW and the EU Convention on Simplified Extradition Procedure can be an advantage for and will contribute to an efficient prosecution of those suspected of trafficking in persons in the future. Both these instruments will reduce the opacity of procedures and will reduce the number of formalities and time-consuming procedures in cooperation in criminal matters.

However, much will continue to depend on the willingness of the particular states. As was concluded in Chapters 5 and 6, the effectiveness of cooperation in criminal matters depends to a large extent on the willingness of states to give priority to the prosecution of trafficking cases and there are no indications that this will change in the future.

7.2.2.1.2 The value of the EU Convention on Mutual Assistance for the prosecution of trafficking in persons

Two important facilities were added to the instruments of cooperation in criminal matters in the EU Convention on Mutual Assistance, namely, the joint investigation teams and the hearing of witnesses by video conference. These two instruments will be examined below concerning their contribution to the prosecution of those suspected of trafficking in persons.

The main advantages of joint teams can be found in the fact that fewer requests for mutual assistance will be necessary and that investigative activities can be more easily executed in accordance with the requirements of the prosecuting state. Besides, information on the legal system of the prosecuting state is available from the representative person of the joint team, which will solve the lack of information problem of the criminal law officers in other states. Furthermore, it will facilitate the establishment of direct contact and diminish the problem of having to identify the competent authorities. With regard to the use of joint teams, it has to be kept in mind that, in trafficking cases, the recruitment practices are often not investigated. These practices often take place in countries with which mutual legal assistance is not easily established, namely, various Eastern European and Western African Countries. Consequently, a complete picture of the organisation of the trafficking is absent. The joint investigation teams could be helpful in correcting this omission in only some of these cases. When the enlargement of the EU is realised in 2004 and after the Convention on Mutual Assistance enters into force, joint investigation teams can also be set up in the applicant countries. However, with regard to states outside the EU, cooperation will take place in accordance with the existing international instruments that have been ratified by the states involved.

The hearing of witnesses by video conference, and in the case of trafficking this often means the victims, would be a great advantage in trafficking cases. The return of the victims, i.e., the witnesses, to their home countries before they are heard is in many cases an obstacle to the prosecution of trafficking.[26] Although the hearing of

[26] See Chapter 6, Section 6.4.2.4.1, and Section 7.1.4 above.

witnesses by video conference may be a solution in certain cases, the reason for the absence of witness reports must not always be sought in the technical or practical problems of contacting victims and witnesses. As stated in Chapter 6, other reasons are that victims and witnesses often suffer from intimidation by the traffickers or their accomplices, that they do not want to be reminded of their terrible experiences, that their family do not know about their activities abroad, or that prostitution and trafficking in persons is a taboo subject in their home country. Introducing the mechanism of video conferencing will not solve these problems. However, this does not take away the fact that, in some cases, hearing by video conference can save time and reduce costs.

7.2.2.1.3 Streamlining the national law on mutual legal assistance

Besides the improvements that can be generated by the new instruments, the system can be further improved by shortening the procedures and by making the system of mutual legal assistance more transparent. This would help to reduce the number of formalities that have to be fulfilled, facilitate the establishment of direct contacts, and contribute to a transparent system for mutual legal assistance. Some of these recommendations were already provided in Chapter 5, Section 5.4.6, but are repeated here. On the basis of the outcome of Chapters 5 and 6, it is necessary that states review their mutual legal assistance system, taking into account the following recommendations.

- States should eliminate the steps in the mutual legal assistance chain that are superfluous and that frustrate an efficient operation of the system.
- Requests that are sent to the wrong authority should be automatically forwarded to the competent authority in the requested state.
- Formalisation of documents should not be required in cases of letters rogatory if an examining magistrate has participated, for instance, for the hearing of witnesses abroad.
- The use of the European Judicial Network and liaison officers seconded to the various countries should be intensified. Furthermore, the number of liaisons should be extended especially in countries that are frequently linked to trafficking cases.
- The use of e-mail should be intensified as this is a rapid means of communication and the recipient can read the message at a convenient moment.
- States should set up a system in which the positive experiences of colleagues with practitioners abroad are shared, for instance, by making available a list of existing contacts.

7.2.2.1.4 Conclusion

The conclusion that follows from this study is that the new instruments developed to improve the system of cooperation in criminal matters on a national level are indeed promising. These instruments have generated a transformation in the use of current legal principles, which inevitably leads to the conclusion that such a transformation might facilitate the prosecution of trafficking in persons. However, it is now too early to welcome these instruments as none of them are in force yet and the as ratification of the conventions may take a while. Therefore, it remains to be seen whether they will have the expected positive effects in the future. Besides, the current system of cooperation in criminal matters must be revised in all states before it can be optimised. But even if such a revision takes place, we have to take into account the limitations that are inextricably bound to a system that is based on the different criminal law systems of the member states, such as the limited possibilities to cooperate with other states. Furthermore, the obstacle of an absence of global sociality and adequate (financial) resources will not be solved by these recommendations and will continue to exist. As we have seen, cooperation in criminal matters cannot be effective when states are not willing to invest in and to give priority to a well-functioning system. Therefore, these recommendations can only be effective when states are prepared to make available the adequate (financial) resources and to give priority to the prosecution of trafficking cases. Another obstacle that is not affected by these recommendations is the absence of cooperation in criminal matters with some countries. Following these comments the final conclusion must be that an approach to improve the prosecution of trafficking in persons on the national level is not desirable

7.2.2.2 *The feasibility of an approach on the national level*

In my view, the question of the feasibility of a national approach must be answered in the affirmative for the following reasons. Firstly, the large number of legal instruments that are currently available cover the whole area of cooperation in criminal matters. Secondly, different organisations exist on the European level to accomplish the aims of the states with regard to cooperation in criminal matters, namely, the EU and the Council of Europe. Thirdly, the current system leaves the national competences untouched as much as possible. As appears from this study, most states prefer a system in which they retain their national competence as regards cooperation in criminal matters. However, this does not take away the fact that limitations to cooperation in criminal matters are inextricably bound to an approach on the national level.

7.2.3 The approach to improve the prosecution of trafficking in persons on an EU level

7.2.3.1 *The desirability of an approach on the EU level*

As has been stated several times in this study, an EU approach might be a possibility to improve the prosecution of those suspected of trafficking in persons. Before the question of desirability can be answered, we first have to elaborate on the possible content of such an approach. This will be done by focusing on the new instruments, namely, the proposed establishment of a European Public Prosecutor (EPP) and Eurojust. The contribution to the improvement of trafficking in persons from an EU perspective of the concept of an EPP as described in Chapter 4 and recently adopted in the Draft Constitution of the European Convention will be examined. In the Draft

Constitution the proposed provision only leaves the possibility of setting up an EPP within the framework of Eurojust without further elaborating upon its tasks and competences. When elaborating the concept of the EPP in the following section, the way in which an EPP might be adopted within the framework of Eurojust will be the main focus.

7.2.3.1.1 The value of an EPP to prosecute trafficking in persons

The question must be answered to what extent the proposed EPP can facilitate the prosecution of traffickers at the EU level. As we have seen in Chapter 4, the idea to set up an EPP has been adopted in the Draft Constitution of the European Convention. In Article III-170 of the Draft Constitution, it is proposed that an EPP will be established within the framework of Eurojust. Although the idea is not elaborated at all in this article, the EPP 'shall be responsible for investigating, prosecuting and bringing to judgement, where appropriate in liaison with Europol, the perpetrators of and the accomplices in serious crimes affecting more than one Member States and of offences against the Union's financial interests'. Decisions in this regard must be taken unanimously. Consequently, the competence of the EPP must not be limited to offences against the financial interests of the EU. As trafficking in persons is a serious crime, often affecting several member states, the future EPP can be used to prosecute the perpetrators of trafficking in persons. However, when cooperation with countries outside the EU is required, the traditional instruments for cooperation must be applied. This means that the added value of an EPP for trafficking cases in which a link with third countries exists is nil. Fortunately, the enlargement of the EU with ten Central and Eastern European countries as well as Malta and Cyprus is scheduled for May 2004. As cooperation in trafficking cases often occurs with one or more of these countries, the concept of an EPP could facilitate the prosecution of trafficking cases in the future. Although the concepts of an EPP as described in more detail in the *Corpus Juris* and the Green Paper are limited to Euro-fraud, they may be helpful to elaborate the idea to integrate the EPP within the system of Eurojust.[27] The possible future role for Eurojust in this regard will be focused upon below.

The mandate of Eurojust is described in Article 4 of the Council Decision of 28 February 2002 and includes trafficking in persons.[28] Eurojust is to facilitate judicial cooperation between member states of the EU without the aim of harmonising national laws. However, even without harmonising criminal (procedure) law, as this road seems to be littered with the many obstacles set up by the member states, judicial cooperation between member states can be facilitated by adopting parts of the pro-

[27] The establishment of Eurojust was described in Chapter 4, Section 4.3.2.5. Fijnaut and Groenhuijsen proposed the strengthening of Eurojust instead of establishing an EPP. They are very critical of the concept of an EPP as they think that the remedy is too heavy-handed, complicated, and non-specific to be able to combat EU fraud. C. Fijnaut and M. Groenhuijsen, Een Europees openbaar ministerie: kanttekening bij het Groenboek, in: *NJB*, Volume 77, issue 26, 2002, pp. 1234-1241.

[28] Council Decision of 28 February 2002 on Setting Up Eurojust with a View to Reinforcing the Fight against Serious Crime, OJ L 63, 6.3.2002, Article 4.

posals for an EPP from the *Corpus Juris* and the Green Paper. The parts referred to here are those concerning the admissibility of evidence and the mutual recognition of decisions on coercive measures, including house searches and the interception of telecommunications. In the concept of the EPP, this might mean that, in these cases, legally obtained evidence collected in one member state may be used in the other member states, taking into account the applicable rules in these member states.[29] The principle of *forum regit actum* should be applied in these cases instead of the principle of *locus regit actum.*[30] This would also be in accordance with Article 4 of the EU Convention on Mutual Assistance. However, adopting these rules can only be successful when mutual confidence in each other's legal systems exists. Although some optimists say that after 50 years of integration in the EU, this mutual confidence has become firmly established,[31] not everyone shares this opinion.[32] Besides, the practice in this regard described in Chapter 6 shows another picture, namely, that the reliability of some of the authorities in some other (Southern) member states of the EU must be doubted. Nevertheless, this may not be a reason not to adopt these rules within the framework of Eurojust.

Another advantage that can be achieved when elaborating the integration of an EPP within Eurojust in this way is a solution to the problem of the responsibility of one individual state in a complex case. This problem was described in Chapter 2.[33] It was stated that in cases of transnational crime and trafficking in persons, the extent and the importance of a case often does not appear at the onset. Therefore, the question of which country must have jurisdiction in a particular case can, in many cases, best be answered during the investigative phase or even after this phase when the impact of the crime becomes clear. Therefore, it would be advisable that in cases where the extent of the case is unclear and where there are indications that more states may claim jurisdiction, the question of jurisdiction is not decided upon until after the investigative phase or at least until it is well underway. Until that decision is taken, a shared responsibility on the part of the states involved could be introduced.[34]

---

[29] This was already agreed upon during the Tampere European Council on 15 and 16 October 1999. No. 36 of the presidency conclusions states: 'The principle of mutual recognition should also apply to pre-trial orders, in particular to those which would enable competent authorities quickly to secure evidence and to seize assets which are easily movable; evidence lawfully gathered by one member state's authorities should be admissible before the courts of other member states, taking into account the standards that apply there.'

[30] See Chapter 5, Section 5.3.1.1.

[31] The Green Paper, Section 6.4.2, states that national legal systems are not an obstacle to the mutual recognition of a decision of a judge of freedoms as all prosecution measures are based on the principles of the European Convention on Human Rights.

[32] C. Fijnaut, Justitiële samenwerking en de beheersing van georganiseerde misdaad in de Europese Unie, in: *Delikt en Delinkwent,* Volume 28, issue 10, 1998, pp. 997-1010. G. Leyns, et al., Bescherming van de financiële belangen van de EU, Corpus Juris en Europees Openbaar Ministerie, in: G. Vermeulen and E. de Busser (eds.), *Aspecten van Europees formeel strafrecht,* Maklu, Antwerp, 2002, pp. 116-117.

[33] Chapter 2, Section 2.3.2.2.

[34] Support for the idea to apply the rules to grant jurisdiction more flexibly, in particular to intensify the use of transfer of proceedings and for shared responsibility can be found in A.H. Klip, Geïntegreerde

The coordination problems that occur when the principle of *forum regit actum* with regard to the collection of evidence, the mutual recognition of decisions by the judges of freedoms, and the postponement of the decision on jurisdiction is applied can be met by entrusting this coordination to Eurojust. In this way, a new approach originating on an EU level to prosecute trafficking offences can be developed and Eurojust can easily apply the principle of regional jurisdiction that was mentioned above. Although it might be confusing that different regimes for cooperation in criminal matters are applicable at the same time, namely, the national system and the regional (Eurojust) system, the seriousness of the crimes that are covered by the mandate of Eurojust justify this system.

7.2.3.1.2 Conclusion

The question of whether an approach at an EU level to prosecute trafficking in persons is desirable must be answered in the affirmative. Such an approach must include at least a uniform system of cooperation in criminal matters and the installation of an EPP. A uniform system for cooperation in criminal matters within the EU would solve many of the problems that were identified in Chapters 5 and 6, especially those problems that are caused by differences in procedural law, such as the identification of the competent authorities, lack of knowledge of the legal system of other states, confusion as to what formalities must be fulfilled, and what channels must be used. However, the implementation of such an approach will depend on the national system. National law enforcement officers must cooperate with the EPP, relevant information should be transmitted to and from the EPP, orders must be given to the national authorities, etc., unless a complete law enforcement system is set up at the European level. If this latter approach is chosen, the mandates of Eurojust and Europol must be extended with full operational powers throughout the EU and the mandate of the European Court of Justice must be extended as well with full powers in this regard, including preliminary decisions and an annulment procedure for individuals. Combining such an approach with the harmonisation of substantive and procedural law would mean the development of a European legal order. However, such an approach will still be dependent on the national law enforcement system, but to a lesser extent, as many of the tasks would be executed on the European level. The question is whether it would be desirable to develop such a legal order for police and judicial cooperation in criminal matters. I am inclined to answer this question in the affirmative as well, but only when some constitutional safeguards accompany such a legal order. These constitutional safeguards are, at least, a more democratic legitimisation of legislation, either by the national or the European Parliament and full power for the ECJ. Such a legal order can only be achieved when parts of the sovereign powers of states are transmitted to the EU. This would be a

bescherming van de financiële belangen van de EG: Verschuiving van de staat-staat-benadering naar verticalisering van de procedure? in: J.A.E. Vervaele, *Transnationale handhaving van de financiële belangen van de Europese Unie. Ontwikkelingen in het Verdrag van Amsterdam en de Corpus Juris*, Intersentia, Antwerp, 1999, pp. 105-111.

radical turn in current practice on police and judicial cooperation in criminal matters and a different approach to state sovereignty, namely, diminishing the role of the nation state on these issues in favour of that of the EU. Furthermore, the system of mutual recognition of decisions in the courts of other member states is not excluded in such a system; on the contrary, it can become fully operational. This is also the case in the first pillar, where mutual recognition of procedures and decisions taken in other member states is an important instrument to make the four freedoms workable in practice and is sometimes preferred to harmonisation of legislation.[35]

7.2.3.2 *The feasibility of an approach on the EU level*

The question of whether an approach to prosecuting trafficking in persons that originates in a European legal order is feasible must be answered on the basis of the existing policy in the third pillar and some recent developments.

It is current practice in the third pillar, pursuant to Article 34 paragraph 2, that the Council decides on the basis of unanimity. That means that each member state has the right to veto a proposal. The European Commission has a shared right of initiative with each member state. Furthermore, the role of the European Parliament is limited to non-binding advice on decisions, framework decisions, and conventions made in accordance with Article 34 EU Treaty. This means that it is recognised in the EU Treaty that, in third pillar issues, the member states retain their full powers in the decision-making process. There is no democratic legitimacy at the European level, and the role of the Commission with its executing powers in the first pillar is very limited. Efforts to reduce the powers of the Council of the EU and thus the powers of the member states in the third pillar have, so far, not achieved this effect.

A recent development shows a confirmation of the practice that, in some areas, the member states will remain the decisive entities on third pillar issues in the near future. The establishment of Eurojust must be welcomed but as we have seen in Chapter 4, its competences are rather limited. Eurojust has limited operational power, namely, only at the request of one of the member states if the requesting country and a third country are involved.[36] Pursuant Article 5 and the sixth consideration of the Council Decision to Set up Eurojust, it has to fulfil its tasks through one or more of the national members or acting as a Body. Furthermore, Eurojust is composed of one national member seconded by each member state, being a prosecutor, judge, or police officer of equivalent competence. The competences of the national members are subject to the national law of their member states and the member state will define the right of a national member to act in relation to foreign judicial authorities.[37] It

[35] A.H.J. Swart, *Een ware Europese rechtsruimte. Wederzijdse erkenning van strafrechtelijke beslissingen in de Europese Unie,* Deventer, Gouda Quint, 2001, pp. 10-12.

[36] Council Decision of 28 February 2002 on Setting up Eurojust with a View to Reinforcing the Fight against Serious Crime, OJ L 63, 16.3.2002, Article 3, paragraph 2.

[37] Council Decision on Setting up Eurojust, Article 9.

must be concluded that, for its functioning, Eurojust is dependent on the cooperation of the national members and the competent authorities in the member states. Much will depend on the willingness of states to transmit information to Eurojust but the experiences of Europol in this regard are not promising as states are reluctant to share operational information because they think that this information is sensitive or confidential and they themselves want to control who has possession of this information. Article III-169 of the proposed European Constitution, Volume II, of June 2003 reflects the reluctance to confer far-reaching powers on Eurojust.[38] In this proposal, no operational authority for Eurojust is provided. According to Article III-169 Eurojust's mission shall be to support and strengthen coordination and cooperation between national prosecuting authorities...'. Paragraph 2 of this Article states that 'a European law shall determine Eurojust's structure, workings, scope of action and tasks. These tasks may include the initiation and coordination of criminal prosecutions conducted by competent national authorities...'. It does not appear from this phrase whether Eurojust will be competent to initiate prosecutions itself. However, its competence will be limited as paragraph 3 states that 'in the prosecutions ... formal acts of judicial procedure shall be adopted by the competent national officials. The role of Europol is described in similar wordings in Article III-172 of the Draft Constitution. This means that no operational competence is granted to Europol. In this regard paragraph 3 states explicitly that 'any operational action by Europol must be carried out in liaison and in agreement with the authorities of the Member States whose territory is concerned'.

A development showing the opposite, namely, the strengthening of the powers of the EU institutions on third pillar issues concerns the discussions within the European Convention. In general, it is said that the tendency of the discussions within the European Convention is to strengthen the role of the member states, for instance, by involving the national parliaments in the legislative procedure. However, for the area of freedom, security, and justice, the trend is for more Communautarisation. The following examples originating from several discussions and documents adopted within the European Convention and included in the Draft Constitution show the tendency for further Communautarisation in the third pillar.[39]

Article 41 of the Draft Treaty establishing a Constitution for Europe states that the area of freedom, security, and justice will be achieved by adopting law and framework laws.[40] The former will replace the regulations and the latter will replace the directives of Article 249 EC Treaty. Under Article 34 of the EU Treaty, both the de-

[38] The European Convention, Draft Constitution, Volume II, Brussels, 27 June 2003, CONV 836/03 Article III-169.

[39] These documents are: the final report of working group X 'freedom, security, and justice', European Convention, Brussels, 2 December 2002, CONV 426/02. Draft Treaty establishing a Constitution for Europe, Brussels, 27 June 2003 and 30 June 2003, CONV 820/1/03 REV 1 and CONV 820/2/03 REV 2 respectively. Draft Constitution, Volume II, Brussels, 27 June 2003, CONV 836/03.

[40] Draft Treaty establishing a Constitution for Europe, Brussels, 30 June 2003, CONV 820/2/03 REV 2, Article 41.

cisions and framework decisions are binding but they lack direct effect. Regulations and, under certain circumstances, directives and thus in the future the laws and framework laws, have direct effect.

The decisions would in general be made by using the co-decision procedure and by majority vote. Only in certain areas will unanimous voting be maintained. These areas are related to member states' essential responsibilities, for example, the creation of Union bodies with operational powers, the harmonisation and approximation of criminal law,[41] and operational cooperation between police authorities.[42]

The right of initiative for the Commission in third pillar issues is further extended in the Draft Constitution. Under Article 34 EU Treaty, each member state has the right of initiative together with the Commission. In accordance with Article III-160 of the Draft Constitution, Volume II, acts will be adopted on a proposal from the Commission, or on the initiative of a quarter of the member states. This means that the states lose their independent right of initiative.

Article III-156 of the Draft Constitution, Volume II, introduces an evaluation mechanism whereby 'member states, in collaboration with the Commission, conduct objective and impartial evaluation of the implementation of the Union policies' without prejudice to Articles 226 to 228 of the EC Treaty. This means that, besides the introduction of this evaluation mechanism, the procedure of Article 226 EC Treaty where the Commission can start infringement proceedings before the ECJ seems to be extended to police and judicial cooperation in criminal matters as well. This is an important extension of the powers of the Commission and the ECJ to control member states in third pillar issues.[43]

The competence of the ECJ is further extended in Article III-279 of the Draft Constitution, Volume II. The comment to this article states that, in the area of freedom, security, and justice, the ECJ will have its general competence with the exception that the Court has no jurisdiction for police action and action relating to the maintenance of law and order, which is covered by national law.

Further approximation of legislation in substantive law and procedural law with regard to police and judicial cooperation in criminal matters will be adopted. Furthermore, the requirement of mutual recognition of judicial decisions is provided with a legal basis in Article III-166 of the Draft Constitution, Volume II.

In general, it can be said that, for police and judicial cooperation in criminal matters, there existed a separate regime in the third pillar with some Communautarian as-

---

[41] See Articles III-166 (2), III-167, III-171 (3), Draft Constitution, Volume II, Brussels, 27 June 2003, CONV 836/03.

[42] See Article III-171, (3), Draft Constitution, Volume II, Brussels, 27 June 2003, CONV 836/03.

[43] See also Chapter 5, Section 5.2.2.1.

pects but that it is proposed by the European Convention to incorporate police and judicial cooperation in criminal matters in the Communautarian regime with some separate provisions. In my view, such a development must be supported. The comments of some of the member states that the Communautarisation of third pillar issues is going too far can be tackled by the proposal of the European Convention to strengthen the role of the national parliaments in the legislative procedure. The national parliaments must be able to take notice of the proposals made by the Commission and will be able to give their opinions on the compatibility of the proposal with the principle of subsidiarity. However, even within the far-reaching proposals of the European Convention an approach with real executive power for institutions at the EU level, such as, Europol and Eurojust, is not aimed at and is surrounded with many exceptions. Besides, the resistance of states to setting up a prosecuting and cooperation in criminal matters system originating on the EU level would be an obstacle to its effectiveness. Therefore, the conclusion must be drawn that such a system is not (yet) feasible.

7.2.4 **Conclusion**

With the above analysis of the pros and cons of the two approaches and the relevant developments, the conclusion must be drawn that an approach on a national level is not desirable although it is indeed feasible, and that the opposite holds true for an approach on the EU level, namely, that such an approach is desirable but not (yet) feasible.

7.3 FINAL CONCLUSION ON THIS STUDY

7.3.1 **The dichotomy regarding cooperation in criminal matters**

On the basis of the previous two sections, it can be said that there are proposals within the European Convention that tend to further the Communautarisation of police and judicial cooperation in criminal matters. However, we cannot ignore that the willingness of states to organise cooperation in criminal matters at the EU level and to equip European organisations such as Eurojust and Europol with real operational power independent from the nation states is not very great. This dichotomy between the readiness for further expansion of competences in police and judicial cooperation in criminal matters on the EU level expressed in many policies and the practices and reluctance of member states to give any real power to the competent EU institutions and organisations at the cost of their own powers is characteristic of the efforts to intensify cooperation in criminal matters. This dichotomy is reflected in the first and second disparities underlying this study. In the first disparity, the dichotomy exists in the national competences that have to be used to prosecute a crime with transnational features. In the second disparity, the dichotomy becomes visible in the goals and aims adopted in many policies on trafficking in persons and some instruments that include more competences on the EU level, on the one hand, and the practice of member states to hold on to their national competences in the area of criminal law and many legal instruments confirming the actual primacy of states, on the other. Following this dichotomy, further harmonisation is only possible on those issues where states are prepared to share or transfer powers. Further elaboration of measures on cooperation in criminal matters is being emulated for those matters that states want to keep within their own powers. As long as this dichotomy exists, complete Communautarisation and the establishment of a European legal order for police and judicial cooperation in criminal matters is not to be expected.

7.3.2 A realistic approach to improve the prosecution of trafficking in persons

Now that it is clear that neither an approach solely on the national level nor an approach solely on the EU level will achieve the required improvement of the prosecution of trafficking in persons, we have to find a way in which the positive aspects of both approaches can be combined. For the moment, this will be the most effective way to realise intensified cooperation between states to prosecute trafficking in persons in the near future. This means that a dual track must be chosen as a solution to the existing dichotomy. Such a dual track includes that the operational powers will, for the greater part, remain with the national authorities and that a monitoring institution could be established at the EU level. This could very well be an EPP within the Eurojust framework. The tasks of such a monitoring authority would at least include the coordination of the prosecution of trafficking cases, the monitoring of the national authorities in this regard, and initiating criminal proceedings against those suspected of trafficking in persons before national courts.

It must be concluded that transmission of state sovereignty in the criminal field to the EU level seems to be a step too far for the moment. Instead a transformation of the use of sovereign powers must be chosen. It was stated in Chapter 1 that states find their legitimisation of sovereignty in the ability to protect their citizens and to secure safety on their territory. When states are not able to provide this protection and safety, they lose their legitimacy of sovereign powers and will therefore be obliged to set up appropriate law enforcement systems with sufficient competences for the authorities involved and sufficient judicial procedures.

For transnational crime and thus for trafficking in persons, which must be considered to be a threat to the legal order and the safety of society, states cannot fulfil this obligation by the sole use of national powers on their own territory. The implications of transnational crime, and thus of trafficking in persons, require intensive cooperation with other states. As the impact of transnational crime and thus of trafficking in persons is on the increase, the cooperation between states must be further intensified in order to maintain the legitimisation of sovereignty. This means that states will have to share their powers in criminal matters. Thus, although it sounds contradictory, if states are not prepared to share their powers on criminal matters with other states but persist in using their sovereign powers in a conservative way, namely, by protecting their competences in criminal matters and rejecting any interference from other states, they will ultimately lose the legitimisation of sovereignty.

Therefore, the relevant question is not whether the concept of state sovereignty is being eroded but whether states can better achieve their aims by transforming the use of their sovereign powers. The traditional concept of state sovereignty, where states have the exclusive right to enact criminal law on their territory and will not tolerate interference from other states in these matters must be abandoned. Instead, a concept of state sovereignty must be accepted in which states take their responsibilities to protect their citizens in the most effective way by intensified cooperation with other states and, where necessary, the transmission of some of the powers to a more appropriate level. Only when states are prepared to accept such a form of state sovereignty, can their citizens be effectively protected in the long term and they can maintain their sovereignty. In other words, states only deserve the maintenance of state sovereignty if they cooperate with other states in the most effective way. This can mean intensified cooperation sometimes on a national and sometimes on an EU level. Although it cannot be predicted, it may be proved in the end that the protection of citizens and security and safety in society can best be achieved when member states transmit part of their power in criminal law to the EU.

SUMMARY

The aim of this study was to identify the obstacles to an effective prosecution of those suspected of trafficking in persons in order to improve their prosecution. The three leading disparities in this study are the following. The first is that between the fact that trafficking in persons is a crime with a transnational element and the fact that strategies to combat it are based on national competences. The second disparity is that between the availability of a great number of strategies to combat and prosecute those suspected of trafficking in persons and the unwillingness or inability of states to efficiently use them. The third is the disparity between the application of migration law, on the one hand, and the importance for prosecution and the protection of the victims on the other. These three disparities will be elaborated below, after it has been determined whether trafficking in persons must be considered to be a transnational crime.

Trafficking in persons is one of the crimes that is nowadays committed more often in an international context than it was previously. The developments in globalisation have influenced the internationalisation of trafficking in persons, mainly in two ways. Firstly, the victims of trafficking in persons are more often and more easily moved from one place to another and from one country to another. Secondly, women are more often affected by poverty and unemployment, which must be considered to be the effects of globalisation for states in transition, making women more vulnerable to trafficking practices. It is often indicated that trafficking in persons can be seen as a transnational crime, but without this term being further analysed, however. The significance of qualifying a crime as transnational is that it justifies an approach from a non-national level, for instance a European level, to combat it. Before a crime can be considered a transnational crime four criteria must be fulfilled, namely: 1) a certain level of organisation is needed to commit the crime, 2) it affects the interests of more than one state, 3) the involvement of more states aggravates the problems involved in prosecuting transnational crime, 4) effective solutions are sought beyond national borders. The first two criteria must be met cumulatively while the third and fourth criteria follow from the first and second one and, therefore, must be considered additional criteria. The question that will be answered below is to what extent those four criteria are fulfilled with regard to trafficking in persons and thus justify an approach beyond national borders to combat it.

The *first criterion* is that a certain level of organisation is needed to commit the crime of trafficking in persons.

In order to find out how trafficking in persons is generally organised we have to look at the definition of this crime. For the purpose of this study the following definition of trafficking in persons was developed:

> Trafficking in persons means all acts involved in the coercive transnational recruitment and/or transportation of a person for forced exploitation

The crime of trafficking in persons consists, in other words, of two phases, namely, the recruitment and transport phase, on the one hand, and the exploitation phase, on the other. For the employment of the persons trafficked, contacts are needed with persons who are willing to participate in the illegal activity. Furthermore, recruitment and transportation often take place in different steps, for instance, including the falsification of documents, advertisements, transfer from one place to another, the purchase of flight tickets, arrangements to accommodate victims, etc. It is very unlikely that one and the same person executes all these activities, especially when it concerns trafficking across borders. The conclusion can therefore be drawn that, for the perpetration of trafficking in persons, a certain level of organisation (consisting of different contacts to execute certain elements of the crime) is necessary.

The *second criterion* is that it affects the interests of more than one state.

The factual and physical act of goods or persons crossing the border is not strictly required to meet this criterion. The involvement of more than one state is already present when, for instance, the crime takes place in one and the same country but is organised from another country. Trafficking in persons often takes place from countries with a less stable economic and legal system to countries in which these systems are well organised. However, it is not strictly necessary that the trafficking takes place between countries as it can also occur within one and the same country. With the broad concept of the requirement that more than one state is involved, this criterion will be met in the majority of cases, however. Furthermore, the definition of trafficking in persons as used in this study includes the transnational element of the involvement of more than one state, which means that this criterion is inevitably fulfilled.

The *third criterion* is that because more states are involved, this aggravates the problems involved in prosecuting trafficking in persons.

As it is not so easy to answer the question of whether this third criterion is fulfilled, some more elaborate considerations are required.

One of the consequences of the fact that more than one state is involved in trafficking in persons is that, for the investigation and prosecution of the crime, international agreements must be applied in addition to national laws. In order to answer the question to what extent obstacles in the prosecution of those suspected of trafficking in persons occur, first, the obstacles with regard to the application of these international agreements have been identified in Chapter V, followed by an empirical research of trafficking cases in the Netherlands in Chapter VI. The relevant agreements can be divided into policy documents and legal instruments.

In many policy documents, adopted by the European Union, the Council of Europe, or the Organization for Security and Cooperation in Europe, trafficking in persons is specifically focused upon. The policy documents contain intentions to suppress trafficking in persons more efficiently. Far-reaching provisions on witness protection, cooperation in criminal matters, information exchange, reducing the imbalance in international economic relations, specific training of police officers, the harmonisation of definitions of trafficking, etc., can be found in these documents. However, one of the main characteristics of policy documents is that they lack direct effect. Consequently, the effect of these documents has so far been limited while the phenomenon of trafficking to and within Europe is still growing and states seem to be rather unwilling to act in accordance with their obligations as laid down in these documents.

The legal instruments enacted within the EU and the Council of Europe and which are relevant for the prosecution of trafficking in persons mainly concern cooperation in criminal matters in general. The nature and scope of the problems with regard to the application of these legal instruments on cooperation in criminal matters can be summarised as follows. With regard to the substantive problems it can be said that their impact in general is less serious than is often thought. The procedural problems mainly consist of the absence of transparency as regards which channels must be used, often following from differences in competences between the member states and a lack of knowledge of each other's system. The organisational problems mainly concern the identification of the competent authorities abroad and practical problems in contacting the authorities involved either due to the lack of telephone and fax numbers and other personal details concerning the person concerned, on the one hand, and language problems on the other. Moreover, the lack of (financial) resources is a major obstacle.

After identifying the main obstacles with regard to cooperation in criminal matters the question must be answered to what extent these problems also occur with regard to the prosecution of trafficking in persons. This can be done on the basis of the outcome of an empirical study which was conducted into trafficking cases in the Netherlands. The most important results of it will be focused upon below.

It is most remarkable that, in general, the need for mutual legal assistance is considered by practitioners to be an obstacle in a criminal procedure and is avoided as much as possible, even when this is at the cost of the indictment of one or more related offences.

One of the main obstacles for the prosecution of those suspected of trafficking in persons is the absence of victims and witnesses, often due to the fact that immigration officers have expelled them from the country. A considerable reduction in the problems involved in the prosecution of transnational trafficking cases can be achieved by closer cooperation between the immigration authorities, the police, and the judiciary. This decreases the risk that victims who are essential for the criminal proceedings are sent back to their country of origin before they are heard by the police or, even more important, by the examining magistrate.

Formal communication lines are normally used for the transmission of requests. Even if direct communication is allowed these lines are still used. Practitioners involved persist in following the formalities needed for the transmission of information, unless the requesting person is known to the provider of the information. The formalities surrounding the practice of mutual legal assistance are regularly an obstacle in the process.

Remarkable is that if an answer to a request is per se required within a certain time period, the competent authorities succeed in obtaining the answer within that period.

The absence of double criminality seems no longer to be an obstacle to cooperation in criminal matters. What is recognised as problematic by the prosecutors is the lack of priority and the absence of attention to the phenomenon of trafficking in persons both in the Netherlands and in other countries. They stated that this absence causes serious difficulties and delays with regard to mutual legal assistance in trafficking cases.

As follows from the empirical study the fact that more states are involved in the trafficking results for various reasons in serious problems in the prosecution of this crime. Consequently, the question whether the third criterion is met must be answered in the affirmative.

The *fourth criterion* is that effective solutions to the problems involved in prosecuting trafficking in persons must be sought beyond national borders.

So far, criminal law based on the sovereignty of states has appeared to be not effective and too complicated to prosecute trafficking in persons. As the involvement of different states aggravates the problems involved in prosecuting trafficking in persons, it is obvious that solutions must be sought in cooperation with other countries, i.e., beyond national borders, for instance, at the EU level. This means that also the fourth criterion is fulfilled and therefore trafficking in persons can also for this reason be considered to be a transnational crime.

With the knowledge that it has now been determined that trafficking in persons must be considered a transnational crime and that an approach to combat and prosecute it effectively must be sought beyond national borders, the three disparities described above will now be further elaborated.

The first disparity between the fact that trafficking in persons is a crime with a transnational element and the fact that strategies to combat it are based on national competences is closely related to the changing role of the nation state and the concept of sovereignty. The legitimisation of the sovereignty of states must be sought in the need for citizens to be protected and to be ensured of legal security. Following this legitimisation, states are obliged to set up a legal system that protects their citizens. In order to protect citizens against cross-border crime, such as trafficking in persons, such a system must include provisions on intensified cooperation with other states in criminal matters either at a national or non-national level, for instance, the European level. Recently developed instruments on the European level, such as the European Arrest Warrant, the EU Conventions on Extradition, and the EU Convention on Mutual Assistance, and the proposals to set up a European Public Prosecutor, have adopted a transformation of the use of current principles such as double criminality, the rule of speciality, and grounds to refuse extradition, in order to facilitate cooperation in criminal matters. These current developments can be summarised by stating that cooperation in criminal matters, specifically extradition and mutual legal assistance, must be simplified and extended. Step by step, it is being accepted that some decisions with regard to criminal law are made at the EU level and not solely at the national level. It is quite likely that the Intergovernmental Conference in 2003/2004 will accelerate this process. The conclusion with regard to the first disparity must be that, on the one hand, an approach to prosecuting those suspected of trafficking in persons on the EU level based on the concept of regional jurisdiction seems most appropriate in order to prosecute them more effectively. On the other hand, some interesting developments have taken place at the EU level concerning closer cooperation in criminal matters, which are based on national competences. Both approaches seem to indicate an erosion of state sovereignty. In general there is a tendency that the role of the nation state is changing, but that states are cautious in leaving criminal matters to the EU. One of the main reasons for this caution is the lack of confidence in each other's legal systems.

With regard to the second disparity between the availability of a great number of strategies to combat and prosecute trafficking in persons and the unwillingness or inability of states to efficiently use them, both the policy documents that specifically address trafficking in persons as well as the legal instruments that address it indirectly by facilitating the prosecution of those suspected of trafficking are relevant to the discussion. The effectiveness of these documents and instruments was investigated in order to discover what the obstacles are to effectively prosecuting the traffickers. The main obstacles with regard to the prosecution of trafficking in persons originate partly in the fact that states have, until now, retained their own criminal law systems and partly in the lack of priority and available (financial) resources to prosecute this crime. Therefore, the causes of the ineffective prosecution must partly be sought in the impossibility for states to prosecute as the current regime based on national laws itself includes limitations on cooperation in criminal matters and partly in the unwillingness of states to provide sufficient resources.

The third disparity concerns the disparity in the application of migration law versus the importance for prosecution and the protection of victims. This disparity can best be tackled with practical solutions such as contacting judicial authorities before possible victims are expelled. However, this will not have the intended effect as long as immigration officers are encouraged to expel illegal persons as much as possible. Furthermore, victims must be treated as such and not as criminals. It is therefore a missed opportunity that provisions on victim protection have not been adopted in the Council Framework Decision on Trafficking in Human Beings and that the proposed Council Directive on the Short-Term Residence Permit does not explicitly adopt victim and witness protection as its aim. In conclusion it must be said that the system of protection of victims and witnesses of trafficking in persons within the EU is fragmented, complex, and with important lacunas.

After the problems with regard to the prosecution of those suspected of trafficking in persons had been identified and analysed, the remedies to improve this prosecution were focused upon. This was done on the basis of the desirability and feasibility of the approaches at the national and the EU level to improve the prosecution of those suspected of trafficking in persons. The conclusions of this examination will follow below.

The approach to improve the prosecution of trafficking in persons on a national level

With regard to the desirability of an approach at the national level to improve the prosecution of those suspected of trafficking in persons it must be concluded that the new instruments developed to improve the system of cooperation in criminal matters seem to be promising at first sight. These instruments have adopted a transformation in the use of current principles which inevitably leads to the conclusion that such a transformation might facilitate the prosecution of trafficking in persons. However, it is now too early to celebrate the emergence of these instruments as none of them are in force yet and the ratification of the conventions can take a while. Therefore, it remains to be seen whether they will have the expected positive effects in the future. Besides, the current system on cooperation in criminal matters must be revised in all states before cooperation in criminal matters can be processed more effectively. But even if such a revision has taken place we have to take into account the limitations that are inextricably bound to a system that is based on the different criminal law systems of the member states, such as the limited possibilities to cooperate with other states. Furthermore, the absence of global sociality and appropriate (financial) resources will not be tackled by these recommendations and they remain in existence. Therefore, an approach exclusively at the national level to improve the prosecution of those suspected of trafficking in persons is not sufficient and therefore not desirable.

The question of the feasibility of an approach at the national level must be answered in the affirmative for the following three reasons. Firstly, because of the great number of legal instruments that are currently available in the field of cooperation in criminal matters. Secondly, because of the different organisations in charge of cooperation in criminal matters both at the national and European levels. Thirdly, because such an approach leaves the national competences untouched as far as possible, which is preferred by states.

The approach to improve the prosecution of trafficking in persons on an EU level

The question whether an approach at an EU level to improve the prosecution of those suspected of trafficking in persons is desirable must be answered in the affirmative. Such an approach must include at least a uniform system for cooperation in criminal matters and the installation of a European Public Prosecutor (EPP). The execution of such an approach will remain dependent on the national system, unless a complete law enforcement system is set up at the European level. When this latter approach is chosen the mandate of Eurojust and Europol must be extended with full operational powers throughout the EU and the mandate of the European Court of Justice must also be extended with full powers in this regard. When such an approach is combined with the harmonisation of substantive and procedural law, this will mean the development of a European legal order. Only when some constitutional safeguards accompany such a legal order, is its development desirable. Furthermore, such a legal order can only be achieved when parts of the sovereign powers of states are transferred to the EU.

With regard to the feasibility of an approach at the EU level it can be said that it seems to be too early to give institutions at the EU level any real executive power. Besides, the resistance of states to set up a prosecuting and cooperation in criminal matters system at the EU level would be an obstacle to its effectiveness. Therefore, the conclusion must be drawn that such a system is not (yet) feasible.

Following the conclusions on the desirability and feasibility of both approaches to improve the prosecution of those suspected of trafficking in persons, the adoption of either one of the approaches will not be effective. This will not change as long as the dichotomy between the willingness for the further expansion of competences in police and judicial cooperation on the EU level and the practices and reluctance of member states to give real power to the competent EU institutions and organisations at the cost of their own powers remains in existence. This means that a dual track must be followed as an alternative solution to the existing dichotomy. Such a dual track will include that the operational powers remain for the greater part with the national authorities but that a monitoring institution could be established at the EU level. This could very well be an EPP within the Eurojust framework.

As said before, states, if they wish to retain their sovereign powers, are obliged to set up an appropriate mechanism to protect their citizens. For transnational crime in general, and for trafficking in persons in particular, states cannot fulfil this obligation by the sole use of national powers on their own territory but have to set up mechanisms for intensified cooperation in order to combat trafficking in persons effectively. States only deserve to maintain their legitimisation of state sovereignty when they cooperate with other states in the most effective way and in that sense are willing to share their sovereign powers with other states. This can mean intensified cooperation sometimes on a national and sometimes on an EU level. It might in the end be proved that the protection of citizens and ensuring safety in society can best be achieved when member states transfer part of their sovereign powers in criminal law to the EU.

SAMENVATTING
MENSENHANDEL
VERVOLGING VANUIT EEN EUROPEES PERSPECTIEF

Het doel van deze studie was het identificeren van belemmeringen voor een effectieve vervolging van mensenhandel, om uiteindelijk die vervolging te verbeteren. De drie tegenstellingen die ten grondslag lagen aan deze studie kunnen als volgt worden omschreven. De eerste is de tegenstelling tussen het feit dat mensenhandel een misdrijf is met een transnationale dimensie en het feit dat remedies ter bestrijding van mensenhandel veelal zijn gebaseerd op nationale bevoegdheden. De tweede tegenstelling volgt uit, aan de ene kant het bestaan van een groot aantal strategieën om mensenhandel te bestrijden en verdachten van mensenhandel te vervolgen en, aan de andere kant de onwilligheid of onmogelijkheid van staten om deze strategieën effectief aan te wenden. De derde tegenstelling is die tussen het gebruik van immigratiewetgeving enerzijds en het belang voor strafrechtelijke vervolging en bescherming van slachtoffers van mensenhandel anderzijds. Nadat was bepaald of mensenhandel een transnationaal misdrijf is, werden deze drie tegenstellingen verder uitgewerkt.

Mensenhandel vindt in toenemende mate in een internationale context plaats. De ontwikkelingen op het gebied van globalisering hebben de internationalisering van mensenhandel op twee manieren beïnvloed. Ten eerste worden slachtoffers steeds vaker en steeds makkelijker verplaatst van de ene naar de andere stad en van het ene land naar het andere land. Ten tweede worden vrouwen in het algemeen vaker getroffen door armoede en werkloosheid, twee effecten van globalisering, waardoor zij kwetsbaarder zijn voor mensenhandelpraktijken. Vaak wordt gesteld dat mensenhandel gezien kan worden als een transnationaal misdrijf, zonder dat deze laatste term verder wordt gedefinieerd. Het belang om mensenhandel te kwalificeren als een transnationaal misdrijf is gelegen in het feit dat een transnationaal misdrijf een benadering vanuit een niet-nationaal perspectief ter bestrijding ervan rechtvaardigt. Om een misdrijf te kwalificeren als een transnationaal misdrijf moeten de volgende vier criteria worden vervuld: 1) een bepaalde mate van organisatie is nodig om het misdrijf te plegen, 2) de belangen van meer dan één staat zijn betrokken bij het misdrijf, 3) de betrokkenheid van meerdere staten verergeren de problemen in de vervolging van het misdrijf, 4) effectieve oplossingen moeten worden gezocht voorbij nationale grenzen. De eerste twee criteria dienen cumulatief te worden vervuld, terwijl het derde en vierde criterium kunnen worden gezien als een gevolg van de eerste twee en daarom als aanvullende criteria moeten worden beschouwd. De vraag die in het navolgende zal worden beantwoord is in hoeverre aan deze vier criteria is voldaan met betrekking tot het misdrijf mensenhandel en dus of een rechtvaardiging is te vinden voor een benadering vanuit een niet-nationaal perspectief.

Het eerste criterium is dat een bepaalde mate van organisatie nodig is om het misdrijf te kunnen plegen.

Om te kunnen bepalen hoe het misdrijf mensenhandel in het algemeen wordt georganiseerd, dienen we te kijken naar de definitie ervan. In het kader van deze studie werd de volgende definitie voor mensenhandel ontwikkeld:

> Met mensenhandel wordt bedoeld alle activiteiten die worden aangewend in de gedwongen transnationale rekrutering en/of het gedwongen transnationale transport van een persoon met de bedoeling deze persoon onder dwang uit te buiten.

Met andere woorden, het misdrijf mensenhandel bestaat uit twee fasen, nl. de fase van rekrutering en transport en de fase van exploitatie. Voor de tewerkstelling van slachtoffers van mensenhandel zijn contacten nodig met personen die bereid zijn deel te nemen aan deze illegale activiteit. Verder brengen de rekrutering en het transport vaak verschillende activiteiten met zich mee, zoals het vervalsen van paspoorten, het plaatsen van advertenties, het vervoer van slachtoffers van de ene locatie naar de andere, het verkrijgen van vliegtickets, het huisvesten van slachtoffers, etc. Het is niet aannemelijk dat al deze activiteiten door één en dezelfde persoon worden uitgevoerd, met name niet wanneer het mensenhandel over de grenzen betreft. De conclusie kan daarom worden getrokken dat voor de uitvoering van het misdrijf mensenhandel een bepaalde mate van organisatie nodig is, die bestaat uit het aangaan van verschillende contacten om de verschillende elementen van het misdrijf uit te voeren.

Het tweede criterium is dat de belangen van meer dan één staat betrokken zijn bij het misdrijf.

Het feitelijk en fysiek passeren van een landsgrens is niet perse nodig om aan dit criterium te voldoen. De betrokkenheid van meerdere staten is ook aanwezig wanneer bijvoorbeeld het misdrijf in één en hetzelfde land plaatsvindt maar dat het is georganiseerd vanuit een ander land. Mensenhandel vindt vaak plaats van landen met een minder stabiel economisch en wettelijk systeem naar landen met een strikter systeem. Toch is het niet strikt noodzakelijk dat de mensenhandel tussen landen plaatsvindt omdat het misdrijf mensenhandel ook binnen één en hetzelfde land kan plaatsvinden. Met een brede opvatting van het vereiste van de betrokkenheid van meerdere staten zal dit criterium vervuld zijn in de meerderheid van de gevallen van mensenhandel. Bovendien is het transnationale element een element in de definitie zoals die werd gebruikt in deze studie, zodat dit criterium altijd is vervuld.

Het derde criterium is dat de betrokkenheid van meerdere staten de problemen in de vervolging van transnationale misdrijven verergeren. Omdat het niet gemakkelijk is om te bepalen in hoeverre dit criterium is vervuld is een verdere verdieping in de problemen bij de vervolging van mensenhandel noodzakelijk.

Een van de gevolgen van het feit dat meerdere landen betrokken zijn bij een geval van mensenhandel is dat voor het strafrechtelijk onderzoek en de vervolging van het misdrijf een beroep gedaan moet worden op internationale overeenkomsten naast de nationale wetgeving. Om de vraag te kunnen beantwoorden in welke mate zich belemmeringen voordoen bij de vervolging van mensenhandel werden eerst de belemmeringen op het gebied van het gebruik van deze overeenkomsten onderzocht in hoofdstuk V waarna een empirisch onderzoek plaatsvond naar mensenhandelzaken in Nederland. De resultaten hiervan werden beschreven in hoofdstuk VI. De relevante overeenkomsten kunnen worden onderverdeeld in beleidsdocumenten en wettelijke instrumenten.

Veel beleidsdocumenten die zijn aangenomen binnen de EU, de Raad van Europa en de Organisatie voor Veiligheid en Samenwerking in Europa hebben betrekking op mensenhandel. Deze documenten behelzen de intentie om mensenhandel effectiever te bestrijden. Vergaande bepalingen met betrekking tot slachtofferbescherming, strafrechtelijke samenwerking, specifieke training voor politieambtenaren, harmonisatie van de definitie van mensenhandel, etc., zijn neergelegd in deze documenten. Echter, een van de belangrijkste kenmerken van beleidsdocumenten is dat ze geen directe werking hebben. Het gevolg is dat het effect van deze documenten tot nu toe beperkt is terwijl mensenhandel naar en in Europa toeneemt en staten niet echt bereid lijken om te handelen in overeenstemming met hun verplichtingen zoals die zijn neergelegd in de beleidsdocumenten.

De relevante wettelijke instrumenten voor de vervolging van mensenhandel aangenomen binnen de EU en de Raad van Europa betreffen met name strafrechtelijke samenwerking in het algemeen. De aard en omvang van de problemen met betrekking tot het gebruik van deze instrumenten kunnen als volgt worden samengevat. Met betrekking tot materieelrechtelijke problemen kan worden gesteld dat hun aandeel naar verhouding niet zo groot is als vaak wordt verondersteld. De procedurele problemen bestaan met name in het gebrek aan transparantie met betrekking tot de communicatiekanalen die gebruikt (moeten) worden, vaak ten gevolge van verschillen in bevoegdheden tussen betrokken instanties in de lidstaten en een gebrek aan kennis over elkanders rechtssysteem. De organisatorische problemen betreffen met name de identificatie van de bevoegde instanties in het betrokken land en praktische problemen in het leggen van contact met de betrokken autoriteiten, bijvoorbeeld door de afwezigheid van telefoon- en faxnummers en andere personalia of door taalproblemen. Verder vormt het gebrek aan (financiële) middelen een belangrijke belemmering in de strafrechtelijke samenwerking.

Nadat de belangrijkste belemmeringen met betrekking tot de strafrechtelijke samenwerking waren vastgesteld, werd de vraag beantwoord in hoeverre deze belemmeringen zich voordoen met betrekking tot de vervolging van mensenhandel. Hiertoe werd een empirisch onderzoek uitgevoerd in mensenhandelzaken in Nederland, waarvan de belangrijkste resultaten hieronder worden weergegeven.

Het is opvallend dat, in het algemeen, de noodzaak van strafrechtelijke samenwerking door de betrokken Officieren van Justitie wordt gezien als een belemmering in een strafprocedure en daarom zoveel mogelijk wordt vermeden, zelfs als dat ten koste gaat van de mogelijkheid één of meerdere gerelateerde misdrijven ten laste te leggen.

Een van de belangrijkste belemmeringen voor een effectieve vervolging van mensenhandel is de afwezigheid van slachtoffers en getuigen, vaak ten gevolge van het feit dat zij het land zijn uitgezet door de vreemdelingenpolitie. Een belangrijke vermindering van de obstakels in de vervolging van mensenhandel kan worden bereikt door een verbeterde samenwerking tussen de vreemdelingenpolitie, en politie en justitie, met name de Officieren van Justitie. Dit zou het risico verminderen dat slachtoffers en getuigen, die in mensenhandelzaken essentieel zijn voor een succesvolle vervolging, worden teruggestuurd naar hun land van herkomst nog voordat zij zijn gehoord door de politie of, nog belangrijker, door de rechter-commissaris.

Formele communicatiekanalen worden normaliter gebruikt voor het versturen van rechtshulpverzoeken, zelfs wanneer directe communicatie tussen de bevoegde instanties is toegestaan. De betrokken functionarissen volgen strikt de formaliteiten nodig voor het uitwisselen van informatie, tenzij de vragende persoon bekend is bij de verstrekkende persoon. De formaliteiten die vervuld dienen te worden bij strafrechtelijke samenwerking worden in het algemeen ervaren als een belemmering voor het proces van strafrechtelijke samenwerking.

Opvallend is voorts dat, als een antwoord op een rechtshulpverzoek perse noodzakelijk was binnen een bepaalde tijdsperiode, de betrokken personen erin slaagden om op tijd een antwoord te krijgen.

De afwezigheid van dubbele strafbaarheid lijkt geen belemmering meer te zijn voor strafrechtelijke samenwerking. Wat echter wel wordt gezien als een belemmering is het gebrek aan prioriteitstelling en het gebrek aan aandacht voor mensenhandel, zowel in Nederland als in andere landen. De betrokken functionarissen stelden dat dit gebrek een belangrijke oorzaak is voor vertragingen in de strafrechtelijke samenwerking in mensenhandelzaken.

De conclusie op basis van het empirisch onderzoek moet daarom zijn dat de betrokkenheid van meerdere staten de problemen in de vervolging van mensenhandel verergeren. De vraag of het derde criterium is vervuld moet daarom bevestigend worden beantwoord.

Het vierde criterium is dat effectieve oplossingen moeten worden gezocht voorbij nationale grenzen.

Tot nu toe is het strafrecht, gebaseerd op de soevereiniteit van staten, niet effectief en te gecompliceerd gebleken om mensenhandel effectief te vervolgen. Omdat de betrokkenheid van meerdere staten de problemen in de vervolging van mensenhandel verergeren is het logisch dat oplossingen moeten worden gezocht in de samenwerking met andere staten, dus voorbij nationale grenzen, bijvoorbeeld op Europees niveau. Dit betekent dat het vierde criterium ook is vervuld en dat mensenhandel dus kan worden gekwalificeerd als een transnationaal misdrijf.

Met de wetenschap dat mensenhandel een transnationaal misdrijf is en dat een benadering om dit misdrijf effectief te bestrijden en te vervolgen moet worden gezocht voorbij nationale grenzen, kunnen de drie tegenstellingen die aan het begin van deze samenvatting werden beschreven verder worden uitgewerkt.

De eerste tegenstelling tussen het feit dat mensenhandel een misdrijf is met een transnationale dimensie en het feit dat remedies ter bestrijding van mensenhandel veelal zijn gebaseerd op nationale bevoegdheden is nauw verbonden met de veranderende rol van de soevereine staat en staatssoevereiniteit. De legitimatie van staatssoevereiniteit moet worden gezocht in de rechtszekerheid en de bescherming van onderdanen. Ten gevolge van deze legitimatie zijn staten verplicht een dusdanig wettelijk systeem op te zetten dat burgers in voldoende mate beschermt. Om burgers te beschermen tegen grensoverschrijdende misdaad, zoals mensenhandel, moet zo'n systeem voorzieningen op het gebied van intensievere samenwerking in strafzaken met andere staten inhouden, ofwel op een nationaal ofwel op een niet-nationaal, bijvoorbeeld een Europees, niveau. Recent ontwikkelde instrumentent op Europees niveau, zoals the Europees Arrestatie Bevel, de EU Verdragen betreffende uitlevering, en het EU Verdrag betreffende wederzijdse samenwerking, naast het voorstel om een Europees Openbaar Ministerie op te zetten, laten een verandering zien in het gebruik van bestaande principes (zoals de dubbele strafbaarheid, het specialiteitsbeginsel, en de uitleveringsexcepties) die de strafrechtelijke samenwerking vergemakkelijkt. Deze recente ontwikkelingen kunnen worden samengevat door te stellen dat samenwerking in strafzaken, met name uitlevering en wederzijdse rechtshulp, dient te worden versimpeld en uitgebreid. Het lijkt langzaam maar zeker meer geaccepteerd te worden dat sommige beslissingen met betrekking tot het strafrecht op Europees niveau worden genomen en niet louter en alleen op nationaal niveau. Het is aannemelijk dat de komende Intergouvernementele Conferentie in 2003/2004 dit proces zal versnellen. Daarom dient de conclusie met betrekking tot de eerste tegenstelling te zijn dat enerzijds een benadering om mensenhandel te vervolgen op een Europees niveau gebaseerd op het beginsel van regionale jurisdictie het meest effectief lijkt. Anderzijds vinden er interessante ontwikkelingen plaats binnen Europa die het huidige systeem van strafrechtelijke samenwerking versterken en dus gebaseerd zijn op nationale bevoegdheden. Toch lijken beide benaderingen een erosie van de staatssoevereiniteit in te houden. In het algemeen is er een tendens dat de rol van de soevereine staat verandert maar dat staten erg voorzichtig zijn om strafrechtelijke aangelegenheden over te laten aan de EU. Een van belangrijkste redenen voor deze terughoudendheid is het gebrek aan vertrouwen in elkanders rechtssysteem.

Met betrekking tot de tweede tegenstelling, tussen het bestaan van een groot aantal strategieën om mensenhandel te bestrijden en verdachten van mensenhandel te vervolgen en de onwilligheid of onmogelijkheid van staten om deze strategieën effectief aan te wenden, zijn zowel de beleidsdocumenten betreffende mensenhandel als de wettelijke instrumenten die de vervolging van mensenhandel vergemakkelijken belangrijk voor de discussie. De effectiviteit van deze documenten en instrumenten werd onderzocht om de belemmeringen voor een effectieve vervolging van mensenhandel vast te kunnen stellen. De belangrijkste belemmeringen met betrekking tot de vervolging van mensenhandel volgen deels uit het feit dat staten, tot op heden, hun eigen strafrechtsystemen hebben behouden, en deels uit het gebrek aan prioriteit en beschikbare (financiële) middelen om mensenhandel te vervolgen. Daarom dient de reden voor de ineffectieve vervolging deels te worden gezocht in de onmogelijkheid voor staten om adequaat te vervolgen omdat een beperking op het gebied van strafrechtelijke samenwerking inherent is aan het huidige systeem gebaseerd op nationale wetten, en deels aan de onwil van staten om toereikende middelen beschikbaar te stellen.

De derde tegenstelling betreft die tussen het gebruik van immigratiewetgeving enerzijds en het belang voor strafrechtelijke vervolging en bescherming van slachtoffers van mensenhandel anderzijds. Deze tegenstelling kan het best worden bestreden met praktische oplossingen zoals het contacteren van justitiële autoriteiten door de vreemdelingenpolitie voordat slachtoffers worden uitgezet. Echter, een dergelijke oplossing zal niet het gewenste resultaat opleveren zolang de vreemdelingendienst wordt aangemoedigd om zoveel mogelijk illegaal in Nederland verblijvende personen uit te zetten. Voorts dienen slachtoffers van mensenhandel als zodanig behandeld te worden en niet als criminelen. Het is daarom een gemiste kans dat voorzieningen met betrekking tot slachtofferbescherming niet zijn opgenomen in het Kaderbesluit van de Raad betreffende mensenhandel en dat getuigen- en slachtofferbescherming niet als een van de doelstellingen is opgenomen in het voorstel voor een Richtlijn betreffende de verblijfstitel met een korte geldigheidsduur. De conclusie met betrekking tot de derde tegenstelling is dat binnen de EU het systeem voor de bescherming van slachtoffers en getuigen van mensenhandel gefragmenteerd en complex is en belangrijke hiaten vertoont.

Nadat de problemen met betrekking tot de vervolging van mensenhandel werden geïdentificeerd en geanalyseerd, werden de oplossingen voor verbetering van de vervolging onderzocht. Hiertoe werden de wenselijkheid en de haalbaarheid van de benaderingen op nationaal en EU niveau bepaald om de vervolging van mensenhandel te verbeteren. De conclusies van deze afweging volgen hieronder.

Benadering op nationaal niveau om de vervolging van mensenhandel te verbeteren

De nieuwe instrumenten die op nationaal niveau zijn ontwikkeld om het systeem van de strafrechtelijke samenwerking te verbeteren, lijken op het eerste gezicht veelbelovend. Deze instrumenten brengen een verandering in het gebruik van bestaande principes die waarschijnlijk de vervolging van mensenhandel zal vergemakkelijken. Het is echter te vroeg om deze ontwikkelingen toe te juichen omdat op dit moment geen van deze instrumenten in werking is getreden en de ratificatie van sommige nog een tijd op zich kan laten wachten. Daarom zal moeten worden afgewacht of deze instrumenten ook het beoogde positieve effect zullen hebben in de toekomst. Daarnaast zal het huidige systeem van strafrechtelijke samenwerking in alle lidstaten moeten worden herzien voordat deze meer effectief kan worden aangewend. Maar zelfs als een dergelijke herziening heeft plaatsgevonden zullen we rekening moeten houden met de beperkingen die inherent zijn aan een systeem dat gebaseerd is op de verschillende strafrechtssystemen van de lidstaten. Verder zullen deze oplossingen het gebrek aan algehele betrokkenheid en adequate (financiële) middelen niet verhelpen. Daarom moet de algehele conclusie zijn dat een benadering om de vervolging van mensenhandel te verbeteren op een nationaal niveau niet toereikend is en daarom niet wenselijk.

De vraag naar de haalbaarheid van een benadering op nationaal niveau kan om de drie navolgende redenen bevestigend worden beantwoord: ten eerste om het grote aantal wettelijke instrumenten dat momenteel beschikbaar is op het gebied van de strafrechtelijke samenwerking, ten tweede vanwege de verschillende organisaties die zich bezighouden met strafrechtelijke samenwerking zowel op nationaal als Europees niveau, en ten derde omdat een dergelijke benadering de nationale bevoegdheden van de staten veelal onaangetast laat, een uitgangspunt waarvoor de lidstaten een voorkeur hebben.

Benadering op Europees niveau om de vervolging van mensenhandel te verbeteren
De vraag of een benadering ter verbetering van de vervolging van mensenhandel op Europees niveau wenselijk is dient bevestigend te worden beantwoord. Een dergelijke benadering moet minimaal een uniform systeem voor strafrechtelijke samenwerking en de oprichting van een Europees Openbaar Ministerie inhouden. De uitvoering van een dergelijke benadering zal voor een deel afhankelijk blijven van de nationale systemen, tenzij een compleet nieuw rechtshandhavingsysteem wordt opgezet op Europees niveau. Als voor deze laatste benadering wordt gekozen dan dient het mandaat van zowel Eurojust als Europol uitgebreid te worden met volledige operationele bevoegdheden binnen de EU, evenals het mandaat van het Europees Hof van Justitie. Wanneer een dergelijke benadering wordt gecombineerd met de harmonisatie van materieel strafrecht en strafprocesrecht, zou dit de ontwikkeling van een eigen Europees strafrechtsstelsel betekenen. Deze ontwikkeling is alleen wenselijk wanneer verschillende constitutionele waarborgen worden gegarandeerd binnen dit Europees strafrechtsstelsel. Overigens is dit alleen haalbaar wanneer delen van de staatssoevereiniteit worden overgedragen aan de EU.

Met het oog op de haalbaarheid van een benadering op Europees niveau kan worden gesteld dat het momenteel nog een stap te ver lijkt om instituties binnen de EU uit te rusten met operationele bevoegdheden. Daarnaast zal de weerstand van staten om een rechtshandhavingsysteem en een systeem voor strafrechtelijke samenwerking op te richten op Europees niveau een belemmering vormen voor de effectiviteit van die samenwerking. Daarom dient te worden gesteld dat een benadering op Europees niveau momenteel (nog) niet haalbaar is.

Op grond van de conclusies met betrekking tot de wenselijkheid en de haalbaarheid van beide benaderingen om de vervolging van mensenhandel te verbeteren moet worden geconcludeerd dat een keuze voor een van beide niet effectief zal zijn. Hierin zal geen verandering komen zolang de tweedeling blijft bestaan tussen de bereidheid op Europees niveau om verdere uitbreiding van bevoegdheden op het gebied van politiële en justitiële samenwerking te bewerkstelligen en de praktijk en terughoudendheid van lidstaten om daadwerkelijke macht te verlenen aan Europese instituties en organisaties ten koste van hun eigen macht. Dit betekent dat een 'tweesporenbeleid' gevolgd dient te worden als een alternatieve oplossing voor de bestaande tweedeling. Een dergelijk beleid zal inhouden dat de operationele macht grotendeels bij de nationale autoriteiten zal blijven liggen maar dat een coördinerend en ondersteunend orgaan opgericht kan worden op Europees niveau. Dit orgaan zou goed passen binnen de plannen om een Europees Openbaar Ministerie binnen het kader van Eurojust op te richten.

Zoals eerder gesteld, zijn staten verplicht om een adequaat systeem voor de bescherming van hun onderdanen op te stellen willen zij hun soevereine macht behouden. Voor transnationale misdrijven in het algemeen en voor mensenhandel in het bijzonder geldt dat staten niet aan deze verplichting kunnen voldoen door alleen gebruik te maken van hun nationale bevoegdheden op hun eigen grondgebied maar dat zij een systeem voor intensievere samenwerking op moeten zetten om mensenhandel effectief te bestrijden. Staten verdienen het behoud van soevereiniteit alleen wanneer zij bereid zijn om samen te werken met andere staten op de meest effectieve manier en in die zin bereid zijn om hun soevereine bevoegdheden te delen met andere staten. Dit kan intensievere samenwerking betekenen, soms op een nationaal en soms op een Europees niveau. Op de lange termijn is het echter heel wel mogelijk dat blijkt dat de bescherming van onderdanen en het garanderen van veiligheid in een maatschappij het best kan worden bereikt als lidstaten bereid zijn een deel van hun soevereine bevoegdheden op het gebied van het strafrecht over te dragen aan de EU.

APPENDIX 1
ORGANISATION CHART

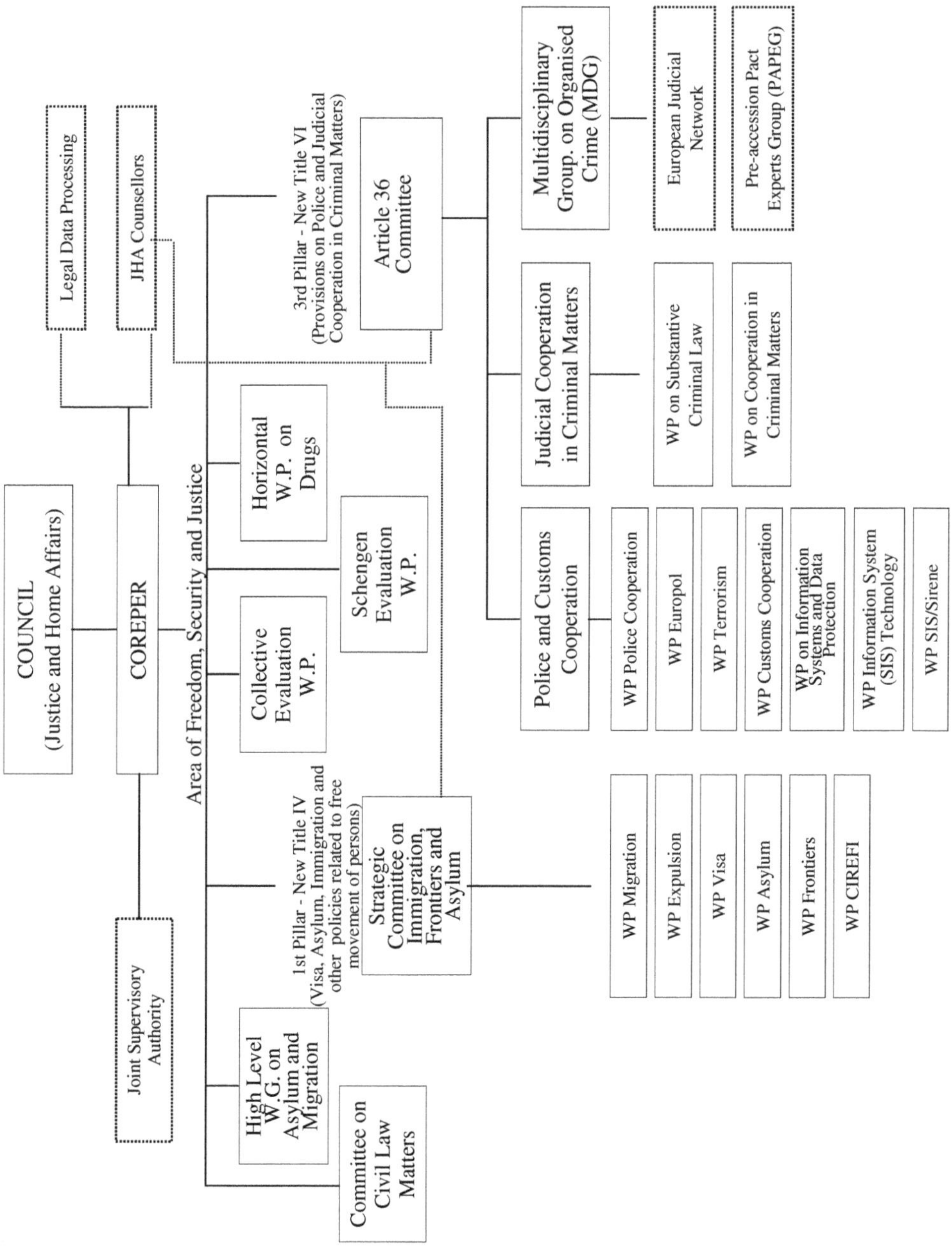

APPENDIX 2
FILE SCREENING LIST

- Name of the offender ....
- File number ....
- Court concerned ....
- Prosecutor concerned ....
- Date of registration ....
- Date of judgement...
- Size of the file ....
- Is criminal cooperation categorised separately? ....
- Prosecution on the basis of Article 250*ter*, 250a, and/or 197a...............
- What other crimes were included in the indictment? ....
- Is the case transnational? ....
- What does the transnational character consist of? ....
- Is the case related to other cases. If yes, how and to which? ....
- Was the case dismissed?...
- What was the reason for dismissal?....................................
- Was an appeal lodged (date)? ....
- By who and where was the appeal lodged?..............................
- Current state of affairs regarding the appeal ....
- Estimation of the time needed for studying this file ....
- What penalty was imposed and on what grounds ....

APPENDIX 3
RESEARCH QUESTIONS OF THE FILE STUDY

I. Questions in the substantive area

a. If prosecution takes place on the basis of Article 197a Dutch Penal Code does it concern a veiled case of trafficking?

b. Is evidence excluded if the requested information is gathered in accordance with the national law of the requested state?

c. Is double criminality a reason to refuse criminal cooperation?

d. Does a different interpretation of terms between states and within states cause any problems? If yes, what problems?

II. Questions in the procedural area

a. Are the authorities involved acquainted with the use of direct communication channels and to what extent are these channels used? Is the European Judical Network used? If yes, does this contribute to adequate criminal cooperation?

b. To what extent does duplication of efforts exists with regard to the control and registration of a request?

c. To what extent are problems concerning criminal cooperation in case of trafficking caused by miscommunication between the police and the judiciary?

d. To what extent are problems caused by confusion as to what formalities must be fulfilled for drafting a request and what channels must be used for sending a request?

e. To what extent are appeals used to delay criminal proceedings?

III. Questions in the organisational area

a. To what extent do problems occur with regard to the identification of the competent judicial authorities for criminal cooperation?

b. What practical problems are encountered in contacting relevant authorities abroad?

c. To what extent do problems exist regarding language?

IV. Additional questions based on the interviews

a. What problems occur as a result of the fact that victims and/or witnesses have returned to their country of origin
   i. with regard to their willingness to testify?
   ii. with regard to the cooperation of the authorities in tracing the victims and/or witnesses?
   iii. with regard to the application of local law on criminal procedure when the victim and/or witness is heard in her country of origin?
   iv. How is the cooperation with the immigration police?

b. What problems cast doubts on the reliability of the authorities on the local level in the requested country?

c. What are the obstacles to the establishment of a relationship based on mutual trust with victims and/or witnesses? To what extent are victims and/or witnesses influenced in this matter by the perpetrators?

d. What is the added value when insight is provided with regard to the recruitment practices in the countries of origin?

e. What problems are experienced as a consequence of the absence of cooperation with African countries in general and with Nigeria in particular (for instance, with regard to falsification of passports, look-alikes, the application of different identities)?

f. What problems are experienced in the criminal cooperation with Spain?

g. What problems are experienced with regard to the investigation of financial data and assets in the requested country?

V. Other problems

a. Which other problems can be identified from the files with regard to the criminal cooperation?

BIBLIOGRAPHY

Adamoli, S., *Organised Crime around the World*, European Institute for Crime Prevention and Control, affiliated with the United Nations, HEUNI publications series, Helsinki, 1998

Advisory Committee on Human Rights and Foreign Policy of the Dutch Ministry of Foreign Affairs, *The Traffic in Persons*, Advice no. 14, The Hague, 1992

Asher, J., How the United States is Violating its International Agreements to Combat Slavery, in: *Emory International Law Review*, Volume 8, issue 1, 1994, pp. 215-253

Baeveghem, P. van, et al., *Trafficking in Migrants through Poland*, Maklu, Antwerp, 1999

Barents, R., *Het Verdrag van Amsterdam in werking*, Europese Monografieën 62, Kluwer, Deventer, 1999

Barents, R. and Brinkhorst, L.J., *Grondlijnen van Europees Recht*, W.E.J. Tjeenk Willink, Deventer, 2001

Bassiouni, M.C., An Appraisal of the Growth and Developing Trends of International Criminal Law, in: *International Review of Penal Law*, Volume 45, 1974, pp. 405-433

Bassiouni, M.C., *A Draft International Criminal Code and Draft Statute for an International Criminal Tribunal*, Nijhoff, Dordrecht, 1987

Bassiouni, M.C., Enslavement as an International Crime, in: *New York University Journal of International Law and Politics*, Volume 23, issue 2, 1991, pp. 445-517

Bassiouni, M.C., Policy Considerations on Inter-State Cooperation in Criminal Matters, in: A. Eser and O. Lagodny (eds.), *Principles and Procedures for a New Transnational Criminal Law*, Max Planck Institute, Freiburg im Breisgau, 1992

Bassiouni, M.C., et al., *International Criminal Law. Cases and Materials*, Carolina Academic Press, Durham, North Carolina, 1996

Bassiouni, M.C., The Penal Characteristics of Conventional International Criminal Law, in: J. Dugard and Ch. van den Wyngaert, *International Criminal Law and Procedure*, Dartmouth, Aldershot, 1996

Bassiouni, M.C., *International Criminal Law, Volume I, Crimes*, second edition, Transnational Publishers, Ardsley, 1999

Bassiouni, M.C. and Vetere, E., Organized Crime and its Transnational Manifestations, in: M.C. Bassiouni, *International Criminal Law, Volume I, Crimes*, second edition, Transnational Publishers, Ardsley, 1999

Beare, M.E., *Criminal Conspiracies: Organised Crime in Canada*, Nelson Canada, Scarborough, 1996

Beken, T. Vander, *Forumkeuze in het internationale strafrecht. Verdeling van misdrijven met aanknopingspunten in meerdere staten*, Maklu, Antwerp, 1999

Besselink, L.F.M., *Europese Unie en nationale soevereiniteit*, W.E.J. Tjeenk Willink, Deventer, 1997

Bhattacharyya, R., Establishing a Rule-of-Law International Criminal Justice System, in: *Texas International Law Journal*, Volume 31, issue 1, 1996, pp. 57-99

Blakesly, C.L. and Lagodny, O., Competing National Laws: Network or Jungle?, in: A. Eser and O. Lagodny (eds.), *Principles and Procedures for a New Transnational Criminal Law*, Max Planck Institute, Freiburg im Breisgau, 1992

Blekxtoon, R., Europees Arrestatiebevel, in: *NJB*, Volume 77, issue 22, 2002, pp. 1058-1061

Boer, M. den and Corrado, L., For the Record or Off the Record: Comments About the Incorporation of Schengen into the EU, in: *European Journal of Migration and Law*, Volume 1, issue 4, 1999, pp. 397-418

Boer, M. den, Incorporation Without Change? Police Cooperation from Schengen to the EU, paper presented at the Madrid Seminar on Immigration, Asylum and Border Controls, February 2000, not published

Boer, M. den and Kerchove, G. de, A Hurdled Admission: The Integration of the Candidate Countries into the Area of Freedom, Security and Justice, in: V. Kronenberger (ed.), *The European Union and the International Legal Order: Discord or Harmony?* T.M.C. Asser Press, The Hague, 2001

Boot, M., *Nullum Crimen Sine Lege and the Subject Matter Jurisdiction of the International Criminal Court. Genocide, Crimes against Humanity, War Crimes*, Intersentia, Antwerp, 2002

Boot-Matthijssen, M. and Elst, R. van, Wetsvoorstel internationale misdrijven, in: *NJB*, Volume 77, issue 35, 2002, pp. 1742-1750

Bossard, A., *Transnational Crime and Criminal Law*, The Office of International Criminal Justice, University of Illinois, Chicago, 1990

Bossuyt, M.J., *Guide to the 'Travaux Préparatoires' of the International Covenant on Civil and Political Rights*, Nijhoff, Dordrecht, 1987

Brouwer, A. de, Note to the Kunarac, Kovac and Vukovic Case (Foča), in: *Tilburg Foreign Law Review*, Volume 9, issue 2, 2001, pp. 221-236

Brownlie, I., *Principles of Public International Law*, Clarendon Press, Oxford, 1990

Bureau Nationaal Rapporteur Mensenhandel, *Mensenhandel. Eerste rapportage van de Nationaal Rapporteur*, Bureau NRM, The Hague, 2002

Bureau Nationaal Rapporteur Mensenhandel, *Mensenhandel. Aanvullende kwantitatieve gegevens*, second report, Bureau NRM, The Hague, 2003

Castells, M., *The Information Age, Volume III, End of Millennium*, Blackwell, Cambridge, 1998

Castiglione, D. and Bellamy, R., Building the Union: The Nature of Sovereignty in the Political Architecture of Europe, in: N. MacCormick, *Constructing Legal Systems: 'European Union' in Legal Theory*, Kluwer Academic Publishers, Dordrecht, 1997

Chayes, A. and Handler Chayes, A., *The New Sovereignty. Compliance with International Regulatory Agreement*, Harvard University Press, Cambridge, 1995

Chinkin, C., The Protection of Victims and Witnesses, in: G.K. MacDonald and O. Swaak-Goldman, *Substantive and Procedural Aspects of International Criminal Law. The Experience of International and National Courts*, Kluwer Law International, The Hague, 2000

Chuang, J., Redirecting the Debate over Trafficking in Women: Definitions, Paradigms, and Contexts, in: *Harvard Human Rights Journal*, Volume 11, issue spring, 1998, pp. 65-107

Corstens, G.J.M., *Het Nederlandse strafprocesrecht*, Gouda Quint, Arnhem, 1993

Corstens, G.J.M. and Praedel, J., *European Criminal Law*, Kluwer Law International, The Hague, 2002

Cullen, D., Monar, J. and Myers, Ph., *Cooperation in Justice and Home Affairs. An Evaluation of the Third Pillar in Practice,* European Interuniversity Press, Brussels, 1996

Curtin, D.M. and Pouw, J.F.M., Samenwerking op het gebied van justitie en binnenlandse zaken in de Europese Unie-pre-Maastricht-nostalgie?, in: *SEW*, Volume 43, issue 9, 1995, pp. 579-605

Daalder, A., *Het bordeelverbod opgeheven, Prostitutie in 2000-2001*, WODC report 200, 2002

Delmas-Marty, M. and Summers, M.A., *What Kind of Criminal Policy for Europe?* Kluwer Law International, The Hague, 1996

Delmas-Marty, M. and Wyngaert, Ch. van den, *Corpus Juris*, Intersentia Rechtswetenschappen, Antwerp, 1998

Delmas-Marty, M. and Vervaele, J.A.E., *The Implementation of the Corpus Juris in the Member States,* Volume I-IV, Intersentia, Antwerp, 2000

Dijk, R. van, et al., *Een schijn van voodoo. Culturele achtergronden van de handel in Nigeriaanse meisjes voor de Nederlandse prostitutie: een verkenning*, African Study Centre, Leyden, 2000.

Dugard, J. and Wyngaert, Ch. van den, *International Criminal Law and Procedure*, Dartmouth, Aldershot, 1996

ECPAT Europe Law Enforcement Group, *Extraterritorial Legislation as a Tool to Combat Sexual Exploitation of Children*, Defence for Children International, Amsterdam, 1999

Farrior, S., The International Law on Trafficking in Women and Children for Prostitution: Making it Live Up to its Potential, in: *Harvard Human Rights Journal*, Volume 10, issue spring, 1997, pp. 213-255

Fennelly, N., Preserving the Legal Coherence within the New Treaty, in: M. den Boer et al., *Coping with Flexibility and Legitimacy after Amsterdam*, Current European Issues/ EIPA, Maastricht, 1998

Fijnaut, C., Justitiële samenwerking en de beheersing van georganiseerde misdaad in de Europese Unie, in: *Delikt en Delinkwent*, Volume 28, issue 10, 1998, pp. 988-1033

Fijnaut, C., Transnational Crime and the Role of the United Nations in its Containment through International Cooperation: A Challenge for the 21st Century, in: *European Journal of Crime, Criminal Law and Criminal Justice*, Volume 8, issue 2, 2000, pp. 119-127

Fijnaut, C., De strafrechtelijke bescherming van de financiële belangen van de Gemeenschap tegen fraude, in: *Delikt en Delinkwent*, Volume 30, issue 10, 2000, pp. 972-988

Fijnaut, C., Europol en Eurojust. Politiële en justitiële samenwerking in strafzaken, in: *Justitiële Verkenningen*, Volume 27, issue 2, 2001, pp. 11-24

Fijnaut, C. and Groenhuijsen, M.S., Een Europees openbaar ministerie. Kanttekening bij het Groenboek, in: *NJB*, Volume 77, issue 26, 2002, pp. 1234-1241

Frijhoff, W., Eigenzinnig Nederland, Europa en de toekomst van een cultuurnatie, in: A. van Staden, *De nationale staat, onhoudbaar maar onmisbaar? Het perspectief van Europese integratie en mondialisering*, Van Gorcum, Assen, 1996

Frimpong, K., Punishing Offences Committed Abroad: Practical (National) Relevance or Theoretical Claim, in: A. Eser and O. Lagodny (eds.), *Principles and Procedures for a New Transnational Criminal Law*, Max Planck Institute, Freiburg im Breisgau, 1992

Gelder, J.C.F. van, *De keten op de keeper beschouwd, Rapportage Project intensivering strafrechtelijke aanpak mensensmokkel, mensenhandel en ama's*, National Public Prosecutor's Office [Landelijk Parket Openbaar Ministerie], Rotterdam, April 2002, not published

Genugten, W.J.M. van (ed.), *Human Rights Reference Handbook*, Netherlands Ministry of Foreign Affairs, The Hague, 1999

Gully-Hart, P., Loss of Time Through Formal and Procedural Requirements in International Co-operation, in: A. Eser and O. Lagodny (eds.), *Principles and Procedures for a New Transnational Criminal Law*, Max Planck Institute, Freiburg im Breisgau, 1992

Harris, D.J., *Cases and Materials on International Law*, Sweet & Maxwell, London, 1998

Hauber, L., The Trafficking of Women for Prostitution: A Growing Problem within the European Union, in: *Boston College International & Comparative Law Review*, Volume 21, issue 1, 1998, pp. 183-199

Haveman, R., Slavernij of reguliere arbeid – Prostitutie en vrouwenhandel in internationaal perspectief, in: *Nemesis*, Volume 11, issue 4, 1995, pp. 97-102

Haveman, R., *Voorwaarden voor strafbaarstelling van vrouwenhandel*, Gouda Quint, Deventer, 1998

Higgins, R., *Problems & Process. International Law and How We Use it*, Clarendon Press, Oxford, 1994

Hirsch Ballin, E.H.M., *Wereldburgers: personen in het internationale recht*, W.E.J. Tjeenk Willink, Zwolle, 1995

Hirsch Ballin, E.H.M., Soevereiniteit in de Europese Unie, in: *NJB*, Volume 72, issue 44, 1997, pp. 2005-2010

Hirsch Ballin, E.H.M., De zaak-Pinochet, in: *Ars Aequi*, Volume 49, issue 6, 2000, pp. 481-488

Hirsch Ballin, E.H.M., Yerodia, Rechtsmacht, immuniteit en vervolgingsbeleid, in: *Ars Aequi*, Volume 51, issue 11, 2002, pp. 829-839

Ingelse, Ch. and Wilt, H. van der, De Zaak Pinochet. Over Universele Rechtsmacht en Hollandse Benepenheid, in: *NJB*, Volume 72, issue 8, 1996, pp. 280-285

International Human Rights Law Institute, DePaul University College of Law, *In Modern Bondage: Sex Trafficking in the Americas*, IHRLI, DePaul University, Chicago, 2002

International Organisation for Migration, *Trafficking of Women to the European Union: Characteristics, Trends and Policy Issues*, Conference paper submitted by the IOM at the Conference on Trafficking in Women for Sexual Exploitation, Vienna, June 1996

Kamminga, M.T. and Tijssen, M.E.M., Pinochet, Nederland en het VN-Verdrag tegen Foltering, in: *NJCM-Bulletin*, Volume 20, issue 8, 1995, pp. 986-995

Kelsen, H., and Tucker, R.W., *Principles of International Law*, second edition, Holt, Rinehart and Winston, New York, 1966

Kittichaisaree, K., *International Criminal Law*, Oxford University Press, Oxford, 2001

Klerk, Y., Definition of 'Traffic in Persons', in: M. Klap, Y. Klerk, and J.A. Smith (eds.), *Combating Traffic in Persons: Proceedings of the Conference on Traffic in Persons held from 15-19 November 1994 in Utrecht and Maastricht*, SIM special no. 17, Utrecht, 1995

Klip, A.H., Amsterdams Uniestrafrecht. Beschouwingen over de internationaal strafrechtelijke samenwerking na het Verdrag van Amsterdam, in: *NJB*, Volume 73, issue 18, 1998, pp. 811-816

Klip, A.H., Geïntegreerde bescherming van de financiële belangen van de EG: Verschuiving van de staat-staat-benadering naar verticalisering van de procedure? in: J.A.E. Vervaele, *Transnationale handhaving van de financiële belangen van de Europese Unie. Ontwikkelingen in het Verdrag van Amsterdam en de Corpus Juris,* Intersentia, Antwerp, 1999

Klip, A.H., Soevereiniteit in het strafrecht, in: G.J.M. Corstens, and M.S. Groenhuijsen (eds.), *Recht en Rede, Liber Amicorum Nico Keijzer*, Gouda Quint, Deventer, 2000

Koers, J., *Nederland als verzoekende staat bij de wederzijdse rechtshulp in strafzaken. Achtergronden, grenzen en mogelijkheden*, Wolf Legal Publishers, Nijmegen, 2001

Kortenhorst, P.C. and Verrest, P.A.M., De magistrat de liaison. Een pionier in de internationale samenwerking, in: *Justitiële Verkenningen*, Volume 27, issue 2, 2001, pp. 56-67

Lahti, R., Sub-Regional Co-operation in Criminal Matters: The Experience of the Nordic Countries, in: A. Eser and O. Lagodny (eds.), *Principles and Procedures for a New Transnational Criminal Law*, Max Planck Institute, Freiburg im Breisgau, 1992

Lap-Chew, L. and Wijers, M., *Trafficking in Women, Forced Labour, and Slavery-Like Practices in Marriage, Domestic Labour, and Prostitution*, Foundation against Trafficking in Women, Utrecht, 1997

Lauterpacht, H. and Oppenheim, L., *International Law, A Treatise, Volume I, Peace*, Longmans, London, 1961

Lee, R.S. and Friman, H. (eds.), *The International Criminal Court. Elements of Crimes and Rules of Procedure and Evidence*, Transnational Publishers, Ardsley, 2001

Leyns, G., et al., Bescherming van de financiële belangen van de EU, Corpus Juris en Europees Openbaar Ministerie, in: G. Vermeulen and E. de Busser (eds.), *Aspecten van Europees formeel strafrecht*, Maklu, Antwerp, 2002

Lubbers, R., *'Globalisering: naar een nieuwe kijk op political economy'*, Center for Economic Research, Tilburg University, Tilburg, 1995

Lubbers, R. and Koorevaar, J., *Primary Globalization, Secondary Globalization and the Sustainable Development Paradigm – Opposing Forces in the 21st Century*, Paper for the Conference on 21st Century Social Dynamics: Towards the Creative Society, Berlin, 2000

Malanczuk, P., *Akehurst's Modern Introduction to International Law*, Routledge, London, 1997

Malekian, F., *International Criminal Law: The Legal and Critical Analysis of International Crimes,* Malekian, Uppsala, 1991

Malekian, F., *The Monopolization of International Criminal Law in the United Nations. A Jurisprudential Approach*, second edition, Almqvist & Wiksell International, Stockholm, 1995

MacCormick, N., Democracy, Subsidiarity, and Citizenship in the 'European Commonwealth', in: N. MacCormick, *Constructing Legal Systems: 'European Union' in Legal Theory*, Kluwer Academic Publishers, Dordrecht, 1997

Malone, L.A., Economic Hardship as Coercion under the Protocol on International Trafficking in Persons by Organized Crime Elements, in: *Fordham International Law Journal*, Volume 25, issue 1, 2001, pp. 54-94

Manunza, E., *EG-aanbestedingsrechtelijke problemen bij privatiseringen en bij de bestrijding van corruptie en georganiseerde criminaliteit*, Kluwer, Deventer, 2001

MacDonald, G.K., Trial Procedures and Practices, in: G.K. MacDonald and O. Swaak-Goldman, *Substantive and Procedural Aspects of International Criminal Law. The Experience of International and National Courts*, Kluwer Law International, The Hague, 2000

McCormack, T.L.H. and Simpson, G.J., A New International Criminal Law Regime?, in: *Netherlands International Law Review,* Volume 42, issue 2, 1995, pp. 177-206

McCormack, T.L.H. and Simpson, G.J., The International Law Commission's Draft Code of Crimes against the Peace and Security of Mankind: An Appraisal of the Substantive Provisions, in: J. Dugard and Ch. van den Wyngaert, *International Criminal Law and Procedure*, Dartmouth, Aldershot, 1996

Mittelman, J.H. and Johnston, R., The Globalization of Organized Crime, the Courtesan State, and the Corruption of Civil Society, in: *Global Governance*, Volume 5, issue 1, 1999, pp. 103-126

Monar, J. and Morgan, R., *The Third Pillar of the European Union. Cooperation in the Fields of Justice and Home Affairs*, European Interuniversity Press, Brussels, 1994

Monar, J., Legitimacy of EU Action in Justice and Home Affairs: An Assessment in the Light of the Reforms of the Treaty of Amsterdam, in: M. den Boer, et al., *Coping with Flexibility and Legitimacy after Amsterdam*, Current European Issues/EIPA, Maastricht, 1998

Monar, J., Justice and Home Affairs in the Treaty of Amsterdam: Reform at the Price of Fragmentation, in: *European Law Review*, Volume 23, issue 4, 1998, pp. 320-335

Mueller, G.O.W. and Besharov, D.J., Evolution and Enforcement of International Criminal Law, in: M.C. Bassiouni, *International Criminal Law, Volume I, Crimes*, second edition, Transnational Publishers, Ardsley, 1999

Nigerian Democratic Movement in the Netherlands and Terre des Hommes, *Handel in Nigeriaanse meisjes naar Nederland*, Amsterdam, September 1999

Nijboer, J.F., Recommendations. Over het 'zachte' (straf)recht van de Raad van Europa, in: *Justitiële Verkenningen*, Volume 27, issue 2, 2001, pp. 81-87

Nowak, M., *U.N. Covenant on Civil and Political Rights, CCPR Commentary*, N.P. Engel Publisher, Kehl, 1993

Ooik, R.H. van, *De keuze der rechtsgrondslag voor besluiten van de Europese Unie*, Europese Monografieën 63, Kluwer, Deventer, 1999

Organization for Security and Cooperation in Europe, *Trafficking in Human Beings: Implications for the OSCE*, Review Conference, ODIHR Background Paper 1999/3, September 1999

Packer, J., The Origin and Nature of the Lund Recommendations on the Effective Participation of National Minorities in Public Life, in: *Helsinki Monitor*, Volume 11, issue 4, 2000, pp. 29-45

Passas, N., *Transnational Crime*, Dartmouth, Aldershot, 1999

Paust, J.J., *International Criminal Law: Cases and Materials*, Carolina Academic Press, Durham, 1996

Peers, S., Caveat Emptor? Integrating the Schengen Acquis into the European Union Legal Order, in: *Cambridge Yearbook of European Legal Studies*, Volume 2, 1999, pp. 87-124

Polakiewicz, J., *Treaty-making in the Council of Europe*, Council of Europe Publishing, Strasbourg, 1999

Pouw, E., Het gemeenschappelijk optreden in de 'Derde Pijler' van de EU, in: *Regelmaat*, Volume 12, issue 3, 1997, pp. 108-118

Rantala, M., A Treaty Labyrinth of Legal Cooperation in Criminal Matters: Can Europe Find Ariadne's Thread?, in: V. Kronenberger, *The European Union and the International Legal Order: Discord or Harmony?*, T.M.C. Asser Press, The Hague, 2001

Rehof, L.A., *Guide to the Travaux préparatoires of the United Nations Convention on the Elimination of All Forms of Discrimination against Women*, Nijhoff, Dordrecht, 1993

Rijken, C., Van asielzoekster tot prostituee. De aanpak van handel in Nigeriaanse alleenstaande minderjarige asielzoeksters, in: *Nemesis*, Volume 16, issue 1, 2000, pp. 4-11

Rijken, C. and Kronenberger, V., The United Nations Convention on Transnational Organised Crime and the European Union, in: V. Kronenberger, *The EU and the International Legal Order*, T.M.C. Asser Press, The Hague, 2001

Roermund, B. van, Jurisprudential Dilemmas of European Law, in: N. MacCormick, *Constructing Legal Systems: 'European Union' in Legal Theory*, Kluwer Academic Publishers, Dordrecht, 1997

Rupert, M., *Ideologies of Globalization. Contending Visions of a New World Order*, Routledge, London, 2000

Ruyver, B. de, et al., *Strategies of the EU and the US in Combating Transnational Organised Crime*, Maklu, Antwerp, 2002

Schwarzenberger, G., The Problem of an International Criminal Law, in: J. Dugard and Ch. van den Wyngaert, *International Criminal Law and Procedure*, Dartmouth, Aldershot, 1996

Shaw, M.N., *International Law*, third edition, Cambridge University Press, Cambridge, 1995

Shelley, L.I., Post-Soviet Organised Crime, Implication for Economic, Social and Political Development, in: N. Passas, *Transnational Crime*, Dartmouth, Aldershot, 1999

Sjöcrona, J.M. and Orie, A.M.M., *Internationaal Strafrecht vanuit Nederlands perspectief*, Kluwer, Deventer, 2002

Smet, B. de, *Internationale samenwerking in strafzaken tussen Angelsaksische en continentale landen*, Intersentia, Antwerp, 1999

Smit, M., Mensenhandel: een moderne vorm van slavernij, in: *Tijdschrift voor Criminologie*, Volume 43, issue 4, 2001, pp. 378-389

Solomon, J.S., Forming a More Secure Union: The Growing Problem of Organised Crime in Europe as a Challenge to National Sovereignty, in: *Dickens Journal of International Law*, Volume 13, issue 3, 1995, pp. 623-648

Staden, A. van, *De nationale staat, onhoudbaar maar onmisbaar? Het perspectief van Europese integratie en mondialisering*, Van Gorcum, Assen, 1996

Sunga, L.S., *The Emerging System of International Criminal Law. Developments in Codification and Implementation*, Kluwer Law International, The Hague, 1997

Swart, A.H.J., *Goede rechtsbedeling en internationale rechtshulp in Strafzaken*, Kluwer, Deventer, 1983

Swart, A.H.J., Human Rights and the Abolition of Traditional Principles, in: A. Eser and O. Lagodny (eds.), *Principles and Procedures for a New Transnational Criminal Law*, Max Planck Institute, Freiburg im Breisgau, 1992

Swart, A.H.J., *Een ware Europese rechtsruimte. Wederzijdse erkenning van strafrechtelijke beslissingen in de Europese Unie*, Gouda Quint, Deventer, 2001

Thomas, F., *Internationale Rechtshulp in Strafzaken*, Story-Scientia, Brussels, 1998

UNICEF, UNOHCHR and OSCE-ODIHR, *Trafficking in Human Beings in Southeastern Europe*, UNICEF, 2002

Vellinga, F.R., *West-Afrikaanse AMA's: vermist, maar ook gemist?*, Police North-East Gelderland, Apeldoorn, 1999

Verdross, A., Dynamisches Naturrecht, in: H. Kelsen, A. Merkl, and A. Verdross. *Die Wiener Rechtstheoretische Schule*, part I, Europa Verlag, Wien, 1968

Vermeulen, G., *Wederzijdse rechtshulp in strafzaken in de Europese Unie: naar een volwaardige eigen rechtshulpruimte voor de Lid-Staten?* Maklu, Antwerp, 1999

Vermeulen, G., International Trafficking in Women and Children, General Report, in: *International Review of Penal Law*, Volume 72, issue 3-4, 2001, pp. 837-890

Vervaele, J.A.E., *Transnationale handhaving van de financiële belangen van de Europese Unie. Ontwikkelingen in het Verdrag van Amsterdam en de Corpus Juris*, Intersentia, Antwerp, 1999

Vleuten, N. van der, *Survey on 'Traffic in Women'*, Vena working paper no. 91/1, Policies and Policy Research in an International Context, Research and Documentation Centre Women and Autonomy, Leyden University, Leyden, 1991

Vocks, J. and Nijboer, J., *Land van belofte. Een onderzoek naar slachtoffers van vrouwenhandel uit Centraal- en Oost-Europa*, Rijksuniversiteit Groningen, Groningen, 1999

Wagner, E., The Intergration of Schengen into the Framework of the European Union, in: *Legal Issues of European Intergration*, Volume 25, issue 2, 1998, pp. 1-60

Walker, N., Current Developments: EC Law; Justice and Home Affairs, in: *International and Comparative Law Quarterly*, Volume 47, issue 1, 1998, pp. 231-238

Wiarda, J., Trends in de wetgeving inzake mensensmokkel en mensenhandel, *Tijdschrift voor Criminologie*, Volume 43, issue 4, 2001, pp. 368-377

Williams, Ph. and Savona, E.U. (eds.), *The United Nations and Transnational Organised Crime*, Cass, London, 1996

Williams, Ph., Transnational Criminal Organisations and International Security, in: N. Passas, *Transnational Crime*, Dartmouth, Aldershot, 1999

Williams, Ph. and Vlassis, D. (eds.), *Combating Transnational Crime. Concepts, Activities and Responses*, Frank Cass, London, 2001

Wise, E.M., Terrorism and the Problems of an International Criminal Law, in: J. Dugard and Ch. van den Wyngaert, *International Criminal Law and Procedure*, Dartmouth, Aldershot, 1996

Wolswijk, H.D., *Locus delicti en rechtsmacht*, Gouda Quint, Deventer, 1998

WRR, *De toekomst van de Nationale Rechtsstaat,* Sdu Publishers, The Hague, 2002

Wyngaert, Ch. van den, Rethinking the Law of International Criminal Cooperation: The Restrictive Function of International Human Rights Through Individual-Oriented Bars, in: A. Eser and O. Lagodny (eds.), *Principles and Procedures for a New Transnational Criminal Law*, Max Planck Institute, Freiburg im Breisau, 1992

Wyngaert, Ch. van den and Stessens, G., Mutual Legal Assistance in Criminal Matters in the European Union, in: J. Dugard and Ch. van den Wyngaert, *International Criminal Law and Procedure*, Dartmouth, Aldershot, 1996

Wyngaert, Ch. van den, *Strafrecht en strafprocesrecht in hoofdlijnen*, Bruylant, Brussels, 1998

Wyngaert, Ch. van den, The Transformations of International Criminal Law in Response to the Challenge of Organized Crime, in: *International Review of Penal Law*, Volume 70, issue 1-2, 1999, pp. 35-132

Yarnold, B.M., The Doctrinal Basis for the International Criminalization Process, in: M.C. Bassiouni, *International Criminal Law, Volume I, Crimes*, second edition, Transnational Publishers, Ardsley, New York, 1999

Zegveld, L., The Combat of Traffic in Persons within the Framework of the United Nations, in: M. Klap, Y. Klerk, and J.A. Smith (eds.), *Combating Traffic in Persons: Proceedings of the Conference on Traffic in Persons held from 15-19 November 1994 in Utrecht and Maastricht*, SIM special no. 17, Utrecht, 1995

Zoglin, K., United Nations Action against Slavery: A Critical Evaluation, in: *Human Rights Quarterly*, Volume 8, issue 1, 1986, pp. 306-339

Zwaan, J.W. de and Bultena, A.J., *Ruimte van vrijheid, veiligheid en rechtvaardigheid. De samenwerking op het gebied van Justitie en Binnenlandse Zaken in de Europese Unie,* Sdu Publishers, The Hague, 2002

TABLE OF TREATIES, DOCUMENTS, AND CASES

United Nations

UN treaties

International Convention for the Suppression of the White Slave Traffic, 18 May 1904, 35 Stat. 426, 1 LNTS 83, as amended by the Protocol signed at Lake Success, New York, 4 May 1949 and which entered into force on 21 June 1951

International Convention for the Suppression of White Slave Traffic, 4 May 1910, III LNTS 278, as amended by the Protocol signed at Lake Success, New York, 4 May 1949 and which entered into force on 14 August 1951

International Convention for the Suppression of Traffic in Women and Children, 30 September 1921, 9 LNTS 416, as amended by the Protocol signed at Lake Success, New York, 12 November 1947 and which entered into force on 24 April 1950

Slavery Convention of 1926, 25 September 1926, 60 LNTS 253, entered into force on 9 March 1927

Convention Concerning Forced or Compulsory Labour (ILO no. 29), 39 UNTS 55, entered into force on 1 May 1932

International Convention for the Suppression of the Traffic in Women of Full Age, 11 October 1933, 150 LNTS 431, as amended by the Protocol signed at Lake Success, New York, 12 November 1947 and which entered into force on 24 April 1950

Convention for the Suppression of the Traffic in Persons and of the Exploitation of the Prostitution of Others, 2 December 1949, 96 UNTS 271, entered into force on 25 July 1951

Supplementary Convention on the Abolition of Slavery, the Slave Trade, and Institutions and Practices Similar to Slavery, 7 September 1956, 226 UNTS 3, entered into force on 30 April 1957

Abolition of Forced Labour Convention (ILO no. 105), 25 June 1957, 320 UNTS 291, entered into force on 17 January 1959

Convention on the Elimination of All Forms of Discrimination against Women, 18 December 1979, GA Res. 34/180, 34 UN GAOR Supp. (no. 46) at 193, UN Doc. A/34/46, 1249 UNTS 13, entered into force on 3 September 1981

Vienna Convention on the Law of Treaties, 1155 UNTS 331, entered into force on 27 January 1980

Optional Protocol to the Convention on the Rights of the Child on the Sale of Children, Child Prostitution and Child Pornography, GA Res. 54/263, Annex II, 54 UN GAOR Supp. (no. 49), UN Doc. A/54/49, entered into force on 18 January 2002

United Nations Convention against Transnational Organized Crime, 12-15 December 2000, GA Res. 55/25, annex I, 55 UN GAOR Supp. (no. 49) at 44, UN Doc. A/45/49 (Vol. I), not yet in force

Other UN documents

S/RES/827
UN Security Council Resolution 827 on the International Criminal Tribunal for the Former Yugoslavia (ICTY, Yugoslavia Tribunal), 25 May 1993

S/RES/955
UN Security Council Resolution 955 on the establishment of an International Tribunal and adoption of the Statute of the Tribunal (ICTR, Rwanda Tribunal), 8 November 1994

A4-0326/95
Report on Trafficking in Human Beings of the Committee on Civil Liberties and Internal Affairs, 14 December 1995

A/31/10
Report of the International Law Commission on the work of its twenty-eighth session, 3 May to 23 July 1976

A/47/38
CEDAW General Recommendation no. 19, *Violence against Women*, 29 January 1992

A/50/369
Report of the Secretary-General, *Traffic in Women and Girls*, 24 August 1995

A/50/433
Report of the Secretary-General on the implementation of General Assembly Resolution 49/150 on the Naples Political Declaration and Global Action against Organised Transnational Crime, *Crime Prevention and Criminal Justice*, 18 September 1995

A/Res/44/39
The General Assembly, *International criminal responsibility of individuals and entities engaged in illicit trafficking in narcotic drugs across national frontiers and other transnational criminal activities: establishment of an international criminal court with jurisdiction over such crimes*, 4 December 1989

A/Res/46/54
The General Assembly, Report of the International Law Commission on the work of its forty-third session, 9 December 1991

A/Res/56/83
The General Assembly Resolution, Responsibility of States for Internationally Wrongful Acts, 28 January 2002

A/55/383/Add.1
Report of the Ad Hoc Committee on the elaboration of a Convention against Transnational Organized Crime on the work of its first to eleventh sessions, *Interpretative notes for the official records (travaux préparatoires) of the negotiations of the United Nations Convention on Transnational Organized Crime and the Protocols thereto*

A/AC.254/4/add.3/Rev.5
Ad Hoc Committee on the elaboration of a Convention against Transnational Organized Crime, *Revised draft Protocol to Prevent, Suppress and Punish Trafficking in Persons, Especially Women and Children, supplementing the United Nations Convention against Transnational Organized Crime*

A/AC.254/4/add.3/Rev.6
Ad Hoc Committee on the elaboration of a Convention against Transnational Organized Crime, *Revised draft Protocol to Prevent, Suppress and Punish Trafficking in Persons, Especially Women and Children, supplementing the United Nations Convention against Transnational Organized Crime*

A/AC.254/4/add.3/Rev.7
Ad Hoc Committee on the elaboration of a Convention against Transnational Organized Crime, *Revised draft Protocol to Prevent, Suppress and Punish Trafficking in Persons, Especially Women and Children, supplementing the United Nations Convention against Transnational Organized Crime*

A/AC.254/33
Ad Hoc Committee on the elaboration of a Convention against Transnational Organized Crime, *Official records (travaux préparatoires) of the negotiation of the United Nations Convention against Transnational Organised Crime*, 4 July 2000

A/Conf.183/10
Rome Statute of the International Criminal Court, adopted 17 July 1998 and which entered into force on 1 July 2002

PCNICC/2000/1/Add.2
Report of the Preparatory Commission for the International Criminal Court, *Part II, Finalised Draft Text of the Elements of Crimes*, 2 November 2000

E/CN.4/RES/1994/45
Commission on Human Rights Res. 1994/45, *Question of integrating the rights of women into the human rights mechanisms of the United Nations and the elimination of violence against women*

E/CN.4/1995/42
Letter dated 3 July 1995 from the Permanent Mission of the Federal Republic of Yugoslavia to the United Nations Office at Geneva addressed to the Chairman of the Sub-Commission on Prevention of Discrimination and Protection of Minorities

E/CN.4/1997/47
Report of the Special Rapporteur on violence against women, its causes and consequences, Ms. Radhika Coomaraswamy, *Further Promotion and encouragement of human rights and*

fundamental freedoms, including the question of the programme and methods of work of the Commission. Alternative approaches and ways and means within the United Nations system for improving the effective enjoyment of human rights and fundamental freedoms

E/CN.4/Sub.2/1991/41
Report of the Working Group on Contemporary Forms of Slavery

E/CN/4/Sub.2/1991/41, Annex I
Report of the Working Group on Contemporary Forms of Slavery on its sixteenth session, *Draft programme of action for the Prevention of Traffic in Persons and the Exploitation of the Prostitution of Others*

E/CN.4/Sub.2/1995/28/Add.1
Report of the Working Group on Contemporary Forms of Slavery, *Draft programme of action on the traffic in persons and the exploitation of the prostitution of others*

E/CN.6/1994/4
Economic and Social Council, Commission on the Status of Women, *Peace: Measures to Eradicate Violence against Women in the Family and Society*, 21 January 1994

E/CN.15/1996/2
Economic and Social Council, Implementation of the Naples Political Declaration and Global Action Plan against Organized Transnational Crime, Report of the Secretary-General, 4 April 1996

L/2863
Press Release, Preparatory Committee on International Criminal Court hears divergent views on convening of informal organizational meeting before Rome, 3 April 1998

Economic and Social Council, Resolution 1998/20, *Action to combat international trafficking in women and children*, 44th plenary meeting, 28 July 1998

UN Office for Drug Control and Crime Prevention, 'A Convention against Transnational Crime', Speech by Pino Arlacchi, Buenos Aires, Argentina, 31 August 1998

United Nations High Commissioner for Human Rights, *Observations by the UNHCHR and the UNHCR on the Proposal for a EU Council Framework Decision on Combating Trafficking in Human Beings*. See: http://www.unhchr.ch/Huridocda/ Huridoca.nsf/TestFrame/ dff9762c0421980ec1256a7f00514e2f?Opendocument (visited 11 July 2003)

Council of Europe

Council of Europe treaties

European Convention on Extradition, ETS no. 024, signed on 13 December 1957 and entered into force on 18 April 1960

European Convention on Mutual Assistance in Criminal Matters, ETS no. 030, signed on 20 April 1959 and entered into force on 12 June 1962

European Agreement on Travel by Young Persons on Collective Passports between the Member Countries of the Council of Europe, ETS no. 037, signed on 16 December 1961 and entered into force on 17 January 1962

European Convention on the International Validity of Criminal Judgments, ETS no. 070, signed on 28 May 1970 and entered into force on 26 July 1974

European Convention on the Transfer of Proceedings in Criminal Matters, ETS no. 073, signed on 15 May 1972 and entered into force on 30 March 1978

Additional Protocol to the European Convention on Extradition, ETS no. 086, signed on 15 October 1975 and entered into force on 20 August 1979

Second Additional Protocol to the European Convention on Extradition, ETS no. 098, signed on 17 March 1978 and entered into force on 5 June 1982

Additional Protocol to the European Convention on Mutual Assistance in Criminal Matters, ETS no. 099, signed on 17 March 1978 and entered into force on 12 April 1982

Convention on the Transfer of Sentenced Persons, ETS no. 112, signed on 21 March 1983 and entered into force on 1 July 1985

Convention on Laundering, Search, Seizure and Confiscation of the Proceeds from Crime, ETS no. 141, signed on 8 December 1990 and entered into force on 1 September 1993

Additional Protocol to the Convention on the Transfer of Sentenced Persons, ETS no. 167, signed on 18 December 1997 and entered into force on 1 June 2000

Criminal Law Convention on Corruption, ETS no. 173, signed on 27 January 1999 and entered into force on 1 July 2002

Second Additional Protocol to the European Convention on Mutual Assistance in Criminal Matters, ETS no. 182, signed on 8 November 2001 and which has not yet entered into force

Convention on Cyber Crime, ETS no. 185, signed on 23 November 2001 and which has not yet entered into force

Other Council of Europe documents

Council of Europe, Seminar on action against traffic in women and forced prostitution as violations of human rights and human dignity, Strasbourg, 25-27 September 1991, EG/prost (91) 13 prov. Sub. II

Specific Terms of Reference from the Multi-sectoral Group on Action against Trafficking in Human Beings for the Purpose of Sexual Exploitation, 587th meeting of the Ministers' Deputies, 1.4.1997, Appendix 2

Parliamentary Assembly, Recommendation 1325 on Traffic in Women and Forced Prostitution in Council of Europe Member States, 23.4.1997

Reply from the Committee of Ministers adopted at the 645th meeting of the Ministers' Deputies (15 and 18 October 1998) to Parliamentary Assembly Recommendation 1325, 28.10.1998, Doc. 8246

Committee on Equal Opportunities for Women and Men, Rapporteur: Mrs. Ruth-Gaby Vermot-Mangold, Council of Europe, *Violence against Women in Europe*, Parliamentary Assembly, 15.3.2000, Doc. 8667

Recommendation no. R (2000) 11 of the Committee of Ministers to Member States on Action against Trafficking in Human Beings for the Purpose of Sexual Exploitation, adopted by the Committee of Ministers on 19.5.2000, at the 710th meeting of the Ministers' Deputies

European Union

EU treaties

Convention Applying the Schengen Agreement of 14 June 1985 between the Governments of the States of the Benelux Economic Union, the Federal Republic of Germany and the French Republic, on the Gradual Abolition of Checks at Their Common Borders, signed on 19 June 1990, in force since March 1995 (the Schengen Convention)

Convention Drawn Up on the Basis of Article K.3 of the Treaty on European Union, on Simplified Extradition Procedure between the Member States of the European Union, OJ C 078, 30.3.1995, p. 2

Convention Based on Article K.3 of the Treaty on European Union, on the Establishment of a European Police Office (Europol Convention), OJ C 316, 27.11.1995, p. 2

Convention Drawn Up on the Basis of Article K.3 of the Treaty on European Union, Relating to Extradition Between the Member States of the European Union – Joint Declaration on the right of asylum – Declaration by Denmark, Finland and Sweden concerning Article 7 of this Convention – Declaration on the concept of 'nationals' – Declaration by Greece regarding Article 5 – Declaration by Portugal on extradition requested for an offence punishable by a life sentence or detention order – Council declaration on the follow up to the Convention, OJ C 313, 23.10.1996, p. 12

Convention on Simplified Extradition Procedure between the Member States of the European Union, Explanatory Report, OJ C 375, 12.12.1996, p. 4

Convention Relating to Extradition between the Member States of the European Union, Explanatory Report, OJ C 191, 23.6.1997, p. 13

Council Act of 29 May 2000 Establishing in Accordance With Article 34 of the Treaty on European Union the Convention on Mutual Assistance in Criminal Matters between the Member States of the European Union, OJ C 197, 12.7.2000, p. 1

Single European Act, signed on 28 February 1986 and in force since 1 July 1987, OJ L 169, 29.6.1987, p. 1

Treaty establishing the European Union, signed in Maastricht on 7 February 1992 and in force since 1 November 1993, OJ C 224, 31.8.1992, p. 1

Treaty of Amsterdam amending the Treaty on European Union, the Treaties establishing the European Communities and certain related acts, signed in Amsterdam on 2 October 1997 and in force since 1 May 1999, OJ C 340, 10.11.1997, p. 1

Treaty of Nice amending the Treaty on European Union, the Treaties establishing the European Communities and certain related acts, signed in Nice on 26 February 2001 and in force since 1 February 2003, OJ C 80, 10.3.2001, p. 1

Framework decisions

2001/220/JHA: Council Framework Decision of 15 March 2001 on the Standing of Victims in Criminal Proceedings, OJ L 82, 22.3.2001, p. 1

Council Framework Decision of 13 June 2002 on Combating Terrorism, OJ L 164, 22.6.2002, p. 3

2002/584/JHA: Council Framework Decision of 13 June 2002 on the European Arrest Warrant and the Surrender Procedures between Member States – Statements Made by Certain Member States on the Adoption of the Framework Decision, OJ L 190, 18.7.2002, p. 1

2002/629/JHA: Council Framework Decision of 19 July 2002 on Combating Trafficking in Human Beings, OJ L 203, 1.8.2002, p. 1

Joint actions

96/277/JHA: Joint Action of 22 April 1996 Adopted by the Council on the Basis of Article K.3 of the Treaty on European Union, Concerning a Framework for the Exchange of Liaison Magistrates to Improve Judicial Cooperation Between the Member States of the European Union, OJ L 105, 27.4.1996, p. 1

96/700/JHA: Joint Action of 29 November 1996 Adopted by the Council on the Basis of Article K.3 of the Treaty on European Union, Establishing an Incentive and Exchange Programme for Persons Responsible for Combating Trade in Human Beings and the Sexual Exploitation of Children, OJ L 322, 12.12.1996, p. 7

96/748/JHA: Joint Action of 16 December 1996 Adopted by the Council on the Basis of Article K.3 of the Treaty on European Union Extending the Mandate Given to the Europol Drugs Unit, OJ L 342, 31.12.1996, p. 4

97/154/JHA: Joint Action of 24 February 1997 Adopted by the Council on the Basis of Article K.3 of the Treaty on European Union Concerning Action to Combat Trafficking in Human Beings and Sexual Exploitation of Children, OJ L 063, 4.3.1997, p. 2

97/827/JHA: Joint Action of 5 December 1997 Adopted by the Council on the Basis of Article K.3 of the Treaty on European Union, Establishing a Mechanism for Evaluating the Application and Implementation at National Level of International Undertakings in the Fight against Organized Crime, OJ L 344, 15.12.1997, p. 7

98/245/JHA: Joint Action of 19 March 1998 Adopted by the Council, on the Basis of Article K.3 of the Treaty on European Union, Establishing a Programme of Exchanges, Training and Cooperation for Persons Responsible for Action to Combat Organised Crime (Falcone programme), OJ L 99, 31.3.1998, p. 8

98/427/JHA: Joint Action of 29 June 1998 Adopted by the Council on the Basis of Article K.3 of the Treaty on European Union, on Good Practice in Mutual Legal Assistance in Criminal Matters, OJ L 191, 7.7.1998, p. 1

98/428/JHA: Joint Action of 29 June 1998 Adopted by the Council on the Basis of Article K.3 of the Treaty on European Union, on the Creation of a European Judicial Network, OJ L 191, 7.7.1998, p. 4

98/733/JHA: Joint Action of 21 December 1998 Adopted by the Council on the Basis of Article K.3 of the Treaty on European Union, on Making it a Criminal Offence to Participate in a Criminal Organisation in the Member States of the European Union, OJ L 351, 29.12.1998, p. 1

Decisions

Decision of the Council of the European Union of 17 March 1999 Concerning the Responsibilities of Council Bodies in the Field of Justice and Home Affairs Following Entry Into Force of the Treaty of Amsterdam, Brussels, 6166/2/99 CK 4 12 REV 2

1999/435/EC: Council Decision of 20 May 1999 Concerning the Definition of the Schengen Acquis for the Purpose of Determining, in Conformity with the Relevant Provisions of the Treaty Establishing the European Community and the Treaty on European Union, the Legal Basis for Each of the Provisions or Decisions which Constitute the Acquis, OJ L 176, 10.7.1999, p. 1

1999/436/EC: Council Decision of 20 May 1999 Determining, in Conformity with the Relevant Provisions of the Treaty Establishing the European Community and the Treaty on European Union, the Legal Basis for Each of the Provisions or Decisions which Constitute the Schengen Acquis, OJ L 176, 10.7.1999, p. 17

2000/293/EC: Decision of the European Parliament and of the Council of 24 January 2000 Adopting a Programme of Community Action (the Daphne programme) (2000 to 2003) on Preventive Measures to Fight Violence against Children, Young Persons and Women, OJ L 034, 9.2.2000, p. 1

The Schengen Acquis as referred to in Article 1(2) of Council Decision 1999/435/EC of 20 May 1999, OJ L 239, 22.9.2000, p. 1

2002/187/JHA: Council Decision of 28 February 2002 Setting Up Eurojust with a View to Reinforcing the Fight against Serious Crime, OJ L 063, 6.3.2002, p. 1

Other EU documents

Documents of the European Commission
COM/96/567 final, Communication from the Commission to the Council and the European Parliament on Trafficking in Women for the Purpose of Sexual Exploitation, 20.11.1996

COM/98/0726 final, Communication from the Commission to the Council and the European Parliament – For Further Actions in the Fight against Trafficking in Women, 9.12.1998

COM/2000/854 final/2, Communication from the Commission to the Council and the European Parliament Combating Trafficking in Human Beings and Combating the Sexual Exploitation of Children and Child Pornography, 21.12.2000

COM/2000/854 final/2 – CNS/2001/0025, Proposal for a Council Framework Decision on Combating the Sexual Exploitation of Children and Child Pornography, 21.12.2000

COM/2000/854 final/2 – CNS/2001/0024, Proposal for a Council Framework Decision on Combating Trafficking in Human Beings, 21.12.2000

COM/2001/715 final, Green Paper on Criminal-Law Protection of the Financial Interests of the Community and the Establishment of a European Prosecutor, 11.12.2001

COM/2003/54 final – COD 2003/0025, Proposal for a Decision of the European Parliament and of the Council Establishing a Second Phase of a Programme of Community Action (2004-2008) to Prevent Violence against Children, Young People and Women and to Protect Victims and Groups At-Risk (the Daphne II programme), 4.2.2002

COM/2002/71 final – CNS 2002/0043, Proposal for a Council Directive on the Short-Term Residence Permit Issued to Victims of Action to Facilitate Illegal Immigration or Trafficking in Human Beings Who Cooperate with the Competent Authorities, 11.2.2002, OJ C 126 E, 28.5.2002, p. 393

COM/2002/247 final, Communication from the Commission – A Project for the European Union, 22.5.2002

COM/2002/728 final/2, For the European Union: Peace, Freedom, Solidarity – Communication of the Commission on the Institutional Architecture, 4.12.2002

COM/2003/075 final, Green Paper from the Commission – Procedural Safeguards for Suspects and Defendants in Criminal Proceedings Throughout the European Union, 19.2.2003

COM/2003/323 final, Communication from the Commission to the European Parliament and the Council in view of the European Council of Thessaloniki, on the Development of a Common Policy on Illegal Immigration, Smuggling and Trafficking of Human Beings, External Borders and the Return of Illegal Residents, 3.6.2003

Commission Decision of 25 March 2003, Setting Up a Consultative Group, to be known as the 'Experts Group on Trafficking in Human Beings', OJ L 79, 26.3.2003

Documents of the European Parliament

Resolution on Violence against Women, OJ C 176, 14.7.1986, p. 73

Resolution on the Exploitation of Prostitution and the Traffic in Human Beings, OJ C 120, 16.5.1989, p. 352

Resolution on Trade in Women, OJ C 268, 4.10.1993, p. 141

Resolution on Trafficking in Human Beings, OJ C 032, 5.2.1996, p. 88

Resolution on the Need to Establish a European Union Wide Campaign for Zero Tolerance of Violence against Women, OJ C 304, 6.10.1997, p. 55

Documents of the European Convention

Final Report of the Working group X 'Freedom, Security and Justice', Brussels, 2.12.2002, CONV 426/02

Feasibility Study, Contribution to a Preliminary Draft, Constitution of the European Union, Working Document Under the Responsibility of F. Lamoureux, European Commission, 4.12.2002

Draft of Articles 1 to 16 of the Constitutional Treaty, Brussels, 6.2.2003, CONV 528/03

Draft of Articles 24 to 33 of the Constitutional Treaty, Brussels, 26.2.2003, CONV 571/03

Area of Freedom, Security and Justice, Draft Article 31 (Part One) and Draft Articles from Part Two, Brussels, 14 March 2003, CONV 614/03

Union Finances: draft Articles 38 to 40, Brussels, 14.3.2003, CONV 602/03

Draft Constitution, Volume II, Brussels, 27 June 2003, CONV 836/03

Draft Treaty establishing a Constitution for Europe, Brussels, 27 June 2003, CONV 820/1/03 REV 1

Draft Treaty establishing a Constitution for Europe, Brussels, 30 June 2003, CONV 820/2/03 REV 2

Documents of the Council of the EU

Council Act of 10 March 1995 Drawing Up the Convention on Simplified Extradition Procedure between the Member States of the European Union, OJ C 078, 30.3.1995, p. 1

Council Act of 27 September 1996 Drawing Up the Convention Relating to Extradition Between the Member States of the European Union, OJ C 313, 23.10.1996, p. 11

The Hague Ministerial Declaration on European Guidelines for Effective Measures to Prevent and Combat Trafficking in Women for the Purpose of Sexual Exploitation, The Hague, 26 April 1997

Action plan to Combat Organized Crime (Adopted by the Council on 28 April 1997), OJ C 251, 15.8.1997, p. 1

Pre-Accession Pact on Organised Crime between the Member States of the European Union and the Applicant Countries of Central and Eastern Europe and Cyprus (Text approved by the JHA Council on 28 May 1998), OJ C 220, 15.7.1998, p. 1

Action Plan of the Council and the Commission on How Best to Implement the Provisions of the Treaty of Amsterdam on an Area of Freedom, Security and Justice – Text Adopted by the Justice and Home Affairs Council of 3 December 1998, OJ C 019, 23.1.1999, p. 1

The Prevention and Control of Organised Crime: a European Union Strategy for the Beginning of the New Millennium, OJ C 124, 3.5.2000, p. 1

Initiative of the Federal Republic of Germany with a View to the Adoption of a Council Decision Setting Up a Eurojust Team, OJ C 206, 19.7.2000, p. 1

Proposal for a Comprehensive Plan to Combat Illegal Immigration and Trafficking of Human Beings in the European Union, OJ C 142, 14.6.2002, p. 23

Implementation of Action Plan to Combat Organized Crime, 29 September 1998, 11537/98 crimorg 139

Evaluation Report on Luxembourg on Mutual Legal Assistance and Urgent Requests for the Tracing and Restraint of Property, 15 February 1999, 5932/99 crimorg 21

Evaluation Report on Ireland on Mutual Legal Assistance and Urgent Requests for the Tracing and Restraint of Property, 18 August 1999, 9079/99 crimorg 70

Evaluation Report on The Netherlands on Mutual Legal Assistance and Urgent Requests for the Tracing and Restraint of Property, 18 August 1999, 10595/99 crimorg 124

Evaluation Report on Greece on Mutual Legal Assistance and Urgent Requests for the Tracing and Restraint of Property, 23 August 1999, 10596/99 crimorg 125

Evaluation Report on Denmark on Mutual Legal Assistance and Urgent Requests for the Tracing and Restraint of Property, 9 September 1999, 10860/99 crimorg 128

Evaluation Report on Spain on Mutual Legal Assistance and Urgent Requests for the Tracing and Restraint of Property, 22 March 2000, 5819/00 crimorg 16

Evaluation Report on Italy on Mutual Legal Assistance and Urgent Requests for the Tracing and Restraint of Property, 22 March 2000, 7254/00 crimorg 52

Evaluation Report on Belgium on Mutual Legal Assistance and Urgent Requests for the Tracing and Restraint of Property, 16 May 2000, 7704/00 crimorg 60

Evaluation Report on Finland on Mutual Legal Assistance and Urgent Requests for the Tracing and Restraint of Property, 7 July 2000, 9392/00 crimorg 94

Evaluation Report on France on Mutual Legal Assistance and Urgent Requests for the Tracing and Restraint of Property, 10 October 2000, 12000/00 crimorg 131

Evaluation Report on Germany on Mutual Legal Assistance and Urgent Requests for the Tracing and Restraint of Property, 11 December 2000, 13365/00 crimorg 153

Evaluation Report on Austria on Mutual Legal Assistance and Urgent Requests for the Tracing and Restraint of Property, 22 December 2000, 14911/00 crimorg 170

Evaluation Report on United Kingdom on Mutual Legal Assistance and Urgent Requests for the Tracing and Restraint of Property, 26 March 2001, 7249/01 crimorg 31

Evaluation Report on Sweden on Mutual Legal Assistance and Urgent Requests for the Tracing and Restraint of Property, 27 March 2001, 7250/01 crimorg 32

Evaluation Report on Portugal on Mutual Legal Assistance and Urgent Requests for the Tracing and Restraint of Property, 2 April 2001, 7251/01 crimorg 33

Final Report on the First Evaluation Exercise – Mutual Legal Assistance in Criminal Matters, OJ C 216, 1.8.2001, p. 14

Good Practices on Mutual Legal Assistance in Criminal Cases. Statements of the Member States of the EU, February 2000, SN 1371/00

Request for Mutual Legal Assistance in Criminal Matters, Brussels, 23 February 2001, 5873/01

Documents of the European Council
Presidency Conclusions, Tampere European Council 15 and 16 October 1999, SI (1999) 800

Documents of the Organization for Security and Cooperation in Europe

Conference for Security and Cooperation in Europe, Third Conference on the Human Dimension of the OSCE, Moscow, 10 September – 15 October 1991

Stockholm Declaration Adopted by the OSCE Parliamentary Assembly, Towards a Common and Comprehensive Security Model for Europe in the Twenty-first Century, 9 July 1996

Conference for Security and Co-operation in Europe, Seventh Meeting of the Ministerial Council, Oslo Ministerial Declaration, December 1998

OSCE-ODIHR, Proposed Action Plan 2000 for Activities to Combat Trafficking in Human Beings, Warsaw, November 1999

OSCE, Supplementary Human Dimension Meeting on Trafficking in Human Beings, Final Report, Vienna, 19 June 2000

Cases

ICJ

Jurisdiction of the Courts of Danzig case, Advisory Opinion PCIJ, Series B no. 15

Case concerning the Barcelona Traction, Light and Power Company, Limited, Preliminary objections and Second phase (1962-1970)

Case concerning *Belgium* v. *Congo*, 14 February 2002

European Court of Justice

Case 26/62, Judgement of 5.2.1963, *Van Gend en Loos / Administratie der Belastingen*, Jur. 1963, p. 3

C-268/99, Judgement of 20.11.2001, *Jany and others*, Jur. 2001, p. I-8615

International tribunals

Judgement of the Women's International War Crimes Tribunal 2000 for the Trial of Japanese Military Sexual Slavery in the matter of the *Prosecutors and the Peoples of the Asia-Pacific Region* v. *Emperor Hirohito et al. and the Government of Japan*, 4 December 2001

United States

Judgement of the Supreme Court, *United States* v. *Shackney*, 333 F.2d 475 (2nd Cir. 1981)

Judgement of the Supreme Court, *United States* v. *Mussry*, 726 F.2d 1448, 1453 (9th Cir. 1984)

Judgement of the Supreme Court, *United States* v. *Kozminski*, 821 F.2d 1186/1192 (6th Cir. 1987)

United Kingdom

UK House of Lords: *Regina* v. *Bartle and the Commissioner of Police for the Metropolis and Others, Ex Parte Pinochet*, 25 November 1998

Germany

Federal Constitutional Court of Germany, 18 June 1997, GER-1997-2-009 in the Codices database

The Netherlands

Dutch Supreme Court, Bouterse case, 18 September 2001, no. 749/01

Belgium

Court of Appeal, Sharon case, Brussels, 26 June 2002, Following a Complaint Filed against Sharon for Massacres in the Refuge Camps Subra and Shatila in 1982

Other documents

Europol Documents

Europol Report on Albanian Prostitution Networks, The Hague, 18 April 2000, not published

Europol 1999 General Situation Report on Trafficking in Human Beings, Open Version, Europol, December 2000, File no: 2565-35rev1

Nordic Agreements Documents

Agreement on Cooperation Between the Nordic Prosecution Services of 6 February 1970

Nordic Agreement of 26 April 1974 between Finland, Iceland, Norway, Sweden and Denmark

IOM Documents

International Organisation for Migration, *Trafficking in Women to Italy for Sexual Exploitation*, 1996

International Organisation for Migration, Trafficking of Women to the European Union: Characteristics, Trends and Policy Issues. Conference paper submitted by the IOM at the Conference on Trafficking in Women for Sexual Exploitation, Vienna, June 1996

International Organisation for Migration, 'Statement by Mr. Marco Gramegna, Preparatory meeting on Trafficking in Women', Brussels, 1-2 December 1995

Miscellaneous Documents

Penn State report 1992, 'Convention on the Elimination of All Forms of Sexual Exploitation of Women' presented by UNESCO and the 'Coalition against Trafficking in Women', which rejects the distinctions between 'free' and 'forced' prostitution

Memorie van Toelichting bij het op 10 december 1984 te New York tot stand gekomen Verdrag tegen foltering en andere wrede, onmenselijke of onterende behandeling of bestraffing, *Kamerstukken II*, 1985-1986, 19 617 (R1312), no. 3, pp. 6-8, 15-16. [Parliamentary documents on the memorandum of understanding to the Torture Convention]

'Rouvoet Motion'. Wijziging van het Wetboek van Strafvordering in verband met de regeling van enige bijzondere bevoegdheden tot opsporing en wijziging van enige andere bevoegdheden (bijzondere opsporingsbevoegdheden), *Kamerstukken II*, 1998-1999, 25403, no. 30. [Parliamentary documents on special investigative powers]

College van Procureurs-Generaal, Aanwijzing aanpak mensenhandel en andere vormen van uitbuiting in de prostitutie, Staatscourant 28 September 2000, no. 188, in force since 1 October 2000, [Directive of the Board of Prosecutors General on the strategy in trafficking in persons cases]

College van Procureurs-Generaal, Aanwijzing bejegening slachtoffers van zedendelicten, Staatscourant, 2 April 2001, no. 64, in force since 1 April 2001, [Directive of the Board of Prosecutors General on the treatment of victims of indecent offences]

Regels met betrekking tot ernstige schendingen van het internationaal humanitair recht (Wet internationale misdrijven), *Kamerstukken II*, 2001/2002, 28 337, no. 3. [Parliamentary documents on the memorandum of understanding to the International Crimes Act]

Wetsontwerp tot wijziging van de wet van 16 juni 1993 betreffende de bestraffing van ernstige schendingen van het internationaal humanitair recht en van artikel 144*ter* van het Gerechtelijk Wetboek, DOC 50 2265/010, April 2003 [Proposal to amend the Belgian Act on international humanitarian law]

INDEX

A

abolitionism, 56
abolitionist, 61, 67
appeal(s), 176, 186, 203, 222, 235,
applicant countries, 196, 197, 211, 248, 251, 260
arranged marriages, 58,
Article 197a, 217
assets, 234, 235
aut dedere aut judicare, 139

B

B9 procedure, 205, 207, 227, 228, 231, 255
binding effect, 151,
binding force, 157, 249

C

COREPER, 109
categorisation, 26-43
centralization, 50,
child abuse, 38
coercion, 53-55, 57, 59-64, 66, 67, 69-73, 78, 87, 89, 250
coercive measures, 119
Cold War, 2
common positions, 109, 110, 155, 156,
Communautarisation, 246, 267, 269, 270
communication, 168, 169, 208, 226
communication techniques, 2, 6
community, 29
competences, 189, 269, 279
complex crimes, 4, 5
complexity, 50
computer developments, 2
concurrent jurisdiction, 49, 209, 246
confidence, 11, 14, 95, 96, 167, 207, 212, 244, 248, 249, 264, 277
confidentiality, 167, 168, 199
consent(s), 19, 20, 55, 57, 61, 63, 66, 67, 70, 72, 73, 124, 258
convention(s), 109, 110, 155-158, 160, 266
Convention for the Suppression of the Traffic in Persons and of the Exploitation of the Prostitution of Others, 55, 56
Convention on Laundering, Search, Seizure and Confiscation of the Proceeds from Crime, 144-146
Convention on the Elimination of All Forms of Discrimination against Woman (CEDAW), 56, 58, 65
Convention on the Transfer of Sentenced Persons, 142-144, 158
cooperation, 7, 10-17, 20, 24, 25, 35, 41, 48-51, 82, 88, 89, 91-97, 99, 101-104, 106, 107, 110, 111, 116, 124, 130, 136-138, 151-152, 162-164, 170, 197-199, 201-212, 209, 210, 212, 224, 227, 232, 233, 234, 240, 241, 244, 245, 248, 250, 251, 253, 254, 258, 260-263, 265, 267-270, 275-278
  international, 11, 34,
  intensified, 5, 7, 9, 10, 20, 271, 276
  police, 112
  police and judicial, 35, 107-109, 111, 117, 121, 122, 133-135, 151, 245, 246, 249, 265, 266, 268, 269, 279
Corpus Juris, 108, 118-120, 263, 264
corruption, 82, 83
Council of Europe, 91, 100-102, 107, 122, 138-151, 157, 158, 160, 161, 164, 197, 198, 253, 254, 274
criminal(s), 1, 3, 4, 10
criminal group(s), 3, 228
criminal law, 9, 10, 12, 15, 16, 19-21,
criminal organisation(s), 1, 4, 10, 46, 82, 84-86, 223, 229, 232, 237
criminal procedure, 258
criminal networks, 97, 103
criteria, 49

D

data, 53, 79, 102
debt bondage, 59, 62, 63, 75, 76, 87,
deception, 59, 62, 63, 66, 87
decisions, 110, 155, 157, 160, 266-268
de lege lata, 28
definition, 7, 16, 27, 53, 57-66, 68, 70, 72, 83-89, 93, 94, 210, 250, 273
desirability, 258-266, 278, 279
development(s), 136-138
development aid, 15
dichotomy, 20, 24, 45, 249, 269, 270, 279
direct communication, 129, 142, 162, 168, 176, 177-179, 190, 197, 198, 208, 218, 219, 225, 231, 234, 239, 250-252, 276
direct effect, 106, 110, 123, 155, 158, 268, 275
disparity(ies), 1, 7, 8, 12, 243, 249, 254, 257, 273, 276, 277
double criminality, 15, 25, 39, 126, 128, 133, 135, 137, 138, 141, 143, 145, 147, 149, 166, 172,

174, 175, 215, 216, 236, 240, 244, 249, 258, 276
Draft Constitution, 121, 122, 262, 263, 267, 268
dual track, 270, 279

E

economic coercion, 62
effects doctrine, 37
e-mail, 168, 189, 192, 221, 225, 261
emancipation, 61
empirical research, 201
empirical study, 202, 211, 213, 214, 239, 240, 275, 276
empowerment, 61
enforceability, 22, 24, 48, 49, 154
enforceable, 156
enforcement, 31-36, 42, 48-52, 56, 159, 199
enlargement, 171, 256, 260, 263
enslavement, 77, 93
equality, 9, 22, 31, 33, 34, 36
EU level, 51, 262- 269, 270
EU Convention on Mutual Assistance, 17, 130-133, 137, 138, 142, 162, 165, 168, 172, 244, 258, 260, 261, 277
EU Conventions on Extradition, 277
EU Convention on Simplified Extradition Procedure, 124-126, 137, 258-260
EU Convention Relating to Extradition, 126-128
EU Council Framework Decision on Combating Trafficking in Human Beings, 54
Eurojust, 14, 17, 108, 114-116, 121, 122, 262-267, 269, 270, 279
European Agreement on Travel by Young Persons on Collective Passports 148, 149, 161
European Arrest Warrant, 17, 128-130, 137, 166, 244, 258-260, 277
European Constitution, 267
European Convention(s), 108, 118, 245, 249, 262, 263, 267, 269,
European Convention on Extradition 138-140, 244
European Convention on Mutual Assistance in Criminal Matters, 140-142
European Convention on the International Validity of Criminal Judgments, 149-151
European Convention on the Transfer of Proceedings in Criminal Matters, 146-148
European Court of Justice (ECJ), 108, 112, 116, 117, 159, 160, 265, 268, 279
European Judicial Network (EJN), 99, 114, 116, 169, 176, 179-181, 193, 195, 197, 218, 219, 221, 252, 261
European legal order, 265, 270, 279
European Public Prosecutor (EPP), 14, 17, 108, 118-122, 137, 152, 244, 262-265, 270, 277-279
Europol, 14, 93, 97, 108, 113-116, 118, 121, 162, 218, 219, 263, 265, 267, 269, 279
Europol Convention, 113
evaluation report(s), 153, 164, 171, 172, 176, 180, 187, 199, 203, 212, 214, 218, 224, 251, 252
evidence, 5, 165, 187, 207, 230, 265
exploitation, 54-61, 63-70, 72, 73, 75, 77, 79, 85, 86, 88, 89, 93, 94, 97, 98, 274,
expulsion, 16, 94, 204, 206, 207, 255
extradite, 33
extradition, 5, 13, 15, 17, 25, 35, 43, 48, 92, 111, 124-130, 134, 135, 137-140, 233, 244, 248, 259, 277
Extradition Procedure, 17
Extraterritorial jurisdiction, 36

F

feasibility, 262, 266-269, 278, 279
file study, 202, 203, 214-236, 243, 252, 259
first pillar, 108, 111, 135, 160, 266
force, 72, 210
forced labour, 53, 58-60, 66, 67, 76, 78, 86, 87
forced marriage, 76
formalities, 185, 186, 209, 221, 222, 239, 251, 265
forum regit actum, 164
Framework Decision on
Combating Trafficking in Human Beings, 54, 63, 65, 68, 99, 107, 122, 123, 250, 256, 257, 277
framework decisions, 110, 155, 157, 160, 245, 247, 266, 267
fraud, 118-120

G

GAATW, 59, 60, 62, 65, 74, 86, 87
global sociality, 252, 253, 262, 278
globalisation, 1-9, 46, 82, 246, 273
guidelines, 97, 106, 184, 185, 210, 214

H

harmonisation, 10, 68, 110, 111, 121, 176, 245, 249, 265, 270, 279
human rights, 25, 27

I

ICJ, 160
ILO, 76
IOM, 66-71, 81, 104
identity, 9
illegal immigrants, 256, 257
illegal immigration, 136, 255-257
immigrants, 15, 16
immigration, 72, 95, 98, 109
immigration law, 93, 95, 103, 135

immigration officers, 255, 257, 275, 277
immigration police, 204, 207, 212, 227, 228, 239
immunity, 33, 34
improvement, 201, 257, 270
indictment, 210, 211, 236, 237, 275
institutional framework, 107-122
instructions, 184, 185, 214
instruments, 48, 52
intent, 63, 84
intention, 59, 63
interception, 132, 133, 145,172, 264
Intergovernmental Conference, 245, 277
Intergovernmental organisation, 2
international community, 27, 28, 39, 42, 43, 45, 247
International cooperation, 144-146
International crimes, 21, 23, 25-34, 42, 43, 45, 49
International Criminal Court, 24, 27, 34, 39, 43, 44, 77, 93
International criminal law, 11, 16, 19-52,
international law, 19-21
international level, 49, 51
international organisations, 2
internationalisation, 5, 13, 14, 19, 34, 47, 273
Internet, 4
Interpol, 97, 132, 146, 147, 150-151, 162, 180, 218, 219, 225
interpreter(s), 226, 231, 236
interviews, 17, 202-212, 221, 225, 228, 236-238, 239
intimidation, 83
inventions, 2
investigation, 4
Iron Curtain, 2, 3

J

Jany case, 211
joint actions, 109, 155
joint investigation teams, 131, 137, 142, 260
judicial cooperation, 111, 116, 263
jurisdiction, 4, 5, 11, 13, 19, 21, 33, 34, 36-43, 45, 56, 57, 116, 117, 120, 123, 127, 146, 147, 156, 244, 246-248, 264, 268
jus cogens, 24, 43, 74, 79

L

language problems, 170, 189-190, 198, 199, 225, 226, 230, 250, 253, 275
language, 93, 207, 209
legal basis, 154-159
legal framework, 92
legal instruments *see also* instruments 12-14, 16, 17, 48, 90, 91, 107-154, 198, 199, 201, 249, 262, 275, 277
legally binding, 106, 107, 110, 123
legitimisation, 270, 276
liaison officers, 100, 115, 134, 180, 208, 210, 217-219, 224, 229, 252, 261
look-alikes, 212, 228, 233
locus delicti, 36, 37, 139, 147
locus regit actum, 164-166, 199
lover-boy, 230

M

matrix, 193, 194, 199
migration, 68, 71, 72, 103
migration law, 15, 16, 73, 74, 243, 254-257, 273, 277
minors, 54, 87, 94, 98,
miscommunication, 190, 225
modus operandi, 94, 102
morally binding, 154, 158, 159
Moscow mechanism, 161
mutual (legal) assistance, 5, 13, 15, 35, 38, 48, 92, 96, 99, 102, 112, 128, 134, 135, 153, 162-164, 166, 170-199, 220, 224, 237-241, 250-254, 260, 261, 275-277
mutual recognition, 95, 97, 120, 121, 128, 246, 248, 258, 264-266, 268

N

nation state(s) *see also* nation, 3, 8, 9, 50, 266, 269, 276
nation(s), 4, 10
national law, 21
national level, 10, 11, 14, 17, 20, 49, 51, 258-262
national competences, 1
natural law, 26
new initiatives, 14
non-national level, 10, 46, 273
non-national approach, 48

O

obstacle(s), 13, 14, 17, 88, 93, 107, 152, 153, 164-199, 204, 210, 212, 257, 263, 274
ODIHR, 103-105, 159,
old boys network, 180, 199, 252
organisational problems, 164, 170, 186, 197, 199, 202, 212, 224-227, 250, 275
organised crime, 13, 46, 47, 54, 81-86, 97, 114, 115, 163
organised crime group(s), 46, 49, 69, 84, 85, 87
OSCE, 91, 102-106, 158, 159, 161, 162, 198, 275
ownership, 59,

P

penalties, 214, 222-224
personal details, 189, 199, 275

Pinochet, 33, 34
policies, 92, 153, 198,
policy documents, 12-14, 16, 17, 91, 92-107, 151, 153, 154, 198, 249, 277
political organisation, 2
politically binding, 154, 156, 158, 159
positivism, 26
positivist, 24
poverty, 6, 15, 62, 94, 95, 103, 123, 273
praesidium 121
primary problems 204-209
principle(s), 15, 19, 92
  active nationality, 36, 38, 39, 42
  aut dedere aut judicare *see also,* aut dedere aut judicare, 34, 48
  confidentiality *see also* confidentiality, 167
  current, 14, 15, 17
  double criminality, 166, 277
  extraterritoriality, 38, 41, 196
  forum regit actum *see also* forum regit actum 121, 132, 169, 173, 244, 264, 264
  immunity, 32
  jurisdiction *see also* jurisdiction, 36-41
  locus regit actum, *see also* locus regit actum 120, 169, 172, 264
  ne bis in idem, 39, 129, 134, 139, 145, 148, 151
  objective territoriality, 37
  passive, nationality 36
  proportionality, 120
  protective, 36, 39,
  rule of speciality, 277
  speciality, 125, 127, 129, 137, 139, 150
  subjective territoriality, 37
  subsidiarity, 119, 120, 269
  territoriality *see also* territoriality, 36-39, 41, 123, 146, 244, 246-248
  universal jurisdiction, 40, 246-248
  universality, 15, 36, 39-41, 48
privacy, 26
problems, 162, 204-212,
procedural, 25, 153
procedural criminal law, 10, 42, 245,
procedural law, 268, 279
procedural problems, 164, 168-170, 176-186, 197, 199, 202, 212, 218-224, 250, 275
profits, 93, 101, 102
proposal for a Council Directive on the Short-Term Residence Permit, 74, 135, 136, 256, 257, 277
prostitution, 16, 53-60, 64-67, 71, 76, 79-81, 87, 93, 101, 103, 105, 158, 206, 210, 211, 229, 230, 250, 261
protection, 9, 10, 64
purpose, 61, 63, 66
pursuit, 134, 135

R

rapporteur, 56, 68, 97, 203
ratification(s), 163, 164, 199, 278
recommendation(s), 58, 65, 94, 98, 101, 102, 104-106, 158, 193-196, 257, 261
recruitment, 55-61, 66, 68-70, 75, 79, 85, 86, 88, 89, 210, 212, 232, 241, 274
regional jurisdiction, 246-249, 265, 277
regional level, 51
regional universality, 123
relationship, 230, 231
reliability, 208, 212, 228, 229
research question, 1, 7-13
reservations 163, 164, 199,
residence permit(s), 73, 74, 101, 104, 136, 205, 206, 217, 227, 255, 257
residence status, 94, 95, 97, 107,
resolutions, 92
resources, 170, 176, 181-183, 184, 192, 193, 198, 199, 219, 220, 241, 250, 252, 253, 262, 275, 277, 278
Rouvoet Motion, 211
rule of speciality, 244
Rwanda Tribunal, 27, 43, 44

S

safeguard(s), 95, 96, 129, 130, 167, 256, 265
Schengen acquis, 108, 110-113
Schengen Agreement, 111, 112
Schengen Convention, 111, 112, 130, 133-135, 142, 162, 177-179,
Schengen Protocol, 112
scope, 53, 79-81, 88
search, 191, 215, 235
secondary problems, 204, 209, 210
second pillar, 108
security, 103, 117, 133, 145
Security Council, 22, 23
seizure, 191, 215, 234-235
self-determination, 57, 58, 61, 62
self-executing, 158
self-executory, 156
serfdom, 75, 76
Serious Crimes Departments, 238, 253
servitude, 66, 69, 76, 78
sex industry, 64, 80
sex market, 6
Single European Act, 108, 109
slave trade, 75, 76, 79
slavery, 7, 16, 26, 54, 56, 66, 67, 69, 70, 74-79, 89
slavery-like practices, 7, 16, 54, 59, 60, 67, 74-79, 86, 89

smuggling, 54, 66, 71-74, 89, 95, 211, 222, 223, 257
socio-economic relations, 1-3
solutions, 14, 49, 50, 276
source countries, 80
sovereign power(s), 9, 10, 20, 49, 52, 249, 265, 270, 271, 279
sovereignty, 9, 20, 31, 32, 34-36, 41, 44, 89, 107, 140, 145, 244-246, 249, 258, 266, 270, 271, 276, 277
speciality rule, 15
standardised form(s), 195, 221
state-report, 78
state sovereignty *see also* sovereignty, 8-11, 17, 20, 118
stricto sensu, 44, 154, 158, 159, 198
substantive, 25, 27, 279
substantive law, 258, 268
substantive criminal law, 10, 42, 245, 249
substantive problems, 164-168, 172-176, 197, 199, 202, 212, 215-217, 275
supranational, 23, 44
supranational level, 11
surveillance, 134, 135

T
technological improvements, 4
technological inventions, 4
telephone conference, 131, 137, 142, 175
telephone taps, 216, 228, 232
territory, 9, 20, 32, 39, 41, 42, 49, 119, 129, 139, 206, 210, 258, 270, 279
territoriality, 20
third pillar, 12, 13, 107-111, 116, 117, 122, 135, 154, 155-157, 159, 160, 249, 266-269
time-consuming, 14
Trafficking Protocol, 53, 63, 65, 66, 67, 69, 123, 136, 250, 254
transactions, 2
transition, 3, 6
transnational, 1, 10, 29, 47, 48, 69, 83, 85, 86, 122, 213, 214
transnational crime, 5, 7, 16, 19-53, 87-89, 99, 118, 122, 198, 238, 240, 241, 243-249, 264, 270, 273, 279
transport, 55, 57-61, 63, 65, 68, 70, 73, 75, 86, 88, 89, 241, 274,
transportation, 2, 6, 57, 59, 66, 69, 79
Treaty of Amsterdam, 109, 111, 154-157
Treaty of Maastricht, 108, 109
trends, 79-81, 89,
TREVI (group), 113
tribunals, 21

U
ubiquity, 37
undercover, 131
unemployment, 3, 6, 95, 103, 123, 273
universal jurisdiction, 40
United Nations, 2, 23
United Nations Convention on Transnational Organised Crime (UNCTOC), 47, 53
universal jurisdiction, 30
urgent, 176, 216

V
values, 24
victim(s), 16, 58, 62, 66, 67, 72-74, 80, 81, 88, 92-95, 97, 101, 102, 105, 123, 136, 204, 206, 207, 210-213, 222, 223, 226-231, 233, 239, 243, 249, 252-257, 273, 275, 277, 278
victim protection, 99, 103, 104, 106, 256
video conference, 131, 132, 137, 142, 175, 260, 261
Vienna mechanism, 161
violence, 59, 62, 77, 80, 82, 83, 87, 98, 102, 230, 232
Voodoo, 216, 230

W
witness protection, 93, 107, 275
witness protection programmes, 231
working conditions, 60, 63, 64, 80, 87
world community, 45

Y
Yugoslavia Tribunal, 27, 43, 44, 77

GPSR Compliance
The European Union's (EU) General Product Safety Regulation (GPSR) is a set of rules that requires consumer products to be safe and our obligations to ensure this.

If you have any concerns about our products, you can contact us on

ProductSafety@springernature.com

In case Publisher is established outside the EU, the EU authorized representative is:

Springer Nature Customer Service Center GmbH
Europaplatz 3
69115 Heidelberg, Germany

www.ingramcontent.com/pod-product-compliance
Lightning Source LLC
Chambersburg PA
CBHW071239230926
51849CB00001B/159
* 9 7 8 9 0 6 7 0 4 1 6 7 6 *